OXFORD SHAKESPEARE CONCORDANCES

OXFORD SHAKESPEARE CONCORDANCES

.THE
TWO GENTLEMEN
OF VERONA

A CONCORDANCE TO THE TEXT
OF THE FIRST FOLIO

OXFORD
AT THE CLARENDON PRESS
1969

Oxford University Press, Ely House, London W.1

GLASGOW NEW YORK TORONTO MELBOURNE WELLINGTON
CAPE TOWN SALISBURY IBADAN NAIROBI LUSAKA ADDIS ABABA
BOMBAY CALCUTTA MADRAS KARACHI LAHORE DACCA
KUALA LUMPUR SINGAPORE HONG KONG TOKYO

FILMSET BY COMPUTAPRINT LIMITED
AND PRINTED IN GREAT BRITAIN
AT THE UNIVERSITY PRESS, OXFORD
BY VIVIAN RIDLER
PRINTER TO THE UNIVERSITY

THE TWO GENTLEMEN OF VERONA

Professor Charlton Hinman (*Printing and Proof-Reading*, Oxford, 1963, v. 1, pp. 253–6), notes that the Lee facsimile of the First Folio (Oxford, 1902) from which the concordance to *The Two Gentlemen of Verona* was made shows the corrected pages B4^v, C4, the second probably corrected with reference to copy. His table (v. 2, p. 514) of the order of printing for this portion of the Folio reads:

Cy Ax ‖ Cy Ax ‖ Cy Ax ‖ Ax Cy ‖ Ax Cy ‖ Cy Ax   Cy Ax ‖ Cy Ax
B3:4^v ‖ B2^v:5 ‖ B2:5^v ‖ B1^v:6 ‖ B1:6^v ‖ C3^v:4   C3:4^v ‖ C2^v:5

Cy Ax ‖ Cy Ax   Cy Ax ‖ Ax Cy ‖ Ax Cy ‖ A* C   C C   C C ‖
C2:5^v ‖ C1^v:6   C1:6^v ‖ D3^v:4 ‖ D3:4^v ‖ D2^v:5   D2:5^v D1^v:6 ‖

TABLE OF LINE AND ACT/SCENE NUMBERS

Page	Col.	Comp.	F line nos.	Globe act/scene nos.
B4^v	a	A	1–49	1.1.1–1.1.45
	b	A	50–99	1.1.100
B5	a	A	100–58	1.2.5
	b	A	159–224	1.2.68
B5^v	a	A	225–90	1.2.131
	b	A	291–349	1.3.47
B6	a	C	350–409	2.1.12
	b	C	410–75	2.1.89
B6^v	a	C	476–541	2.2.156
	b	C	542–95	2.3.4
C1	a	C	596–656	2.4.1
	b	C	657–722	2.4.72
C1^v	a	C	723–88	2.4.136
	b	C	789–854	2.4.199
C2	a	C	855–914	2.5.48
	b	C	915–73	2.6.43
C2^v	a	C	974–1035	2.7.60
	b	C	1036–95	3.1.26
C3	a	C	1096–1161	3.1.92
	b	C	1162–1226	3.1.156
C3^v	a	C	1227–1292	3.1.222
	b	C	1293–1358	3.1.294
C4	a	A	1359–1424	3.1.372
	b	A	1425–84	3.2.38

Page	Col.	Comp.	F line nos.	Globe act/scene nos.
C4ᵛ	a	A	1485–1547	4.1.1
.	b	A	1548–1613	4.1.67
C5	a	A	1614–71	4.2.47
	b	A	1672–1736	4.2.112
C5ᵛ	a	A	1737–95	4.3.25
	b	A	1796–1854	4.4.39
C6	a	A	1855–1920	4.4.104
	b	A	1921–86	4.4.170
C6ᵛ	a	A	1987–2042	5.2.1
	b	A	2043–2103	5.3.1
D1	a	C	2104–64	5.4.43
	b	C	2165–2230	5.4.104
D1ᵛ	a	C	{2231–65, 2301–6 (Names)}	5.4.138
	b	C2	{2266–2300, 2307–16 (Names)}	5.4.173

The following misprints, etc. have been corrected in the text:

B6	378	*Panthmo*;		C6ᵛ	2097	*Siluas*
C2ᵛ	989	*Iul:*		D1	2127	distrestes,
	1075	yonr			2178	*Pre.*
C3ᵛ	1262	t'is			2183	*Pre.*
C5	1723	returneₐ				

June 1968   T. H. H.

PREFACE

ALTHOUGH responsibility for the text and arrangement of the concordances is solely that of the editor, their preparation has entailed the laborious collaboration of many individuals and organizations, to whom the Press and the editor are very grateful. The texts were prepared at the English Electric Computers Ltd. Data Processing Bureau, London, under the supervision of Mr. David Lyon; Mrs. Elizabeth Lyon undertook the first proof-reading of the uncorrected texts. The main concordance programmes were written and tested by Miss Patricia Fell of the Bureau Support Group, English Electric Computers, Ltd., Kidsgrove, Staffs., and were run on the KDF9 computer at the Oxford University Computing Laboratory, Oxford. Without the continued and valued co-operation of the Director, staff, and (particularly) operators at the Laboratory, this project would have come to nothing. The magnetic tapes were prepared for publication by filmsetting by Computaprint, Ltd., London. The editor is greatly obliged to the secretarial staff of the Clarendon Press, who encouraged him to undertake this work and who continually supported him through all the vicissitudes of its preparation. What good lies in these concordances must be credited, after Shakespeare, to these people and others too numerous to mention.

T. H. HOWARD-HILL

'Trevenny'
Noke, Oxford

GENERAL INTRODUCTION

IN this series of Oxford Shakespeare Concordances, a separate volume is devoted to each of the plays. The text for each concordance is the one chosen as copy-text by Dr. Alice Walker for the Oxford Old Spelling Shakespeare now in preparation.

Each concordance takes account of every word in the text, and represents their occurrence by frequency counts, line numbers, and reference lines, or a selection of these according to the interest of the particular word. The number of words which have frequency counts only has been kept as low as possible. The introduction to each volume records the facsimile copy of the text from which the concordance was prepared, a table of Folio through line numbers and Globe edition act and scene numbers, a list of the misprints corrected in the text, and an account of the order of printing, and the proof-reading, abstracted from Professor Charlton Hinman's *The Printing and Proof-Reading of the First Folio of Shakespeare* (Oxford, 1963).

The following notes on the main features of the concordances may be helpful.[1]

A. *The Text*

The most obvious misprints have been corrected, on conservative principles, and have been listed for each play in the introduction to the corresponding concordance. Wrong-fount letters have been silently corrected.

Obvious irregularities on the part of the original compositor—for example the anomalous absence of full stops after speech prefixes—have been normalized and noted. Colons, semicolons, exclamation and interrogation marks after italicized words have been modernized to roman fount after current practice, since this aspect of

---

[1] An account of the principles and methods by which the concordances were edited appears in *Studies in Bibliography*, vol. 22, 1969.

compositorial practice would not normally be studied from a concordance. The spacing of words in the original printed texts, particularly in 'justified' lines, is extremely variable; spacing has been normalized on the basis of the compositor's practice as revealed in the particular column or page.

For ease of reference, the contractions *S.*, *L.*, *M.*, and forms such as *Mist.* and tildes, have been expanded when the compositor's own preferred practice is clear, and the expansion has been noted in the text. For M^r, the superior character has been lowered silently. Superior characters like the circumflex in *baâ* and those in ẙ, ẙ, ẙ, and ẘ, have been ignored. The reader should find little difficulty in distinguishing the original form of the pronominal contractions when they are encountered in the text. They are listed under Y and W respectively.

B. *Arrangement of entries*

The words in the text are arranged alphabetically, with numerals and & and &c listed at the end. Words starting with I and J, and U and V, will be found together under I and V respectively. The reader should note that the use of U for the medial V (and I for J) leads in some cases to an unfamiliar order of entry. For example, ADUISED is listed before ADULTERY. The reader will usually find the word he wants if he starts his inquiry at the modern spelling, for when the old spelling differs considerably from the modern spelling, a reference such as 'ENFORCE *see* inforce' will direct the reader to the entry in the concordance.

In hyphenated compounds where the hyphen is the second or third character of the heading-word (as in A-BOORD), the hyphenated form may be listed some distance from other occurrences of the same word in un-hyphenated form. In significant cases, references are given to alert the user.

Under the heading-word, the line numbers or lines of context are in the order of the text. The heading-word is followed by a frequency count of the words in short and long (that is, marked with an asterisk) lines, and the reference lines. When a word has been treated as one to have a frequency count only, or a list of the line numbers and count, any further count which follows will refer to the reference lines listed under the same heading. Where there are two counts but no reference lines (as with AN), the first count refers to the speech prefix.

C. *Special Forms*

(*a*) The following words have not been given context lines and line references but are dealt with only by the counting of their frequency:

A AM AND ARE AT BE BY HE I IN IS IT OF ON SHE THE THEY TO WAS WE WITH YOU

These forms occur so often in most texts that the reader can locate them more easily by examining the text of the play than he could by referring to an extensive listing in the concordance.

Homographs of these words (for example I = *ay*) have been listed in full and are given separate counts under the same heading-word.

(*b*) A larger number of words, consisting mainly of variant spellings, have been given line references as well as frequency counts.

These words are: ACTUS AN AR ART ATT AU BEE BEEING BEEN BEENE BEING BENE BIN BUT CAN CANST CE COULD COULDST DE DECIMA DES DID DIDD DIDDEST DIDDST DO DOE DOES DOEST DOETH DONE DOO DOOE DOOES DOOEST DOOING DOON DOONE DOOS DOOST DOOTH DOS DOST DOTH DU E EN EST ET ETC FINIS FOR FROM HA HAD HADST HAH HAS HAST HATH HAUE HEE HEEL HEELE HEL HELL HER HIM HIR HIS IE IF IL ILL ILLE INTO LA LE LES MA MAIE MAIEST MAIST MAY ME MEE MIGHT MIGHTEST MIGHTST MINE MOI MOY MY NE NO NOE NON NONA NOR NOT O OCTAUA OFF OH OR OU OUR OUT PRIMA PRIMUS QUARTA QUARTUS QUE QUINTA QUINTUS SCAENA SCENA SCOENA SECUNDA SECUNDUS SEPTIMA SEPTIMUS SEXTA SHAL SHALL SHALT SHEE SHOLD SHOLDE SHOLDST SHOULD SHOULDE SHOULDST SIR SO SOE TE TERTIA TERTIUS THAT THEE THEIR THEIRE THEM THEN THER THERE THESE THEYR THIS THOSE THOU THY TIS TU VN VNE VOS VOSTRE VOUS VS WAST WEE WER WERE WERT WHAT WHEN WHER WHERE WHICH WHO WHOM WHOME WHY WIL WILL WILT WILTE WOLD WOLDE WOLDST WOULD WOULDE WOULDEST WOULDST YE YEE YF YOUE YOUR YT & &c 1 2 3 4.

Homographs of words on this list (e.g. *bee* = n.) have been listed in full, and also have separate counts.

(*c*) All speech prefixes, other than *All.*, *Both.*, and those which represent the names of actors, have been treated as count-only words. In some cases, however, where a speech prefix corresponds to a form already on the count-only list (e.g. *Is.*), a full entry has been given. In some other cases, when two counts are given for the same heading-word for no apparent reason, the count which does not correspond to the following full references or to the list of line references is that of the speech prefix form (for example AN in *The Tempest*).

(*d*) Hyphenated compounds such as *all-building-law* have been listed under the full form, and also under each main constituent after the first. In this example there are entries under ALL-BUILDING-LAW, BUILDING, and LAW. When, however, one of the constituents of the compound is a word on the count- or location-only list ((*a*) or (*b*) above), it is dealt with in whichever of these two lists applies. References such as 'AT *see also* bemock't-at-stabs' are given to assist the reader in such cases.

Simple or non-hyphenated compounds such as *o'th'King* have been listed only under the constituent parts—in this example under OTH and KING.

(*e*) 'Justified' lines where the spellings *may* have been affected by the compositor's need to fit the text to his measure are distinguished by an asterisk at the beginning of the reference line. If only location is being given, the asterisk occurs before the line reference. If only frequency counts are being given, the number *after* the asterisk records the frequency of forms occurring in 'justified' lines. Lines which do not extend to the full width of the compositor's measure have not been distinguished as 'justified' lines, even though in many cases the shorter line may have affected the spelling.

D. *Line Numbers*

The lines in each text have been numbered from the first *Actus Primus* or stage direction and thereafter in normal reading order, including all stage directions and act and scene divisions. Each typographical line has been counted as a unit when it contains matter for inclusion in the concordance. Catchwords are not included in the count. The only general exception is that turn-overs are regarded as belonging to their base-lines; where a turn-over occurs on a line by itself, it has been reckoned as part of the base-line, and the line containing only the turn-over has not been counted as a separate line. Turn-overs may readily be distinguished by vertical stroke and single bracket after the last word of the base-line; for example *brought with* | (*child,*.

When two or more lines have been joined in order to provide a fuller context, the line-endings are indicated by a vertical stroke |, and the line reference applies to that part of the line before the vertical stroke. For the true line-numbers of words in the following part of the context line, the stated line-number should be increased by one each time a vertical stroke occurs, save when the next word is a turn-over.

The numbering of the quarto texts has been fitted to that of the corresponding Folio texts; lines in the Quarto which do not occur in the Folio are prefixed by +. The line references are similarly specified. The line references of these concordances therefore provide a consistent permanent numbering of each typographical line of text, based on the First Folio.

THE TWO GENTLEMEN OF VERONA

A = 226*86, 7*⊩
  Panth. *Launce*, away, away: a Boord: thy Master is   626
  And heere he meanes to spend his time a while,   730
  Duke. Sir *Thurio*, giue vs leaue (I pray) a while,   1070
  Duk. Nay then no matter: stay with me a while,   1127
  Val. By seauen a clock, ile get you such a Ladder.   1195
  Let's tune: and too it lustily a while.   1650
  And at that time I made her weepe a good,   1986
  Loue, lend me patience to forbeare a while.   2148
ABBEY = 1
  Out at the Posterne by the Abbey wall;   2036
ABC = *1
  *to sigh, like a Schoole-boy that had lost his *A.B.C.* to   417
ABHORD = 1
  Vaine *Thurio* (whom my very soule abhor'd.)   1787
ABLE = *1
  *were drie, I am able to fill it with my teares: if the winde   645
ABOAD = 1
  To *Mantua*, where I heare, he makes aboad;   1793
ABOARDE *see also* boord = 1
  Which cannot perish hauing thee aboarde,   147
ABOUE = 2
  Lest it should burne aboue the bounds of reason.   998
  Therefore, aboue the rest, we parley to you: 1606
ABOUT = 5*2
  We haue some secrets to confer about.   1071
  Du. About it Gentlemen.   1541
  Du. Euen now about it, I will pardon you. *Exeunt*.   1544
  3.Out. Stand sir, and throw vs that you haue about'ye.   1549
  Sil. How tall was she? | *Iul*. About my stature: for at *Pentecost*,   1978
  Therefore I know she is about my height,   1985
  And now it is about the very houre   2029
ABRIDGE = 1
  Besides, thy staying will abridge thy life: 1315
ABROAD = 1
  To see the wonders of the world abroad,   9
ABSENCE = 1
  Betideth here in absence of thy Friend: 63

1

ABURNE = 1
  Her haire is *Aburne*, mine is perfect *Yellow*;   2009
ACCESSE = 3
  That no man hath accesse by day to her.   1178
  Vpon this warrant, shall you haue accesse,   1507
  I haue accesse my owne loue to prefer.   1628
ACCOMPLISHD = 1
  Valiant, wise, remorse-full, well accomplish'd.   1783
ACCORDING = 4
  According to my shallow simple skill.   161
  Duk. Welcome him then according to his worth: 733
  (According to our Proclamation) gon?   1458
  According to your Ladiships impose,   1778
ACCORDS = 1
  Pro. Why this it is: my heart accords thereto,   392
ACCOUNT = *1
  Val. How esteem'st thou me? I account of her beauty.   455
ACCURST = 1
  The priuate wound is deepest: oh time, most accurst.   2196
ACQUAINTED = *1
  *third) hang him vp (saies the Duke.) I hauing bin ac-|quainted   1842
ACTED = 1
  Which I so liuely acted with my teares: 1990
ACTION = *1
  Pro. What dangerous action, stood it next to death   2162
ACTORS = 1
  The names of all the Actors.   2301
ACTUS *l*.1 395 1067 1545 2026 = 5
ADEW = 1
  Pro. Wilt thou be gone? Sweet *Valentine* adew,   14
ADIEU = 1
  Once more adieu: my Father at the Road   57
ADIEW = 1
  Pro. Adiew, my Lord, Sir *Valentine* is comming.   1119
ADMIRED = 1
  that she might admired be.   1667
ADOE = *1
  *I did the thing you wot of: he makes me no more adoe,   1847
ADORD = 1
  Thou shalt be worship'd, kiss'd, lou'd, and ador'd;   2019
ADORE = 2
  At first I did adore a twinkling Starre,   938
  To worship shadowes, and adore false shapes,   1755
ADUANTAGE *see also* vantage = 1*1
  Made vse, and faire aduantage of his daies: 718
  Du. Where your good word cannot aduantage him,   1488
ADUENTURE = 1
  So bold *Leander* would aduenture it.   1189
ADUERSITIE = 1
  A man I am, cross'd with aduersitie: 1558
ADUICE = 4
  How shall I doate on her with more aduice,   862
  That thus without aduice begin to loue her?   863
  (Vpon aduice) hath drawne my loue from her,   1142
  Th. And thy aduice, this night, ile put in practise: 1535
ADUISD = 1
  Ant. I like thy counsaile: well hast thou aduis'd: 336

2

ADUISE = 2
Aduise me, where I may haue such a Ladder.   1191
To giue the on-set to thy good aduise.   1540
AFFAIRES = 4
Ile leaue you to confer of home affaires,   770
In these affaires to aid me with thy counsaile.   840
I am to breake with thee of some affaires   1128
Of all that may concerne thy Loue-affaires: 1324
AFFECT = 1
Whom I affect: but she is nice, and coy,   1151
AFFECTED = 2
Ant. And how stand you affected to his wish?   362
Val. In conclusion, I stand affected to her.   477
AFFECTION = 1*1
Wer't not affection chaines thy tender dayes   6
Speed. I would you were set, so your affection would | cease.   478
AFTER = 7*5
Pro. He after Honour hunts, I after Loue;   67
Ant. Look what thou want'st shalbe sent after thee: 376
*Lions: when you fasted, it was presently after dinner: 423
*ship'd, and thou art to post after with oares; what's the   627
Is gone with her along, and I must after,   831
Lau. Marry after they cloas'd in earnest, they parted | very fairely in
iest.   883
And there Ile rest, as after much turmoile   1012
*Ile after, to reioyce in the boyes correctio(n). *Exeunt.*   1444
After your dire-lamenting Elegies,   1528
Pro. We'll wait vpon your Grace, till after Supper,   1542
Ile after; more to be reueng'd on *Eglamoure,*   2095
AFTERWARD = 1
And afterward determine our proceedings.   1543
AFTER-LOUE = 1
For scorne at first, makes after-loue the more.   1164
AGAINE = 12
It were a shame to call her backe againe,   205
And yet, take this againe: and yet I thanke you: 508
But (since vnwillingly) take them againe. | Nay, take them.   514
Or else for want of idle time, could not againe reply,   556
Moist it againe: and frame some feeling line,   1522
Here haue I brought him backe againe.   1872
Pro. Goe, get thee hence, and finde my dog againe,   1878
Or nere returne againe into my sight.   1879
Sil. I pray thee let me looke on that againe.   1946
And once againe, I doe receiue thee honest;   2204
Doe not name *Siluia* thine: if once againe,   2255
Cancell all grudge, repeale thee home againe,   2270
AGAINST *see also* 'gainst = 7*1
To whisper, and conspire against my youth?   196
I throw thy name against the bruzing-stones,   271
Hath he excepted most against my loue.   385
Except thou wilt except against my Loue.   809
And manage it, against despairing thoughts: 1317
How she opposes her against my will?   1472
Especially against his very friend.   1487
*thou see me heaue vp my leg, and make water against a   1856
AGE = 4
Which would be great impeachment to his age,   317

3

AGE *cont.*

To cloath mine age with Angel-like perfection:	716
It would be much vexation to your age.	1085
And where I thought the remnant of mine age	1143

AGED = 1

And naught esteemes my aged eloquence.	1152

AGENT = 2

Here is her hand, the agent of her heart;	348
Eglamoure: Agent for Siluia in her escape.	2307

AGONE = 1

(For long agone I haue forgot to court,	1154

AGOOD *see* good

AGREED *see* 'greed

AH = 1

Sweet Ornament, that deckes a thing diuine, | Ah *Siluia, Siluia.*	401

AID = 1

In these affaires to aid me with thy counsaile.	840

AIMED = 1

That my discouery be not aimed at:	1114

AIRE *see* ayre

AL = *1

Val. Now tell me: how do al from whence you came?	773

ALAS = 9

Alas, this parting strikes poore Louers dumbe. | *Exeunt.*	589
Luc. Alas, the way is wearisome and long.	983
Iul. Alas. | *Pro.* Why do'st thou cry alas?	1896
And thinking on it, makes me cry alas.	1905
Alas poore *Protheus,* thou hast entertain'd	1912
Alas, poore foole, why doe I pitty him	1914
Alas (poore Lady) desolate, and left;	1995
Alas, how loue can trifle with it selfe:	2003

ALE = 3*1

*himselfe in Loue. If thou wilt goe with me to the Ale-|house:	920
to goe to the Ale with a Christian: Wilt thou goe?	925
Sp. Item, she brewes good Ale.	1366
La. And thereof comes the prouerbe: (*Blessing of* | *your heart, you brew good Ale.*)	1367

ALE-HOUSE = *1

Speed. Come-on you mad-cap: Ile to the Ale-house	879

ALIDE = 1

And heire and Neece, alide vnto the Duke.	1595

ALIUE = 3

I will forget that *Iulia* is aliue,	956
Foster'd, illumin'd, cherish'd, kept aliue.	1254
I haue one friend aliue; thou wouldst disproue me:	2191

ALL = 56*9

Inhabits in the finest wits of all.	48
And all the faire effects of future hopes.	54
Pro. All happinesse bechance to thee in *Millaine.*	65
I loue my selfe, my friends, and all for loue:	69
Sp. Sir, I could perceiue nothing at all from her;	136
Iul. Of all the faire resort of Gentlemen,	157
Iu. Why not on *Protheus,* as of all the rest?	173
Iul. Why he, of all the rest, hath neuer mou'd me.	180
Lu. Yet he, of all the rest, I thinke best loues ye.	181
Lu. Fire that's closest kept, burnes most of all.	183
And presently, all humbled kisse the Rod?	213

ALL *cont.*

For any, or for all these exercises,	313
Which now shewes all the beauty of the Sun,	388
And by and by a clowd takes all away.	389
Val. Are all these things perceiu'd in me?	427
Speed. They are all perceiu'd without ye.	428
Speed. That's because the one is painted, and the o- | ther out of all	
count.	450
All this I speak in print, for in print I found it.	559
*weeping: all the kinde of the *Launces*, haue this very	594
*Catte wringing her hands, and all our house in a great	600
*now the dogge all this while sheds not a teare: nor	623
Comes all the praises that I now bestow.)	722
With all good grace, to grace a Gentleman.	724
Thur. They say that Loue hath not an eye at all.	746
Val. And how doe yours? | *Pro.* I left them all in health.	775
Soueraigne to all the Creatures on the earth.	806
Val. Pardon me (*Protheus*) all I can is nothing,	819
As twenty Seas, if all their sand were pearle,	825
With all the cunning manner of our flight	835
The Ladder made of Cords, and all the means	837
Lau. Why, stand-vnder: and vnder-stand is all one.	901
Who (all inrag'd) will banish *Valentine*:	967
Who art the Table wherein all my thoughts	978
I feare me he will scarce be pleas'd with all.	1042
Luc. All these are seruants to deceitfull men.	1047
All that is mine I leaue at thy dispose,	1061
Thanke me for this, more then for all the fauors	1231
Which (all too-much) I haue bestowed on thee.	1232
Time is the Nurse, and breeder of all good;	1313
Of all that may concerne thy Loue-affaires:	1324
*that's all one, if he be but one knaue: He liues not now	1333
That all the Trauailers doe feare so much.	1552
Say I, and be the captaine of vs all:	1611
And show thee all the Treasure we haue got;	1621
Which, with our selues, all rest at thy dispose. *Exeunt.*	1622
And notwithstanding all her sodaine quips,	1636
That all our Swaines commend her?	1664
He lou'd her out of all nicke.	1697
As much, I wish all good befortune you.	1811
*thing, when a Cur cannot keepe himselfe in all compa- | nies:	1831
*him to be a dog indeede, to be, as it were, a dog at all	1833
*all the chamber smelt him: out with the dog (saies one)	1840
When all our Pageants of delight were plaid,	1980
Which serued me as fit, by all mens iudgements,	1983
If that be all the difference in his loue,	2010
Into a thousand oathes; and all those oathes,	2169
Sil. All men but *Protheus*.	2177
'Mongst all foes that a friend should be the worst?	2197
All that was mine, in *Siluia*, I giue thee.	2209
Iul. Behold her, that gaue ayme to all thy oathes,	2227
*Fils him with faults: makes him run through all th'sins;	2238
Know then, I heere forget all former greefes,	2269
Cancell all grudge, repeale thee home againe,	2270
Come, let vs goe, we will include all iarres,	2287
The names of all the Actors.	2301

5

ALLYCHOLLY = *1
  Ho. Now, my yong guest; me thinks your' allycholly;   1651
ALMOST = 2
  Trust me, I thinke 'tis almost day.   1764
  Iul. Almost as well as I doe know my selfe.   1964
ALOFT = 1
  Duk. Her chamber is aloft, far from the ground,   1183
ALONE = 7*1
  Iul. But say *Lucetta* (now we are alone)   154
  *to walke alone like one that had the pestilence: 416
  Shee is alone. | *Pro*. Then let her alone.   821
  For why, the fooles are mad, if left alone.   1168
  Duk But harke thee: I will goe to her alone,   1196
  That I may venture to depart alone.   1806
  Here can I sit alone, vn-seene of any,   2125
ALONG = 7
  Had come along with me, but that his Mistresse   738
  Is gone with her along, and I must after,   831
  Luc. But in what habit will you goe along?   1014
  Regard thy danger, and along with me.   1326
  I giue consent to goe along with you,   1809
  Val. And as we walke along, I dare be bold   2289
  Val. Please you, Ile tell you, as we passe along,   2295
ALPHONSO = 1
  Pan. To morrow, may it please you, *Don Alphonso*,   341
ALREADY = 5
  Sp. Twenty to one then, he is ship'd already,   76
  So much of bad already hath possest them.   1276
  Val. Oh, I haue fed vpon this woe already,   1289
  You are already loues firme votary,   1505
  Pro. Already haue I bin false to *Valentine*,   1625
ALSO = 1
  Du. And also, I thinke, thou art not ignorant   1471
ALTAR = 1
  Pro. Say that vpon the altar of her beauty   1519
ALTERD = 1
  Val. I *Protheus*, but that life is alter'd now,   780
ALTHOUGH = 1
  I see things too, although you iudge I winke.   298
ALWAIES = 1*3
  Val. I know it wel sir, you alwaies end ere you begin.   683
  *not welcome. I reckon this alwaies, that a man is neuer   875
  Ho. You would haue them alwaies play but one thing.   1692
  Iu. I would alwaies haue one play but one thing.   1693
AM = 36*10
AMEN = 2
  Sil. Amen, Amen: goe on (good *Eglamoure*)   2035
AMENDS = 3
  Ile kisse each seuerall paper, for amends: 268
  La. That makes amends for her soure breath.   1391
  Returne, returne, and make thy loue amends: 1723
AMONG = 1*1
  La. Oh villaine, that set this downe among her vices;   1396
  Iu. Is he among these? | *Ho*. I: but peace, let's heare'm.   1661
AMONGST *see* 'mongst

6

AN *l*.197 198 367 387 *433 *434 549 *552 *692 714 726 727 746 798 894
  *921 958 1044 1104 1208 *1443 1453 1486 1586 2068 2115 2185 2232
  2268 = 23*6, 1
  A Slaue, that still an end, turnes me to shame: 1881
ANCESTRY = 1
  Now, by the honor of my Ancestry,   2266
ANCHORING = 1
  To cast vp, with a paire of anchoring hookes,   1187
AND = 334*66, 2*1   •
  And if the Shepheard be awhile away.   79
  Val. I pray thee *Launce*, and if thou seest my Boy   1327
  *Well, ile haue her: and if it be a match, as nothing is | impossible.   1429
ANGELLS = 1
  Though nere so blacke, say they haue Angells faces,   1172
ANGEL-LIKE = 1
  To cloath mine age with Angel-like perfection: 716
ANGER = 2
  You would be fingring them, to anger me.   261
  Vrge not my fathers anger (*Eglamoure*)   1797
ANGERLY = 1
  How angerly I taught my brow to frowne,   216
ANGRED = 2
  To be so angred with another Letter.   263
  Iu. Nay, would I were so angred with the same: 264
ANGRY = 2
  Val. She gaue me none, except an angry word.   549
  Sil. What, angry, Sir *Thurio*, do you change colour?   677
ANOTHER = 11*2
  Pro. It shall goe hard but ile proue it by another.   89
  Sp. Such another proofe will make me cry baa.   97
  To be so angred with another Letter.   263
  Thus will I fold them, one vpon another;   288
  Speed. And yet you will: and yet, another yet.   510
  Val. Please you, Ile write your Ladiship another.   520
  Euen as one heate, another heate expels,   847
  Or as one naile, by strength driues out another.   848
  Send her another: neuer giue her ore,   1163
  Would serue to scale another *Hero's* towre,   1188
  Ile get me one of such another length.   1203
  *keepe shut: Now, of another thing shee may, and that | cannot I helpe.
  Well, proceede.   1412
  *what cur is that (saies another) whip him out (saies the   1841
ANSWERE = 3
  Pro. A silly answere, and fitting well a Sheepe.   85
  My father staies my comming: answere not: 581
  Come; answere not: but to it presently,   1064
ANSWERS = 1
  And yet a thousand times it answer's no. | *Exeunt. Finis*.   393
ANT = 8*3
ANTHEME = 1
  As ending Antheme of my endlesse dolor.   1310
ANTHONIO = 1
  Anthonio: father to Protheus.   2305
ANTONIO see also Ant. = 3
  Enter Antonio and Panthino. Protheus.   301
  Duk. Know ye *Don Antonio*, your Countriman?   704
  Panthion: seruant to Antonio.   2312

ANY = 9*1
For any, or for all these exercises,	313
the Tide, if you tarry any longer.	629
vnkindest Tide, that euer any man tide.	631
To any happy messenger from thence.	703
Val. Sweet: except not any,	808
That I had any light from thee of this.	1118
Vnder a cloake, that is of any length.	1199
Val. Why any cloake will serue the turn (my Lord)	1204
2.*Out*. Tell vs this: haue you any thing to take to?	1588
Here can I sit alone, vn-seene of any,	2125

ANYTHING *see* thing
APPARANT = 1
Without apparant hazard of his life.	1185

APPEARE = 1
And that my loue may appeare plaine and free,	2208

APPEARES = 1
For it appeares by their bare Liueries	694

APPEASD = 1
By Penitence th'Eternalls wrath's appeas'd:	2207

APPLAUD = 2
O that our Fathers would applaud our loues	350
I doe applaud thy spirit, *Valentine*,	2267

APPROACH = *1
Sil. By thy approach thou mak'st me most vnhappy.	2152

APPROCHETH = *1
Iul. And me, when he approcheth to your presence.	2153

APPROUD = 1
Oh 'tis the curse in Loue, and still approu'd	2164

APRILL = 1
The vncertaine glory of an Aprill day,	387

ARE *see also* they're, your' = 59*13
ARIADNE = 1
(Madam) 'twas *Ariadne*, passioning	1988

ARMES = 1*1
*learn'd (like Sir *Protheus*) to wreath your Armes like a	414
Ile wooe you like a Souldier, at armes end,	2180

ART *l*.56 96 *627 894 895 *921 978 1190 1222 1287 1318 *1435 1471 1734
1735 1781 1784 2263 2273 = 16*3
ARTICLE = *1
*mine, twice or thrice in that last Article: rehearse that ∣ once more.	1417

AS = 115*21
Euen as I would, when I to loue begin.	13
Pro. Yet Writers say; as in the sweetest Bud,	46
Val. And Writers say; as the most forward Bud	49
Val. As much to you at home: and so farewell. *Exit*.	66
No, not so much as a ducket for deliuering your letter:	137
*I feare she'll proue as hard to you in telling your minde.	139
Giue her no token but stones, for she's as hard as steele.	140
Sp. No, not so much as take this for thy pains:	142
Lu. As of a Knight, well-spoken, neat, and fine;	163
That I (vnworthy body as I am)	171
Iu. Why not on *Protheus*, as of all the rest?	173
Iul. As little by such toyes, as may be possible:	239
As in reuenge of thy ingratitude,	270
Poore wounded name: my bosome, as a bed,	274
Pro. As one relying on your Lordships will,	363

AS *cont.*

Speed. Shee that you gaze on so, as she sits at supper?	437
Val. Not so faire (boy) as well fauour'd.	443
Speed. That shee is not so faire, as (of you) well-fa-|uourd?	446
Val. No (Boy) but as well as I can do them:	485
Val. As you inioynd me; I haue writ your Letter	494
(Please you command) a thousand times as much: | And yet---	504
*As a nose on a mans face, or a Wethercocke on a steeple:	527
Speed. Ile warrant you, 'tis as well:	554
*for, looke you, she is as white as a lilly, and as	612
*small as a wand: this hat is *Nan* our maid: I am the	613
Val. I knew him as my selfe: for from our Infancie	712
He is as worthy for an Empresse loue,	726
As meet to be an Emperors Councellor:	727
Val. To see such Louers, *Thurio*, as your selfe,	747
And hath so humbled me, as I confesse	789
And I as rich in hauing such a Iewell	824
As twenty Seas, if all their sand were pearle,	825
Euen as one heate, another heate expels,	847
Or as one naile, by strength driues out another.	848
And that I loue him not as I was wont:	859
Lau. No; they are both as whole as a fish.	890
Lau. A notable Lubber: as thou reportest him to | bee.	913
Spee. Why? | *Lau.* Because thou hast not so much charity in thee as	923
Ayming at *Siluia* as a sweeter friend.	959
As thou hast lent me wit, to plot this drift. | *Exit.*	972
Of such diuine perfection as Sir *Protheus.*	988
Thou wouldst as soone goe kindle fire with snow	994
As seeke to quench the fire of Loue with words.	995
Ile be as patient as a gentle streame,	1009
And there Ile rest, as after much turmoile	1012
As may beseeme some well reputed Page.	1018
Iul. That fits as well, as tell me (good my Lord)	1025
Iul. Lucetta, as thou lou'st me let me haue	1032
His heart, as far from fraud, as heauen from earth.	1053
Iul. Now, as thou lou'st me, do him not that wrong,	1055
Done to me (vndeseruing as I am)	1076
Beseeming such a Wife, as your faire daughter:	1135
Nor fearing me, as if I were her father:	1140
Duk. Now as thou art a Gentleman of blood	1190
Duk. A cloake as long as thine will serue the turne? | *Val.* I my good Lord.	1200
Oh, could their Master come, and goe as lightly,	1212
But as thou lou'st thy life, make speed from hence.	1239
As if but now they waxed pale for woe:	1298
As ending Antheme of my endlesse dolor.	1310
As thou lou'st *Siluia* (though not for thy selfe)	1325
Sp. Why man? how blacke? | *La.* Why, as blacke as Inke.	1353
La. That's as much as to say (*Can she so?*)	1370
La. That's as much as to say *Bastard-vertues*: that	1381
*Well, ile haue her: and if it be a match, as nothing is | impossible.	1429
Du. This weake impresse of Loue, is as a figure	1452
By one, whom she esteemeth as his friend.	1483
Th. Therefore, as you vnwinde her loue from him;	1497
Which must be done, by praising me as much	1500
As you, in worth dispraise, sir *Valentine.*	1501
Pro. As much as I can doe, I will effect:	1513

9

AS *cont.*

Such as the fury of vngouern'd youth	1591
1.*Out*. And I, for such like petty crimes as these.	1598
As we doe in our quality much want.	1604
And liue as we doe in this wildernesse?	1609
Loue thee, as our Commander, and our King.	1613
And now I must be as vniust to *Thurio*,	1626
Is she kinde as she is faire?	1668
Sil. Sir *Protheus*, as I take it.	1713
And make it but a shadow, as I am.	1752
Pro. As wretches haue ore-night	1758
Eg. As many (worthy Lady) to your selfe:	1777
As when thy Lady, and thy true-loue dide,	1790
As full of sorrowes, as the Sea of sands,	1803
Wreaking as little what betideth me,	1810
As much, I wish all good befortune you.	1811
*taught him (euen as one would say precisely, thus I	1826
*would teach a dog) I was sent to deliuer him, as a pre-|sent	1827
*I would haue (as one should say) one that takes vp-|on	1832
*him to be a dog indeede, to be, as it were, a dog at all	1833
*for't: sure as I liue he had suffer'd for't: you shall iudge:	1836
*not I bid thee still marke me, and doe as I do; when did'st	1855
*As big as ten of yours, & therefore the guift the greater.	1877
Iul. Because, me thinkes that she lou'd you as well	1900
As you doe loue your Lady *Siluia*:	1901
As (heauen it knowes) I would not haue him speed.	1928
As easily as I doe teare his paper.	1952
Iul. Almost as well as I doe know my selfe.	1964
She, in my iudgement, was as faire as you.	1972
That now she is become as blacke as I.	1977
Which serued me as fit, by all mens iudgements,	1983
As if the garment had bin made for me:	1984
Were full as louely, as is this of hers;	2006
Her eyes are grey as glasse, and so are mine.	2012
I, but her fore-head's low, and mine's as high:	2013
Thu. 'Tis true, such Pearles as put out Ladies eyes,	2054
As he, in pennance wander'd through the Forrest:	2082
Whose life's as tender to me as my soule,	2158
And full as much (for more there cannot be)	2159
I tender't heere: i doe as truely suffer, | As ere I did commit.	2201
To make such meanes for her, as thou hast done,	2264
Dispose of them, as thou knowst their deserts.	2286
Val. And as we walke along, I dare be bold	2289
Val. Please you, Ile tell you, as we passe along,	2295

ASCEND = 1

How he her chamber-window will ascend,	1108

ASHAMD = 2

I am betroth'd; and art thou not asham'd	1735
Be thou asham'd that I haue tooke vpon me,	2231

ASIDE = 1

Iu. Peace, stand aside, the company parts.	1702

ASKD = 1

*you shall heare Musique, and see the Gentleman that | you ask'd for.	1655

ASKE = 3*1

And you aske me if she did nod, and I say I.	118
And aske remission, for my folly past.	219
Lau. Aske my dogge, if he say I, it will: if hee say	903

ASKE *cont.*
  To grant one Boone that I shall aske of you.   2277
ASLEEPE = 2
  Haply when they haue iudg'd me fast asleepe,   1094
  Ho. By my hallidome, I was fast asleepe.   1761
ASPIRE = 1
  Wilt thou aspire to guide the heauenly Car?   1223
ASSE = 3*1
  *matter? why weep'st thou man? away asse, you'l loose   628
  Spee. What an asse art thou, I vnderstand thee not.   894
  Spee. Why, thou whorson Asse, thou mistak'st me,   915
  Thu. Wherefore? | *Iul.* That such an Asse should owe them.   2068
ASSIST = 1
  Iul. Counsaile, *Lucetta*, gentle girle assist me,   976
ASSURE = 1
  Assure thy selfe, my loue is buried.   1739
ASTRAY = *1
  Pro. Nay, in that you are astray: 'twere best pound | you.   107
AT = 41*8
ATCHIEUD = 1
  Experience is by industry atchieu'd,   324
ATTEND = 3
  Pro. Wee'll both attend vpon your Ladiship.   772
  And then Ile presently attend you.   844
  Tarry I heere, I but attend on death,   1256
ATTENDED = 1
  I feare I am attended by some Spies.   2037
ATTENDS = 2
  Attends the Emperour in his royall Court.   329
  One that attends your Ladiships command.   1775
AUGHT *see also* ought = 1
  (Though you respect not aught your seruant doth)   2141
AUGURY = 1
  Which (if my Augury deceiue me not)   1887
AWAY = 16*4
  And if the Shepheard be awhile away.   79
  Lu. I: if you thought your loue not cast away.   179
  Be calme (good winde) blow not a word away,   278
  To the sweet Iulia: that ile teare away: 285
  Some, to discouer Islands farre away: 311
  And by and by a clowd takes all away.   389
  Panth. Launce, away, away: a Boord: thy Master is   626
  *matter? why weep'st thou man? away asse, you'l loose   628
  Panth. Come: come away man, I was sent to call | thee.   647
  This night intends to steale away your daughter: 1080
  And should she thus be stolne away from you,   1084
  And thence she cannot be conuay'd away.   1106
  Duk. Sir *Valentine*, whether away so fast?   1120
  For, get you gon, she doth not meane away.   1170
  But flie I hence, I flie away from life.   1257
  For practising to steale away a Lady,   1594
  Away, I say: stayest thou to vexe me here;   1880
  And threw her Sun-expelling Masque away,   1974
  2 *Out.* Come, bring her away.   2107
AWFULL = 1
  Thrust from the company of awfull men.   1592

AWHILE = 1
  And if the Shepheard be awhile away.   79
AY *see* I
AYME = 2
  But fearing lest my iealous ayme might erre,   1097
  Iul. Behold her, that gaue ayme to all thy oathes,   2227
AYMING = 1
  Ayming at *Siluia* as a sweeter friend.   959
AYRE = 2*1
  *can feed on the ayre, I am one that am nourish'd by my   563
  then liue in your ayre.   680
  The ayre hath staru'd the roses in her cheekes,   1975
BAA = 1
  Sp. Such another proofe will make me cry baa.   97
BABBLE = 1
  Iu. This babble shall not henceforth trouble me;   258
BABE = 1
  That (like a testie Babe) will scratch the Nurse,   212
BACKE = 4
  It were a shame to call her backe againe,   205
  My pennance is, to call *Lucetta* backe   218
  Here haue I brought him backe againe.   1872
  Val. *Thurio* giue backe; or else embrace thy death: 2253
BAD = 7
  Val. Why sir, who bad you call her?   406
  Loue bad mee sweare, and Loue bids me for-sweare; 935
  To learne his wit, t'exchange the bad for better;   942
  Fie, fie, vnreuerend tongue, to call her bad,   943
  So much of bad already hath possest them.   1276
  For they are harsh, vn-tuneable, and bad.   1278
  La. Marry Sir, I carried Mistris *Siluia* the dogge you | bad me. 1865
BADE *see* bad
BANISH = 1
  Who (all inrag'd) will banish *Valentine*:   967
BANISHD = 8
  And *Siluia* is my selfe: banish'd from her   1242
  Pro. That thou art banish'd: oh that's the newes, 1287
  Doth *Siluia* know that I am banish'd?   1291
  Now *Valentine* is banish'd from her sight.   1448
  1.*Out*. What, were you banish'd thence?   1569
  2.*Out*. Indeede because you are a banish'd man, 1605
  I beare vnto the banish'd *Valentine*:   1785
  Val. These banish'd men, that I haue kept withall, 2279
BANISHED = 2
  My selfe was from *Verona* banished,   1593
  Your Grace is welcome to a man disgrac'd, | Banished *Valentine*. 2249
BANISHMENT = 1
  Is selfe from selfe. A deadly banishment: 1243
BANISHT = 2
  To die, is to be banisht from my selfe,   1241
  But were you banisht for so small a fault?   1577
BANKRUPT = 1
  Thu. Sir, if you spend word for word with me, I shall | make your wit
  bankrupt.   690
BARE = 3*1
  For it appeares by their bare Liueries   694
  That they liue by your bare words.   695

BARE *cont.*
  *much in a bare Christian: Heere is the Cate-log of her   1341
  3.*Out.* By the bare scalpe of *Robin Hoods* fat Fryer,   1582
BARGAINE = 1
  Iul. And seale the bargaine with a holy kisse.   575
BASE = 9
  Iu. The meane is dround with you vnruly base.   256
  Lu. Indeede I bid the base for *Protheus.*   257
  To beare my Ladies traine, lest the base earth   813
  Iul. Base men, that vse them to so base effect;   1048
  Goe base Intruder, ouer-weening Slaue,   1227
  Without false vantage, or base treachery.   1575
  3.*Out.* No, we detest such vile base practises.   1619
  Duke. The more degenerate and base art thou   2263
BASTARD-VERTUES = *1
  **La.* That's as much as to say *Bastard-vertues*: that   1381
BE *see also* shalbe, wilbe = 121*24
BEADES-MAN = 1
  For I will be thy beades-man, *Valentine.*   21
BEARD = *1
  *3.*Out.* I by my beard will we: for he is a proper man.   1556
BEARE = 7*3
  **Sp.* Well, I perceiue I must be faine to beare with you.   123
  Pro. Why Sir, how doe you beare with me?   124
  *Except mine own name: That, some whirle-winde beare   280
  To beare my Ladies traine, lest the base earth   813
  To beare a hard opinion of his truth: 1056
  That stayes to beare my Letters to my friends,   1122
  Val. It will be light (my Lord) that you may beare it   1198
  I beare vnto the banish'd *Valentine*:   1785
  To beare me company, and goe with me: 1804
  **Pro.* Beare witnes (heauen) I haue my wish for euer.   2245
BEARES = 2
  Beares no impression of the thing it was.)   857
  Feare not: he beares an honourable minde.   2115
BEARING = 1
  Pro. No, no, you shall haue it for bearing the letter.   122
BEAST = 1
  I would haue beene a break-fast to the Beast,   2155
BEAUTEOUS = 1
  Blacke men are Pearles, in beauteous Ladies eyes.   2053
BEAUTIFIDE = 1
  And partly seeing you are beautifide   1601
BEAUTIFULL = 2
  And still I see her beautifull.   460
  A vertuous gentlewoman, milde, and beautifull.   2000
BEAUTY = 7*1
  Which now shewes all the beauty of the Sun,   388
  Val. I meane that her beauty is exquisite, | But her fauour infinite.   448
  **Speed.* Marry sir, so painted to make her faire, that no | man counts of
  her beauty.   453
  **Val.* How esteem'st thou me? I account of her beauty.   455
  Then let her beauty be her wedding dowre: 1147
  Pro. Say that vpon the altar of her beauty   1519
  When to her beauty I commend my vowes,   1633
  For beauty liues with kindnesse: 1669

BECAME = *1
*Wringing her hands, whose whitenes so became them,   1297
BECAUSE = 10*5
I thinke him so, because I thinke him so.   177
*Speed. That's because the one is painted, and the o-|ther out of all count.   450
*Speed. Because Loue is blinde: O that you had mine   463
Because thou seest me doate vpon my loue: 828
Spee. Why? | *Lau. Because thou hast not so much charity in thee as   923
Because my selfe doe want my seruants fortune.   1217
Wilt thou reach stars, because they shine on thee?   1225
*La. I care not for that neither: because I loue crusts.   1403
Because we know (on *Valentines* report)   1504
2.*Out.* Indeede because you are a banish'd man,   1605
Iu. Marry (mine *Host*) because I cannot be merry.   1653
Iul. Because, me thinkes that she lou'd you as well   1900
Because he loues her, he despiseth me,   1916
Because I loue him, I must pitty him.   1917
*For thy sweet Mistris sake, because thou lou'st her. Fare-|(well.   1998
BECHANCE = 1
Pro. All happinesse bechance to thee in *Millaine.*   65
BECOME = 7
He being her Pupill, to become her Tutor.   529
thou that that my master is become a notable Louer?   910
Spee. I tell thee, my Master is become a hot Louer.   918
To be fantastique, may become a youth   1022
Will well become such sweet complaining grieuance: 1532
But, since your falsehood shall become you well   1754
That now she is become as blacke as I.   1977
BED = 2*1
Poore wounded name: my bosome, as a bed,   274
Speed. True sir: I was in loue with my bed, I thanke   474
That presently you hie you home to bed: 1718
BEE *l.*564 *593 *608 913 = 1*3
BEEING *l.*469 *470 = *2
BEENE *see also* bin *l.*457 714 732 1144 1581 2154 2155 = 7
BEES = 1
And kill the Bees that yeelde it, with your stings;   267
BEFORE = 3*2
Pro. Goe on before: I shall enquire you forth: 841
Th. How now, sir *Protheus*, are you crept before vs?   1642
Ho. How now? are you sadder then you were before;   1678
*with the smell before, knew it was Crab; and   1843
Vnlesse it be to come before their time,   2032
BEFORTUNE = 1
As much, I wish all good befortune you.   1811
BEG = 1
(A smaller boone then this I cannot beg,   2145
BEGET = 1
But rather to beget more loue in you.   1166
BEGGAR = *1
*feares robbing: to speake puling, like a beggar at Hal-|low-Masse: 420
BEGIN = 2*1
Euen as I would, when I to loue begin.   13
Val. I know it wel sir, you alwaies end ere you begin.   683
That thus without aduice begin to loue her?   863

BEGINS = 2
Egl. The Sun begins to guild the westerne skie,   2028
Inconstancy falls-off, ere it begins: 2239
BEGOT = 1
La. I will try thee: tell me this: who begot thee?   1358
BEGUILD = 1
Thou hast beguil'd my hopes; nought but mine eye   2189
BEHAUIOUR = 1
But chiefely, for thy face, and thy behauiour,   1886
BEHELD = 1
'Tis but her picture I haue yet beheld,   864
BEHINDE = 1
And in a word (for far behinde his worth   721
BEHOLD = 1
Iul. Behold her, that gaue ayme to all thy oathes,   2227
BEHOLDING = 1
Sil. She is beholding to thee (gentle youth)   1994
BEING *l.*138 148 192 323 *409 500 529 531 743 969 1001 1090 1319 1491
  1672 2084 2109 = 16*1, 1
My health, and happy being at your Court.   1126
BELEEUE = 2
Val. No, beleeue me.   546
Du. So I beleeue: but *Thurio* thinkes not so: 1462
BELEEUING = 1
Speed. No beleeuing you indeed sir: 547
BELIKE = 2*2
Iu. Heauy? belike it hath some burden then?   242
Val. Belike (boy) then you are in loue, for last mor-|(ning   472
She is dead belike? | *Pro.* Not so: I thinke she liues.   1894
Sil. Belike she thinks that *Protheus* hath forsook her?   1967
BELOUD = 2*1
How happily he liues, how well-belou'd,   359
When women cannot loue, where they're belou'd.   2165
Sil. When *Protheus* cannot loue, where he's belou'd: 2166
BELOUED = 2
Iulia: beloued of Protheus.   2313
Siluia: beloued of Valentine.   2314
BENDED = 1
But neither bended knees, pure hands held vp,   1299
BENEFIT = 1
Omitting the sweet benefit of time   715
BESEECH = 1*1
Val. Welcome, deer *Protheus*: Mistris, I beseech you   750
I now beseech you (for your daughters sake)   2276
BESEEME = 1
As may beseeme some well reputed Page.   1018
BESEEMING = 1
Beseeming such a Wife, as your faire daughter: 1135
BESET = 2
Duk. Now, daughter *Siluia*, you are hard beset.   698
The Thicket is beset, he cannot scape.   2113
BESHREW = 2
Pro. Beshrew me, but you haue a quicke wit.   127
Duk. Beshrew me sir, but if he make this good   725
BESIDES = 5
Were rich and honourable: besides, the gentleman   1133
Besides the fashion of the time is chang'd)   1155

BESIDES *cont.*

Besides, her intercession chaf'd him so,	1303
Besides, thy staying will abridge thy life:	1315
Besides she did intend Confession	2085

BEST = 10*4

*Sp. If the ground be ouer-charg'd, you were best | sticke her.	105
*Pro. Nay, in that you are astray: 'twere best pound | you.	107
Lu. Then thus: of many good, I thinke him best.	174
Lu. Yet he, of all the rest, I thinke best loues ye.	181
Best sing it to the tune of *Light O, Loue.*	240
*Lu. She makes it stra(n)ge, but she would be best pleas'd	262
*lu. If you respect them; best to take them vp.	293
Then tell me, whether were I best to send him?	326
Why eu'n what fashion thou best likes (*Lucetta.*)	1027
*Val. A woman somtime scorns what best co(n)tents her.	1162
How shall I best conuey the Ladder thither?	1197
La. Well: the best is, she hath no teeth to bite.	1405
Pro. The best way is, to slander *Valentine,*	1477
Read ouer *Iulia's* heart, (thy first best Loue)	2167

BESTOW = 4

Comes all the praises that I now bestow.)	722
I know you haue determin'd to bestow her	1082
How, and which way I may bestow my selfe	1156
Bestow thy fawning smiles on equall mates,	1228

BESTOWED = 1

Which (all too-much) I haue bestowed on thee.	1232

BETIDETH = 2

Betideth here in absence of thy Friend:	63
Wreaking as little what betideth me,	1810

BETROATHD = *1

*Val. I, and we are betroathd: nay more, our mariage | howre,	834

BETROTHD = 1

I am betroth'd; and art thou not asham'd	1735

BETTER = 10*2

I must goe send some better Messenger,	149
Oh excellent deuise, was there euer heard a better?	530
For truth hath better deeds, then words to grace it.	586
To learne his wit, t'exchange the bad for better;	942
Luc. Better forbeare, till *Protheus* make returne.	989
*onely carry, therefore is shee better then a Iade. *Item.*	1344
*La. For thee? I, who art thou? he hath staid for a bet-|ter man then thee.	1435
Makes me the better to confer with thee.	1465
Would better fit his Chamber, then this Shadow.	1941
Iul. But better indeede, when you hold you peace.	2059
I better brooke then flourishing peopled Townes:	2124
And that's farre worse then none: better haue none	2172

BETWEENE = 1

The match betweene sir *Thurio,* and my daughter? | *Pro.* I doe my Lord.	1469

BE-LIKE = 1

Sil. Be-like that now she hath enfranchis'd them	740

BID = 2*1

Lu. Indeede I bid the base for *Protheus.*	257
Bid him make haste, and meet me at the North-gate.	1328
*not I bid thee still marke me, and doe as I do; when did'st	1855

BIDING = 1

With many bitter threats of biding there.	1306

BIDS = 3

Loue bad mee sweare, and Loue bids me for-sweare;	935
The Law of friendship bids me to conceale,	1074
She bids me thinke how I haue bin forsworne	1634

BIG = *1

*As big as ten of yours, & therefore the guift the greater.	1877

BIN *l.320 1534 1625 1634 1765 *1835 *1839 *1842 *1851 1864 1970
1984 = 8*4

BINDE = 1

To binde him to remember my good will:	1919

BIRTH = 3

Worthy his youth, and noblenesse of birth.	335
But truer starres did gouerne *Protheus* birth,	1049
Thu. What saies she to my birth?	2063

BITE = 1

La. Well: the best is, she hath no teeth to bite.	1405

BITTER = 3

With bitter fasts, with penitentiall grones,	783
Pro. When I was sick, you gaue me bitter pils,	802
With many bitter threats of biding there.	1306

BITTERLY = 1

Wept bitterly: and would I might be dead,	1992

BLACKE = 6

Though nere so blacke, say they haue Angells faces,	1172
Sp. Why man? how blacke? | *La.* Why, as blacke as Inke.	1353
That now she is become as blacke as I.	1977
Thu. Nay then the wanton lyes: my face is blacke.	2051
Blacke men are Pearles, in beauteous Ladies eyes.	2053

BLACKST = 1

La. The black'st newes that euer thou heard'st.	1352

BLASTING = 1

Is turn'd to folly, blasting in the Bud,	52

BLESSE = *1

*had not bin there (blesse the marke) a pissing while, but	1839

BLESSED = 1

A blessed soule doth in *Elizium*.	1013

BLESSING = *2

*come I to my Father; Father, your blessing: now	616
La. And thereof comes the prouerbe: (*Blessing of | your heart, you brew good Ale.*)	1367

BLEST = 2

Doe curse the grace, that with such grace hath blest them,	1216
Let me be blest to make this happy close:	2243

BLIND = 2

Sil. Nay then he should be blind, and being blind	743

BLINDE = 1*3

Speed. Because Loue is blinde: O that you had mine	463
*no eyes, looke you, wept her selfe blinde at my parting:	605
There is no reason, but I shall be blinde.	867
*foure of his blinde brothers and sisters went to it: I haue	1825

BLINDED = 1

If this fond Loue, were not a blinded god.	2016

BLINDNESSE = 1

To helpe him of his blindnesse:	1671

BLOCKE = 1

Lau. What a blocke art thou, that thou canst not?	895

BLOOD = 1
Duk. Now as thou art a Gentleman of blood   1190
BLOT = 1
It is the lesser blot modesty findes,   2234
BLOUD = *1
Thu. That hath more minde to feed on your bloud,   679
BLOW = 2
Is eaten by the Canker ere it blow,   50
Be calme (good winde) blow not a word away,   278
BLUNT = 1
By some slie tricke, blunt *Thurio's* dull proceeding.   970
BLUSH = 1
Oh *Protheus*, let this habit make thee blush.   2230
BLUSHES = *1
Duke. I think the Boy hath grace in him, he blushes.   2292
BOAST = 1
Pro. My dutie will I boast of, nothing else.   761
BOATE = 1
were downe, I could driue the boate with my sighes.   646
BODY = 2
That I (vnworthy body as I am)   171
His Body, for a Girle that loues him not: 2261
BOLD = 3
So bold *Leander* would aduenture it.   1189
Ile be so bold to breake the seale for once.   1209
Val. And as we walke along, I dare be bold   2289
BOLDER = 1
bolder to chide you, for yours.   476
BONDS = 1
His words are bonds, his oathes are oracles,   1050
BOOKE = 2
Val. And on a loue-booke pray for my successe?   22
Pro. Vpon some booke I loue, I'le pray for thee.   23
BOONE = 2
(A smaller boone then this I cannot beg,   2145
To grant one Boone that I shall aske of you.   2277
BOORD = *1
Panth. Launce, away, away: a Boord: thy Master is   626
BOOTE = *1
Thu. Ile weare a Boote, to make it somewhat roun-|(der.   2047
BOOTES = 2 ˙
Val. 'Tis true; for you are ouer-bootes in loue,   28
Pro. Ouer the Bootes? nay giue me not the Boots.   30
BOOTS = 2
Pro. Ouer the Bootes? nay giue me not the Boots.   30
Val. No, I will not; for it boots thee not. | *Pro.* What?   31
BORE = 1
I euer bore my daughter, or thy selfe.   1237
BORROWES = *1
*And spends what he borrowes kindly in your company.   689
BORROWS = *1
*Sir *Thurio* borrows his wit from your Ladiships lookes,   688
BOSOME = 4
Poore wounded name: my bosome, as a bed,   274
My Herald Thoughts, in thy pure bosome rest-them,   1214
Euen in the milke-white bosome of thy Loue.   1320
Is periured to the bosome? *Protheus*   2193

BOTH = 4
may be both at once deliuered.   132
Pro. Wee'll both attend vpon your Ladiship.   772
Lau. No; they are both as whole as a fish.   890
'Tis true: for Frier *Laurence* met them both   2081
BOTTOME = 1
You must prouide to bottome it on me: 1499
BOUGHT = 1*1
Val. To be in loue; where scorne is bought with | (grones: 33
How euer: but a folly bought with wit,   38
BOUNDS = 1
Lest it should burne aboue the bounds of reason.   998
BOUNTY = 1*1
*To testifie your bounty, I thank you, you haue cestern'd | (me;   143
Is full of Vertue, Bounty, Worth, and Qualities   1134
BOY = 8*4
*to sigh, like a Schoole-boy that had lost his *A.B.C.* to   417
Val. Not so faire (boy) as well fauour'd.   443
Val. Belike (boy) then you are in loue, for last mor-|(ning   472
Val. No (Boy) but as well as I can do them: 485
Spee. Master, Sir *Thurio* frownes on you. | *Val.* I Boy, it's for loue. 657
Pro. Run (boy) run, run, and seeke him out.   1258
Val. I pray thee *Launce*, and if thou seest my Boy   1327
Pro. Looke to the Boy. | *Val.* Why, Boy?   2211
Pro. Where is that ring? boy? | *Iul.* Heere 'tis: this is it.   2216
Duke. I think the Boy hath grace in him, he blushes.   2292
Val. I warrant you (my Lord) more grace, then Boy.   2293
BOYES = 1*1
*Ile after, to reioyce in the boyes correctio(n). *Exeunt.*   1444
By the Hangmans boyes in the market place,   1875
BRAG = *1
*2.*Out.* Thou shalt not liue, to brag what we haue of-|(fer'd.   1615
BRAGADISME = 1
Pro. Why *Valentine*, what Bragadisme is this?   818
BREAK = *1
La. Well: that fault may be mended with a break-|fast: read on.   1388
BREAKE = 6
And in good time: now will we breake with him.   346
Now can I breake my fast, dine, sup, and sleepe,   793
I am to breake with thee of some affaires   1128
Ile be so bold to breake the seale for once.   1209
And full of new-found oathes, which he will breake   1951
She will not faile; for Louers breake not houres,   2031
BREAKING = 1
In breaking faith with *Iulia*, whom I lou'd;   1635
BREAK-FAST = 1
I would haue beene a break-fast to the Beast,   2155
BREAST = *1
*Male-content: to rellish a Loue-song, like a *Robin*-red-|breast: 415
BREATH = 4*1
*there 'tis; heere's my mothers breath vp and downe: 621
If so: I pray thee breath it in mine eare,   1309
Sp. Item, shee is not to be fasting in respect of her | breath.   1386
La. That makes amends for her soure breath.   1391
I dare thee, but to breath vpon my Loue.   2258
BRED = 1
Du. I, much is the force of heauen-bred Poesie.   1518

19

BREECHES = *1
*Luc. What fashion (Madam) shall I make your bree-|(ches?   1024
BREED = 1
Val. How vse doth breed a habit in a man?   2122
BREEDER = 1
Time is the Nurse, and breeder of all good;   1313
BREST = 1
O thou that dost inhabit in my brest,   2128
BREW = 1
*La. And thereof comes the prouerbe: (Blessing of | your heart, you brew
good Ale.)   1367
BREWES = 1
Sp. Item, she brewes good Ale.   1366
BRIEFE = *1
*Pro. Come, come, open the matter in briefe; what | said she.   129
BRIGHT = 1
To be regarded in her sun-bright eye.   1157
BRING = 7*2
Pro. And thither will I bring thee Valentine.   59
Come, goe with vs, we'll bring thee to our Crewes,   1620
*Ho. Come, we'll haue you merry: ile bring you where   1654
To her let vs Garlands bring.   1677
To bring me where to speake with Madam Siluia.   1930
Sil. Vrsula, bring my Picture there,   1938
We must bring you to our Captaine.   2104
2 Out. Come, bring her away.   2107
*1 Out. Come, I must bring you to our Captains caue.   2114
BRINGING = 1
Witnesse good bringing vp, fortune, and truth: 1888
BROKEN = 2
Spee. What, are they broken?   889
Vn-heedfull vowes may heedfully be broken,   940
BROKER = 1
Iul. Now (by my modesty) a goodly Broker: 194
BROOKE = 2
Haue learn'd me how to brooke this patiently.   2106
I better brooke then flourishing peopled Townes: 2124
BROTHER = 1
Wherewith my brother held you in the Cloyster?   303
BROTHERS = *1
*foure of his blinde brothers and sisters went to it: I haue   1825
BROUGHT = 4*1
And being so hard to me, that brought your minde;   138
Till the last step haue brought me to my Loue,   1011
*him (looke you) it goes hard: one that I brought vp of   1823
Here haue I brought him backe againe.   1872
And Iulia her selfe hath brought it hither. | Pro. How? Iulia?   2225
BROW = 1
How angerly I taught my brow to frowne,   216
BRUZING-STONES = 1
I throw thy name against the bruzing-stones,   271
BUD = 3
Pro. Yet Writers say; as in the sweetest Bud,   46
Val. And Writers say; as the most forward Bud   49
Is turn'd to folly, blasting in the Bud,   52
BUILDING = 1
Lest growing ruinous, the building fall,   2130

BUILT = 1
   And built so sheluing, that one cannot climbe it   1184
BURDEN = 1
   Iu. Heauy? belike it hath some burden then?   242
BURIED = 2*1
   *weep like a yong wench that had buried her Grandam: 418
   For I am sure she is not buried.   1732
   Assure thy selfe, my loue is buried.   1739
BURNE = 2*1
   Lau. Why, I tell thee, I care not, though hee burne   919
   Lest it should burne aboue the bounds of reason.   998
   And with thy daring folly burne the world?   1224
BURNES = 2
   Lu. Fire that's closest kept, burnes most of all.   183
   Iul. The more thou dam'st it vp, the more it burnes: 999
BURNING = *1
   Pro. Thus haue I shund the fire, for feare of burning,   380
BURY = 1
   Pro. Then in dumbe silence will I bury mine,   1277
BUSINESSE = 1
   That can with some discretion doe my businesse: 1884
BUT *l.*12 38 55 *75 89 *91 *98 114 126 127 140 154 164 166 175 182 192
   255 *262 277 *358 *399 *431 *434 436 448 485 497 514 518 548 *562
   *624 719 720 725 738 757 764 780 798 833 860 864 866 867 *881 885
   *898 902 *907 *909 939 947 955 969 993 997 1002 1014 1034 1039 1049
   1064 1075 1097 1113 1125 1151 1161 1166 1175 *1180 1182 1196 1233
   1239 1256 1257 1262 1298 1299 1302 *1331 *1332 *1333 *1334 *1336
   *1343 1447 1462 1480 1495 1514 *1548 1574 1577 1589 1599 1614 1629
   1640 1645 1646 1657 1661 1684 *1692 1693 1694 1729 1749 1752 1754
   1765 1798 *1829 *1839 *1848 1870 1886 1898 1925 1927 1973 2001 2013
   2015 2048 2052 2058 2059 2084 2089 2110 2144 2151 2177 2189 2195
   *2222 2237 2240 2257 2258 2260 2297 = 121*27
BY = 71*8, 2
   And by and by a clowd takes all away.   389
   And by and by intend to chide my selfe,   1727
CALL = 11*1
   Pro. So, by your circumstance, you call me foole.   40
   It were a shame to call her backe againe,   205
   My pennance is, to call *Lucetta* backe   218
   Val. Why sir, who bad you call her?   406
   Panth. Come: come away man, I was sent to call | thee.   647
   Lau. Sir: call me what thou dar'st. | *Pant.* Wilt thou goe? 649
   Val. Call her diuine. | *Pro.* I will not flatter her.   799
   Fie, fie, vnreuerend tongue, to call her bad,   943
   But when I call to minde your gracious fauours   1075
   A Sea of melting pearle, which some call teares;   1294
   Sil. Goe to thy Ladies graue and call hers thence,   1741
   Entreated me to call, and know her minde: 1770
CALLS = 1
   Pan. Sir *Protheus*, your Fathers call's for you,   390
CALME = 2
   Be calme (good winde) blow not a word away,   278
   Would I not vndergoe, for one calme looke: 2163
CALS = 1
   Madam, Madam. | *Sil.* Who cals?   1772
CAME = 4*2
   Deliuer'd by a friend, that came from him.   356

CAME *cont.*

Val. Now trust me (Madam) it came hardly-off	499
*Val. Now tell me: how do al from whence you came?	773
1.*Out.* Whence came you? | *Val.* From *Millaine.*	1564
**to Mistris *Siluia,* from my Master; and I came no	1828
Pro. Vnhappy were you (Madam) ere I came:	2150

CAMELEON = *1

*Speed. I, but hearken sir: though the Cameleon Loue	562

CAMELION = *1

*Val. Giue him leaue, Madam, he is a kind of *Camelion.*	678

CAMST = *1

*Pro. But how cam'st thou by this ring? at my depart | I gaue this vnto *Iulia.*	2222

CAN *l.*88 238 426 485 *563 570 748 793 819 868 1194 1269 *1342 *1343 *1345 1356 1364 1369 1370 1371 1373 1374 1377 1378 1489 1492 1493 1513 1861 1884 2003 2015 2125 2179 = 31*4

CANCELL = 1

Cancell all grudge, repeale thee home againe,	2270

CANKER = 2

The eating Canker dwels; so eating Loue	47
Is eaten by the Canker ere it blow,	50

CANNOT = 26*8

Sp. And yet it cannot ouer-take your slow purse.	128
Which cannot perish hauing thee aboarde,	147
Iu. And why not you? | *Lu.* I cannot reach so high.	244
And how he cannot be a perfect man,	322
Pro. My Lord I cannot be so soone prouided,	374
Val. Without me? they cannot.	429
Speed. If you loue her, you cannot see her. | *Val.* Why?	461
**his hose; and you, beeing in loue, cannot see to put on | your hose.	470
I, so true loue should doe: it cannot speake,	585
**shooe is my mother: nay, that cannot bee so neyther:	608
I cannot leaue to loue; and yet I doe:	946
I cannot now proue constant to my selfe,	960
And thence she cannot be conuay'd away.	1106
Cannot your Grace win her to fancie him?	1136
If with his tongue he cannot win a woman.	1174
And built so sheluing, that one cannot climbe it	1184
*Val. My eares are stopt, & cannot hear good newes,	1275
**a horse can doe no more; nay, a horse cannot fetch, but	1343
It was *Eues* legacie, and cannot be t'ane from her.	1401
*La. Of her tongue she cannot; for that's writ downe	1410
**keepe shut: Now, of another thing shee may, and that | cannot I helpe. Well, proceede.	1412
*Du. Where your good word cannot aduantage him,	1488
And cannot soone reuolt, and change your minde.	1506
Will creepe in seruice, where it cannot goe.	1644
Iu. Marry (mine *Host*) because I cannot be merry.	1653
**thing, when a Cur cannot keepe himselfe in all compa-|nies:	1831
Iul. I cannot choose but pitty her.	1898
But cannot be true seruant to my Master,	1925
The Thicket is beset, he cannot scape.	2113
(A smaller boone then this I cannot beg,	2145
And lesse then this, I am sure you cannot giue.)	2146
And full as much (for more there cannot be)	2159
When women cannot loue, where they're belou'd.	2165
*Sil. When *Protheus* cannot loue, where he's belou'd:	2166

CANST *l*.895 1311 1314 1356 1361 = 5
CAP = *1
   Speed. Come-on you mad-cap: Ile to the Ale-house   879
CAPONS-LEG = *1
   *Trencher, and steales her Capons-leg: O, 'tis a foule   1830
CAPTAINE = 3
   Say I, and be the captaine of vs all: 1611
   We must bring you to our Captaine.   2104
   There is our Captaine: Wee'll follow him that's fled,   2112
CAPTAINS = *1
   *1 *Out*. Come, I must bring you to our Captains caue.   2114
CAR = 1
   Wilt thou aspire to guide the heauenly Car?   1223
CARE = 3*3
   And yet I will not name it: and yet I care not.   507
   Lau. Why, I tell thee, I care not, though hee burne   919
   Duke. *Protheus*, I thank thee for thine honest care,   1091
   La. What neede a man care for a stock with a wench,   1372
   La. I care not for that neither: because I loue crusts.   1403
   Thur. Sir *Valentine*, I care not for her, I: 2259
CARES = 1
   You doate on her, that cares not for your loue.   1903
CARRIED = *1
   La. Marry Sir, I carried Mistris *Siluia* the dogge you | bad me.   1865
CARRY = 1*4
   *In requitall whereof, henceforth, carry your letters your   144
   *Condition. *Inprimis*. Shee can fetch and carry: why   1342
   *onely carry, therefore is shee better then a Iade. *Item*.   1344
   *Masters command, hee must carry for a present to his | Lady.   1700
   To carry that, which I would haue refus'd;   1922
CARRYING = *2
   Sp. Nay Sir, lesse then a pound shall serue me for car-|rying your
   Letter.   109
   *'Tis threefold too little for carrying a letter to your louer   113
CAST = 2*1
   Iul. And would'st thou haue me cast my loue on him?   178
   Lu. I: if you thought your loue not cast away.   179
   To cast vp, with a paire of anchoring hookes,   1187
CATCHING = 1
   Yet here they shall not lye, for catching cold.   295
CATE-LOG = *1
   *much in a bare Christian: Heere is the Cate-log of her   1341
CATTE = *1
   *Catte wringing her hands, and all our house in a great   600
CAUE = *1
   *1 *Out*. Come, I must bring you to our Captains caue.   2114
CAUILL = 1
   Pro. 'Tis Loue you cauill at, I am not Loue.   42
CAUSE = *1
   Iul. I thinke she doth: and that's her cause of sorrow.   1968
CEASE = 3
   Valentine. | Cease to perswade, my louing *Protheus*;   3
   Speed. I would you were set, so your affection would | cease.   478
   Pro. Cease to lament for that thou canst not helpe,   1311
CEAZED = 1
   Sil. Had I beene ceazed by a hungry Lion,   2154

CELESTIALL = 2
But now I worship a celestiall Sunne: 939
To climbe celestiall *Siluia's* chamber window,   963
CELL = 3
  Eg. Where shall I meete you? | *Sil.* At *Frier Patrickes* Cell,   1814
  That *Siluia*, at Fryer *Patricks* Cell should meet me,   2030
  At *Patricks* Cell this euen, and there she was not.   2086
CENSURE = 1
Should censure thus on louely Gentlemen.   172
CERTAINE = 1*2
  Speed. Without you? nay, that's certaine: for with-|out   430
  *till some certaine shot be paid, and the Hostesse say wel-|come.   877
  Enter Valentine, Speed, and certaine Out-lawes.   1546
CESTERND = *1
  *To testifie your bounty, I thank you, you haue cestern'd | (me;   143
CHACE = 1
Haue some vnhappy passenger in chace;   2136
CHAFD = 1
Besides, her intercession chaf'd him so,   1303
CHAINES = 1
Wer't not affection chaines thy tender dayes   6
CHAMBER = 8*3
Good *Protheus* goe with me to my chamber,   839
To climbe celestiall *Siluia's* chamber window,   963
And presently goe with me to my chamber   1058
Duk. Her chamber is aloft, far from the ground,   1183
The Picture that is hanging in your chamber: 1746
*sooner into the dyning-chamber, but he steps me to her   1829
*all the chamber smelt him: out with the dog (saies one)   1840
*but whips me out of the chamber: how many Masters   1848
This Letter: that's her chamber: Tell my Lady,   1907
Your message done, hye home vnto my chamber,   1909
Would better fit his Chamber, then this Shadow.   1941
CHAMBER-WINDOW = 2
How he her chamber-window will ascend,   1108
Visit by night your Ladies chamber-window   1529
CHANCE = 1
Should from her vesture chance to steale a kisse,   814
CHANGD = 1
Besides the fashion of the time is chang'd)   1155
CHANGE = 6
Sil. What, angry, Sir *Thurio*, do you change colour?   677
And cannot soone reuolt, and change your minde.   1506
Ho. Harke, what fine change is in the Musique.   1690
Iu. I: that change is the spight.   1691
Can no way change you to a milder forme;   2179
Women to change their shapes, then men their minds.   2235
CHANGING = 1
One *Iulia*, that his changing thoughts forget   1940
CHARACTERD = 1
Are visibly Character'd, and engrau'd,   979
CHARGD = *2
  Sp. If the ground be ouer-charg'd, you were best | sticke her.   105
  Iul. O good sir, my master charg'd me to deliuer a ring   2214
CHARITY = *1
  Spee. Why? | *Lau.* Because thou hast not so much charity in thee as   923

24

CHASD = 1
Loue hath chas'd sleepe from my enthralled eyes,   786
CHASTITIE = 1
Vpon whose Graue thou vow'dst pure chastitie: 1791
CHECKE = 1
If I can checke my erring loue, I will,   868
CHEEKES = 1
The ayre hath staru'd the roses in her cheekes,   1975
CHERISH = 1
Thou gentle Nimph, cherish thy for-lorne swaine.   2133
CHERISHD = 2
Should haue beene cherish'd by her child-like dutie,   1144
Foster'd, illumin'd, cherish'd, kept aliue.   1254
CHID = 2
And pray her to a fault, for which I chid her.   206
How churlishly, I chid *Lucetta* hence,   214
CHIDDE = *1
*to haue, when you chidde at Sir *Protheus*, for going vn- | garter'd.   465
CHIDDEN = *1
Speed. And yet I was last chidden for being too slow.   409
CHIDE = 3
bolder to chide you, for yours.   476
If she doe chide, 'tis not to haue you gone,   1167
And by and by intend to chide my selfe,   1727
CHIEFE = *1
*I pray thee out with't, and place it for her chiefe vertue.   1398
CHIEFELY = 1
But chiefely, for thy face, and thy behauiour,   1886
CHILDE = 2
Neither regarding that she is my childe,   1139
Duk. This very night; for Loue is like a childe   1193
CHILD-LIKE = 1
Should haue beene cherish'd by her child-like dutie,   1144
CHOOSE = 1
Iul. I cannot choose but pitty her.   1898
CHOSE = 1
Thus (for my duties sake) I rather chose   1086
CHRISTALL = 1
Did hold his eyes, lockt in her Christall lookes.   739
CHRISTIAN = 2*1
*if not, thou art an Hebrew, a Iew, and not worth | the name of a
Christian.   921
to goe to the Ale with a Christian: Wilt thou goe?   925
*much in a bare Christian: Heere is the Cate-log of her   1341
CHRONICLED = 1
Me thinkes should not be chronicled for wise.   45
CHURLISH = 1
Those at her fathers churlish feete she tenderd,   1295
CHURLISHLY = 1
How churlishly, I chid *Lucetta* hence,   214
CIRCUMSTANCE = 4
Pro. So, by your circumstance, you call me foole.   40
Val. So, by your circumstance, I feare you'll proue.   41
Sp. Nay, that I can deny by a circumstance.   88
Therefore it must with circumstance be spoken   1482
CITE = 2
For *Valentine*, I need not cite him to it,   735

25

CITE *cont.*
  But to the purpose: for we cite our faults,   1599
CITY = 1
  Let vs into the City presently   1537
CITY-GATE = 1
  Come, Ile conuey thee through the City-gate.   1322
CIUILL = 1
  They are reformed, ciuill, full of good,   2283
CLAIME = 2
  I claime the promise for her heauenly Picture: 1908
  I claime her not, and therefore she is thine.   2262
CLEANE = 1
  *She can milke, looke you, a sweet vertue in a maid with | cleane
  hands.   1345
CLEFT = 1
  How oft hast thou with periury cleft the roote?   2229
CLERKLY = *1
  *Sil. I thanke you (gentle Seruant) 'tis very Clerkly- |(done.   498
CLIMBE = 3
  Determin'd of: how I must climbe her window,   836
  To climbe celestiall *Siluia's* chamber window,   963
  And built so sheluing, that one cannot climbe it   1184
CLOAKE = 5*1
  Vnder a cloake, that is of any length.   1199
  Duk. A cloake as long as thine will serue the turne? | *Val.* I my good
  Lord.   1200
  Duk. Then let me see thy cloake,   1202
  Val. Why any cloake will serue the turn (my Lord)   1204
  Duk. How shall I fashion me to weare a cloake?   1205
  I pray thee let me feele thy cloake vpon me.   1206
CLOASD = *1
  Lau. Marry after they cloas'd in earnest, they parted | very fairely in
  iest.   883
CLOATH = 1
  To cloath mine age with Angel-like perfection: 716
CLOCK = 1
  Val. By seauen a clock, ile get you such a Ladder.   1195
CLOSE = 3
  That to close prison he commanded her,   1305
  La. Close at the heeles of her vertues.   1385
  Let me be blest to make this happy close: 2243
CLOSEST = 1
  Lu. Fire that's closest kept, burnes most of all.   183
CLOWD = 1
  And by and by a clowd takes all away.   389
CLOWNISH = 1
  Speed: a clownish seruant to Valentine.   2310
CLOYSTER = 1
  Wherewith my brother held you in the Cloyster?   303
COCKE = *1
  *like a cocke; when you walk'd, to walke like one of the   422
COD-PEECE = 1*1
  Luc. You must needs haue the(m) with a cod-peece (Ma- |(dam   1028
  Vnlesse you haue a cod-peece to stick pins on.   1031
COILE = 1
  Here is a coile with protestation: 259

COLD = 3
   Yet here they shall not lye, for catching cold. 295
   Me thinkes my zeale to *Valentine* is cold, 858
   I hope my Masters suit will be but cold, 2001
COLDLY = 1
   Yet will I woe for him, but yet so coldly, 1927
COLOUR = 2
   Sil. What, angry, Sir *Thurio*, do you change colour? 677
   Vnder the colour of commending him, 1627
COME = 30*10
   Pro. Come, come, open the matter in briefe; what | said she. 129
   Iu. Come, come, wilt please you goe. *Exeunt.* 299
   Come on *Panthino*; you shall be imployd, 378
   Pro. Goe: I come, I come: 588
   *come I to my Father; Father, your blessing: now 616
   *Now come I to my Mother: Oh that she could speake 619
   *Now come I to my sister; marke the moane she makes: 622
   Panth. Come: come away man, I was sent to call | thee. 647
   Well, Sir: this Gentleman is come to me 728
   Had come along with me, but that his Mistresse 738
   Sil. I wait vpon his pleasure: Come Sir *Thurio*, 768
   If *Protheus* like your iourney, when you come, 1040
   Luc. Pray heau'n he proue so when you come to him. 1054
   Come; answere not: but to it presently, 1064
   That longs for euery thing that he can come by. 1194
   Oh, could their Master come, and goe as lightly, 1212
   Come, Ile conuey thee through the City-gate. 1322
   Pro. Goe sirha, finde him out: Come *Valentine*. 1329
   Sp. Come foole, come: try me in thy paper. 1362
   Come, goe with vs, we'll bring thee to our Crewes, 1620
   Ho. Come, we'll haue you merry: ile bring you where 1654
   I am thus early come, to know what seruice 1779
   No griefe did euer come so neere thy heart, 1789
   Come shadow, come, and take this shadow vp, 2017
   Vnlesse it be to come before their time, 2032
   1.*Out.* Come, come be patient: 2103
   2 *Out.* Come, bring her away. 2107
   1 Out. Come, I must bring you to our Captains caue. 2114
   Val. Come, come: a hand from either: 2242
   Come not within the measure of my wrath: 2254
   Come, let vs goe, we will include all iarres, 2287
   Come *Protheus*, 'tis your pennance, but to heare 2297
COMES = 8*2
   Peace, here she comes. 486
   Sil. No more, gentlemen, no more: | Here comes my father. 696
   Comes all the praises that I now bestow.) 722
   Sil. Haue done, haue done: here comes y gentleman. 749
   And this way comes he with it presently. 1111
   La. And thereof comes the prouerbe: (*Blessing of* | *your heart, you brew*
   good Ale.) 1367
   But here comes *Thurio*; now must we to her window, 1640
   See where she comes: Lady a happy euening. 2034
   Iul. Here comes the Duke. 2071
   Withdraw thee *Valentine*: who's this comes heere? 2139
COME-ON = *1
   Speed. Come-on you mad-cap: Ile to the Ale-house 879

COMMAND = 4*1
    (Please you command) a thousand times as much: | And yet---   504
    Which to requite, command me while I liue.   1092
    *Masters command, hee must carry for a present to his | Lady.   1700
    One that attends your Ladiships command.   1775
    It is your pleasure to command me in.   1780
COMMANDED = 1
    That to close prison he commanded her,   1305
COMMANDER = 1
    Loue thee, as our Commander, and our King.   1613
COMMEND = 6
    Commend thy grieuance to my holy prayers,   20
    selfe; And so Sir, I'le commend you to my Master.   145
    And to commend their seruice to his will.   344
    Flatter, and praise, commend, extoll their graces: 1171
    When to her beauty I commend my vowes,   1633
    That all our Swaines commend her?   1664
COMMENDATION = 1
    With Commendation from great Potentates,   729
COMMENDATIONS = 1
    Of commendations sent from *Valentine*;   355
COMMENDED = *1
    Pro. Your frends are wel, & haue the(m) much com(m)ended.   774
COMMENDING = 1
    Vnder the colour of commending him,   1627
COMMENT = *1
    *not an eye that sees you, but is a Physician to comment | on your
    Malady.   434
COMMING = 5
    Expects my comming, there to see me ship'd.   58
    My father staies my comming: answere not: 581
    Pro. Adiew, my Lord, Sir *Valentine* is comming.   1119
    When will you goe? | *Sil.* This euening comming.   1812
    But by my comming, I haue made you happy.   2151
COMMIT = 1
    I tender't heere: I doe as truely suffer, | As ere I did commit.   2201
COMMITTED = 1
    Forgiue them what they haue committed here,   2281
COMMON = *1
    Val. Thou co(m)mon friend, that's without faith or loue,   2187
COMPANIE = 1
    Sir *Valentine* her companie, and my Court.   1096
COMPANIES = *1
    *thing, when a Cur cannot keepe himselfe in all compa-|nies: 1831
COMPANION = 1
    How his companion, youthfull *Valentine*,   328
COMPANY = 7*3
    I rather would entreat thy company,   8
    Ant. Good company: with them shall *Protheus* go: 345
    *And spends what he borrowes kindly in your company.   689
    Forsworne my company, and rail'd at me,   1450
    Thrust from the company of awfull men.   1592
    Iu. Peace, stand aside, the company parts.   1702
    I doe desire thy worthy company,   1795
    To beare me company, and goe with me: 1804
    *Hee thrusts me himselfe into the company of three or   1837
    And *Eglamoure* is in her Company: 2080

COMPASSE = 3
If not, to compasse her Ile vse my skill. | *Exeunt.*   869
What compasse will you weare your Farthingale?   1026
Sil. What's your will? | *Pro.* That I may compasse yours.   1715
COMPETITOR = 1
My selfe in counsaile his competitor.   964
COMPLAINING = 3
He couples it, to his complaining Names;   287
Will well become such sweet complaining grieuance: 1532
And to the Nightingales complaining Notes   2126
COMPLEAT = 1
He is compleat in feature, and in minde,   723
COMPOSED = 1
By walefull Sonnets, whose composed Rimes   1516
CONCEALE = 1
The Law of friendship bids me to conceale,   1074
CONCEALING = 1
Then (by concealing it) heap on your head   1088
CONCEIT = 1
Protheus, the good conceit I hold of thee,   1463
CONCEITED = 1
With twentie od-conceited true-loue knots: 1021
CONCEITLESSE = 1
Think'st thou I am so shallow, so conceitlesse,   1720
CONCERNE = 1
Of all that may concerne thy Loue-affaires: 1324
CONCERNES = 2
Iul. Then let it lye, for those that it concernes.   233
Lu. Madam, it will not lye where it concernes,   234
CONCERNING = 1
Lu. Nothing concerning me.   232
CONCLUDE = *1
Sp. You conclude that my Master is a Shepheard then, | and I
Sheepe? | *Pro.* I doe   80
CONCLUSION = 2
Val. In conclusion, I stand affected to her.   477
Spee. The conclusion is then, that it will.   906
CONCORD = 1
And marre the concord, with too harsh a descant: 254
CONDITION = *1
Condition. Inprimis. Shee can fetch and carry: why   1342
CONDITIONS = 1
And leaue her on such slight conditions.   2265
CONFER = 4
Ile leaue you to confer of home affaires,   770
We haue some secrets to confer about.   1071
And ere I part with thee, confer at large   1323
Makes me the better to confer with thee.   1465
CONFERRE = 1
Where you, with *Siluia*, may conferre at large.   1508
CONFESSE = 1
And hath so humbled me, as I confesse   789
CONFESSION = 2
Where I intend holy Confession.   1816
Besides she did intend Confession   2085
CONFIRME = 2
Confirme his welcome, with some speciall fauor.   751

CONFIRME *cont.*
These likelihoods confirme her flight from hence; 2087
CONFIRMED = 1
I am my Masters true confirmed Loue, 1924
CONFIRMING = 1
With twenty thousand soule-confirming oathes. 945
CONFOUNDS = 1
Pro. My shame and guilt confounds me: 2198
CONIURE = 1
And eu'n in kinde loue, I doe coniure thee, 977
CONSENT = 1
I giue consent to goe along with you, 1809
CONSENTS = 1
To seale our happinesse with their consents. 351
CONSIDERD = 1
I haue consider'd well, his losse of time, 321
CONSIDERS = 1
Thu. Considers she my Possessions? 2066
CONSORT = 1*1
With some sweet Consort; To their Instruments 1530
*3.*Out.* What saist thou? wilt thou be of our consort? 1610
CONSPIRE = 1
To whisper, and conspire against my youth? 196
CONSTANCIE = 1
Pro. Here is my hand, for my true constancie: 576
CONSTANT = 3
I cannot now proue constant to my selfe, 960
But Constant, he were perfect; that one error 2237
More fresh in *Iulia's*, with a constant eye? 2241
CONSTRUE = 1
Which they would haue the profferer construe, I. 210
CONTEMNING = 1
I haue done pennance for contemning Loue, 781
CONTEMPT = 1
For in reuenge of my contempt of loue, 785
CONTEMPTUOUSLY = 1
Trampling contemptuously on thy disdaine. 272
CONTEND = 1
Now kisse, embrace, contend, doe what you will. 289
CONTENT = 1*1
*Male-content: to rellish a Loue-song, like a *Robin*-red- | breast: 415
Are you content to be our Generall? 1607
CONTENTS = 1*1
Lu. That the Contents will shew. 189
Val. A woman somtime scorns what best co(n)tents her. 1162
CONTINUE = 1
She shall not long continue loue to him: 1494
CONTRARY = 2
Thu. What instance of the contrary? | *Val.* Your folly. 670
'Tis pitty Loue, should be so contrary: 1904
CONUAYD = 1
And thence she cannot be conuay'd away. 1106
CONUERSE = 1
Heare sweet discourse, conuerse with Noble-men, 333
CONUERST = 1
We haue conuerst, and spent our howres together, 713

CONUEY = 2
How shall I best conuey the Ladder thither?   1197
Come, Ile conuey thee through the City-gate.   1322
CORDED-LADDER = 2
This night he meaneth with a Corded-ladder   962
And with a Corded-ladder fetch her downe: 1109
CORDS = 2
The Ladder made of Cords, and all the means   837
Val. Why then a Ladder quaintly made of Cords   1186
CORRECTION = 1*1
There is no woe to his correction,   790
*Ile after, to reioyce in the boyes correctio(n). *Exeunt.*   1444
CORRUPTED = 1
To be corrupted with my worthlesse guifts;   1630
COUER = *1
*couer of the salt, hides the salt, and therefore it is more   1421
COUERS = *1
*then the salt; the haire that couers the wit, is more   1422
COULD *l.*136 *469 473 556 *619 646 744 1212 1301 1525 2190 = 9*2
COULDST *l.*135 = *1
COULOURD = 1
Ile get me such a coulour'd Perrywig: 2011
COUNCELLOR = 1
As meet to be an Emperors Councellor: 727
COUNSAILE = 7
But wherefore waste I time to counsaile thee   55
Warre with good counsaile; set the world at nought;   72
Would'st thou then counsaile me to fall in loue?   155
Ant. I like thy counsaile: well hast thou aduis'd: 336
In these affaires to aid me with thy counsaile.   840
My selfe in counsaile his competitor.   964
Iul. Counsaile, *Lucetta*, gentle girle assist me,   976
COUNT = 2*1
Speed. That's because the one is painted, and the o-|ther out of all
count.   450
Val. How painted? and how out of count?   452
But count the world a stranger for thy sake: 2195
COUNTERFEYT = 1
Thou Counterfeyt, to thy true friend.   2174
COUNTERFEYTS = 1
Thu. So doe Counterfeyts. | *Val.* So doe you.   666
COUNTRIMAN = 2
Duk. Know ye *Don Antonio*, your Countriman?   704
How now sir *Protheus*, is your countriman   1457
COUNTS = 1
Speed. Marry sir, so painted to make her faire, that no | man counts of
her beauty.   453
COUPLES = 1
He couples it, to his complaining Names;   287
COURSE = 3
And perfected by the swift course of time: 325
But when his faire course is not hindered,   1002
Then let me goe, and hinder not my course: 1008
COURT = 7*1
Attends the Emperour in his royall Court.   329
I will dispatch him to the Emperors Court.   340
With *Valentinus*, in the Emperors Court: 369

COURT *cont.*

*Court: I thinke *Crab* my dog, be the sowrest natured	597
Sir *Valentine* her companie, and my Court.	1096
My health, and happy being at your Court.	1126
(For long agone I haue forgot to court,	1154
Will giue thee time to leaue our royall Court,	1235

COWARDIZE = 1*1

With falsehood, cowardize, and poore discent:	1478
Iul. She needes not, when she knowes it cowardize.	2062

COY = 1*1

*Coy looks, with hart-sore sighes: one fading moments | (mirth,	34
Whom I affect: but she is nice, and coy,	1151

CRAB = 1*2

*Court: I thinke *Crab* my dog, be the sowrest natured	597
Lau. Why, he that's tide here, *Crab* my dog.	633
*with the smell before, knew it was Crab; and	1843

CREATURES = 1

Soueraigne to all the Creatures on the earth.	806

CREEPE = 1

Will creepe in seruice, where it cannot goe.	1644

CREPT = 1

Th. How now, sir *Protheus*, are you crept before vs?	1642

CREWES = 1

Come, goe with vs, we'll bring thee to our Crewes,	1620

CRIMES = 1

1.*Out.* And I, for such like petty crimes as these.	1598

CROOKED = 1

If crooked fortune had not thwarted me.	1568

CROSSD = 1

A man I am, cross'd with aduersitie:	1558

CROSSE = 3

But *Valentine* being gon, Ile quickely crosse	969
To crosse my friend in his intended drift,	1087
Iul. And I will follow, more to crosse that loue	2099

CROST = 1

How yong *Leander* crost the *Hellespont*.	25

CROW = *1

*You were wont, when you laughed, to crow	421

CRUELL-HEARTED = *1

*perplexitie, yet did not this cruell-hearted Curre shedde	601

CRUSTS = *1

La. I care not for that neither: because I loue crusts.	1403

CRY = 4

Sp. Such another proofe will make me cry baa.	97
Iul. Alas. | *Pro.* Why do'st thou cry alas?	1896
And thinking on it, makes me cry alas.	1905
Iul. Oh, cry you mercy sir, I haue mistooke:	2220

CRYING = *1

*wayling: my Sister crying: our Maid howling: our	599

CUNNING = 2

With all the cunning manner of our flight	835
That you shall say, my cunning drift excels.	1704

CUNNINGLY = 1

But (good my Lord) doe it so cunningly	1113

CUR = *3

*thing, when a Cur cannot keepe himselfe in all compa-|nies:	1831
*what cur is that (saies another) whip him out (saies the	1841

CUR *cont.*
La. Marry she saies your dog was a cur, and tels you   1868
CURRE = *2
*perplexitie, yet did not this cruell-hearted Curre shedde   601
Lau. When a mans seruant shall play the Curre with   1822
CURRENT = 1
The Current that with gentle murmure glides   1000
CURRISH = 1
currish thanks is good enough for such a present.   1869
CURSE = 3
Doe curse the grace, that with such grace hath blest them,   1216
I curse my selfe, for they are sent by me,   1218
Oh 'tis the curse in Loue, and still approu'd   2164
CURST = 1
Sp. Item, she is curst.   1404
CURTESIE = 1
1.*Out.* But if thou scorne our curtesie, thou dyest.   1614
CUT = 1
Luc. Why then your Ladiship must cut your haire.   1019
DAIES = 1
Made vse, and faire aduantage of his daies: 718
DAIGNE = 1
I feare my *Iulia* would not daigne my lines,   150
DAILY = 2
And daily graced by the Emperor;   360
With nightly teares, and daily hart-sore sighes,   784
DAMST = 1
Iul. The more thou dam'st it vp, the more it burnes: 999
DANCE = 1
Forsake vnsounded deepes, to dance on Sands.   1527
DANGER = 3
When thou do'st meet good hap; and in thy danger,   18
(If euer danger doe enuiron thee)   19
Regard thy danger, and along with me.   1326
DANGEROUS = 1*1
And for the waies are dangerous to passe,   1794
Pro. What dangerous action, stood it next to death   2162
DARE = 5
Dare you presume to harbour wanton lines?   195
Du. And *Protheus*, we dare trust you in this kinde,   1502
Could haue perswaded me: now I dare not say   2190
I dare thee, but to breath vpon my Loue.   2258
Val. And as we walke along, I dare be bold   2289
DARING = 1
And with thy daring folly burne the world?   1224
DARST = 1
Lau. Sir: call me what thou dar'st. | *Pant.* Wilt thou goe?   649
DAUGHTER = 10
Duk. Now, daughter *Siluia*, you are hard beset.   698
For *Thurio* he intends shall wed his daughter,   968
This night intends to steale away your daughter: 1080
On *Thurio*, whom your gentle daughter hates,   1083
To match my friend Sir *Thurio*, to my daughter.   1131
Beseeming such a Wife, as your faire daughter: 1135
I euer bore my daughter, or thy selfe.   1237
Du. My daughter takes his going grieuously?   1460
The match betweene sir *Thurio*, and my daughter? | *Pro.* I doe my Lord.   1469

DAUGHTER *cont.*
  Du. Saw you my daughter? | *Pro.* Neither.   2076
DAUGHTERS = 1
  I now beseech you (for your daughters sake)   2276
DAY = 11
  That euery day with par'le encounter me,   158
  Please you deliberate a day or two.   375
  The vncertaine glory of an Aprill day,   387
  And when that howre ore-slips me in the day,   577
  That no man hath accesse by day to her.   1178
  Vnlesse I looke on *Siluia* in the day,   1250
  There is no day for me to looke vpon.   1251
  Trust me, I thinke 'tis almost day.   1764
  Gentlewoman, good day: I pray you be my meane   1929
  What hallowing, and what stir is this to day?   2134
  That done, our day of marriage shall be yours,   2299
DAYES = 2
  Wer't not affection chaines thy tender dayes   6
  Where haue you bin these two dayes loytering?   1864
DAZELD = 1
  And that hath dazel'd my reasons light: 865
DEAD = 7
  Remembring that my Loue to her is dead.   957
  Val. Is *Siluia* dead? | *Pro.* No, *Valentine.*   1279
  Tune a deploring dumpe: the nights dead silence   1531
  Pro. I grant (sweet loue) that I did loue a Lady, | But she is dead.   1729
  Pro. I likewise heare that *Valentine* is dead.   1737
  She is dead belike? | *Pro.* Not so: I thinke she liues.   1894
  Wept bitterly: and would I might be dead,   1992
DEADLY = 2
  Is selfe from selfe. A deadly banishment: 1243
  I flie not death, to flie his deadly doome,   1255
DEAFE = *1
  Iu. I, I would I were deafe: it makes me haue a slow | (heart.   1687
DEARE = 2
  Lu. Pardon deare Madam, 'tis a passing shame,   170
  For whose deare sake, thou didst then rend thy faith   2168
DEARTH = 1
  Pitty the dearth that I haue pined in,   991
DEATH = 5*2
  Being destin'd to a drier death on shore: 148
  Val. And why not death, rather then liuing torment?   1240
  I flie not death, to flie his deadly doome,   1255
  Tarry I heere, I but attend on death,   1256
  I kil'd a man, whose death I much repent,   1573
  Pro. What dangerous action, stood it next to death   2162
  Val. Thurio giue backe; or else embrace thy death: 2253
DECEITFULL = 1
  Luc. All these are seruants to deceitfull men.   1047
DECEIUD = 1
  That has't deceiu'd so many with thy vowes?   1722
DECEIUE = 1*1
  Iul. If 'twere a substance you would sure deceiue it,   1751
  Which (if my Augury deceiue me not)   1887
DECKES = 1
  Sweet Ornament, that deckes a thing diuine, | Ah *Siluia, Siluia.*   401

DEEDS = 1
For truth hath better deeds, then words to grace it.   586
DEEPE = 3
Val. That's on some shallow Storie of deepe loue,   24
Pro. That's a deepe Storie, of a deeper loue,   26
Sad sighes, deepe grones, nor siluer-shedding teares   1300
DEEPELY = 1
And entertain'd'em deepely in her heart.   2228
DEEPER = 1
Pro. That's a deepe Storie, of a deeper loue,   26
DEEPES = 1
Forsake vnsounded deepes, to dance on Sands.   1527
DEEPEST = 1
The priuate wound is deepest: oh time, most accurst.   2196
DEER = *1
*Val. Welcome, deer *Protheus*: Mistris, I beseech you   750
DEERE = 3
And when the flight is made to one so deere,   987
Val. Oh my deere *Siluia*; haplesse *Valentine*.   1330
Thou art not ignorant what deere good will   1784
DEERER = 1
I to my selfe am deerer then a friend,   952
DEFORMD = 2
Speed. You neuer saw her since she was deform'd.   456
Val. How long hath she beene deform'd?   457
DEFORMITIE = *1
*Speed. Your owne present folly, and her passing de-|formitie: 468
DEGENERATE = 1
Duke. The more degenerate and base art thou   2263
DELIBERATE = 1
Please you deliberate a day or two.   375
DELIGHT = 2
Ho. I perceiue you delight not in Musique.   1688
When all our Pageants of delight were plaid,   1980
DELIGHTS = 1
Val. O flatter me: for Loue delights in praises.   801
DELIUER = 3*2
And I am going to deliuer them.   1123
Pro. I, if his enemy deliuer it.   1481
*would teach a dog) I was sent to deliuer him, as a pre-|sent   1827
Deliuer it to Madam *Siluia*;   1891
*Iul. O good sir, my master charg'**d** me to deliuer a ring   2214
DELIUERD = 4*1
Deliuer'd by a friend, that came from him.   356
*Speed. And y letter hath she deliuer'd, & there an end.   552
Which, being writ to me, shall be deliuer'd   1319
She lou'd me well, deliuer'd it to me.   1892
Deliuer'd you a paper that I should not;   1944
DELIUERED = 1
may be both at once deliuered.   132
DELIUERING = 1
No, not so much as a ducket for deliuering your letter: 137
DENY = 1
Sp. Nay, that I can deny by a circumstance.   88
DEPART = 1*1
That I may venture to depart alone.   1806

35

DEPART *cont.*
Pro. But how cam'st thou by this ring? at my depart | I gaue this vnto
    Iulia.   2222
DEPARTURE = 2
  Is priuiledge for thy departure hence.   1230
  His *Iulia* gaue it him, at his departure: 1956
DEPENDING = 1
  And not depending on his friendly wish.   364
DEPLORING = 1
  Tune a deploring dumpe: the nights dead silence   1531
DERIUD = 2
  Pro. That you are well deriu'd.   2064
  Thou art a Gentleman, and well deriu'd,   2273
DESART = 1
  This shadowy desart, vnfrequented woods   2123
DESCANT = 1
  And marre the concord, with too harsh a descant: 254
DESCENDED = 1
  Descended into periury, to loue me,   2170
DESERT = 3
  And not without desert so well reputed.   707
  And thinke my patience, (more then thy desert)   1229
  (For thou hast showne some signe of good desert)   1464
DESERTS = 1
  Dispose of them, as thou knowst their deserts.   2286
DESERUD = 1
  Take thou thy *Siluia*, for thou hast deseru'd her.   2274
DESERUE = 1
  Onely deserue my loue, by louing him,   1057
DESERUES = 2
  Lu. To plead for loue, deserues more fee, then hate.   201
  Val. I, my good Lord, a Son, that well deserues   709
DESIRE = 4
  That art a votary to fond desire?   56
  I doe desire thy worthy company,   1795
  I doe desire thee, euen from a heart   1802
  Sil. Oh heauen. | *Pro.* Ile force thee yeeld to my desire.   2182
DESIRES = 1
  You must lay Lime, to tangle her desires   1515
DESOLATE = 1
  Alas (poore Lady) desolate, and left;   1995
DESPAIRING = 1
  And manage it, against despairing thoughts: 1317
DESPERATE = 1
  That I am desperate of obtaining her.   1451
DESPISD = 1
  Th. Since his exile she hath despis'd me most,   1449
DESPISE = 1
  That I despise thee, for thy wrongfull suite;   1726
DESPISETH = 2
  That with his very heart despiseth me?   1915
  Because he loues her, he despiseth me,   1916
DESTIND = 1
  Being destin'd to a drier death on shore: 148
DETERMIND = 2
  Determin'd of: how I must climbe her window,   836
  I know you haue determin'd to bestow her   1082

DETERMINE = 1
  And afterward determine our proceedings.   1543
DETEST = 2
  3.*Out.* No, we detest such vile base practises.   1619
  I doe detest false periur'd *Protheus*:   2160
DEUISD = 1
  Pro. Know (noble Lord) they haue deuis'd a meane   1107
DEUISE = 1
  Oh excellent deuise, was there euer heard a better?   530
DEUOTED = 2
  Iul. A true-deuoted Pilgrime is not weary   984
  Is else deuoted, I am but a shadow;   1749
DID *l.*117 118 193 315 548 *601 739 762 855 882 938 1049 1161 1473 1666
  1729 1789 *1835 *1847 *1854 1870 1971 1973 1987 2085 2201
  2224 = 23*4
DIDE = 1
  As when thy Lady, and thy true-loue dide,   1790
DIDST = 4*3
  Lu. Nothing. | *Iu.* Why didst thou stoope then?   228
  Didst thou but know the inly touch of Loue,   993
  Sp. Why didst not tell me sooner? 'pox of your loue | Letters.   1440
  *not I bid thee still marke me, and doe as I do; when did'st   1855
  *Gentlewomans farthingale? did'st thou euer see me doe | such a tricke?   1857
  Pro. What, didst thou offer her this from me?   1873
  For whose deare sake, thou didst then rend thy faith   2168
DIE = 3
  Pro. Ile die on him that saies so but your selfe.   764
  To die, is to be banisht from my selfe,   1241
  But *Valentine*, if he be tane, must die.   1302
DIET = *1
  *to fast, like one that takes diet: to watch, like one that   419
DIFFERENCE = 1
  If that be all the difference in his loue,   2010
DIGNIFIE = 1
  He leaues his friends, to dignifie them more;   68
DIGNIFIED = 1
  Shee shall be dignified with this high honour,   812
DIND *see* dyn'd
DINE = 1
  Now can I breake my fast, dine, sup, and sleepe,   793
DINING *see* dyning
DINNER = 2*2
  Iul. Is't neere dinner time? | *Lu.* I would it were,   222
  Lu. Madam: dinner is ready: and your father staies.   290
  *Lions: when you fasted, it was presently after dinner: 423
  Why muse you sir, 'tis dinner time. | *Val.* I haue dyn'd.   560
DIRECTION-GIUER = 1
  Therefore, sweet *Protheus*, my direction-giuer,   1536
DIRE-LAMENTING = 1
  After your dire-lamenting Elegies,   1528
DISABILITIE = 1
  Val. Leaue off discourse of disabilitie: 759
DISCENT = 1
  With falsehood, cowardize, and poore discent: 1478
DISCIPLINE = 1
  Du. This discipline, showes thou hast bin in loue.   1534

DISCLOSD = 1
That which thy selfe hast now disclos'd to me.   1101
DISCOUER = 2*2
Some, to discouer Islands farre away: 311
*Or fearing els some messe(n)ger, y might her mind discouer   557
*Pro. My gracious Lord, that which I wold discouer,   1073
That may discouer such integrity: 1523
DISCOUERED = 1
The story of your Loues discouered.   2298
DISCOUERY = 1
That my discouery be not aimed at: 1114
DISCOURSE = 8
Heare sweet discourse, conuerse with Noble-men,   333
Val. Leaue off discourse of disabilitie: 759
I know you ioy not in a Loue-discourse.   779
Now, no discourse, except it be of loue: 792
Thu. How likes she my discourse?   2056
Thu. But well, when I discourse of loue and peace.   2058
Therefore I pray you stand, not to discourse,   2088
With our discourse, to make your Grace to smile.   2290
DISCRETION = 1
That can with some discretion doe my businesse: 1884
DISDAINE = 2
Trampling contemptuously on thy disdaine.   272
Disdaine to roote the Sommer-swelling flowre,   816
DISFURNISH = 1
Of which, if you should here disfurnish me,   1560
DISGRACD = 1
Your Grace is welcome to a man disgrac'd, | Banished *Valentine*.   2249
DISGRACE = 1
And so (vnworthily) disgrace the man   1098
DISGUISE = 1
Such an immodest rayment; if shame liue | In a disguise of loue?   2232
DISGUISING = 1
Of their disguising and pretended flight: 966
DISLOYALL = 1
Thou subtile, periur'd, false, disloyall man: 1719
DISOBEDIENT = 1
Prowd, disobedient, stubborne, lacking duty,   1138
DISPATCH = 3
I will dispatch him to the Emperors Court.   340
Onely, in lieu thereof, dispatch me hence: 1063
Dispatch (sweet Gentlemen) and follow me.   2092
DISPLEASD = 1
No matter who's displeas'd, when you are gone: 1041
DISPOSE = 3
All that is mine I leaue at thy dispose,   1061
Which, with our selues, all rest at thy dispose. *Exeunt.*   1622
Dispose of them, as thou knowst their deserts.   2286
DISPRAISD = 1
To praise his faith, which I would haue disprais'd.   1923
DISPRAISE = 2
By ought that I can speake in his dispraise,   1493
As you, in worth dispraise, sir *Valentine*.   1501
DISPROUE = 1
I haue one friend aliue; thou wouldst disproue me: 2191

DISSOLUES = 1
Dissolues to water, and doth loose his forme. 1454
DISTRESSES = 1
Tune my distresses, and record my woes. 2127
DIS-EMBARQUE = 1
I must vnto the Road, to dis-embarque 842
DIUINE = 4
Sweet Ornament, that deckes a thing diuine, | Ah *Siluia, Siluia.* 401
Val. Call her diuine. | *Pro.* I will not flatter her. 799
Val. Then speake the truth by her; if not diuine, 804
Of such diuine perfection as Sir *Protheus.* 988
DO *l.*249 *410 485 677 *773 *898 1055 *1149 1210 1617 *1855 = 6*5
DOATE = 3
Because thou seest me doate vpon my loue: 828
How shall I doate on her with more aduice, 862
You doate on her, that cares not for your loue. 1903
DOE *l.*19 80 124 *184 250 289 512 536 545 585 664 666 775 827 946 977
996 1113 1160 1165 1167 1216 1217 *1343 1469 1475 1485 1492 1513
1552 1604 1609 1612 1646 1679 1782 1795 1802 *1845 *1846 *1849
*1855 *1857 1861 1884 1901 1911 1914 1932 1952 1958 1964 1965 2137
2160 2201 2204 2255 2267 = 53*8
DOES *l.*777 = *1
DOG = 4*8
*Court: I thinke *Crab* my dog, be the sowrest natured 597
Lau. Why, he that's tide here, *Crab* my dog. 633
Ho. Gone to seeke his dog, which to morrow, by his 1699
*would teach a dog) I was sent to deliuer him, as a pre-|sent 1827
*him to be a dog indeede, to be, as it were, a dog at all 1833
*all the chamber smelt him: out with the dog (saies one) 1840
*(quoth I) you meane to whip the dog: I marry doe I 1845
La. Marry she saies your dog was a cur, and tels you 1868
Pro. But she receiu'd my dog? | *La.* No indeede did she not: 1870
And then I offer'd her mine owne, who is a dog 1876
Pro. Goe, get thee hence, and finde my dog againe, 1878
DOGGE = *9
*dogge that liues: My Mother weeping: my Father 598
*more pitty in him then a dogge: a Iew would haue wept 603
*dogge: no, the dogge is himselfe, and I am the dogge: 614
*oh, the dogge is me, and I am my selfe: I; so, so: now 615
*now the dogge all this while sheds not a teare: nor 623
Lau. Aske my dogge, if he say I, it will: if hee say 903
La. Marry Sir, I carried Mistris *Siluia* the dogge you | bad me. 1865
DOGGES = *1
*goes me to the fellow that whips the dogges: friend 1844
DOGS = *1
*foure gentleman-like-dogs, vnder the Dukes table: hee 1838
DOLOR = 1
As ending Antheme of my endlesse dolor. 1310
DON = 2
Pan. To morrow, may it please you, *Don Alphonso,* 341
Duk. Know ye *Don Antonio,* your Countriman? 704
DONE *l.*498 *593 681 *749 771 781 1076 1500 1576 1909 2140 *2215
2264 2299 = 10*5
DOOME = 3
I flie not death, to flie his deadly doome, 1255
Pro. I, I: and she hath offered to the doome 1292
Val. I was, and held me glad of such a doome. 1578

39

DOORES = *1
*Duk. I, but the doores be lockt, and keyes kept safe,   1180
DOST l.18 *98 436 *440 445 638 1896 1963 2128 = 7*2
DOTH l.78 1001 1013 1125 1169 1170 1291 1392 1454 1670 1694 *1968
2122 2141 = 13*1
DOUBLE = 1
Val. Well then, Ile double your folly. | Thu. How?   675
DOUBLET = 1
Thu. My Ierkin is a doublet.   674
DOUBT = 1
Pro. Oh Sir, she makes no doubt of that.   2061
DOUBTFULLY = 1
I writ at randome, very doubtfully.   501
DOWN = *1
*2.Out. If there be ten, shrinke not, but down with'em.   1548
DOWNE = 5*3
But twice, or thrice, was Protheus written downe: 277
Lu. Nay, I was taken vp, for laying them downe.   294
*there 'tis; heere's my mothers breath vp and downe: 621
were downe, I could driue the boate with my sighes.   646
A pack of sorrowes, which would presse you downe   1089
And with a Corded-ladder fetch her downe: 1109
*La. Oh villaine, that set this downe among her vices;   1396
*La. Of her tongue she cannot; for that's writ downe   1410
DOWRE = 1
Then let her beauty be her wedding dowre: 1147
DRAW = 1
Which else, no worldly good should draw from me: 1078
DRAWNE = 1
(Vpon aduice) hath drawne my loue from her,   1142
DREAME = 3
Forgiue me, that I doe not dreame on thee,   827
Luc. Then neuer dreame on Infamy, but go: 1039
Val. How like a dreame is this? I see, and heare: 2147
DREAMES = 1
She dreames on him, that has forgot her loue,   1902
DRENCHD = 1
And drench'd me in the sea, where I am drown'd.   381
DRIE = *1
*were drie, I am able to fill it with my teares: if the winde   645
DRIER = 1
Being destin'd to a drier death on shore: 148
DRIFT = 3
As thou hast lent me wit, to plot this drift. | Exit.   972
To crosse my friend in his intended drift,   1087
That you shall say, my cunning drift excels.   1704
DRIUE = 1
were downe, I could driue the boate with my sighes.   646
DRIUES = 1
Or as one naile, by strength driues out another.   848
DROUND = 1
Iu. The meane is dround with you vnruly base.   256
DROWND = 1
And drench'd me in the sea, where I am drown'd.   381
DROWNING = *1
*a puppy: one that I sau'd from drowning, when three or   1824

DRY = 1
Write till your inke be dry: and with your teares   1521
DU = 16*2
DUCKET = 1
No, not so much as a ducket for deliuering your letter: 137
DUK = 20*1
DUKE see also Du., Duk. = 8*1, 7*3
  Enter Valentine, Siluia, Thurio, Speed, Duke, Protheus.   654
  Enter Duke, Thurio, Protheus, Valentine, | Launce, Speed.   1068
  Enter Duke, Thurio, Protheus.   1446
  And heire and Neece, alide vnto the Duke.   1595
  *third) hang him vp (saies the Duke.) I hauing bin ac-|quainted   1842
  Enter Thurio, Protheus, Iulia, Duke.   2041
  Iul. Here comes the Duke.   2071
  Enter Valentine, Protheus, Siluia, Iulia, Duke, Thurio, | Out-lawes.   2120
  Val. Forbeare, forbeare I say: It is my Lord the *Duke*.   2248
  Duke: Father to Siluia.   2302
DUKES = *1
  *foure gentleman-like-dogs, vnder the Dukes table: hee   1838
DULL = 2
  By some slie tricke, blunt *Thurio's* dull proceeding.   970
  Vpon the dull earth dwelling.   1676
DULLY = 1
  Then (liuing dully sluggardiz'd at home)   10
DUMBE = 3
  Alas, this parting strikes poore Louers dumbe. | *Exeunt.*   589
  Dumbe Iewels often in their silent kinde   1159
  Pro. Then in dumbe silence will I bury mine,   1277
DUMPE = 1
  Tune a deploring dumpe: the nights dead silence   1531
DUST = *1
  *speakes a word: but see how I lay the dust with my | teares.   624
DUTIE = 4
  Pro. My dutie will I boast of, nothing else.   761
  Sil. And dutie neuer yet did want his meed.   762
  My dutie pricks me on to vtter that   1077
  Should haue beene cherish'd by her child-like dutie,   1144
DUTIES = 1
  Thus (for my duties sake) I rather chose   1086
DUTY = 2
  But for my duty to your Ladiship.   497
  Prowd, disobedient, stubborne, lacking duty,   1138
DWELLING = 1
  Vpon the dull earth dwelling.   1676
DWELS = 1
  The eating Canker dwels; so eating Loue   47
DYEST = 1
  1.*Out.* But if thou scorne our curtesie, thou dyest.   1614
DYND = 1
  Why muse you sir, 'tis dinner time. | *Val.* I haue dyn'd.   560
DYNING-CHAMBER = *1
  *sooner into the dyning-chamber, but he steps me to her   1829
EACH = 4
  Ile kisse each seuerall paper, for amends: 268
  Till I haue found each letter, in the Letter,   279
  And make a pastime of each weary step,   1010
  She excels each mortall thing   1675

EARE = 3

If so: I pray thee breath it in mine eare,	1309
And giue some euening Musique to her eare.	1641
Ho. You haue a quicke eare.	1686

EARES = *1

*Val. My eares are stopt, & cannot hear good newes,	1275

EARLY = 1

I am thus early come, to know what seruice	1779

EARNEST = 1 *1

But did you perceiue her earnest?	548
*Lau. Marry after they cloas'd in earnest, they parted │ very fairely in iest.	883

EARTH = 7

Nor to his Seruice, no such ioy on earth:	791
Soueraigne to all the Creatures on the earth.	806
To beare my Ladies traine, lest the base earth	813
His heart, as far from fraud, as heauen from earth.	1053
Vpon the dull earth dwelling.	1676
Pro. Sweet Lady, let me rake it from the earth.	1740
Is nor of heauen, nor earth; for these are pleas'd:	2206

EARTHLY = 1

Pro. No; But she is an earthly Paragon.	798

EASILY = 1

As easily as I doe teare his paper.	1952

EATEN = 1

Is eaten by the Canker ere it blow,	50

EATING = 2

The eating Canker dwels; so eating Loue	47

EFFECT = 3

Iul. Base men, that vse them to so base effect;	1048
Du. Thou know'st how willingly, I would effect	1468
Pro. As much as I can doe, I will effect:	1513

EFFECTS = 1

And all the faire effects of future hopes.	54

EFFECTUALL = 1

(Which vn-reuerst stands in effectuall force)	1293

EG = 5

EGL = 3

EGLAMORE see also Eg., Egl. = 2

Enter Eglamore, Siluia.	1768
Sil. Sir *Eglamore*, a thousand times good morrow.	1776

EGLAMOURE = 12

Iu. What thinkst thou of the faire sir *Eglamoure*?	162
Sil. Oh *Eglamoure*, thou art a Gentleman:	1781
Sir *Eglamoure*: I would to *Valentine*	1792
Vrge not my fathers anger (*Eglamoure*)	1797
Sil. Good morrow, kinde Sir *Eglamoure. Exeunt.*	1819
Enter Eglamore, Siluia.	2027
Sil. Amen, Amen: goe on (good *Eglamoure*)	2035
Which of you saw *Eglamoure* of late?	2073
And *Eglamoure* is in her Company:	2080
Ile after; more to be reueng'd on *Eglamoure*,	2095
Then hate of *Eglamoure* that goes with her.	2098
Eglamoure: Agent for Siluia in her escape.	2307

EITHER = 1

Val. Come, come: a hand from either:	2242

ELEGIES = 1
    After your dire-lamenting Elegies,   1528
ELIZIUM = 1
    A blessed soule doth in *Elizium*.   1013
ELOQUENCE = 1
    And naught esteemes my aged eloquence.   1152
ELS = *1
    *Or fearing els some messe(n)ger, y might her mind discouer   557
ELSE = 13*1
    Or else a wit, by folly vanquished.   39
    Of thy successe in loue; and what newes else   62
    Or else returne no more into my sight.   200
    Speed. Your worship sir, or else I mistooke.   407
    *you were so simple, none else would: but you are   431
    Or else for want of idle time, could not againe reply,   556
    Pro. My dutie will I boast of, nothing else.   761
    Which else, no worldly good should draw from me: 1078
    This, or else nothing, will inherit her.   1533
    Or else I often had beene often miserable.   1581
    Pro. Sir, but I doe: or else I would be hence.   1646
    Is else deuoted, I am but a shadow;   1749
    That vs'd me so: or else by *Ioue*, I vow,   2023
    Val. *Thurio* giue backe; or else embrace thy death: 2253
EM *see also* heare'm = 1*1
    2.Out. If there be ten, shrinke not, but down with'em.   1548
    And entertain'd'em deepely in her heart.   2228
EMBARQUE = 1*1
    Pro. But now he parted hence to embarque for *Millain*.   75
    I must vnto the Road, to dis-embarque   842
EMBRACE = 2
    Now kisse, embrace, contend, doe what you will.   289
    Val. *Thurio* giue backe; or else embrace thy death: 2253
EMPERIOUS = 1
    Whose high emperious thoughts haue punish'd me   782
EMPEROR = 2
    Are iournying, to salute the *Emperor*,   343
    And daily graced by the Emperor;   360
EMPERORS = 3
    I will dispatch him to the Emperors Court.   340
    With *Valentinus*, in the Emperors Court: 369
    As meet to be an Emperors Councellor: 727
EMPEROUR = 1
    Attends the Emperour in his royall Court.   329
EMPLOY *see also* imploy = 1
    Ther's some great matter she'ld employ me in.   1771
EMPLOY'D *see* imployd
EMPLOYMENT = 1
    And fit for great employment (worthy Lord.)   2284
EMPRESSE = 2
    He is as worthy for an Empresse loue,   726
    And thinke thee worthy of an Empresse loue: 2268
ENAMELD = 1
    He makes sweet musicke with th'enameld stones,   1003
ENCOUNTER = 1
    That euery day with par'le encounter me,   158
ENCOUNTERS = 1
    The loose encounters of lasciuious men: 1016

END = 4*2

For what I will, I will, and there an end:	367
*Speed. And y letter hath she deliuer'd, & there an end.	552
*Val. I know it wel sir, you alwaies end ere you begin.	683
A Slaue, that still an end, turnes me to shame:	1881
Goe thou with her to the West end of the wood,	2111
Ile wooe you like a Souldier, at armes end,	2180

ENDAMAGE = 1

Your slander neuer can endamage him;	1489

ENDANGER = 1

I hold him but a foole that will endanger	2260

ENDING = 1

As ending Antheme of my endlesse dolor.	1310

ENDLESSE = 1

As ending Antheme of my endlesse dolor.	1310

ENDUD = 1

Are men endu'd with worthy qualities:	2280

ENDURE = 1

Sil. O Valentine: this I endure for thee.	Exeunt.	2117

ENEMIE = 1

And Valentine Ile hold an Enemie,	958

ENEMIES = 1

Val. My friends.	1.Out. That's not so, sir: we are your enemies.	1553

ENEMY = 1

Pro. I, if his enemy deliuer it.	1481

ENFORCD = 1

When inward ioy enforc'd my heart to smile?	217

ENFORCE = 1

Nor how my father would enforce me marry	1786

ENFRANCHISD = 1

Sil. Be-like that now she hath enfranchis'd them	740

ENFRANCHISE = 1

What's here? Siluia, this night I will enfranchise thee.	1220

ENGINE = 1

And heere an Engine fit for my proceeding,	1208

ENGRAUD = 1

Are visibly Character'd, and engrau'd,	979

ENIOYND see also inioynd = 1

Val. Last night she enioyn'd me,	480

ENOUGH = 5

Speed. Sir, I know that well enough.	444
Pro. Enough; I read your fortune in your eye:	795
But you sir Thurio, are not sharpe enough:	1514
currish thanks is good enough for such a present.	1869
If we recouer that, we are sure enough. Exeunt.	2039

ENQUIRE = 1

Pro. Goe on before: I shall enquire you forth:	841

ENRAGD see inrag'd

ENSUING = 1

The next ensuing howre, some foule mischance	579

ENTER = 18*1

Enter Iulia and Lucetta.	153
Enter Antonio and Panthino. Protheus.	301
Enter Valentine, Speed, Siluia.	396
Enter Protheus, Iulia, Panthion.	567
Enter Launce, Panthion.	592
Enter Valentine, Siluia, Thurio, Speed, Duke, Protheus.	654

ENTER *cont.*

Enter Speed and Launce.	872
Enter Protheus *solus.*	929
Enter Iulia *and* Lucetta.	975
Enter Duke, Thurio, Protheus, Valentine, | Launce, Speed.	1068
Val. What letts but one may enter at her window?	1182
Enter Duke, Thurio, Protheus.	1446
Enter Valentine, Speed, and certaine Out-lawes.	1546
Enter Protheus, Thurio, Iulia, Host, Musitian, Siluia.	1624
Enter Eglamore, Siluia.	1768
Enter Launce, Protheus, Iulia, Siluia.	1821
Enter Eglamoure, Siluia.	2027
Enter Thurio, Protheus, Iulia, Duke.	2041
*Enter Valentine, Protheus, Siluia, Iulia, Duke, Thurio, | Out-lawes.	2120

ENTERTAIND = 2

Alas poore *Protheus,* thou hast entertain'd	1912
And entertain'd'em deepely in her heart.	2228

ENTERTAINE = 3

Val. Mistris, it is: sweet Lady, entertaine him	754
Sweet Lady, entertaine him for your Seruant.	760
Therefore know thee, for this I entertaine thee.	1889

ENTERTAINED = 1

Sebastian, I haue entertained thee,	1882

ENTHRALLED = 1

Loue hath chas'd sleepe from my enthralled eyes,	786

ENTREAT = 1

I rather would entreat thy company,	8

ENTREATED *see also* intreated = 1

Entreated me to call, and know her minde:	1770

ENUIRON = 1

(If euer danger doe enuiron thee)	19

EQUALL = 1

Bestow thy fawning smiles on equall mates,	1228

ERE = 7*3

Is eaten by the Canker ere it blow,	50
*Launce. Nay, 'twill bee this howre ere I haue done	593
*Val. I know it wel sir, you alwaies end ere you begin.	683
And ere I part with thee, confer at large	1323
That ere I watch'd, and the most heauiest.	1766
*Iul. And she shall thanke you for't, if ere you know | (her.	1999
Pro. Vnhappy were you (Madam) ere I came:	2150
I tender't heere: I doe as truely suffer, | As ere I did commit.	2201
Inconstancy falls-off, ere it begins:	2239
Duke. I grant it (for thine owne) what ere it be.	2278

ERRE = 1

But fearing lest my iealous ayme might erre,	1097

ERRING = 1

If I can checke my erring loue, I will,	868

ERROR = 1

But Constant, he were perfect; that one error	2237

ESCAPE = 1

Eglamoure: Agent for Siluia in her escape.	2307

ESPECIALLY = 1

Especially against his very friend.	1487

ESSENCE = 1

Shee is my essence, and I leaue to be;	1252

ESTEEME = 1
With other Gentlemen of good esteeme 342
ESTEEMES = 2
For me, and my possessions she esteemes not. 1148
And naught esteemes my aged eloquence. 1152
ESTEEMETH = 1
By one, whom she esteemeth as his friend. 1483
ESTEEMST = *1
*Val. How esteem'st thou me? I account of her beauty. 455
ESTIMATION = 1
To be of worth, and worthy estimation, ... 706
ETERNALLS = 1
By Penitence th'Eternalls wrath's appeas'd: 2207
ETHIOPE = 1
Shewes *Iulia* but a swarthy Ethiope. 955
EUEN *see also* ev'n = 12*2
Euen as I would, when I to loue begin. 13
Euen so by Loue, the yong, and tender wit 51
Loosing his verdure, euen in the prime, ... 53
Euen with the speediest expedition, ... 339
Val. Hast thou obseru'd that? euen she I meane. 438
Val. Euen She; and is she not a heauenly Saint? 797
Euen as one heate, another heate expels, ... 847
Euen in the milke-white bosome of thy Loue. 1320
Du. Euen now about it, I will pardon you. *Exeunt.* 1544
Sil. You haue your wish: my will is euen this, ... 1717
Euen for this time I spend in talking to thee. 1728
I doe desire thee, euen from a heart 1802
*taught him (euen as one would say precisely, thus I 1826
At *Patricks* Cell this euen, and there she was not. 2086
EUENING *see also* eu'n, euen = 3
And giue some euening Musique to her eare. 1641
When will you goe? | *Sil.* This euening comming. 1812
See where she comes: Lady a happy euening. 2034
EUER *see also* ere = 12*3
*Home-keeping youth, haue euer homely wits, ... 5
(If euer danger doe enuiron thee) 19
How euer: but a folly bought with wit, ... 38
Speed. Euer since you lou'd her. 458
Val. I haue lou'd her euer since I saw her, ... 459
Oh excellent deuise, was there euer heard a better? 530
vnkindest Tide, that euer any man tide. 631
(A rashnesse that I euer yet haue shun'd) 1099
The key whereof, my selfe haue euer kept: 1105
Take no repulse, what euer she doth say, ... 1169
I euer bore my daughter, or thy selfe. 1237
La. The black'st newes that euer thou heard'st. 1352
No griefe did euer come so neere thy heart, ... 1789
*Gentlewomans farthingale? did'st thou euer see me doe | such a tricke? 1857
Pro. Beare witnes (heauen) I haue my wish for euer. 2245
EUERLASTINGLY = 1
And make rough winter euerlastingly. 817
EUERY = 4
That euery day with par'le encounter me, ... 158
And be in eye of euery Exercise 334
Giuing a gentle kisse to euery sedge 1004
That longs for euery thing that he can come by. 1194

EUERYTHING *see* euery
EUES = 1
  It was *Eues* legacie, and cannot be t'ane from her.   1401
EVN = 4*1
  Speed. Oh, 'giue ye-good-ev'n: heer's a million of | manners.   490
  And ev'n that Powre which gaue me first my oath   933
  And eu'n in kinde loue, I doe coniure thee,   977
  Why eu'n what fashion thou best likes (*Lucetta*.)   1027
  Pro. Madam: good eu'n to your Ladiship.   1708
EXCEED = 1
  By heauen, my wrath shall farre exceed the loue   1236
EXCEEDING = *1
  Speed. Oh excellent motion; oh exceeding Puppet: 487
EXCELLENT = 1*1
  Speed. Oh excellent motion; oh exceeding Puppet: 487
  Oh excellent deuise, was there euer heard a better?   530
EXCELLING = 1
  That Siluia is excelling;   1674
EXCELS = 2
  She excels each mortall thing   1675
  That you shall say, my cunning drift excels.   1704
EXCEPT = 7*1
  *Except mine own name: That, some whirle-winde beare   280
  Val. She gaue me none, except an angry word.   549
  Now, no discourse, except it be of loue: 792
  Pro. Except my Mistresse.   807
  Val. Sweet: except not any,   808
  Except thou wilt except against my Loue.   809
  Except I be by *Siluia* in the night,   1248
EXCEPTED = 1
  Hath he excepted most against my loue.   385
EXCEPTIONS = 2
  Least he should take exceptions to my loue,   383
  And yet she takes exceptions at your person.   2044
EXCESSE = 1
  And now excesse of it will make me surfet.   1290
EXCHANGE = 2
  Pro. Why then wee'll make exchange; | Here, take you this.   573
  To learne his wit, t'exchange the bad for better;   942
EXCHEQUER = *1
  Val. I know it well sir: you haue an Exchequer of | (words,   692
EXCUSD = 1
  That they may hold excus'd our lawlesse liues;   1600
EXCUSE = 4
  Excuse it not: for I am peremptory.   373
  And with the vantage of mine owne excuse   384
  Teach me (thy tempted subiect) to excuse it.   937
  Be gone, I will not heare thy vaine excuse,   1238
EXECUTED = *1
  *he had bin executed: I haue stood on the Pillorie for   1851
EXECUTION = 2
  The execution of it shall make knowne;   338
  That wait for execution in the morne.   1759
EXERCISE = 1
  And be in eye of euery Exercise   334
EXERCISES = 1
  For any, or for all these exercises,   313

EXEUNT = 15*2

Iu. Come, come, wilt please you goe. *Exeunt.*	299
And yet a thousand times it answer's no. | *Exeunt. Finis.*	393
your Mistresse, be moued, be moued. *Exeunt.*	565
Alas, this parting strikes poore Louers dumbe. | *Exeunt.*	589
Laun. Well, I will goe. | *Exeunt.*	651
If not, to compasse her Ile vse my skill. | *Exeunt.*	869
Spee. At thy seruice. | *Exeunt.*	926
I am impatient of my tarriance. | *Exeunt.*	1065
*Ile after, to reioyce in the boyes correctio(n). *Exeunt.*	1444
Du. Euen now about it, I will pardon you. *Exeunt.*	1544
Which, with our selues, all rest at thy dispose. *Exeunt.*	1622
Sil. Good morrow, kinde Sir *Eglamoure. Exeunt.*	1819
To make my Master out of loue with thee. *Exeunt.*	2025
If we recouer that, we are sure enough. *Exeunt.*	2039
Then hate for *Siluia*, that is gone for loue. *Exeunt.*	2100
Sil. O *Valentine*: this I endure for thee. | *Exeunt.*	2117
One Feast, one house, one mutuall happinesse. *Exeunt.*	2300

EXHIBITION = 1

Like exhibition thou shalt haue from me,	371

EXILE = 2

Th. Since his exile she hath despis'd me most,	1449
And let them be recall'd from their Exile:	2282

EXIT = 6

Val. As much to you at home: and so farewell. *Exit.*	66
Receiuing them from such a worthlesse post. *Exit.*	151
Iul. Will ye be gon? | *Lu.* That you may ruminate. *Exit.*	202
And so good-morrow Seruant. *Exit. Sil.*	525
Val. Will you make haste? *Exit.* | *Pro.* I will.	845
As thou hast lent me wit, to plot this drift. | *Exit.*	972

EXPECTS = 1

Expects my comming, there to see me ship'd.	58

EXPEDITION = 4

Euen with the speediest expedition,	339
To hasten on his Expedition.	379
But if thou linger in my Territories | Longer then swiftest expedition	1233
So much they spur their expedition.	2033

EXPELLING = 1

And threw her Sun-expelling Masque away,	1974

EXPELS = 1

Euen as one heate, another heate expels,	847

EXPERIENCE = 2

Experience is by industry atchieu'd,	324
His yeares but yong, but his experience old:	719

EXPOSTULATE = 1

The time now serues not to expostulate,	1321

EXQUISITE = 1

Val. I meane that her beauty is exquisite, | But her fauour infinite.	448

EXTOLL = 1

Flatter, and praise, commend, extoll their graces:	1171

EXTREAME = 1

But qualifie the fires extreame rage,	997

EYE = 6*1

And be in eye of euery Exercise	334
*not an eye that sees you, but is a Physician to comment | on your Malady.	434
Thur. They say that Loue hath not an eye at all.	746

EYE *cont.*

Pro. Enough; I read your fortune in your eye:	795
To be regarded in her sun-bright eye.	1157
Thou hast beguil'd my hopes; nought but mine eye	2189
More fresh in *Iulia's*, with a constant eye?	2241

EYES = 8*3

*eyes, or your owne eyes had the lights they were wont	464
*no eyes, looke you, wept her selfe blinde at my parting:	605
Did hold his eyes, lockt in her Christall lookes.	739
Val. Why Lady, Loue hath twenty paire of eyes.	745
Loue hath chas'd sleepe from my enthralled eyes,	786
Loue doth to her eyes repaire,	1670
Her eyes are grey as glasse, and so are mine.	2012
I should haue scratch'd out your vnseeing eyes,	2024
Blacke men are Pearles, in beauteous Ladies eyes.	2053
Thu. 'Tis true, such Pearles as put out Ladies eyes,	2054

FACE = 6*1

*As a nose on a mans face, or a Wethercocke on a steeple:	527
But chiefely, for thy face, and thy behauiour,	1886
And pinch'd the lilly-tincture of her face,	1976
If I had such a Tyre, this face of mine	2005
Thu. What saies she to my face?	2049
Thu. Nay then the wanton lyes: my face is blacke.	2051
What is in *Siluia's* face, but I may spie	2240

FACES = 1

Though nere so blacke, say they haue Angells faces,	1172

FACTION = 1

This fellow were a King, for our wilde faction.	1583

FADING = *1

*Coy looks, with hart-sore sighes: one fading moments | (mirth,	34

FAILE = 2

Eg. I will not faile your Ladiship:	1817
She will not faile; for Louers breake not houres,	2031

FAINE = *2

Sp. Well, I perceiue I must be faine to beare with you.	123
*victuals; and would faine haue meate: oh bee not like	564

FAIRE = 19*2

And all the faire effects of future hopes.	54
Iul. Of all the faire resort of Gentlemen,	157
Iu. What thinkst thou of the faire sir *Eglamoure?*	162
Val. Not so faire (boy) as well fauour'd.	443
Speed. That shee is not so faire, as (of you) well-fa- |uourd?	446
Speed. Marry sir, so painted to make her faire, that no | man counts of	
her beauty.	453
Made vse, and faire aduantage of his daies:	718
Shee is faire: and so is *Iulia* that I loue,	854
To loue faire *Siluia*; shall I be forsworne?	931
And *Siluia* (witnesse heauen that made her faire)	954
But when his faire course is not hindered,	1002
Beseeming such a Wife, as your faire daughter:	1135
If I be not by her faire influence	1253
But *Siluia* is too faire, too true, too holy,	1629
Holy, faire, and wise is she,	1665
Is she kinde as she is faire?	1668
Sil. Is she not passing faire?	1969
She, in my iudgement, was as faire as you.	1972
Pro. She saies it is a faire one.	2050

49

FAIRE *cont.*

    Pro. But Pearles are faire; and the old saying is,   2052
    Vouchsafe me for my meed, but one faire looke: 2144
FAIRELY = 1

    Lau. Marry after they cloas'd in earnest, they parted | very fairely in
    iest.   883
FAIRER = 1

    Iul. She hath bin fairer (Madam) then she is,   1970
FAITH = 6*1

    In breaking faith with *Iulia*, whom I lou'd;   1635
    Vpon whose faith and honor, I repose.   1796
    To praise his faith, which I would haue disprais'd.   1923
    For whose deare sake, thou didst then rend thy faith 2168
    Thou hast no faith left now, vnlesse thou'dst two,   2171
    Then plurall faith, which is too much by one: 2173
    Val. Thou co(m)mon friend, that's without faith or loue, 2187
FALL = 3

    Would'st thou then counsaile me to fall in loue?   155
    Lu. To take a paper vp, that I let fall.   230
    Lest growing ruinous, the building fall,   2130
FALLS-OFF = 1

    Inconstancy falls-off, ere it begins: 2239
FALSE = 13

    Vnlesse it haue a false Interpreter.   235
    Her true perfection, or my false transgression?   852
    Without false vantage, or base treachery.   1575
    Pro. Already haue I bin false to *Valentine*,   1625
    Ho. Why, my pretty youth? | *Iu.* He plaies false (father.) 1681
    Iu. Not so: but yet | So false that he grieues my very heart-strings. 1684
    Thou subtile, periur'd, false, disloyall man: 1719
    Iu. 'Twere false, if I should speake it;   1731
    To worship shadowes, and adore false shapes,   1755
    Vnlesse I proue false traitor to my selfe.   1926
    Though his false finger haue prophan'd the Ring,   1957
    Rather then haue false *Protheus* reskue me: 2156
    I doe detest false periur'd *Protheus*:   2160
FALSEHOOD = 3

    With falsehood, cowardize, and poore discent: 1478
    She twits me with my falsehood to my friend;   1632
    But, since your falsehood shall become you well   1754
FANCIE = 1

    Cannot your Grace win her to fancie him?   1136
FANTASTIQUE = 1

    To be fantastique, may become a youth   1022
FAR = 3

    And in a word (for far behinde his worth   721
    His heart, as far from fraud, as heauen from earth. 1053
    Duk. Her chamber is aloft, far from the ground,   1183
FAREWELL = 3*1

    Val. As much to you at home: and so farewell. *Exit.* 66
    Iulia, farewell: what, gon without a word?   584
    Th. Where meete we? | *Pro.* At Saint *Gregories* well. | *Th.* Farewell. 1705
    *For thy sweet Mistris sake, because thou lou'st her. Fare-|(well. 1998
FARRE = 4

    Some, to discouer Islands farre away: 311
    By heauen, my wrath shall farre exceed the loue   1236
    I am so farre from granting thy request,   1725

FARRE *cont.*
And that's farre worse then none: better haue none — 2172
FARTHINGALE = 1*1
What compasse will you weare your Farthingale? — 1026
*Gentlewomans farthingale? did'st thou euer see me doe | such a tricke? — 1857
FASHION = 4*1
*Luc. What fashion (Madam) shall I make your bree- |(ches? — 1024
Why eu'n what fashion thou best likes (*Lucetta*.) — 1027
Besides the fashion of the time is chang'd) — 1155
Duk. How shall I fashion me to weare a cloake? — 1205
Thou friend of an ill fashion. | *Pro. Valentine.* — 2185
FAST = 5*2
*to fast, like one that takes diet: to watch, like one that — 419
Now can I breake my fast, dine, sup, and sleepe, — 793
Haply when they haue iudg'd me fast asleepe, — 1094
Duk. Sir *Valentine*, whether away so fast? — 1120
La. Well: that fault may be mended with a break- |fast: read on. — 1388
1.*Out-l.* Fellowes, stand fast: I see a passenger. — 1547
Ho. By my hallidome, I was fast asleepe. — 1761
FASTED = *1
*Lions: when you fasted, it was presently after dinner: — 423
FASTING = *1
Sp. Item, shee is not to be fasting in respect of her | breath. — 1386
FASTS = 1
With bitter fasts, with penitentiall grones, — 783
FAT = 1
3.*Out.* By the bare scalpe of *Robin Hoods* fat Fryer, — 1582
FATHER = 14*9
Once more adieu: my Father at the Road — 57
Lu. Madam: dinner is ready: and your father staies. — 290
I fear'd to shew my Father *Iulias* Letter, — 382
My father staies my comming: answere not: — 581
*dogge that liues: My Mother weeping: my Father — 598
*nay, Ile shew you the manner of it. This shooe is my fa- |ther: — 606
*no, this left shooe is my father; no, no, this left — 607
*with the hole in it, is my mother: and this my father: — 610
*come I to my Father; Father, your blessing: now — 616
*now should I kisse my Father; well, hee weepes on: — 618
Sil. No more, gentlemen, no more: | Here comes my father. — 696
Sir *Valentine*, your father is in good health, — 699
The honor, and regard of such a father. — 710
Thur. Madam, my Lord your father wold speak with | (you. — 767
My foolish Riuall that her Father likes — 829
Now presently Ile giue her father notice — 965
Nor fearing me, as if I were her father: — 1140
Sp. Marry, the son of my Grand-father. — 1359
Ho. Why, my pretty youth? | *Iu.* He plaies false (father.) — 1681
Nor how my father would enforce me marry — 1786
Duke: Father to Siluia. — 2302
Anthonio: father to Protheus. — 2305
FATHERS = 4*1
O that our Fathers would applaud our loues — 350
Pan. Sir *Protheus*, your Fathers call's for you, — 390
Those at her fathers churlish feete she tenderd, — 1295
*indeede know not their fathers; and therefore haue no | names. — 1382
Vrge not my fathers anger (*Eglamoure*) — 1797

FAULT = 3*3
Did in your name receiue it: pardon the fault I pray.	193
And pray her to a fault, for which I chid her.	206
*fault: I haue receiu'd my proportion, like the prodigious	595
*La. Well: that fault may be mended with a break- |fast: read on.	1388
But were you banisht for so small a fault?	1577
*things. If I had not had more wit then he, to take a fault	1834

FAULTS = 6*1
faults then haires, and more wealth then faults.	1415
Sp. And more faults then haires.	1425
Sp. And more wealth then faults.	1427
La. Why that word makes the faults gracious:	1428
But to the purpose: for we cite our faults,	1599
*Fils him with faults: makes him run through all th'sins;	2238

FAUOR = 2
Confirme his welcome, with some speciall fauor.	751
And of so great a fauor growing proud,	815

FAUORS = 1
Thanke me for this, more then for all the fauors	1231

FAUOUR = 1
Val. I meane that her beauty is exquisite,	But her fauour infinite.	448

FAUOURD = 2*1
Speed. Is she not hard-fauour'd, sir?	442
Val. Not so faire (boy) as well fauour'd.	443
*Speed. That shee is not so faire, as (of you) well-fa- |uourd?	446

FAUOURS = 1
But when I call to minde your gracious fauours	1075

FAWNETH = 1
The more it growes, and fawneth on her still;	1639

FAWNING = 1
Bestow thy fawning smiles on equall mates,	1228

FEALTY = 1
Vpon some other pawne for fealty.	741

FEARD = 1
I fear'd to shew my Father Iulias Letter,	382

FEARE = 13*2
Val. So, by your circumstance, I feare you'll proue.	41
*I feare she'll proue as hard to in telling your minde.	139
I feare my Iulia would not daigne my lines,	150
*Pro. Thus haue I shund the fire, for feare of burning,	380
Laun. For feare thou shouldst loose thy tongue.	639
I feare me it will make me scandaliz'd.	1036
I feare me he will scarce be pleas'd with all.	1042
Iul. That is the least (Lucetta) of my feare:	1043
And that thou maist perceiue my feare of this,	1102
Du. Sir Thurio, feare not, but that she will loue you	1447
That all the Trauailers doe feare so much.	1552
Pro. Sir Thurio, feare not you, I will so pleade,	1703
I feare I am attended by some Spies.	2037
Egl. Feare not: the Forrest is not three leagues off,	2038
Feare not: he beares an honourable minde.	2115

FEAREFULL = 1
Vnto a ragged, fearefull, hanging Rocke,	281

FEARES = *1
*feares robbing: to speake puling, like a beggar at Hal- |low-Masse:	420

FEARING = 2*1
*Or fearing els some messe(n)ger, y might her mind discouer	557

FEARING *cont.*
But fearing lest my iealous ayme might erre, 1097
Nor fearing me, as if I were her father: 1140
FEAST = 1
One Feast, one house, one mutuall happinesse. *Exeunt.* 2300
FEATURE = 1
He is compleat in feature, and in minde, 723
FED = 1
Val. Oh, I haue fed vpon this woe already, 1289
FEE = 1
Lu. To plead for loue, deserues more fee, then hate. 201
FEEBLE = 1
To measure Kingdomes with his feeble steps, 985
FEED = 1*2
*can feed on the ayre, I am one that am nourish'd by my 563
Thu. That hath more minde to feed on your bloud, 679
And feed vpon the shadow of perfection. 1247
FEEDE = 1
Iniurious Waspes, to feede on such sweet hony, 266
FEELE = 1
I pray thee let me feele thy cloake vpon me. 1206
FEELING = 1
Moist it againe: and frame some feeling line, 1522
FEETE = 1
Those at her fathers churlish feete she tenderd, 1295
FELLOW = 1*1
This fellow were a King, for our wilde faction. 1583
*goes me to the fellow that whips the dogges: friend 1844
FELLOWES = 1
1.*Out-l.* Fellowes, stand fast: I see a passenger. 1547
FELLOW-SERUANT = 1
To be my fellow-seruant to your Ladiship. 755
FELT = 1
If I in thought felt not her very sorrow. 1993
FETCH = 1*2
And with a Corded-ladder fetch her downe: 1109
*Condition. *Inprimis.* Shee can fetch and carry: why 1342
*a horse can doe no more; nay, a horse cannot fetch, but 1343
FIE = 5
Fie, fie: how way-ward is this foolish loue; 211
Fie, fie, vnreuerend tongue, to call her bad, 943
La. Fie on thee Iolt-head, thou canst not read. | *Sp.* Thou lyest: I can. 1356
FIGHT = 1
But yet I slew him manfully, in fight, 1574
FIGURE = 2*1
Val. To whom? | *Speed.* To your selfe: why, she woes you by a figure. 538
Val. What figure? | *Speed.* By a Letter, I should say. 540
Du. This weake impresse of Loue, is as a figure 1452
FILL = 1*1
There wanteth but a Meane to fill your Song. 255
*were drie, I am able to fill it with my teares: if the winde 645
FILS = *1
*Fils him with faults: makes him run through all th'sins; 2238
FINDE = 7
If I loose them, thus finde I by their losse, 950
I gaue him gentle lookes, thereby to finde 1100
Pro. What seest thou? | *Lau.* Him we goe to finde, 1260

FINDE *cont.*

  Pro. Goe sirha, finde him out: Come *Valentine.*   1329
  Pro. Goe, get thee hence, and finde my dog againe,   1878
  Where thou shalt finde me sad, and solitarie.   1910
  Pro. Oh Sir, I finde her milder then she was,   2043

FINDES = 1

  It is the lesser blot modesty findes,   2234

FINE = 2*1

  Lu. As of a Knight, well-spoken, neat, and fine;   163
  Sil. A fine volly of words, gentleme(n), & quickly shot off   684
  Ho. Harke, what fine change is in the Musique.   1690

FINEST = 1

  Inhabits in the finest wits of all.   48

FINGER = 1

  Though his false finger haue prophan'd the Ring,   1957

FINGRING = 1

  You would be fingring them, to anger me.   261

FINIS *l.*393 2315 = 2

FIRE = 6*1

  Lu. Fire that's closest kept, burnes most of all.   183
  Pro. Thus haue I shund the fire, for feare of burning,   380
  Val. Your selfe (sweet Lady) for you gaue the fire,   687
  Which like a waxen Image 'gainst a fire   856
  Thou wouldst as soone goe kindle fire with snow   994
  As seeke to quench the fire of Loue with words.   995
  Luc. I doe not seeke to quench your Loues hot fire,   996

FIRES = 1

  But qualifie the fires extreame rage,   997

FIRME = 1

  You are already loues firme votary,   1505

FIRST = 4*1

  Speed. Marry by these speciall markes: first, you haue   413
  And ev'n that Powre which gaue me first my oath   933
  At first I did adore a twinkling Starre,   938
  For scorne at first, makes after-loue the more.   1164
  Read ouer *Iulia's* heart, (thy first best Loue)   2167

FISH = 1

  Lau. No; they are both as whole as a fish.   890

FIT = 6

  And you an officer fit for the place: 198
  Gentle *Lucetta,* fit me with such weedes   1017
  And heere an Engine fit for my proceeding,   1208
  Would better fit his Chamber, then this Shadow.   1941
  Which serued me as fit, by all mens iudgements,   1983
  And fit for great employment (worthy Lord.)   2284

FITS = 1

  Iul. That fits as well, as tell me (good my Lord)   1025

FITTING = 1

  Pro. A silly answere, and fitting well a Sheepe.   85

FIUE = *2

  *with you presently; where, for one shot of fiue pence,   880
  *thou shalt haue fiue thousand welcomes: But sirha, how   881

FLAT = 1

  Lu. Nay, now you are too flat;   253

FLATTER = 5

  Val. Call her diuine. | *Pro.* I will not flatter her.   799
  Val. O flatter me: for Loue delights in praises.   801

FLATTER *cont.*

Flatter, and praise, commend, extoll their graces:	1171
Thinke not I flatter (for I sweare I doe not)	1782
Vnlesse I flatter with my selfe too much.	2008

FLATTER'D = 1

And yet the Painter flatter'd her a little,	2007

FLATTERY = 1

To be seduced by thy flattery,	1721

FLED = 3

Du. Why then | She's fled vnto that pezant, *Valentine*;	2078
That leads toward *Mantua*, whether they are fled:	2091
There is our Captaine: Wee'll follow him that's fled,	2112

FLIE = 5

Much lesse shall she that hath Loues wings to flie,	986
I flie not death, to flie his deadly doome,	1255
But flie I hence, I flie away from life.	1257

FLIES = 1

That flies her fortune when it followes her:	2094

FLIGHT = 5

With all the cunning manner of our flight	835
Of their disguising and pretended flight:	966
And when the flight is made to one so deere,	987
For *Thesus* periury, and vniust flight;	1989
These likelihoods confirme her flight from hence;	2087

FLOOD = *2

Pant. Tut, man: I meane thou'lt loose the flood, and	634
*in loosing the flood, loose thy voyage, and in loosing thy	635

FLOURISHING = 1

I better brooke then flourishing peopled Townes:	2124

FLOWRE = 1

Disdaine to roote the Sommer-swelling flowre,	816

FLYING = 2

And slaues they are to me, that send them flying.	1211
And on the iustice of my flying hence,	1799

FODDER = *1

Pro. The Sheepe for fodder follow the Shepheard,	93

FOES = 2

'Mongst all foes that a friend should be the worst?	2197
'Twere pitty two such friends should be long foes.	2244

FOLD = 3

Sp. From a pound to a pin? fold it ouer and ouer,	112
Thus will I fold them, one vpon another;	288
Prouokes me to this three-fold periurie.	934

FOLLIES = *2

*so without these follies, that these follies are within you,	432

FOLLOW = 6*1

Pro. The Sheepe for fodder follow the Shepheard,	93
Sp. Here follow her vices.	1384
Dispatch (sweet Gentlemen) and follow me.	2092
Pro. And I will follow, more for *Siluias* loue	2097
Iul. And I will follow, more to crosse that loue	2099
But *Moyses* and *Valerius* follow him:	2110
There is our Captaine: Wee'll follow him that's fled,	2112

FOLLOWERS = 1

And I thinke, no other treasure to giue your followers:	693

FOLLOWES = 3*1

*the Shepheard for foode followes not the Sheepe: thou	94

FOLLOWES *cont.*
followes not thee: therefore thou art a Sheepe.	96
It followes not that she will loue sir *Thurio.*	1496
That flies her fortune when it followes her:	2094

FOLLOWEST = *1
*for wages followest thy Master, thy Master for wages	95

FOLLY = 9*1
How euer: but a folly bought with wit,	38
Or else a wit, by folly vanquished.	39
Is turn'd to folly, blasting in the Bud,	52
Lu. Lord, Lord: to see what folly raignes in vs.	168
And aske remission, for my folly past.	219
Speed. Your owne present folly, and her passing de-|formitie:	468
Thu. What instance of the contrary? | *Val.* Your folly.	670
Thu. And how quoat you my folly?	672
Val. Well then, Ile double your folly. | *Thu.* How?	675
And with thy daring folly burne the world?	1224

FOND = 2
That art a votary to fond desire?	56
If this fond Loue, were not a blinded god.	2016

FOOD = 1*1
Iul. Oh, know'st y not, his looks are my soules food?	990
By longing for that food so long a time.	992

FOODE = *1
*the Shepheard for foode followes not the Sheepe: thou	94

FOOLE = 7*2
Pro. So, by your circumstance, you call me foole.	40
And he that is so yoked by a foole,	44
What 'foole is she, that knowes I am a Maid,	207
Lau. Why Foole, I meant not thee, I meant thy | Master.	916
Launce. I am but a foole, looke you, and yet I haue	1331
Sp. Come foole, come: try me in thy paper.	1362
Alas, poore foole, why doe I pitty him	1914
Iul. True: from a Gentleman, to a foole.	2065
I hold him but a foole that will endanger	2260

FOOLES = 1
For why, the fooles are mad, if left alone.	1168

FOOLISH = 4
Fie, fie: how way-ward is this foolish loue;	211
My foolish Riuall that her Father likes	829
For 'tis no trusting to yond foolish Lowt;	1885
Thurio: a foolish riuall to Valentine.	2306

FOOTE = 1
Vpon the rising of the Mountaine foote	2090

FOOTED = 1
3 *Out.* Being nimble footed, he hath out-run vs.	2109

FOR *l.*21 22 23 27 28 31 43 45 69 *75 *93 *94 *95 102 *103 *109 *113
*120 122 126 *133 137 140 142 198 201 206 219 233 241 257 268 294
295 313 349 367 373 *380 390 *399 *409 *424 *430 *465 *469 *472 *475
476 497 500 516 518 521 524 555 556 559 572 576 578 580 586 587 *612
*617 *630 639 657 681 687 *690 694 712 717 721 726 735 741 752 756
760 781 785 801 *823 830 832 838 855 *874 *880 942 951 953 968 992
1015 1035 1086 1091 1110 1115 1148 1154 1164 1168 1170 1193 1194
1208 1209 1218 1221 1222 1230 1231 1251 1278 1281 1298 1304 1311
1312 1325 *1338 *1339 *1372 *1375 1378 1391 *1393 *1398 *1403 1408
*1410 *1411 *1423 1432 1434 *1435 *1438 *1442 1464 1486 1509 1510
1524 *1556 1570 1572 1577 1583 1594 1596 1598 1599 1643 1647 *1649

FOR *cont.*
   1655 1669 *1700 1709 1724 1726 1728 1732 1738 1745 1748 1759 1782
   1794 *1849 *1850 *1851 1869 1885 1886 1889 1903 1908 1921 1927 1936
   1954 1955 1978 1984 1987 1989 *1998 2018 2022 2031 2055 2081 2096
   2097 2100 2117 2140 2144 2159 2163 2168 2188 2195 2200 2206 *2245
   2259 2261 2264 2274 2276 2278 2284 2307 = 178*49

FORBEARE = 4*2

Luc. Better forbeare, till *Protheus* make returne.	989
Pro. Villaine, forbeare.	1272
Pro. Sirha, I say forbeare: friend *Valentine*, a word.	1274
Loue, lend me patience to forbeare a while.	2148
*Val. Forbeare, forbeare I say: It is my Lord the *Duke*.	2248

FORBID = 1

And oftentimes haue purpos'd to forbid	1095

FORCD = 1

That would haue forc'd your honour, and your loue,	2143

FORCE = 5

And would not force the letter to my view?	208
(Which vn-reuerst stands in effectuall force)	1293
Du. I, much is the force of heauen-bred Poesie.	1518
And loue you 'gainst the nature of Loue: force ye.	2181
Sil. Oh heauen. | *Pro.* Ile force thee yeeld to my desire.	2182

FORE-HEADS = 1

I, but her fore-head's low, and mine's as high:	2013

FOREUER *see* euer

FORGET = 4

I will forget that *Iulia* is aliue,	956
What might we doe to make the girle forget	1475
One *Iulia*, that his changing thoughts forget	1940
Know then, I heere forget all former greefes,	2269

FORGETFULNESSE = 1

Torment me for my Loues forgetfulnesse:	580

FORGIUE = 3

Forgiue me, that I doe not dreame on thee,	827
Forgiue me *Valentine*: if hearty sorrow	2199
Forgiue them what they haue committed here,	2281

FORGOT = 3

(For long agone I haue forgot to court,	1154
And worthlesse *Valentine* shall be forgot.	1456
She dreames on him, that has forgot her loue,	1902

FORGOTTEN = 1

Is by a newer obiect quite forgotten,	850

FORLORNE = 1

Poore forlorne Protheus, passionate Protheus:	284

FORME = 3

Dissolues to water, and doth loose his forme.	1454
For 'tis thy riuall: O thou sencelesse forme,	2018
Can no way change you to a milder forme;	2179

FORMER = 2

So the remembrance of my former Loue	849
Know then, I heere forget all former greefes,	2269

FORREST = 2

Egl. Feare not: the Forrest is not three leagues off,	2038
As he, in pennance wander'd through the Forrest:	2082

FORSAKE = 1

Forsake vnsounded deepes, to dance on Sands.	1527

FORSOOK = *1
  Sil. Belike she thinks that *Protheus* hath forsook her?   1967
FORSWEARE = *1
  Laun. Forsweare not thy selfe, sweet youth, for I am   874
FORSWORNE = 7
  Pro. To leaue my *Iulia*; shall I be forsworne?   930
  To loue faire *Siluia*; shall I be forsworne?   931
  To wrong my friend, I shall be much forsworne.   932
  Hath she forsworne me? | *Pro.* No, *Valentine.*   1282
  Val. No *Valentine*, if *Siluia* haue forsworne me.   1284
  Forsworne my company, and rail'd at me,   1450
  She bids me thinke how I haue bin forsworne   1634
FORT = *4
  *for't: sure as I liue he had suffer'd for't: you shall iudge: 1836
  *Geese he hath kil'd, otherwise he had sufferd for't: thou   1852
  Iul. And she shall thanke you for't, if ere you know | (her.   1999
FORTH = 2
  Put forth their Sonnes, to seeke preferment out.   309
  Pro. Goe on before: I shall enquire you forth: 841
FORTUNE = 9
  Some to the warres, to try their fortune there;   310
  Wishing me with him, partner of his fortune.   361
  Pro. Enough; I read your fortune in your eye: 795
  Because my selfe doe want my seruants fortune.   1217
  If crooked fortune had not thwarted me.   1568
  Val. Nothing but my fortune.   1589
  Which heauen and fortune still rewards with plagues.   1801
  Witnesse good bringing vp, fortune, and truth: 1888
  That flies her fortune when it followes her: 2094
FORTUNED = 1
  That you will wonder what hath fortuned: 2296
FORWARD = 2
  Val. And Writers say; as the most forward Bud   49
  Val. Well: you'll still be too forward.   408
FOR-LORNE = 1
  Thou gentle Nimph, cherish thy for-lorne swaine.   2133
FOR-SWEARE = 1
  Loue bad mee sweare, and Loue bids me for-sweare;   935
FOSTERD = 1
  Foster'd, illumin'd, cherish'd, kept aliue.   1254
FOULE = 1*1
  The next ensuing howre, some foule mischance   579
  *Trencher, and steales her Capons-leg: O, 'tis a foule   1830
FOUND = 3
  Till I haue found each letter, in the Letter,   279
  All this I speak in print, for in print I found it.   559
  And full of new-found oathes, which he will breake   1951
FOURE = *2
  *foure of his blinde brothers and sisters went to it: I haue   1825
  *foure gentleman-like-dogs, vnder the Dukes table: hee   1838
FOXE = 1
  A Foxe, to be the Shepheard of thy Lambs;   1913
FRAME = 1
  Moist it againe: and frame some feeling line,   1522
FRAUD = 1
  His heart, as far from fraud, as heauen from earth.   1053

FRAUGHT = 1
Should be full fraught with seruiceable vowes. 1517
FREE = 1
And that my loue may appeare plaine and free, 2208
FRENDS = *1
*Pro. Your frends are wel, & haue the(m) much com(m)ended. 774
FRESH = 1
More fresh in *Iulia's*, with a constant eye? 2241
FRIEND = 26*2
Betideth here in absence of thy Friend: 63
Deliuer'd by a friend, that came from him. 356
Vnto the secret, nameles friend of yours: 495
Val. That's the Letter I writ to her friend. 551
To wrong my friend, I shall be much forsworne. 932
I to my selfe am deerer then a friend, 952
Ayming at *Siluia* as a sweeter friend. 959
Know (worthy Prince) Sir *Valentine* my friend 1079
To crosse my friend in his intended drift, 1087
For, loue of you, not hate vnto my friend, 1115
To match my friend Sir *Thurio*, to my daughter. 1131
Pro. Sirha, I say forbeare: friend *Valentine*, a word. 1274
From hence, from *Siluia*, and from me thy friend. 1288
By one, whom she esteemeth as his friend. 1483
Especially against his very friend. 1487
Being intreated to it by your friend. 1491
To hate yong *Valentine*, and loue my friend. 1512
She twits me with my falsehood to my friend; 1632
Sil. Say that she be: yet *Valentine* thy friend 1733
Eg. Your seruant, and your friend; 1774
*goes me to the fellow that whips the dogges: friend 1844
Thou Counterfeyt, to thy true friend. 2174
Pro. In Loue, | Who respects friend? 2175
Thou friend of an ill fashion. | *Pro*. *Valentine*. 2185
Val. Thou co(m)mon friend, that's without faith or loue, 2187
For such is a friend now: treacherous man, 2188
I haue one friend aliue; thou wouldst disproue me: 2191
'Mongst all foes that a friend should be the worst? 2197
FRIENDLY = 1
And not depending on his friendly wish. 364
FRIENDS = 9
He leaues his friends, to dignifie them more; 68
I loue my selfe, my friends, and all for loue: 69
What maintenance he from his friends receiues, 370
What say you to a Letter from your friends | Of much good newes? 700
That stayes to beare my Letters to my friends, 1122
Duk. But she I meane, is promis'd by her friends 1175
And (for your friends sake) will be glad of you; 1510
Val. My friends. | 1.*Out*. That's not so, sir: we are your enemies. 1553
'Twere pitty two such friends should be long foes. 2244
FRIENDSHIP = 1
The Law of friendship bids me to conceale, 1074
FRIER = 2
Eg. Where shall I meete you? | *Sil*. At *Frier Patrickes* Cell, 1814
'Tis true: for Frier *Laurence* met them both 2081
FROM *I*.61 112 *135 136 *146 151 188 *191 355 356 370 371 536 *688 700
703 712 729 753 771 *773 786 814 *907 1052 1053 1078 1084 1118 1142
1177 1183 1239 1241 1242 1243 1257 1288 *1335 1401 1448 1495 1497

FROM *cont.*
1564 1592 1593 1596 1725 1740 1800 1802 *1824 *1828 1873 1874 1918
1934 1939 2065 2087 2138 2142 2242 2282 = 59*9
FROWARD = 1
Duk. No, trust me, She is peeuish, sullen, froward,   1137
FROWNE = 2
How angerly I taught my brow to frowne,   216
If she doe frowne, 'tis not in ňate of you,   1165
FROWNES = 1
Spee. Master, Sir *Thurio* frownes on you. | *Val.* I Boy, it's for loue.   657
FROZEN = 1
A little time will melt her frozen thoughts,   1455
FRYER = 2
3.*Out.* By the bare scalpe of *Robin Hoods* fat Fryer,   1582
That *Siluia*, at Fryer *Patricks* Cell should meet me,   2030
FULL = 10
For Loue (thou know'st is full of iealousie.)   832
Is full of Vertue, Bounty, Worth, and Qualities   1134
I now am full resolu'd to take a wife,   1145
Should be full fraught with seruiceable vowes.   1517
Valiant, wise, remorse-full, well accomplish'd.   1783
As full of sorrowes, as the Sea of sands,   1803
And full of new-found oathes, which he will breake   1951
Were full as louely, as is this of hers;   2006
And full as much (for more there cannot be)   2159
They are reformed, ciuill, full of good,   2283
FURNISH = 1
To furnish me vpon my longing iourney: 1060
FURY = 1
Such as the fury of vngouern'd youth   159ʰ
FUTURE = 1
And all the faire effects of future hopes.   54
GAINE = 1
If hap'ly won, perhaps a haplesse gaine;   36
GAINST = 2
Which like a waxen Image 'gainst a fire   856
And loue you 'gainst the nature of Loue: force ye.   2181
GARLANDS = 1
To her let vs Garlands bring.   1677
GARMENT = 1
As if the garment had bin made for me: 1984
GARTER = *1
*for hee beeing in loue, could not see to garter   469
GATE = 3
Come, Ile conuey thee through the City-gate.   1322
Bid him make haste, and meet me at the North-gate.   1328
La. Why then, will I tell thee, that thy Master staies | for thee at the
North gate.   1432
GAUE = 11*2
Sp. I Sir: I (a lost-Mutton) gaue your Letter to her   100
*(a lac'd-Mutton) and she (a lac'd-Mutton) gaue mee (a   101
Iul. Say, say: who gaue it thee?   190
Val. She gaue me none, except an angry word.   549
Val. Your selfe (sweet Lady) for you gaue the fire,   687
Pro. When I was sick, you gaue me bitter pils,   802
And ev'n that Powre which gaue me first my oath   933
I gaue him gentle lookes, thereby to finde   1100

GAUE *cont.*

This Ring I gaue him, when he parted from me,	1918
His *Iulia* gaue it him, at his departure:	1956
Pro. How? let me see. | Why this is the ring I gaue to *Iulia*.	2218
**Pro.* But how cam'st thou by this ring? at my depart | I gaue this vnto	
Iulia.	2222
Iul. Behold her, that gaue ayme to all thy oathes,	2227

GAUST = *1

**Pro.* But do'st thou heare: gau'st thou my Letter | to *Iulia*?	98

GAZE = *1

**Speed.* Shee that you gaze on so, as she sits at supper?	437

GAZING = *1

**Val.* Do'st thou know her by my gazing on her, and | yet know'st her	
not?	440

GEESE = *1

**Geese he hath kil'd, otherwise he had sufferd for't: thou	1852

GENERALL = 1

Are you content to be our Generall?	1607

GENTLE = 16*1

Iu. What think'st thou of the gentle *Protheus*?	167
**Sil.* I thanke you (gentle Seruant) 'tis very Clerkly- |(done.	498
Pro. Haue patience, gentle *Iulia*:	568
O gentle *Protheus*, Loue's a mighty Lord,	788
Iul. Counsaile, *Lucetta*, gentle girle assist me,	976
The Current that with gentle murmure glides	1000
Giuing a gentle kisse to euery sedge	1004
Ile be as patient as a gentle streame,	1009
Gentle *Lucetta*, fit me with such weedes	1017
On *Thurio*, whom your gentle daughter hates,	1083
I gaue him gentle lookes, thereby to finde	1100
Pro. I gentle *Thurio*, for you know that loue	1643
Pro. Sir *Protheus* (gentle Lady) and your Seruant.	1714
Good morrow (gentle Lady.)	1818
Sil. She is beholding to thee (gentle youth)	1994
Thou gentle Nimph, cherish thy for-lorne swaine.	2133
Pro. Nay, if the gentle spirit of mouing words	2178

GENTLEMAN = 13*2

Val. I, my good Lord, I know the Gentleman	705
With all good grace, to grace a Gentleman.	724
Well, Sir: this Gentleman is come to me	728
Val. This is the Gentleman I told your Ladiship	737
**Sil.* Haue done, haue done: here comes y gentleman.	749
Were rich and honourable: besides, the gentleman	1133
Vnto a youthfull Gentleman of worth,	1176
Duk. Now as thou art a Gentleman of blood	1190
'Tis an ill office for a Gentleman,	1486
2.*Out.* And I from *Mantua*, for a Gentleman,	1596
*you shall heare Musique, and see the Gentleman that | you ask'd for.	1655
Sil. Oh *Eglamoure*, thou art a Gentleman:	1781
Iul. True: from a Gentleman, to a foole.	2065
1 *Out.* Where is the Gentleman that was with her?	2108
Thou art a Gentleman, and well deriu'd,	2273

GENTLEMAN-LIKE-DOGS = *1

*foure gentleman-like-dogs, vnder the Dukes table: hee	1838

GENTLEMEN = 11*2

Iul. Of all the faire resort of Gentlemen,	157
Should censure thus on louely Gentlemen.	172

61

GENTLEMEN *cont.*

With other Gentlemen of good esteeme	342
Sil. A fine volly of words, gentleme(n), & quickly shot off	684
Sil. No more, gentlemen, no more: | Here comes my father.	696
To sort some Gentlemen, well skil'd in Musicke.	1538
Du. About it Gentlemen.	1541
3.*Out.* Know then, that some of vs are Gentlemen,	1590
Th. I thanke you for your owne: Now Gentlemen	1649
Sil. I thanke you for your Musique (Gentlemen)	1709
Dispatch (sweet Gentlemen) and follow me.	2092
Valentine. | *Protheus. the two Gentlemen.*	2303
THE | Two Gentlemen of Verona.	2317

GENTLEWOMAN = 4

Often resort vnto this Gentlewoman?	1695
Gentlewoman, good day: I pray you be my meane	1929
Poore Gentlewoman, my Master wrongs her much.	1962
A vertuous gentlewoman, milde, and beautifull.	2000

GENTLEWOMANS = *1

*Gentlewomans farthingale? did'st thou euer see me doe | such a tricke?	1857

GET = 6*2

Goe, get you gone: and let the papers lye:	260
Lau. Thou shalt neuer get such a secret from me, but | by a parable.	907
Spee. 'Tis well that I get it so: but *Launce*, how saist	909
For, get you gon, she doth not meane away.	1170
Val. By seauen a clock, ile get you such a Ladder.	1195
Ile get me one of such another length.	1203
Pro. Goe, get thee hence, and finde my dog againe,	1878
Ile get me such a coulour'd Perrywig:	2011

GHESSE = 1

Sil. A pretty period: well: I ghesse the sequell;	506

GIFT *see also* guift = *1

Val. I thank your Grace, y gift hath made me happy:	2275

GIFTS *see also* guifts = 1

Val. Win her with gifts, if she respect not words,	1158

GINGERLY = 1

Iu. What is't that you | Tooke vp so gingerly?	226

GIRLE = 5

Iul. Counsaile, *Lucetta*, gentle girle assist me,	976
Iul. No girle, Ile knit it vp in silken strings,	1020
What might we doe to make the girle forget	1475
Thu. Why this it is, to be a peeuish Girle,	2093
His Body, for a Girle that loues him not:	2261

GIUE = 19*3

Pro. Ouer the Bootes? nay giue me not the Boots.	30
Giue her no token but stones, for she's as hard as steele.	140
Giue me a Note, your Ladiship can set	238
Val. Ha? Let me see: I, giue it me, it's mine:	400
Speed. Oh, 'giue ye-good-ev'n: heer's a million of | manners.	490
Speed. He should giue her interest: & she giues it him.	493
Val. Giue him leaue, Madam, he is a kind of *Camelion.*	678
And I thinke, no other treasure to giue your followers:	693
Now presently Ile giue her father notice	965
Duke. Sir *Thurio*, giue vs leaue (I pray) a while,	1070
Send her another: neuer giue her ore,	1163
Will giue thee time to leaue our royall Court,	1235
To giue the on-set to thy good aduise.	1540
And giue some euening Musique to her eare.	1641

GIUE *cont.*

I giue consent to goe along with you,	1809
Pro. Well: giue her that Ring, and therewithall	1906
Goe, giue your Master this: tell him from me,	1939
Here youth: there is my purse; I giue thee this	1997
And lesse then this, I am sure you cannot giue.)	2146
All that was mine, in *Siluia,* I giue thee.	2209
Iul. And *Iulia* her selfe did giue it me,	2224
Val. Thurio giue backe; or else embrace thy death:	2253

GIUEN = 2

He would haue giuen it you, but I being in the way,	192
Speed. Why she hath giuen you a Letter.	550

GIUER = 2

Val. 'Tis indeed, Madam, we thank the giuer.	685
Therefore, sweet *Protheus,* my direction-giuer,	1536

GIUES = *1

*Speed. He should giue her interest: & she giues it him.	493

GIUING = 1

Giuing a gentle kisse to euery sedge	1004

GLAD = 2

And (for your friends sake) will be glad of you;	1510
Val. I was, and held me glad of such a doome.	1578

GLASSE = 2

But since she did neglect her looking-glasse,	1973
Her eyes are grey as glasse, and so are mine.	2012

GLAUNCES = 1

To the sweet glaunces of thy honour'd Loue,	7

GLIDES = 1

The Current that with gentle murmure glides	1000

GLORY = 1

The vncertaine glory of an Aprill day,	387

GLOUE = 1

Speed. Sir, your Gloue. | *Valen.* Not mine: my Gloues are on.	397

GLOUES = 1

Speed. Sir, your Gloue. | *Valen.* Not mine: my Gloues are on.	397

GO = 3*4

*Pro. Go, go, be gone, to saue your Ship from wrack,	146
*Ant. Good company: with them shall *Protheus* go:	345
He is in hast, therefore I pray you go.	391
*Luc. If you thinke so, then stay at home, and go not.	1037
Luc. Then neuer dreame on Infamy, but go:	1039
Go presently, and take this Ring with thee,	1890

GOD = 1

If this fond Loue, were not a blinded god.	2016

GOE = 38*2

Pro. It shall goe hard but ile proue it by another.	89
I must goe send some better Messenger,	149
Goe, get you gone: and let the papers lye:	260
Iu. Well, let vs goe.	291
Iu. Come, come, wilt please you goe. *Exeunt.*	299
To morrow be in readinesse, to goe,	372
No more of stay: to morrow thou must goe;	377
*Val. Goe to, sir, tell me: do you know Madam *Siluia?*	410
Pro. Goe: I come, I come:	588
Lau. Sir: call me what thou dar'st. | *Pant.* Wilt thou goe?	649
Laun. Well, I will goe. | *Exeunt.*	651
Goe with me: once more, new Seruant welcome;	769

GOE *cont.*

Good *Protheus* goe with me to my chamber,	839
Pro. Goe on before: I shall enquire you forth:	841
*himselfe in Loue. If thou wilt goe with me to the Ale-|house:	920
to goe to the Ale with a Christian: Wilt thou goe?	925
Thou wouldst as soone goe kindle fire with snow	994
Then let me goe, and hinder not my course:	1008
Luc. But in what habit will you goe along?	1014
And presently goe with me to my chamber	1058
Duk But harke thee: I will goe to her alone,	1196
Oh, could their Master come, and goe as lightly,	1212
Goe base Intruder, ouer-weening Slaue,	1227
Pro. What seest thou? | *Lau.* Him we goe to finde,	1260
Pro. Goe sirha, finde him out: Come *Valentine.*	1329
Sp. And must I goe to him?	1437
Come, goe with vs, we'll bring thee to our Crewes,	1620
Will creepe in seruice, where it cannot goe.	1644
Sil. Goe to thy Ladies graue and call hers thence,	1741
Iul. Host, will you goe?	1760
To beare me company, and goe with me:	1804
I giue consent to goe along with you,	1809
When will you goe? | *Sil.* This euening comming.	1812
Pro. Goe, get thee hence, and finde my dog againe,	1878
Goe, giue your Master this: tell him from me,	1939
Sil. Amen, Amen: goe on (good *Eglamoure*)	2035
Goe thou with her to the West end of the wood,	2111
Val. Ruffian: let goe that rude vnciuill touch,	2184
Come, let vs goe, we will include all iarres,	2287

GOES = 2*2

For being ignorant to whom it goes,	500
*him (looke you) it goes hard: one that I brought vp of	1823
*goes me to the fellow that whips the dogges: friend	1844
Then hate of *Eglamoure* that goes with her.	2098

GOING = 3*2

*to haue, when you chidde at Sir *Protheus,* for going vn-|garter'd.	465
*Sonne, and am going with Sir *Protheus* to the Imperialls	596
And I am going to deliuer them.	1123
that going will scarce serue the turne.	1439
Du. My daughter takes his going grieuously?	1460

GOLD = 1

The water, Nectar, and the Rocks pure gold.	826

GOLDEN = 1

Whose golden touch could soften steele and stones;	1525

GON = 6

Iul. Will ye be gon? | *Lu.* That you may ruminate. *Exit.*	202
Iulia, farewell: what, gon without a word?	584
But *Valentine* being gon, Ile quickely crosse	969
For, get you gon, she doth not meane away.	1170
(According to our Proclamation) gon?	1458
Pro. Gon, my good Lord.	1459

GONE = 9*2

Pro. Wilt thou be gone? Sweet *Valentine* adew,	14
Pro. Go, go, be gone, to saue your Ship from wrack,	146
Goe, get you gone: and let the papers lye:	260
Is gone with her along, and I must after,	831
No matter who's displeas'd, when you are gone:	1041
For which, the youthfull Louer now is gone,	1110

GONE *cont*.

If she doe chide, 'tis not to haue you gone,	1167
Be gone, I will not heare thy vaine excuse,	1238
Ho. Gone to seeke his dog, which to morrow, by his	1699
Then hate for *Siluia*, that is gone for loue. *Exeunt*.	2100
Therefore be gone, sollicit me no more.	2161

GOOD = 43*7

When thou do'st meet good hap; and in thy danger,	18
Warre with good counsaile; set the world at nought;	72
Lu. Then thus: of many good, I thinke him best.	174
Be calme (good winde) blow not a word away,	278
Pan. 'Twere good, I thinke, your Lordship sent him | (thither,	331
With other Gentlemen of good esteeme	342
Ant. Good company: with them shall *Protheus* go:	345
And in good time: now will we breake with him.	346
Speed. Oh, 'giue ye-good-ev'n: heer's a million of | manners.	490
Spee. 'Twere good you knockt him.	661
Sir *Valentine*, your father is in good health,	699
What say you to a Letter from your friends | Of much good newes?	700
Val. I, my good Lord, I know the Gentleman	705
Val. I, my good Lord, a Son, that well deserues	709
With all good grace, to grace a Gentleman.	724
Duk. Beshrew me sir, but if he make this good	725
Good *Protheus* goe with me to my chamber,	839
To lesson me, and tell me some good meane	980
Iul. That fits as well, as tell me (good my Lord)	1025
Which else, no worldly good should draw from me:	1078
But (good my Lord) doe it so cunningly	1113
Duk. A cloake as long as thine will serue the turne? | *Val*. I my good Lord.	1200
Val. My eares are stopt, & cannot hear good newes,	1275
Time is the Nurse, and breeder of all good;	1313
Sp. Item, she brewes good Ale.	1366
La. And thereof comes the prouerbe: (*Blessing of | your heart, you brew good Ale*.)	1367
La. If her liquor be good, she shall: if she will not,	1407
I will; for good things should be praised.	1408
Pro. Gon, my good Lord.	1459
Protheus, the good conceit I hold of thee,	1463
(For thou hast showne some signe of good desert)	1464
Du. Where your good word cannot aduantage him,	1488
Least it should rauell, and be good to none,	1498
To giue the on-set to thy good aduise.	1540
Pro. Madam: good eu'n to your Ladiship.	1708
Send to me in the morning, and ile send it: | And so, good rest.	1756
Sil. Sir *Eglamore*, a thousand times good morrow.	1776
Thou art not ignorant what deere good will	1784
As much, I wish all good befortune you.	1811
Good morrow (gentle Lady.)	1818
Sil. Good morrow, kinde Sir *Eglamoure*. *Exeunt*.	1819
currish thanks is good enough for such a present.	1869
Witnesse good bringing vp, fortune, and truth:	1888
To binde him to remember my good will:	1919
Gentlewoman, good day: I pray you be my meane	1929
Iul. It may not be: good Madam pardon me.	1947
And at that time I made her weepe a good,	1986
Sil. Amen, Amen: goe on (good *Eglamoure*)	2035

GOOD *cont.*
  Iul. O good sir, my master charg'd me to deliuer a ring   2214
  They are reformed, ciuill, full of good,   2283
GOODLY = 2
  Iul. Now (by my modesty) a goodly Broker: 194
  With goodly shape; and by your owne report,   1602
GOODS = 1
  My goods, my Lands, my reputation,   1062
GOOD-MORROW = 1
  And so good-morrow Seruant. *Exit. Sil.*   525
GOOD-MORROWS = *1
  Val. Madam & Mistres, a thousand good-morrows.   489
GOSSIPS = *1
  *not a maid: for shee hath had Gossips: yet 'tis a maid,   1338
GOT = 2
  And show thee all the Treasure we haue got;   1621
  Our youth got me to play the womans part,   1981
GOUERNE = 1
  But truer starres did gouerne *Protheus* birth,   1049
GOWNE = 1
  And I was trim'd in Madam *Iulias* gowne,   1982
GRACE = 13*4
  For truth hath better deeds, then words to grace it.   586
  With all good grace, to grace a Gentleman.   724
  Val. Please it your Grace, there is a Messenger   1121
  Cannot your Grace win her to fancie him?   1136
  Val. What would your Grace haue me to do in this?   1149
  Doe curse the grace, that with such grace hath blest them,   1216
  Pro. Longer then I proue loyall to your Grace,   1466
  Let me not liue, to looke vpon your Grace.   1467
  Pro. We'll wait vpon your Grace, till after Supper,   1542
  The heauen such grace did lend her,   1666
  Your Grace is welcome to a man disgrac'd, | Banished *Valentine.*   2249
  Val. I thank your Grace, y gift hath made me happy: 2275
  With our discourse, to make your Grace to smile.   2290
  Duke. I think the Boy hath grace in him, he blushes.   2292
  Val. I warrant you (my Lord) more grace, then Boy.   2293
GRACED = 1
  And daily graced by the Emperor;   360
GRACES = 1
  Flatter, and praise, commend, extoll their graces: 1171
GRACIOUS = 2*1
  Pro. My gracious Lord, that which I wold discouer,   1073
  But when I call to minde your gracious fauours,   1075
  La. Why that word makes the faults gracious: 1428
GRANDAM = *2
  *weep like a yong wench that had buried her Grandam: 418
  *to haue seene our parting: why my Grandam hauing   604
GRAND-FATHER = 1
  Sp. Marry, the son of my Grand-father.   1359
GRAND-MOTHER = 1
  Grand-mother: this proues that thou canst not read.   1361
GRANT = 3
  Pro. I grant (sweet loue) that I did loue a Lady, | But she is dead.   1729
  To grant one Boone that I shall aske of you.   2277
  Duke. I grant it (for thine owne) what ere it be.   2278

GRANTING = 1
I am so farre from granting thy request,   1725
GRAUE = 4
(Being vnpreuented) to your timelesse graue.   1090
Sil. And so suppose am I; for in her graue   1738
Sil. Goe to thy Ladies graue and call hers thence,   1741
Vpon whose Graue thou vow'dst pure chastitie: 1791
GREAT = 6*1
Now trust me, 'tis an office of great worth,   197
Which would be great impeachment to his age,   317
*Catte wringing her hands, and all our house in a great   600
With Commendation from great Potentates,   729
And of so great a fauor growing proud,   815
Ther's some great matter she'ld employ me in.   1771
And fit for great employment (worthy Lord.)   2284
GREATER = 1*2
Of greater time then I shall shew to be.   1023
*then the wit; for the greater hides the lesse: What's | next?   1423
*As big as ten of yours, & therefore the guift the greater.   1877
GREED = 1
Plotted, and 'greed on for my happinesse.   838
GREEFES = 1
Know then, I heere forget all former greefes,   2269
GREGORIES = 1
Th. Where meete we? | *Pro.* At Saint *Gregories* well. | *Th.* Farewell. 1705
GREY = 1
Her eyes are grey as glasse, and so are mine.   2012
GRIEFE = 4
Pro. A little time (my Lord) will kill that griefe.   1461
No griefe did euer come so neere thy heart,   1789
But thinke vpon my griefe (a Ladies griefe)   1798
GRIEUANCE = 2
Commend thy grieuance to my holy prayers,   20
Will well become such sweet complaining grieuance: 1532
GRIEUANCES = 1
Egl. Madam, I pitty much your grieuances,   1807
GRIEUES = 1
Iu. Not so: but yet | So false that he grieues my very heart-strings.   1684
GRIEUOUS = 1
If lost, why then a grieuous labour won;   37
GRIEUOUSLY = 1
Du. My daughter takes his going grieuously?   1460
GRONES = 3
Val. To be in loue; where scorne is bought with | (grones: 33
With bitter fasts, with penitentiall grones,   783
Sad sighes, deepe grones, nor siluer-shedding teares   1300
GROUND = 1*1
Sp. If the ground be ouer-charg'd, you were best | sticke her.   105
Duk. Her chamber is aloft, far from the ground,   1183
GROWES = 1
The more it growes, and fawneth on her still;   1639
GROWING = 2
And of so great a fauor growing proud,   815
Lest growing ruinous, the building fall,   2130
GRUDGE = 1
Cancell all grudge, repeale thee home againe,   2270

GUESD = 1
Him he knew well: and guesd that it was she,   2083
GUESSE *see* ghesse
GUEST = *1
  Ho. Now, my yong guest; me thinks your' allycholly;   1651
GUIDE = 1
Wilt thou aspire to guide the heauenly Car?   1223
GUIFT = *1
  *As big as ten of yours, & therefore the guift the greater.   1877
GUIFTS = 1
To be corrupted with my worthlesse guifts;   1630
GUILD = 1
  Egl. The Sun begins to guild the westerne skie,   2028
GUILT = 1
  Pro. My shame and guilt confounds me: 2198
HA *l*.400 = 1
HABILIMENTS = 1
My riches, are these poore habiliments,   1559
HABIT = 3
  Luc. But in what habit will you goe along?   1014
  Val. How vse doth breed a habit in a man?   2122
Oh *Protheus*, let this habit make thee blush.   2230
HAD *l*.204 215 *416 *417 *418 *463 *464 519 732 738 1118 *1338 1568
  1581 *1834 *1835 *1836 *1839 *1851 *1852 1984 2005 2055
  2154 = 12*13
HADST *see* thou'dst
HAIRE = 4*3
  Luc. Why then your Ladiship must cut your haire.   1019
There's not a haire on's head, but 'tis a *Valentine*.   1262
  Sp. Item, shee hath more haire then wit, and more   1414
  Sp. Item, she hath more haire then wit.   1419
  La. More haire then wit: it may be ile proue it: The   1420
  *then the salt; the haire that couers the wit, is more   1422
Her haire is *Aburne*, mine is perfect *Yellow*;   2009
HAIRES = 2
faults then haires, and more wealth then faults.   1415
  Sp. And more faults then haires.   1425
HALLIDOME = 1
  Ho. By my hallidome, I was fast asleepe.   1761
HALLOWING = 1
What hallowing, and what stir is this to day?   2134
HALLOW-MASSE = *1
  *feares robbing: to speake puling, like a beggar at Hal-|low-Masse: 420
HAMERING = 1
Whereon, this month I haue bin hamering.   320
HAND = 4
Here is her hand, the agent of her heart;   348
  Pro. Here is my hand, for my true constancie: 576
Who should be trusted, when ones right hand   2192
  Val. Come, come: a hand from either: 2242
HANDS = 3*2
Oh hatefull hands, to teare such louing words;   265
  *Catte wringing her hands, and all our house in a great   600
  *Wringing her hands, whose whitenes so became them,   1297
But neither bended knees, pure hands held vp,   1299
  *She can milke, looke you, a sweet vertue in a maid with | cleane
  hands.   1345

HANG = *1
    *third) hang him vp (saies the Duke.) I hauing bin ac-|quainted   1842
HANGD = *2
    *vndon till hee be hang'd, nor neuer welcome to a place,   876
    *vpon me that he did, I thinke verily hee had bin hang'd   1835
HANGING = 2
    Vnto a ragged, fearefull, hanging Rocke,   281
    The Picture that is hanging in your chamber: 1746
HANGMANS = 1
    By the Hangmans boyes in the market place,   1875
HAP = 1
    When thou do'st meet good hap; and in thy danger,   18
HAPLESSE = 2
    If hap'ly won, perhaps a haplesse gaine;   36
    Val. Oh my deere *Siluia*; haplesse *Valentine.*   1330
HAPLY = 4
    Thinke on thy *Protheus*, when thou (hap'ly) seest   15
    If hap'ly won, perhaps a haplesse gaine;   36
    Thu. Seeme you that you are not? | *Val.* Hap'ly I doe.   664
    Haply when they haue iudg'd me fast asleepe,   1094
HAPPILY = 1
    How happily he liues, how well-belou'd,   359
HAPPINESSE = 5
    Wish me partaker in thy happinesse,   17
    Pro. All happinesse bechance to thee in *Millaine.*   65
    To seale our happinesse with their consents.   351
    Plotted, and 'greed on for my happinesse.   838
    One Feast, one house, one mutuall happinesse. *Exeunt.*   2300
HAPPY = 6*1
    To any happy messenger from thence.   703
    My health, and happy being at your Court.   1126
    Val. My youthfull trauaile, therein made me happy,   1580
    See where she comes: Lady a happy euening.   2034
    But by my comming, I haue made you happy.   2151
    Let me be blest to make this happy close: 2243
    Val. I thank your Grace, y gift hath made me happy: 2275
HARBOUR = 3
    Dare you presume to harbour wanton lines?   195
    My thoughts do harbour with my Siluia *nightly,*   1210
    That they should harbour where their Lord should be.   1219
HARD = 5*2
    Pro. It shall goe hard but ile proue it by another.   89
    And being so hard to me, that brought your minde;   138
    *I feare she'll proue as hard to you in telling your minde.   139
    Giue her no token but stones, for she's as hard as steele.   140
    Duk. Now, daughter *Siluia*, you are hard beset.   698
    To beare a hard opinion of his truth: 1056
    *him (looke you) it goes hard: one that I brought vp of   1823
HARDLY = 2
    Sp. Truely Sir, I thinke you'll hardly win her.   134
    looke on you, I can hardly thinke you my Master.   426
HARDLY-OFF = 1
    Val. Now trust me (Madam) it came hardly-off   499
HARD-FAUOURD = 1
    Speed. Is she not hard-fauour'd, sir?   442
HARKE = 4
    Duk But harke thee: I will goe to her alone,   1196

HARKE *cont.*
 Iu. That will be Musique. | *Ho.* Harke, harke.   1659
 Ho. Harke, what fine change is in the Musique.   1690
HARSH = 2
 And marre the concord, with too harsh a descant: 254
 For they are harsh, vn-tuneable, and bad.   1278
HART = *1
 *Made Wit with musing, weake; hart sick with thought.   73
HART-SORE = 1*1
 *Coy looks, with hart-sore sighes: one fading moments | (mirth,   34
 With nightly teares, and daily hart-sore sighes,   784
HAS *l.**602 1902 = 1*1
HAST *l.*70 336 438 *923 936 944 972 1101 *1438 1464 1534 1722 1788
 1912 2171 2189 2229 2264 2274 2285 = 18*2, 1
 He is in hast, therefore I pray you go.   391
HASTE *see also* hast = 2
 Val. Will you make haste? *Exit.* | *Pro.* I will.   845
 Bid him make haste, and meet me at the North-gate.   1328
HASTEN = 1
 To hasten on his Expedition.   379
HAT = *1
 *small as a wand: this hat is *Nan* our maid: I am the   613
HATE = 8
 Lu. To plead for loue, deserues more fee, then hate.   201
 For, loue of you, not hate vnto my friend,   1115
 If she doe frowne, 'tis not in hate of you,   1165
 Three things, that women highly hold in hate.   1479
 Du. I, but she'll thinke, that it is spoke in hate.   1480
 To hate yong *Valentine*, and loue my friend.   1512
 Then hate of *Eglamoure* that goes with her.   2098
 Then hate for *Siluia*, that is gone for loue. *Exeunt.*   2100
HATEFULL = 1
 Oh hatefull hands, to teare such louing words;   265
HATES = 1
 On *Thurio*, whom your gentle daughter hates,   1083
HATH *l.*180 236 242 385 457 528 542 544 550 *552 *558 586 *609 *679
 708 717 740 745 746 786 789 865 986 1116 1142 1173 1178 1181 1216
 1276 1282 1292 *1338 *1340 1380 1390 1402 1405 *1414 1419 *1435
 1449 1765 *1850 *1852 *1967 1970 1975 2109 2225 *2275 *2292
 2296 = 40*13
HAUE *l.*5 77 *120 122 127 *143 175 *178 192 210 215 235 279 296 320
 321 371 *380 *413 459 *465 482 494 519 *535 555 560 *564 568 *593
 *594 *595 *603 *604 681 *692 713 714 732 *749 753 758 771 *774 781
 782 810 864 *881 991 1011 *1028 1031 1032 1071 1082 1093 1094 1095
 1099 1105 1107 1130 1144 *1149 1153 1154 1167 1172 1191 1232 1284
 1289 1308 *1331 *1382 *1416 *1429 1492 1507 1539 *1549 1557 1561
 1566 *1567 1579 1584 1588 *1615 1621 1625 1628 1634 *1654 1686
 *1687 *1692 1693 1717 1758 1788 1805 *1825 *1832 *1849 *1851 1864
 1872 1882 1883 1922 1923 1928 1943 1955 1957 1966 2024 2106 2136
 2137 2140 2143 2151 2155 2156 2172 2190 2191 2220 2231 *2245 2279
 2281 = 101*36
HAUING = 4*2
 Hauing nothing but the word noddy for my paines.   126
 Which cannot perish hauing thee aboarde,   147
 In hauing knowne no trauaile in his youth.   318
 *to haue seene our parting: why my Grandam hauing   604
 And I as rich in hauing such a Iewell   824

HAUING *cont.*
  *third) hang him vp (saies the Duke.) I hauing bin ac-|quainted   1842
HAZARD = 2
  Without apparant hazard of his life.   1185
  To hazard life, ánd reskew you from him,   2142
HE = 68*25
HEAD = 4
  His head vn-mellowed, but his Iudgement ripe;   720
  Then (by concealing it) heap on your head   1088
  There's not a haire on's head, but 'tis a *Valentine*.   1262
  La. Fie on thee Iolt-head, thou canst not read. | *Sp*. Thou lyest: I can.   1356
HEADS = 1
  I, but her fore-head's low, and mine's as high: 2013
HEALD = 1
  Shall lodge thee till thy wound be throughly heal'd;   275
HEALTH = 3
  Sir *Valentine*, your father is in good health,   699
  Val. And how doe yours? | *Pro*. I left them all in health.   775
  My health, and happy being at your Court.   1126
HEAP = 1
  Then (by concealing it) heap on your head   1088
HEAR = *1
  Val. My eares are stopt, & cannot hear good newes,   1275
HEARD = 4
  Oh excellent deuise, was there euer heard a better?   530
  Iul. He heard not that.   1743
  Thy selfe hast lou'd, and I haue heard thee say   1788
  For I haue heard him say a thousand times,   1955
HEARDST = 1
  La. The black'st newes that euer thou heard'st.   1352
HEARE = 12*2
  To *Millaine* let me heare from thee by Letters   61
  Pro. But do'st thou heare: gau'st thou my Letter | to *Iulia*?   98
  Heare sweet discourse, conuerse with Noble-men,   333
  If this be he you oft haue wish'd to heare from.   753
  When you haue done, we looke too heare from you.   771
  Be gone, I will not heare thy vaine excuse,   1238
  2.*Out*. Peace: we'll heare him.   1555
  *you shall heare Musique, and see the Gentleman that | you ask'd for.   1655
  Iu. But shall I heare him speake. | *Ho*. I that you shall.   1657
  Pro. I likewise heare that *Valentine* is dead.   1737
  To *Mantua*, where I heare, he makes aboad;   1793
  To heare me speake the message I am sent on.   1933
  Val. How like a dreame is this? I see, and heare: 2147
  Come *Protheus*, 'tis your pennance, but to heare   2297
HEAREM = 1
  Iu. Is he among these? | *Ho*. I: but peace, let's heare'm.   1661
HEARING = 1
  Speed. Shee is not within hearing Sir.   405
HEARKEN = *1
  Speed. I, but hearken sir: though the Cameleon Loue   562
HEART *see also* hart = 15
  When inward ioy enforc'd my heart to smile?   217
  Here is her hand, the agent of her heart;   348
  Pro. Why this it is: my heart accords thereto,   392
  His teares, pure messengers, sent from his heart,   1052
  His heart, as far from fraud, as heauen from earth.   1053

HEART *cont.*

La. And thereof comes the prouerbe: (*Blessing of | your heart, you brew*
   good Ale.)   1367
You sacrifice your teares, your sighes, your heart: 1520
Who, in my moode, I stab'd vnto the heart.   1597
Iu. I, I would I were deafe: it makes me haue a slow | (heart.   1687
Pro. Madam: if your heart be so obdurate: 1744
No griefe did euer come so neere thy heart,   1789
I doe desire thee, euen from a heart   1802
That with his very heart despiseth me?   1915
Read ouer *Iulia's* heart, (thy first best Loue)   2167
And entertain'd'em deepely in her heart.   2228
HEARTED = *1
*perplexitie, yet did not this cruell-hearted Curre shedde   601
HEARTS = 2
And made them watchers of mine owne hearts sorrow.   787
Pro. One (Lady) if you knew his pure hearts truth,   1711
HEARTY = 1
Forgiue me *Valentine*: if hearty sorrow   2199
HEART-STRINGS = 1
Iu. Not so: but yet | So false that he grieues my very heart-strings. 1684
HEATE = 3
Euen as one heate, another heate expels,   847
Trenched in ice, which with an houres heate   1453
HEAUE = *1
*thou see me heaue vp my leg, and make water against a   1856
HEAUEN = 9*1
And *Siluia* (witnesse heauen that made her faire)   954
His heart, as far from fraud, as heauen from earth.   1053
By heauen, my wrath shall farre exceed the loue   1236
The heauen such grace did lend her,   1666
Which heauen and fortune still rewards with plagues.   1801
As (heauen it knowes) I would not haue him speed.   1928
Oh heauen be iudge how I loue *Valentine*,   2157
Sil. Oh heauen. | *Pro.* Ile force thee yeeld to my desire.   2182
Is nor of heauen, nor earth; for these are pleas'd: 2206
Pro. Beare witnes (heauen) I haue my wish for euer.   2245
HEAUENLY = 4
Pro. Oh heauenly *Iulia*.   352
Val. Euen She; and is she not a heauenly Saint?   797
Wilt thou aspire to guide the heauenly Car?   1223
I claime the promise for her heauenly Picture: 1908
HEAUEN-BRED = 1
Du. I, much is the force of heauen-bred Poesie.   1518
HEAUIEST = 1
That ere I watch'd, and the most heauiest.   1766
HEAUN = *1
Luc. Pray heau'n he proue so when you come to him.   1054
HEAUY = 3
Lu. It is too heauy for so light a tune.   241
Iu. Heauy? belike it hath some burden then?   242
For she is lumpish, heauy, mellancholly,   1509
HEBREW = *1
*if not, thou art an Hebrew, a Iew, and not worth | the name of a
Christian.   921
HEE *l.*469 *618 *876 *903 *904 *919 *1700 *1835 *1837 *1838 = *10

HEEDFULL = 1
    Vn-heedfull vowes may heedfully be broken,   940
HEEDFULLY = 1
    Vn-heedfull vowes may heedfully be broken,   940
HEELES = 1
    La. Close at the heeles of her vertues.   1385
HEERE = 9*1
    And heere he meanes to spend his time a while,   730
    Duk. There is a Lady in *Verona* heere   1150
    And heere an Engine fit for my proceeding,   1208
    Tarry I heere, I but attend on death,   1256
    *much in a bare Christian: Heere is the Cate-log of her   1341
    Withdraw thee *Valentine*: who's this comes heere?   2139
    I tender't heere: I doe as truely suffer, | As ere I did commit.   2201
    Pro. Where is that ring? boy? | *Iul*. Heere 'tis: this is it.   2216
    Verona shall not hold thee: heere she stands,   2256
    Know then, I heere forget all former greefes,   2269
HEERES = 1*1
    *there 'tis; heere's my mothers breath vp and downe: 621
    'Tis so: and heere's the Ladder for the purpose.   1221
HEERS = *1
    Speed. Oh, 'giue ye-good-ev'n: heer's a million of | manners.   490
HEIGHT = 1
    Therefore I know she is about my height,   1985
HEIRE = 1
    And heire and Neece, alide vnto the Duke.   1595
HELD = 3
    Wherewith my brother held you in the Cloyster?   303
    But neither bended knees, pure hands held vp,   1299
    Val. I was, and held me glad of such a doome.   1578
HELLESPONT = 2
    How yong *Leander* crost the *Hellespont*.   25
    And yet you neuer swom the *Hellespont*.   29
HELP = 1
    Val. And I will help thee to prefer her to: 811
HELPD = 1
    And being help'd, inhabits there.   1672
HELPE = 4
    Pro. Cease to lament for that thou canst not helpe,   1311
    And study helpe for that which thou lament'st,   1312
    *keepe shut: Now, of another thing shee may, and that | cannot I helpe.
    Well, proceede.   1412
    To helpe him of his blindnesse: 1671
HENCE = 12*1
    Pro. But now he parted hence to embarque for *Millain*.   75
    How churlishly, I chid *Lucetta* hence,   214
    Onely, in lieu thereof, dispatch me hence: 1063
    Is priuiledge for thy departure hence.   1230
    But as thou lou'st thy life, make speed from hence.   1239
    But flie I hence, I flie away from life.   1257
    From hence, from *Siluia*, and from me thy friend.   1288
    Hope is a louers staffe, walke hence with that   1316
    Thy letters may be here, though thou art hence,   1318
    Pro. Sir, but I doe: or else I would be hence.   1646
    And on the iustice of my flying hence,   1799
    Pro. Goe, get thee hence, and finde my dog againe,   1878
    These likelihoods confirme her flight from hence;   2087

HENCEFORTH = 2*1
*In requital whereof, henceforth, carry your letters your	144
Iu. This babble shall not henceforth trouble me;	258
Meaning henceforth to trouble you no more.	509

HER *I*.*100 105 134 *135 136 140 205 206 215 348 349 406 *418 439 440
448 453 *455 456 458 459 460 461 *468 477 488 *493 528 529 548 551
555 *557 *558 *600 *605 *620 739 799 804 805 811 814 820 821 829 831
836 852 862 863 864 866 869 887 892 943 954 957 965 1082 1096 1104
1108 1109 1136 1140 1142 1144 1146 1147 1157 1158 1161 *1162 1163
1175 1178 1179 1181 1182 1183 1196 1242 1253 1295 1296 *1297 1301
1303 1305 *1339 *1341 1378 1384 1385 *1386 1391 1392 *1393 *1396
*1398 1401 1406 *1407 *1410 *1411 *1416 *1429 1448 1451 1455 1472
1495 1497 1511 1515 1519 1533 1631 1633 1636 1639 1640 1641 1664
1666 1670 1677 1697 1738 1770 *1829 *1830 1873 1876 *1893 1898 1899
1902 1903 1906 1907 1908 1916 1931 1961 1962 1963 1965 *1967 *1968
1971 1973 1974 1975 1976 1986 1993 *1998 1999 2004 2007 2009 2012
2013 2014 2043 2080 2087 2094 2098 2107 2108 2111 2224 2225 2227
2228 2257 2259 2262 2264 2265 2274 2307 = 170*36

HERALD = 1
My Herald Thoughts, in thy pure bosome rest-them,	1214

HERE = 30*3
Betideth here in absence of thy Friend:	63
Pro. Well Sir: here is for your paines: what said she?	133
When willingly, I would have had her here?	215
Here is a coile with protestation:	259
Looke, here is writ, kinde *Iulia*: vnkinde *Iulia*,	269
And here is writ, *Loue wounded Protheus*.	273
Loe, here in one line is his name twice writ:	283
Lu. What, shall these papers lye, like Tel-tales here?	292
Yet here they shall not lye, for catching cold.	295
Here is her hand, the agent of her heart;	348
Here is her oath for loue, her honors paune;	349
Peace, here she comes.	486
Pro. Why then wee'll make exchange; | Here, take you this.	573
Pro. Here is my hand, for my true constancie:	576
Lau. Why, he that's tide here, *Crab* my dog.	633
Sil. No more, gentlemen, no more: | Here comes my father.	696
Sil. Haue done, haue done: here comes y gentleman.	749
What Letter is this same? what's here? to *Siluia*?	1207
What's here? *Siluia, this night I will enfranchise thee*.	1220
Here, if thou stay, thou canst not see thy loue:	1314
Thy letters may be here, though thou art hence,	1318
Sp. Here follow her vices.	1384
Pro. She did my Lord, when *Valentine* was here.	1473
Of which, if you should here disfurnish me,	1560
But here comes *Thurio*; now must we to her window,	1640
Th. I, but I hope, Sir, that you loue not here.	1645
Here haue I brought him backe againe.	1872
Away, I say: stayest thou to vexe me here;	1880
Here youth: there is my purse; I giue thee this	1997
Here is her Picture: let me see, I thinke	2004
Iul. Here comes the Duke.	2071
Here can I sit alone, vn-seene of any,	2125
Forgiue them what they haue committed here,	2281

HERES = *1
Pro. Here's too small a Pasture for such store of | Muttons.	103

HEROS = 1
Would serue to scale another *Hero's* towre,   1188
HERS = 4
And may I say to thee, this pride of hers,   1141
Sil. Goe to thy Ladies graue and call hers thence,   1741
Or at the least, in hers, sepulcher thine.   1742
Were full as louely, as is this of hers;   2006
HERSELF *see* self
HERSELFE *see* selfe
HES = *1
Sil. When *Protheus* cannot loue, where he's belou'd: 2166
HETHER = 1
Sil. His worth is warrant for his welcome hether,   752
HEUEN = *1
Pro. Then men their minds? tis true: oh heuen, were man   2236
HIDE = 1
If not, to hide what I haue said to thee,   1805
HIDES = *2
*couer of the salt, hides the salt, and therefore it is more   1421
*then the wit; for the greater hides the lesse: What's | next?   1423
HIE = 1
That presently you hie you home to bed: 1718
HIGH = 5
Iu. And why not you? | *Lu.* I cannot reach so high.   244
Sil. Too low a Mistres for so high a seruant.   756
Whose high emperious thoughts haue punish'd me   782
Shee shall be dignified with this high honour,   812
I, but her fore-head's low, and mine's as high: 2013
HIGHLY = 1
Three things, that women highly hold in hate.   1479
HIM *l.*77 174 177 *178 305 307 316 326 *331 340 346 356 361 *493 *603
661 *678 711 712 733 735 736 754 760 764 859 861 885 *892 911 *913
*1054 1055 1057 1100 1112 1136 1258 1260 1303 1328 1329 1373 1437
*1438 1484 *1488 1489 1494 1497 1555 1574 1584 1627 1657 1671 1712
1736 *1823 *1826 *1827 *1833 *1840 *1841 *1842 *1846 1872 1902 1914
1917 1918 1919 1927 1928 1939 1954 1955 1956 2083 2110 2112 2142
*2238 2260 2261 *2292 = 68*21
HIMSELF = *1
*Her self hath taught her Loue himself, to write vnto her | (louer.   558
HIMSELFE = 3*5
Lu. Well of his wealth; but of himselfe, so, so.   166
To himselfe should write the Letter?   532
*dogge: no, the dogge is himselfe, and I am the dogge: 614
*himselfe in Loue. If thou wilt goe with me to the Ale- | house: 920
Himselfe would lodge where (senceles) they are lying.   1213
*An vnmannerly slaue, that will thrust himselfe into se- | crets: 1443
*thing, when a Cur cannot keepe himselfe in all compa- | nies: 1831
*Hee thrusts me himselfe into the company of three or   1837
HINDER = 1
Then let me goe, and hinder not my course: 1008
HINDERED = 1
But when his faire course is not hindered,   1002
HIS *see also* on's *l.*53 68 *83 166 *169 182 186 283 287 304 307 316 317
318 321 328 329 335 344 361 362 364 365 370 379 *417 *470 *688 717
718 719 720 721 730 733 738 739 744 751 752 762 768 790 791 830 860
*904 942 964 968 985 *990 1002 1005 1044 1050 1051 1052 1053 1056
1087 1174 1185 1255 1265 1449 1454 1460 1481 1483 1487 1493 1671

HIS *cont.*
1696 *1699 *1700 1711 1712 *1825 *1849 1915 1923 1940 1941 1952
1956 1957 1958 2010 2020 2261 = 88*12

HITHER *see also* hether = 2

I will send him hither to you presently.	736
And *Iulia* her selfe hath brought it hither. | *Pro.* How? *Iulia?*	2225

HO = 11*5
HOE = 1

What hoe: *Lucetta.* | *Lu.* What would your Ladiship?	220

HOLD = 9

Did hold his eyes, lockt in her Christall lookes.	739
And *Valentine* Ile hold an Enemie,	958
Protheus, the good conceit I hold of thee,	1463
Three things, that women highly hold in hate.	1479
That they may hold excus'd our lawlesse liues;	1600
Sil. There, hold: | I will not looke vpon your Masters lines:	1948
Iul. But better indeede, when you hold you peace.	2059
Verona shall not hold thee: heere she stands,	2256
I hold him but a foole that will endanger	2260

HOLDS = *1

Val. Nay sure, I thinke she holds them prisoners stil.	742

HOLE = *1

*with the hole in it, is my mother: and this my father:	610

HOLY = 5

Commend thy grieuance to my holy prayers,	20
Iul. And seale the bargaine with a holy kisse.	575
But *Siluia* is too faire, too true, too holy,	1629
Holy, faire, and wise is she,	1665
Where I intend holy Confession.	1816

HOMAGE = 1

We'll doe thee homage, and be rul'd by thee,	1612

HOME = 8*1

Then (liuing dully sluggardiz'd at home)	10
Val. As much to you at home: and so farewell. *Exit.*	66
Would suffer him, to spend his youth at home,	307
To let him spend his time no more at home;	316
Ile leaue you to confer of home affaires,	770
Luc. If you thinke so, then stay at home, and go not.	1037
That presently you hie you home to bed:	1718
Your message done, hye home vnto my chamber,	1909
Cancell all grudge, repeale thee home againe,	2270

HOMELY = 1*1

*Home-keeping youth, haue euer homely wits,	5
Vpon a homely obiect, Loue can winke.	748

HOME-KEEPING = *1

*Home-keeping youth, haue euer homely wits,	5

HONEST = 2

Duke. *Protheus,* I thank thee for thine honest care,	1091
And once againe, I doe receiue thee honest;	2204

HONESTY = 1

Speed. Launce, by mine honesty welcome to *Padua.*	873

HONOR = 4

The honor, and regard of such a father.	710
Duke. Vpon mine Honor, he shall neuer know	1117
Vpon whose faith and honor, I repose.	1796
Now, by the honor of my Ancestry,	2266

HONORS = 1
  Here is her oath for loue, her honors paune;   349
HONOUR = 4
  Pro. He after Honour hunts, I after Loue;   67
  Shee shall be dignified with this high honour,   812
  How with my honour I may vndertake   981
  That would haue forc'd your honour, and your loue,   2143
HONOURABLE = 3
  Were rich and honourable: besides, the gentleman   1133
  It's an honourable kinde of theeuery.   1586
  Feare not: he beares an honourable minde.   2115
HONOURD = 1
  To the sweet glaunces of thy honour'd Loue,   7
HONY = 1
  Iniurious Waspes, to feede on such sweet hony,   266
HOODS = 1
  3.*Out.* By the bare scalpe of *Robin Hoods* fat Fryer,   1582
HOOKES = 1
  To cast vp, with a paire of anchoring hookes,   1187
HOPE = 5
  Hope is a louers staffe, walke hence with that   1316
  The least whereof would quell a louers hope: 1637
  Th. I, but I hope, Sir, that you loue not here.   1645
  Pro. I hope thou wilt.   1862
  I hope my Masters suit will be but cold,   2001
HOPES = 2
  And all the faire effects of future hopes.   54
  Thou hast beguil'd my hopes; nought but mine eye   2189
HORNES = *2
  Sp. Why then my hornes are his hornes, whether I | wake or sleepe.   83
HORSE = *3
  *Teeme of horse shall not plucke that from me: nor who   1335
  *a horse can doe no more; nay, a horse cannot fetch, but   1343
HOSE = 2*1
  *his hose; and you, beeing in loue, cannot see to put on | your hose.   470
  Luc. A round hose (Madam) now's not worth a pin   1030
HOST see also Ho. = 5
  Enter Protheus, Thurio, Iulia, Host, Musitian, Siluia.   1624
  Iu. Marry (mine *Host*) because I cannot be merry.   1653
  But Host, doth this Sir *Protheus*, that we talke on,   1694
  Iul. Host, will you goe?   1760
  Host: where Iulia lodges.   2308
HOSTESSE = *1
  *till some certaine shot be paid, and the Hostesse say wel-|come.   877
HOT = 2
  Spee. I tell thee, my Master is become a hot Louer.   918
  Luc. I doe not seeke to quench your Loues hot fire,   996
HOUGH = 2
  Lau. So-hough, Soa hough---   1259
HOURE = 2
  Eg. This is the houre that Madam *Siluia*   1769
  And now it is about the very houre   2029
HOURES = 2
  Trenched in ice, which with an houres heate   1453
  She will not faile; for Louers breake not houres,   2031
HOUSE = 2*3
  *Catte wringing her hands, and all our house in a great   600

HOUSE *cont.*

Speed. Come-on you mad-cap: Ile to the Ale-house	879
*himselfe in Loue. If thou wilt goe with me to the Ale-|house:	920
Iul. Pray you, where lies Sir *Protheus*? | *Ho*. Marry, at my house:	1762
One Feast, one house, one mutuall happinesse. *Exeunt*.	2300

HOW = 58*14

How yong *Leander* crost the *Hellespont*.	25
How euer: but a folly bought with wit,	38
Pro. Why Sir, how doe you beare with me?	124
Iu. How now? what meanes this passion at his name?	169
Fie, fie: how way-ward is this foolish loue;	211
How churlishly, I chid *Lucetta* hence,	214
How angerly I taught my brow to frowne,	216
Iu. Let's see your Song: | How now Minion?	246
And how he cannot be a perfect man,	322
How his companion, youthfull *Valentine*,	328
And that thou maist perceiue how well I like it,	337
Ant. How now? What Letter are you reading there?	353
How happily he liues, how well-belou'd,	359
Ant. And how stand you affected to his wish?	362
Oh, how this spring of loue resembleth	386
Speed. Madam *Siluia*: Madam *Siluia*. | *Val*. How now Sirha?	403
Val. Why, how know you that I am in loue?	412
Val. How painted? and how out of count?	452
Val. How esteem'st thou me? I account of her beauty.	455
Val. How long hath she beene deform'd?	457
Val. How now Sir? | What are you reasoning with your selfe?	533
*speakes a word: but see how I lay the dust with my | teares.	624
Thu. And how quoat you my folly?	672
Val. Well then, Ile double your folly. | *Thu*. How?	675
How could he see his way to seeke out you?	744
Val. Now tell me: how do al from whence you came?	773
Val. And how doe yours? | *Pro*. I left them all in health.	775
Val. How does your Lady? & how thriues your loue?	777
Determin'd of: how I must climbe her window,	836
How shall I doate on her with more aduice,	862
*thou shalt haue fiue thousand welcomes: But sirha, how	881
Spee. How then? shall he marry her? | *Lau*. No, neither.	887
Spee. Why then, how stands the matter with them?	891
Spee. 'Tis well that I get it so: but *Launce*, how saist	909
Lau. I neuer knew him otherwise. | *Spee*. Then how?	911
How with my honour I may vndertake	981
But tell me (wench) how will the world repute me	1034
How he her chamber-window will ascend,	1108
How, and which way I may bestow my selfe	1156
How shall I best conuey the Ladder thither?	1197
Duk. How shall I fashion me to weare a cloake?	1205
Speed. How now Signior *Launce*? what newes with | your Mastership?	1347
Sp. Why man? how blacke? | *La*. Why, as blacke as Inke.	1353
How now sir *Protheus*, is your countriman	1457
Du. Thou know'st how willingly, I would effect	1468
How she opposes her against my will?	1472
She bids me thinke how I haue bin forsworne	1634
Th. How now, sir *Protheus*, are you crept before vs?	1642
Ho. How now? are you sadder then you were before;	1678
How doe you, man? the Musicke likes you not.	1679
Ho. How, out of tune on the strings.	1683

HOW *cont.*
Nor how my father would enforce me marry	1786
*but whips me out of the chamber: how many Masters	1848
How now you whor-son pezant,	1863
Iul. How many women would doe such a message?	1911
Sil. How tall was she? | *Iul.* About my stature: for at *Pentecost*,	1978
Alas, how loue can trifle with it selfe:	2003
Thu. How likes she my discourse?	2056
Du. How now sir *Protheus*; how now *Thurio*?	2072
Haue learn'd me how to brooke this patiently.	2106
Val. How vse doth breed a habit in a man?	2122
Val. How like a dreame is this? I see, and heare:	2147
Oh heauen be iudge how I loue *Valentine*,	2157
*Why wag: how now? what's the matter? look vp: speak.	2213
Pro. How? let me see. | Why this is the ring I gaue to *Iulia*.	2218
Pro. But how cam'st thou by this ring? at my depart | I gaue this vnto *Iulia*.	2222
And *Iulia* her selfe hath brought it hither. | *Pro.* How? *Iulia*?	2225
How oft hast thou with periury cleft the roote?	2229

HOWEUER *see* how
HOWLING = *1
*wayling: my Sister crying: our Maid howling: our	599

HOWRE = 3*1
And when that howre ore-slips me in the day,	577
The next ensuing howre, some foule mischance	579
Launce. Nay, 'twill bee this howre ere I haue done	593
Val. I, and we are betroathd: nay more, our mariage | (howre,	834

HOWRES = 1
We haue conuerst, and spent our howres together,	713

HUGE = 2
(Onely for his possessions are so huge)	830
Make Tygers tame, and huge *Leuiathans*	1526

HUMBLE = 1
With them vpon her knees, her humble selfe,	1296

HUMBLED = 2
And presently, all humbled kisse the Rod?	213
And hath so humbled me, as I confesse	789

HUNDRED = 1
That I haue wept a hundred seuerall times.	1966

HUNGRY = 1
Sil. Had I beene ceazed by a hungry Lion,	2154

HUNTS = 1
Pro. He after Honour hunts, I after Loue;	67

HYE = 1
Your message done, hye home vnto my chamber,	1909

I = 460*92, 35*11
Sp. I Sir: I (a lost-Mutton) gaue your Letter to her	100
Pro. But what said she? | *Sp.* I.	114
And you aske me if she did nod, and I say I.	118
Luc. I Madam, so you stumble not vnheedfully.	156
Lu. I: if you thought your loue not cast away.	179
Which they would haue the profferer construe, I.	210
Lu. I: and melodious were it, would you sing it,	243
Lu. I (Madam) you may say what sights you see;	297
Val. Ha? Let me see: I, giue it me, it's mine:	400
Silu. I, I: you writ them Sir, at my request,	517
Speed. I, but hearken sir: though the Cameleon Loue	562

I *cont.*

I, so true loue should doe: it cannot speake,	585
*oh, the dogge is me, and I am my selfe: I; so, so: now	615
Spee. Master, Sir *Thurio* frownes on you. | *Val.* I Boy, it's for loue.	657
Val. You haue said Sir. | *Thu.* I Sir, and done too for this time.	681
Val. I, my good Lord, I know the Gentleman	705
Val. I, my good Lord, a Son, that well deserues	709
Val. I *Protheus*, but that life is alter'd now,	780
Val. I, and we are betroathd: nay more, our mariage | (howre,	834
Lau. I, and what I do too: looke thee, Ile but leane,	898
Lau. Aske my dogge, if he say I, it will: if hee say	903
Duk. I, but the doores be lockt, and keyes kept safe,	1180
Duk. A cloake as long as thine will serue the turne? | *Val.* I my good Lord.	1200
Pro. I, I: and she hath offered to the doome	1292
Sp. Inprimis she can milke. | *La.* I that she can.	1364
La. For thee? I, who art thou? he hath staid for a bet-|ter man then thee.	1435
Du. I, and peruersly, she perseuers so:	1474
Du. I, but she'll thinke, that it is spoke in hate.	1480
Pro. I, if his enemy deliuer it.	1481
Du. I, much is the force of heauen-bred Poesie.	1518
3.Out. I by my beard will we: for he is a proper man.	1556
Say I, and be the captaine of vs all:	1611
Pro. I gentle *Thurio*, for you know that loue	1643
Th. I, but I hope, Sir, that you loue not here.	1645
Th. Who, *Siluia*? | *Pro.* I, *Siluia*, for your sake.	1647
Iu. But shall I heare him speake. | *Ho.* I that you shall.	1657
Iu. Is he among these? | *Ho.* I: but peace, let's heare'm.	1661
Iu. I, I would I were deafe: it makes me haue a slow | (heart.	1687
Iu. I: that change is the spight.	1691
*(quoth I) you meane to whip the dog: I marry doe I	1845
La. I Sir, the other Squirrill was stolne from me	1874
Sil. Oh: he sends you for a Picture? | *Iul.* I, Madam.	1936
I, but her fore-head's low, and mine's as high:	2013
Pro. Oh, I: and pitties them.	2067

IADE = *1

*onely carry, therefore is shee better then a Iade. *Item.*	1344

IARRES = 1

Come, let vs goe, we will include all iarres,	2287

IARS = 1

Iu. Not a whit, when it iars so.	1689

ICE = 1

Trenched in ice, which with an houres heate	1453

IDLE = 2

Or else for want of idle time, could not againe reply,	556
And though my selfe haue beene an idle Trewant,	714

IDLENESSE = 1

Weare out thy youth with shapelesse idlenesse.	11

IDOLATRY = 1

And were there sence in his Idolatry,	2020

IDOLL = 2

Was this the Idoll, that you worship so?	796
Sil. I am very loath to be your Idoll Sir;	1753

IEALOUS = 1

But fearing lest my iealous ayme might erre,	1097

IEALOUSIE = 1
    For Loue (thou know'st is full of iealousie.)   832
IERKIN = 2
    Val. I quoat it in your Ierkin.   673
    Thu. My Ierkin is a doublet.   674
IEST = 3
    Speed. Oh Iest vnseene: inscrutible: inuisible,   526
    Why, doe you not perceiue the iest?   545
    *Lau. Marry after they cloas'd in earnest, they parted | very fairely in
    iest.   883
IEW = *2
    *more pitty in him then a dogge: a Iew would haue wept   603
    *if not, thou art an Hebrew, a Iew, and not worth | the name of a
    Christian.   921
IEWELL = 2
    And I as rich in hauing such a Iewell   824
    Pro. And what saies she to my little Iewell?   1867
IEWELS = 1
    Dumbe Iewels often in their silent kinde   1159
IF *l.*19 36 37 79 *105 118 179 293 461 522 523 524 571 629 *630 *644 *645
    *690 725 753 804 825 868 869 *903 *904 *920 *921 936 949 950 *1037
    1040 1112 1140 1158 1165 1167 1168 1174 1233 1244 1245 1253 1284
    1298 1302 1309 1314 1327 *1333 *1407 *1429 1481 1492 *1548 1550
    1560 1568 1576 1614 1711 1731 1744 *1751 1805 *1834 1887 1931 1932
    1984 1993 *1999 2005 2010 2016 2039 2178 2199 2232 2255 = 65*19
IGNORANT = 4
    Pan. I thinke your Lordship is not ignorant   327
    For being ignorant to whom it goes,   500
    Du. And also, I thinke, thou art not ignorant   1471
    Thou art not ignorant what deere good will   1784
ILE *l.*23 89 145 *160 268 285 520 554 *606 675 764 770 844 869 *879 *898
    958 965 969 1009 1012 1020 1195 1203 1209 1273 1322 *1411 *1416
    *1420 *1429 *1444 1535 *1654 1747 1756 *1849 1861 2011 2022 *2047
    2095 2180 2182 2295 = 34*12
ILL = 3
    'Tis an ill office for a Gentleman,   1486
    Pro. Ill, when you talke of war.   2057
    Thou friend of an ill fashion. | *Pro. Valentine.*   2185
ILLFAUOURD = 1
    Iul. Out, out, (*Lucetta*) that wilbe illfauourd.   1029
ILLITERATE = *1
    *La. Oh illiterate loyterer; it was the sonne of thy   1360
ILLUMIND = 1
    Foster'd, illumin'd, cherish'd, kept aliue.   1254
IMAGE = 1
    Which like a waxen Image 'gainst a fire   856
IMMACULATE = 1
    His loue sincere, his thoughts immaculate,   1051
IMMODEST = 1
    Such an immodest rayment; if shame liue | In a disguise of loue?   2232
IMPATIENT = 1
    I am impatient of my tarriance. | *Exeunt.*   1065
IMPATIENTLY = 1
    (Thou know'st) being stop'd, impatiently doth rage: 1001
IMPEACHMENT = 1
    Which would be great impeachment to his age,   317

IMPERIALLS = *1
 *Sonne, and am going with Sir *Protheus* to the Imperialls   596
IMPLOY = 1
 And will imploy thee in some seruice presently.   1860
IMPLOYD = 1
 Come on *Panthino*; you shall be imployd,   378
IMPORT = 1
 Duk. Be they of much import?   1124
IMPORTUNACY = 1
 To wrong him, with thy importunacy?   1736
IMPORTUNE = 3
 And did request me, to importune you   315
 Ant. Nor need'st thou much importune me to that   319
 While I (their King) that thither them importune   1215
IMPOSE = 1
 According to your Ladiships impose,   1778
IMPOSSIBLE = 1
 *Well, ile haue her: and if it be a match, as nothing is | impossible.   1429
IMPRESSE = 1
 Du. This weake impresse of Loue, is as a figure   1452
IMPRESSION = 1
 Beares no impression of the thing it was.)   857
IN = 143*33
INCLUDE = 1
 Come, let vs goe, we will include all iarres,   2287
INCONSTANCY = 1
 Inconstancy falls-off, ere it begins: 2239
INDEED = 5
 Speed. No beleeuing you indeed sir: 547
 Sil. Seruant, you are sad. | *Val*. Indeed, Madam, I seeme so.   662
 Val. 'Tis indeed, Madam, we thank the giuer.   685
 Spee. It stands vnder thee indeed.   900
 Val. No *Valentine* indeed, for sacred *Siluia*,   1281
INDEEDE = 5*2
 Pro. Indeede a Sheepe doth very often stray,   78
 Lu. Indeede I bid the base for *Protheus*.   257
 *indeede know not their fathers; and therefore haue no | names.   1382
 2.*Out*. Indeede because you are a banish'd man,   1605
 *him to be a dog indeede, to be, as it were, a dog at all   1833
 Pro. But she receiu'd my dog? | *La*. No indeede did she not: 1870
 Iul. But better indeede, when you hold you peace.   2059
INDIFFERENT = 1
 Therefore the office is indifferent,   1490
INDUSTRY = 1
 Experience is by industry atchieu'd,   324
INFAMY = 1
 Luc. Then neuer dreame on Infamy, but go: 1039
INFANCIE = 1
 Val. I knew him as my selfe: for from our Infancie   712
INFINITE = 2
 Val. I meane that her beauty is exquisite, | But her fauour infinite.   448
 And instances of infinite of Loue,   1045
INFLUENCE = 1
 If I be not by her faire influence   1253
INGRATITUDE = 1
 As in reuenge of thy ingratitude,   270

INHABIT = 1
O thou that dost inhabit in my brest,   2128
INHABITS = 2
Inhabits in the finest wits of all.   48
And being help'd, inhabits there.   1672
INHERIT = 1
This, or else nothing, will inherit her.   1533
INIOYND = 1
Val. As you inioynd me; I haue writ your Letter   494
INIURIOUS = 1
Iniurious Waspes, to feede on such sweet hony,   266
INKE = 2
Sp. Why man? how blacke? | *La.* Why, as blacke as Inke.   1353
Write till your inke be dry: and with your teares   1521
INLY = 1
Didst thou but know the inly touch of Loue,   993
INPRIMIS = 1*1
Condition. Inprimis. Shee can fetch and carry: why   1342
Sp. Inprimis she can milke. | *La.* I that she can.   1364
INRAGD = 1
Who (all inrag'd) will banish *Valentine*:   967
INSCRUTIBLE = 1
Speed. Oh Iest vnseene: inscrutible: inuisible,   526
INSTANCE = 1
Thu. What instance of the contrary? | *Val.* Your folly.   670
INSTANCES = 1
And instances of infinite of Loue,   1045
INSTRUMENTS = 1
With some sweet Consort; To their Instruments   1530
INTEGRITY = 1
That may discouer such integrity: 1523
INTEND = 3
And by and by intend to chide my selfe,   1727
Where I intend holy Confession.   1816
Besides she did intend Confession   2085
INTENDED = 1
To crosse my friend in his intended drift,   1087
INTENDS = 2
For *Thurio* he intends shall wed his daughter,   968
This night intends to steale away your daughter: 1080
INTERCEPT = 1
Where (if it please you) you may intercept him.   1112
INTERCESSION = 1
Besides, her intercession chaf'd him so,   1303
INTEREST = *1
Speed. He should giue her interest: & she giues it him.   493
INTERPRET = 1
Now will he interpret to her.   488
INTERPRETER = 1
Vnlesse it haue a false Interpreter.   235
INTO *l.*200 282 *1443 1537 *1829 *1837 1879 2169 2170 = 6*3
INTREAT = 1
Iul. If you be she, I doe intreat your patience   1932
INTREATED = 1
Being intreated to it by your friend.   1491
INTRUDER = 1
Goe base Intruder, ouer-weening Slaue,   1227

INUISIBLE = 1
    Speed. Oh Iest vnseene: inscrutible: inuisible,   526
INWARD = 1
    When inward ioy enforc'd my heart to smile?   217
IOLT-HEAD = 1
    La. Fie on thee Iolt-head, thou canst not read. | *Sp*. Thou lyest: I can.   1356
IOUE = 1
    That vs'd me so: or else by *Ioue*, I vow,   2023
IOURNEY = 4
    A iourney to my louing *Protheus*.   982
    For vndertaking so vnstaid a iourney?   1035
    If *Protheus* like your iourney, when you come,   1040
    To furnish me vpon my longing iourney: 1060
IOURNYING = 1
    Are iournying, to salute the *Emperor*,   343
IOY = 5
    When inward ioy enforc'd my heart to smile?   217
    I know you ioy not in a Loue-discourse.   779
    Nor to his Seruice, no such ioy on earth: 791
    What ioy is ioy, if *Siluia* be not by?   1245
IS *see also* call's, head's, heer's, here's, he's, it's, life's, Loue's, mine's, now's, she's, *Siluia's*, that's, ther's, there's, 'tis, what's, who's, wrath's = 181*42
ISLANDS = 1
    Some, to discouer Islands farre away: 311
IST = 2
    Iul. Is't neere dinner time? | *Lu*. I would it were,   222
    Iu. What is't that you | Tooke vp so gingerly?   226
IT *see also* is't, may't, on't, 't, tender't, 'tis, wer't, wilt, with't = 137*40
ITEM = 15*3
    *onely carry, therefore is shee better then a Iade. *Item*.   1344
    Sp. Item, she brewes good Ale.   1366
    Sp. Item, she can sowe.   1369
    Sp. Item she can knit.   1371
    Sp. Item, she can wash and scoure.   1374
    Sp. Item, she can spin.   1377
    Sp. Item, she hath many namelesse vertues.   1380
    *Sp. Item, shee is not to be fasting in respect of her | breath.   1386
    Sp. Item, she hath a sweet mouth.   1390
    Sp. Item, she doth talke in her sleepe.   1392
    Sp. Item, she is slow in words.   1395
    Sp. Item, she is proud. | *La*. Out with that too: 1399
    Sp. Item, she hath no teeth.   1402
    Sp. Item, she is curst.   1404
    Sp. Item, she will often praise her liquor.   1406
    Sp. Item, she is too liberall.   1409
    *Sp. Item, shee hath more haire then wit, and more   1414
    Sp. Item, she hath more haire then wit.   1419
ITS = 4*1
    Val. Ha? Let me see: I, giue it me, it's mine: 400
    Sil. And when it's writ: for my sake read it ouer,   521
    Spee. Master, Sir *Thurio* frownes on you. | *Val*. I Boy, it's for loue.   657
    *La. It's no matter for that; so shee sleepe not in her | talke.   1393
    It's an honourable kinde of theeuery.   1586
ITSELFE *see* selfe
IU = 32*2

IUDGD = 1
Haply when they haue iudg'd me fast asleepe, 1094
IUDGE = 2*1
I see things too, although you iudge I winke. 298
*for't: sure as I liue he had suffer'd for't: you shall iudge: 1836
Oh heauen be iudge how I loue *Valentine*, 2157
IUDGEMENT = 2
His head vn-mellowed, but his Iudgement ripe; 720
She, in my iudgement, was as faire as you. 1972
IUDGEMENTS = 1
Which serued me as fit, by all mens iudgements, 1983
IUL = 61*10
*IULIA see also Iu., Iul, = 36*1*
Thou *Iulia*, thou hast metamorphis'd me: 70
*Pro. But do'st thou heare: gau'st thou my Letter | to *Iulia*? 98
I feare my *Iulia* would not daigne my lines, 150
Enter Iulia and Lucetta. 153
Iul. To *Iulia*: say, from whom? 188
Looke, here is writ, kinde *Iulia*: vnkinde *Iulia*, 269
To the sweet Iulia: that ile teare away: 285
Pro. Oh heauenly *Iulia*. 352
Enter Protheus, Iulia, Panthion. 567
Pro. Haue patience, gentle *Iulia*: 568
Wherein I sigh not (*Iulia*) for thy sake, 578
Iulia, farewell: what, gon without a word? 584
Shee is faire: and so is *Iulia* that I loue, 854
did thy Master part with Madam *Iulia*? 882
Pro. To leaue my *Iulia*; shall I be forsworne? 930
Iulia I loose, and *Valentine* I loose, 948
For *Valentine*, my selfe: for *Iulia*, *Siluia*. 951
Shewes *Iulia* but a swarthy Ethiope. 955
I will forget that *Iulia* is aliue, 956
Enter Iulia and Lucetta. 975
Enter Protheus, Thurio, Iulia, Host, Musitian, Siluia. 1624
In breaking faith with *Iulia*, whom I lou'd; 1635
Enter Launce, Protheus, Iulia, Siluia. 1821
One *Iulia*, that his changing thoughts forget 1940
His *Iulia* gaue it him, at his departure: 1956
Mine shall not doe his *Iulia* so much wrong. 1958
Enter Thurio, Protheus, Iulia, Duke. 2041
Enter Valentine, Protheus, Siluia, Iulia, Duke, Thurio, | Out-lawes. 2120
Pro. How? let me see. | Why this is the ring I gaue to *Iulia*. 2218
*Pro. But how cam'st thou by this ring? at my depart | I gaue this vnto *Iulia*. 2222
Iul. And *Iulia* her selfe did giue it me, 2224
And *Iulia* her selfe hath brought it hither. | *Pro.* How? *Iulia*? 2225
Host: where Iulia lodges. 2308
Iulia: beloued of Protheus. 2313
Lucetta: waighting-woman to Iulia. | FINIS. 2315
IULIAS = 5
I fear'd to shew my Father *Iulias* Letter, 382
Keepe this remembrance for thy *Iulia's* sake. 572
And I was trim'd in Madam *Iulias* gowne, 1982
Read ouer *Iulia's* heart, (thy first best Loue) 2167
More fresh in *Iulia's*, with a constant eye? 2241
IUSTICE = 1
And on the iustice of my flying hence, 1799

KEEPE = 5*2

   Lu. Keepe tune there still; so you will sing it out: 248
Keepe this remembrance for thy *Iulia's* sake.   572
If I keepe them, I needs must loose my selfe: 949
*keepe shut: Now, of another thing shee may, and that | cannot I helpe.
   Well, proceede.   1412
To keepe me from a most vnholy match,   1800
*thing, when a Cur cannot keepe himselfe in all compa- | nies: 1831
To keepe them from vnciuill outrages.   2138

KEEPING = *1

   *Home-keeping youth, haue euer homely wits,   5

KEPT = 5*1

   Lu. Fire that's closest kept, burnes most of all.   183
The key whereof, my selfe haue euer kept: 1105
And kept seuerely from resort of men,   1177
Duk. I, but the doores be lockt, and keyes kept safe,   1180
Foster'd, illumin'd, cherish'd, kept aliue.   1254
   Val. These banish'd men, that I haue kept withall,   2279

KEY = 1

The key whereof, my selfe haue euer kept: 1105

KEYES = *1

   Duk. I, but the doores be lockt, and keyes kept safe,   1180

KILD = 1*1

I kil'd a man, whose death I much repent,   1573
*Geese he hath kil'd, otherwise he had sufferd for't: thou   1852

KILL = 3

That you might kill your stomacke on your meat,   224
And kill the Bees that yeelde it, with your stings;   267
   Pro. A little time (my Lord) will kill that griefe.   1461

KIND = *1

   Val. Giue him leaue, Madam, he is a kind of *Camelion.*   678

KINDE = 7*2

Looke, here is writ, kinde *Iulia*: vnkinde *Iulia*,   269
*weeping: all the kinde of the *Launces*, haue this very   594
And eu'n in kinde loue, I doe coniure thee,   977
Dumbe Iewels often in their silent kinde   1159
*the wit to thinke my Master is a kinde of knaue: but   1332
Du. And *Protheus*, we dare trust you in this kinde,   1502
It's an honourable kinde of theeuery.   1586
Is she kinde as she is faire?   1668
   Sil. Good morrow, kinde Sir *Eglamoure. Exeunt.*   1819

KINDLE = 1

Thou wouldst as soone goe kindle fire with snow   994

KINDLY = 1*1

*And spends what he borrowes kindly in your company.   689
Ile vse thee kindly, for thy Mistris sake   2022

KINDNESSE = 1

For beauty liues with kindnesse: 1669

KING = 3

While I (their King) that thither them importune   1215
This fellow were a King, for our wilde faction.   1583
Loue thee, as our Commander, and our King.   1613

KINGDOMES = 1

To measure Kingdomes with his feeble steps,   985

KISSD = 1

Thou shalt be worship'd, kiss'd, lou'd, and ador'd;   2019

KISSE = 7*2
And presently, all humbled kisse the Rod?	213
Ile kisse each seuerall paper, for amends:	268
And thus I search it with a soueraigne kisse.	276
Now kisse, embrace, contend, doe what you will.	289
Iul. And seale the bargaine with a holy kisse.	575
*now should I kisse my Father; well, hee weepes on:	618
*now, like a would-woman: well, I kisse her: why	620
Should from her vesture chance to steale a kisse,	814
Giuing a gentle kisse to euery sedge	1004

KNAUE = *2
*the wit to thinke my Master is a kinde of knaue: but	1332
*that's all one, if he be but one knaue: He liues not now	1333

KNEES = 2
With them vpon her knees, her humble selfe,	1296
But neither bended knees, pure hands held vp,	1299

KNEW = 5*1
Iul. I would I knew his minde.	186
Val. I knew him as my selfe: for from our Infancie	712
Lau. I neuer knew him otherwise. | *Spee.* Then how?	911
Pro. One (Lady) if you knew his pure hearts truth,	1711
*with the smell before, knew it was Crab; and	1843
Him he knew well: and guesd that it was she,	2083

KNIGHT = 1
Lu. As of a Knight, well-spoken, neat, and fine;	163

KNIT = 3
Iul. No girle, Ile knit it vp in silken strings,	1020
Sp. Item she can knit.	1371
When she can knit him a stocke?	1373

KNOCKT = 1
Spee. 'Twere good you knockt him.	661

KNOTS = 1
With twentie od-conceited true-loue knots:	1021

KNOW = 31*7
Lu. Oh, they loue least, that let men know their loue.	185
Ant. I know it well.	330
Val. Goe to, sir, tell me: do you know Madam *Siluia*?	410
Val. Why, how know you that I am in loue?	412
Val. But tell me: do'st thou know my Lady *Siluia*?	436
Speed. Why sir, I know her not.	439
Val. Do'st thou know her by my gazing on her, and | yet know'st her not?	440
Speed. Sir, I know that well enough.	444
Val. What dost thou know?	445
Val. I know it wel sir, you alwaies end ere you begin.	683
Val. I know it well sir: you haue an Exchequer of \] (words,	692
Duk. Know ye *Don Antonio*, your Countriman?	704
Val. I, my good Lord, I know the Gentleman	705
Duk. You know him well?	711
I know you ioy not in a Loue-discourse.	779
Didst thou but know the inly touch of Loue,	993
Know (worthy Prince) Sir *Valentine* my friend	1079
I know you haue determin'd to bestow her	1082
Pro. Know (noble Lord) they haue deuis'd a meane	1107
Duke. Vpon mine Honor, he shall neuer know	1117
Val. I know it well (my Lord) and sure the Match	1132
Doth *Siluia* know that I am banish'd?	1291

KNOW *cont.*

*indeede know not their fathers; and therefore haue no | names.	1382
Because we know (on *Valentines* report)	1504
Val. Then know that I haue little wealth to loose;	1557
3.*Out.* Know then, that some of vs are Gentlemen,	1590
Pro. I gentle *Thurio*, for you know that loue	1643
You would quickly learne to know him by his voice.	1712
Entreated me to call, and know her minde:	1770
I am thus early come, to know what seruice	1779
Which, since I know they vertuously are plac'd,	1808
Therefore know thee, for this I entertaine thee.	1889
I know they are stuft with protestations,	1950
Sil. Do'st thou know her?	1963
Iul. Almost as well as I doe know my selfe.	1964
Therefore I know she is about my height,	1985
Iul. And she shall thanke you for't, if ere you know | (her.	1999
Know then, I heere forget all former greefes,	2269

KNOWES = 2*2

What 'foole is she, that knowes I am a Maid,	207
*that knowes me to be in loue, yet I am in loue, but a	1334
As (heauen it knowes) I would not haue him speed.	1928
Iul. She needes not, when she knowes it cowardize.	2062

KNOWING = 1

Knowing that tender youth is soone suggested,	1103

KNOWNE = 2

In hauing knowne no trauaile in his youth.	318
The execution of it shall make knowne;	338

KNOWST = 5*1

Val. Do'st thou know her by my gazing on her, and | yet know'st her not?	440
For Loue (thou know'st is full of iealousie.)	832
Iul. Oh, know'st y not, his looks are my soules food?	990
(Thou know'st) being stop'd, impatiently doth rage:	1001
Du. Thou know'st how willingly, I would effect	1468
Dispose of them, as thou knowst their deserts.	2286

LA = 16*20
LABOUR = 3

If lost, why then a grieuous labour won;	37
lost-Mutton) nothing for my labour.	102
Sil. Why if it please you, take it for your labour;	524

LACD-MUTTON = *2

*(a lac'd-Mutton) and she (a lac'd-Mutton) gaue mee (a	101

LACKING = 1

Prowd, disobedient, stubborne, lacking duty,	1138

LADDER = 8

The Ladder made of Cords, and all the means	837
This night he meaneth with a Corded-ladder	962
And with a Corded-ladder fetch her downe:	1109
Val. Why then a Ladder quaintly made of Cords	1186
Aduise me, where I may haue such a Ladder.	1191
Val. By seauen a clock, ile get you such a Ladder.	1195
How shall I best conuey the Ladder thither?	1197
'Tis so: and heere's the Ladder for the purpose.	1221

LADIES = 6

To beare my Ladies traine, lest the base earth	813
Visit by night your Ladies chamber-window	1529
Sil. Goe to thy Ladies graue and call hers thence,	1741

LADIES *cont.*

But thinke vpon my griefe (a Ladies griefe)	1798
Blacke men are Pearles, in beauteous Ladies eyes.	2053
Thu. 'Tis true, such Pearles as put out Ladies eyes,	2054

LADISHIP = 13

What hoe: *Lucetta.* | *Lu.* What would your Ladiship?	220
Giue me a Note, your Ladiship can set	238
But for my duty to your Ladiship.	497
Val. What meanes your Ladiship?	511
Val. Please you, Ile write your Ladiship another.	520
Val. This is the Gentleman I told your Ladiship	737
To be my fellow-seruant to your Ladiship.	755
Pro. Wee'll both attend vpon your Ladiship.	772
Luc. Why then your Ladiship must cut your haire.	1019
Pro. Madam: good eu'n to your Ladiship.	1708
Eg. I will not faile your Ladiship:	1817
This is the Letter to your Ladiship.	1945
Iul. Madam, he sends your Ladiship this Ring.	1953

LADISHIPS = 2*1

*Sir *Thurio* borrows his wit from your Ladiships lookes,	688
One that attends your Ladiships command.	1775
According to your Ladiships impose,	1778

LADY = 21*1

Val. But tell me: do'st thou know my Lady *Siluia?*	436
Val. Your selfe (sweet Lady) for you gaue the fire,	687
Val. Why Lady, Loue hath twenty paire of eyes.	745
Val. Mistris, it is: sweet Lady, entertaine him	754
Pro. Not so, sweet Lady, but too meane a seruant	757
Sweet Lady, entertaine him for your Seruant.	760
Val. How does your Lady? & how thriues your loue?	777
O, but I loue his Lady too-too much,	860
Duk. There is a Lady in *Verona* heere	1150
For practising to steale away a Lady,	1594
*Masters command, hee must carry for a present to his | Lady.	1700
Pro. One (Lady) if you knew his pure hearts truth,	1711
Pro. Sir *Protheus* (gentle Lady) and your Seruant.	1714
Pro. I grant (sweet loue) that I did loue a Lady, | But she is dead.	1729
Pro. Sweet Lady, let me rake it from the earth.	1740
Eg. As many (worthy Lady) to your selfe:	1777
As when thy Lady, and thy true-loue dide,	1790
Good morrow (gentle Lady.)	1818
As you doe loue your Lady *Siluia*:	1901
This Letter: that's her chamber: Tell my Lady,	1907
Alas (poore Lady) desolate, and left;	1995
See where she comes: Lady a happy euening.	2034

LAMBS = 1

A Foxe, to be the Shepheard of thy Lambs;	1913

LAMELY = 1

Speed. Are they not lamely writt?	484

LAMENT = 1

Pro. Cease to lament for that thou canst not helpe,	1311

LAMENTABLE = 1

For I did play a lamentable part.	1987

LAMENTING = 1

After your dire-lamenting Elegies,	1528

LAMENTST = 1

And study helpe for that which thou lament'st,	1312

LANDS = 1
My goods, my Lands, my reputation,   1062
LARGE = 2
And ere I part with thee, confer at large   1323
Where you, with *Siluia*, may conferre at large.   1508
LASCIUIOUS = 1
The loose encounters of lasciuious men: 1016
LAST = 2*3
Speed. And yet I was last chidden for being too slow.   409
Val. Belike (boy) then you are in loue, for last mor- |(ning   472
Val. Last night she enioyn'd me,   480
Till the last step haue brought me to my Loue,   1011
*mine, twice or thrice in that last Article: rehearse that | once more.   1417
LATE = 1
Which of you saw *Eglamoure* of late?   2073
LAU = 13*11
LAUGHED = *1
*You were wont, when you laughed, to crow   421
LAUN = 3*3
LAUNCE see also La., Lau., Laun. = *2, 9*3
Enter Launce, Panthion.   592
Panth. Launce, away, away: a Boord: thy Master is   626
Enter Speed and Launce.   872
Speed. Launce, by mine honesty welcome to *Padua*.   873
Spee. 'Tis well that I get it so: but *Launce*, how saist   909
Enter Duke, Thurio, Protheus, Valentine, | Launce, Speed.   1068
Val. I pray thee *Launce*, and if thou seest my Boy   1327
Speed. How now Signior *Launce*? what newes with | your Mastership?   1347
Ho. I tell you what *Launce* his man told me,   1696
Iu. Where is *Launce*?   1698
Enter Launce, Protheus, Iulia, Siluia.   1821
Launce: the like to Protheus.   2311
LAUNCES = *1
*weeping: all the kinde of the *Launces*, haue this very   594
LAURENCE = 1
'Tis true: for Frier *Laurence* met them both   2081
LAW = 2
The Law of friendship bids me to conceale,   1074
These are my mates, that make their wills their Law,   2135
LAWES = 1
Enter Valentine, Speed, and certaine Out-lawes.   1546
LAWLESLY = 1
And will not vse a woman lawlesly.   2116
LAWLESSE = 1
That they may hold excus'd our lawlesse liues;   1600
LAY = 1*1
*speakes a word: but see how I lay the dust with my | teares.   624
You must lay Lime, to tangle her desires   1515
LAYING = 1
Lu. Nay, I was taken vp, for laying them downe.   294
LEADS = 1
That leads toward *Mantua*, whether they are fled: 2091
LEAGUES = 1
Egl. Feare not: the Forrest is not three leagues off,   2038
LEANDER = 2
How yong *Leander* crost the *Hellespont*.   25
So bold *Leander* would aduenture it.   1189

LEANE = *1
 Lau. I, and what I do too: looke thee, Ile but leane,   898
LEARND = 1*1
 *learn'd (like Sir *Protheus*) to wreath your Armes like a   414
 Haue learn'd me how to brooke this patiently.   2106
LEARNE = 2
 To learne his wit, t'exchange the bad for better;   942
 You would quickly learne to know him by his voice.   1712
LEASE = 1
 Pro. That they are out by Lease.   2070
LEAST *see also* lest = 5*1
 Lu. Oh, they loue least, that let men know their loue. 185
 Least he should take exceptions to my loue,   383
 Iul. That is the least (*Lucetta*) of my feare: 1043
 Least it should rauell, and be good to none,   1498
 The least whereof would quell a louers hope: 1637
 Or at the least, in hers, sepulcher thine.   1742
LEAUE = 12*4
 Val. Sweet *Protheus*, no: Now let vs take our leaue: 60
 Val. Giue him leaue, Madam, he is a kind of *Camelion*. 678
 Val. Leaue off discourse of disabilitie: 759
 Ile leaue you to confer of home affaires,   770
 Pro. To leaue my *Iulia*; shall I be forsworne?   930
 I cannot leaue to loue; and yet I doe: 946
 But there I leaue to loue, where I should loue.   947
 All that is mine I leaue at thy dispose,   1061
 Duke. Sir *Thurio*, giue vs leaue (I pray) a while,   1070
 Will giue thee time to leaue our royall Court,   1235
 Shee is my essence, and I leaue to be;   1252
 *seru'd me, when I tooke my leaue of Madam *Siluia*: did 1854
 Iul. It seemes you lou'd not her, not leaue her token: 1893
 Leaue not the Mansion so long Tenant-lesse,   2129
 And leaue no memory of what it was,   2131
 And leaue her on such slight conditions.   2265
LEAUES = 1
 He leaues his friends, to dignifie them more;   68
LEFT = 4*2
 *no, this left shooe is my father; no, no, this left   607
 Val. And how doe yours? | *Pro*. I left them all in health. 775
 For why, the fooles are mad, if left alone.   1168
 Alas (poore Lady) desolate, and left;   1995
 Thou hast no faith left now, vnlesse thou'dst two,   2171
LEG = 1*2
 *Trencher, and steales her Capons-leg: O, 'tis a foule 1830
 *thou see me heaue vp my leg, and make water against a 1856
 Thu. What? that my leg is too long?   2045
LEGACIE = 1
 It was *Eues* legacie, and cannot be t'ane from her.   1401
LEND = 4
 Ant. Lend me the Letter: Let me see what newes.   357
 Loue lend me wings, to make my purpose swift   971
 The heauen such grace did lend her,   1666
 Loue, lend me patience to forbeare a while.   2148
LENGTH = 2
 Vnder a cloake, that is of any length.   1199
 Ile get me one of such another length.   1203

LENT = 1
As thou hast lent me wit, to plot this drift. | *Exit.* 972
LESSE = 4*2
Sp. Nay Sir, lesse then a pound shall serue me for car-|rying your
 Letter. 109
Much lesse shall she that hath Loues wings to flie, 986
*then the wit; for the greater hides the lesse: What's | next? 1423
Then for the loue of reck-lesse *Siluia.* 2096
Leaue not the Mansion so long Tenant-lesse, 2129
And lesse then this, I am sure you cannot giue.) 2146
LESSER = 1
It is the lesser blot modesty findes, 2234
LESSON = 1
To lesson me, and tell me some good meane 980
LEST *see also* least = 4
To beare my Ladies traine, lest the base earth 813
Lest it should burne aboue the bounds of reason. 998
But fearing lest my iealous ayme might erre, 1097
Lest growing ruinous, the building fall, 2130
LET = 29*2
Val. Sweet *Protheus,* no: Now let vs take our leaue: 60
To *Millaine* let me heare from thee by Letters 61
Lu. Oh, they loue least, that let men know their loue. 185
Lu. To take a paper vp, that I let fall. 230
Iul. Then let it lye, for those that it concernes. 233
Goe, get you gone: and let the papers lye: 260
Iu. Well, let vs goe. 291
To let him spend his time no more at home; 316
Ant. Lend me the Letter: Let me see what newes. 357
Val. Ha? Let me see: I, giue it me, it's mine: 400
Yet let her be a principalitie, 805
Shee is alone. | *Pro.* Then let her alone. 821
Then let me goe, and hinder not my course: 1008
Iul. Lucetta, as thou lou'st me let me haue 1032
Then let her beauty be her wedding dowre: 1147
Duk. Then let me see thy cloake, 1202
I pray thee let me feele thy cloake vpon me. 1206
Sp. Let me read them? 1355
Let me not liue, to looke vpon your Grace. 1467
Let vs into the City presently 1537
Then to Siluia, let vs sing, 1673
To her let vs Garlands bring. 1677
Pro. Sweet Lady, let me rake it from the earth. 1740
Sil. I pray thee let me looke on that againe. 1946
Here is her Picture: let me see, I thinke 2004
Val. Ruffian: let goe that rude vnciuill touch, 2184
Pro. How? let me see. | Why this is the ring I gaue to *Iulia.* 2218
Oh *Protheus,* let this habit make thee blush. 2230
Let me be blest to make this happy close: 2243
And let them be recall'd from their Exile: 2282
Come, let vs goe, we will include all iarres, 2287
LETS = 3
Iu. Let's see your Song: | How now Minion? 246
Let's tune: and too it lustily a while. 1650
Iu. Is he among these? | *Ho.* I: but peace, let's heare'm. 1661
LETTER = 20*7
Pro. But do'st thou heare: gau'st thou my Letter | to *Iulia?* 98

LETTER *cont.*

*Sp. I Sir: I (a lost-Mutton) gaue your Letter to her	100
*Sp. Nay Sir, lesse then a pound shall serue me for car- |rying your Letter.	109
*'Tis threefold too little for carrying a letter to your louer	113
Pro. No, no, you shall haue it for bearing the letter.	122
Sp. Marry Sir, the letter very orderly,	125
No, not so much as a ducket for deliuering your letter:	137
Iul. And yet I would I had ore-look'd the Letter;	204
And would not force the letter to my view?	208
To be so angred with another Letter.	263
Till I haue found each letter, in the Letter,	279
*Ant. How now? What Letter are you reading there?	353
Ant. Lend me the Letter: Let me see what newes.	357
I fear'd to shew my Father *Iulias* Letter,	382
Val. As you inioynd me; I haue writ your Letter	494
To himselfe should write the Letter?	532
Val. What figure? | *Speed.* By a Letter, I should say.	540
Speed. Why she hath giuen you a Letter.	550
Val. That's the Letter I writ to her friend.	551
*Speed. And y letter hath she deliuer'd, & there an end.	552
What say you to a Letter from your friends | Of much good newes?	700
What Letter is this same? what's here? to *Siluia?*	1207
*La. Now will he be swing'd for reading my Letter;	1442
This Letter: that's her chamber: Tell my Lady,	1907
Iul. Madam, please you peruse this Letter;	1942
This is the Letter to your Ladiship.	1945

LETTERS = 4*1

To *Millaine* let me heare from thee by Letters	61
**In requital whereof, henceforth, carry your letters your	144
That stayes to beare my Letters to my friends,	1122
Thy letters may be here, though thou art hence,	1318
*Sp. Why didst not tell me sooner? 'pox of your loue | Letters.	1440

LETTS = 1

Val. What letts but one may enter at her window?	1182

LEUIATHANS = 1

Make Tygers tame, and huge *Leuiathans*	1526

LIBERALL = 1

Sp. Item, she is too liberall.	1409

LIES = 1

Iul. Pray you, where lies Sir *Protheus?* | *Ho.* Marry, at my house:	1762

LIEU = 1

Onely, in lieu thereof, dispatch me hence:	1063

LIFE = 8

Pro. Sweet Loue, sweet lines, sweet life,	347
Val. I *Protheus,* but that life is alter'd now,	780
Without apparant hazard of his life.	1185
But as thou lou'st thy life, make speed from hence.	1239
But flie I hence, I flie away from life.	1257
Haue some malignant power vpon my life:	1308
Besides, thy staying will abridge thy life:	1315
To hazard life, and reskew you from him,	2142

LIFES = 1

Whose life's as tender to me as my soule,	2158

LIGHT = 7

Best sing it to the tune of *Light O, Loue.*	240
Lu. It is too heauy for so light a tune.	241

LIGHT *cont.*

And that hath dazel'd my reasons light:	865
That I had any light from thee of this.	1118
Val. It will be light (my Lord) that you may beare it	1198
What light, is light, if *Siluia* be not seene?	1244

LIGHTLY = 1

Oh, could their Master come, and goe as lightly,	1212

LIGHTS = *1

*eyes, or your owne eyes had the lights they were wont	464

LIKE = 20*17

That (like a testie Babe) will scratch the Nurse,	212
And yet me thinkes I do not like this tune.	249
Lu. What, shall these papers lye, like Tel-tales here?	292
Ant. I like thy counsaile: well hast thou aduis'd:	336
And that thou maist perceiue how well I like it,	337
Like exhibition thou shalt haue from me,	371
*learn'd (like Sir *Protheus*) to wreath your Armes like a	414
*Male-content: to rellish a Loue-song, like a *Robin*-red-|breast:	415
*to walke alone like one that had the pestilence:	416
*to sigh, like a Schoole-boy that had lost his *A.B.C.* to	417
*weep like a yong wench that had buried her Grandam:	418
*to fast, like one that takes diet: to watch, like one that	419
*feares robbing: to speake puling, like a beggar at Hal-|low-Masse:	420
*like a cocke; when you walk'd, to walke like one of the	422
*and shine through you like the water in an Vrinall: that	433
Doe you not like it?	512
*victuals; and would faine haue meate: oh bee not like	564
*fault: I haue receiu'd my proportion, like the prodigious	595
*now, like a would-woman: well, I kisse her: why	620
To cloath mine age with Angel-like perfection:	716
Sil. Be-like that now she hath enfranchis'd them	740
And I must minister the like to you.	803
Which like a waxen Image 'gainst a fire	856
Iul. Not like a woman, for I would preuent	1015
If *Protheus* like your iourney, when you come,	1040
Should haue beene cherish'd by her child-like dutie,	1144
Duk. This very night; for Loue is like a childe	1193
1.Out. And I, for such like petty crimes as these,	1598
Yet (Spaniel-like) the more she spurnes my loue,	1638
*foure gentleman-like-dogs, vnder the Dukes table: hee	1838
Pro. Sebastian is thy name: I like thee well,	1859
Val. How like a dreame is this? I see, and heare:	2147
Ile wooe you like a Souldier, at armes end,	2180
Launce: the like to Protheus.	2311

LIKELIHOODS = 1

These likelihoods confirme her flight from hence;	2087

LIKES = 5

My foolish Riuall that her Father likes	829
Why eu'n what fashion thou best likes (*Lucetta*.)	1027
How doe you, man? the Musicke likes you not.	1679
Iu. You mistake: the Musitian likes me not.	1680
Thu. How likes she my discourse?	2056

LIKEWISE = 2

And I likewise will visite thee with mine.	64
Pro. I likewise heare that *Valentine* is dead.	1737

LILLY = *1

*for, looke you, she is as white as a lilly, and as	612

LILLY-TINCTURE = 1
And pinch'd the lilly-tincture of her face,   1976
LIME = 1
You must lay Lime, to tangle her desires   1515
LINE = 2
Loe, here in one line is his name twice writ: 283
Moist it againe: and frame some feeling line,   1522
LINES = 6
I feare my *Iulia* would not daigne my lines,   150
Dare you presume to harbour wanton lines?   195
Pro. Sweet Loue, sweet lines, sweet life,   347
To write some lines to one she loues.   481
Sil. Yes, yes: the lines are very queintly writ,   513
Sil. There, hold: | I will not looke vpon your Masters lines: 1948
LINGER = 1
But if thou linger in my Territories | Longer then swiftest expedition   1233
LINGUIST = 1
A Linguist, and a man of such perfection,   1603
LION = 1
Sil. Had I beene ceazed by a hungry Lion,   2154
LIONS = *1
*Lions: when you fasted, it was presently after dinner: 423
LIQUOR = 1*1
Sp. Item, she will often praise her liquor.   1406
La. If her liquor be good, she shall: if she will not,   1407
LITTLE = 10*1
*'Tis threefold too little for carrying a letter to your louer   113
Iul. His little speaking, shewes his loue but small.   182
Iul. As little by such toyes, as may be possible: 239
And that's the reason I loue him so little.   861
A little time will melt her frozen thoughts,   1455
Pro. A little time (my Lord) will kill that griefe.   1461
Val. Then know that I haue little wealth to loose;   1557
Wreaking as little what betideth me,   1810
Pro. And what saies she to my little Iewell?   1867
And yet the Painter flatter'd her a little,   2007
Pro. No, that it is too little.   2046
LIUE = 7*2
then liue in your ayre.   680
That they liue by your bare words.   695
Which to requite, command me while I liue.   1092
Let me not liue, to looke vpon your Grace.   1467
And liue as we doe in this wildernesse?   1609
2.Out. Thou shalt not liue, to brag what we haue of-|(fer'd.   1615
Val. I take your offer, and will liue with you,   1616
*for't: sure as I liue he had suffer'd for't: you shall iudge: 1836
Such an immodest rayment; if shame liue | In a disguise of loue?   2232
LIUELY = 1
Which I so liuely acted with my teares: 1990
LIUERIES = 1
For it appeares by their bare Liueries   694
LIUES = 4*2
How happily he liues, how well-belou'd,   359
*dogge that liues: My Mother weeping: my Father   598
*that's all one, if he be but one knaue: He liues not now   1333
That they may hold excus'd our lawlesse liues;   1600
For beauty liues with kindnesse: 1669

LIUES *cont.*
    She is dead belike? | *Pro.* Not so: I thinke she liues.   1894
LIUING = 2*1
    Then (liuing dully sluggardiz'd at home)   10
    Val. And why not death, rather then liuing torment?   1240
    La. Then may I set the world on wheeles, when she | can spin for her
    liuing.   1378
LOATH = 2
    Pro. And that (my Lord) I shall be loath to doe: 1485
    Sil. I am very loath to be your Idoll Sir;   1753
LOATHES = 1
    Pro. But loue will not be spurd to what it loathes.   2048
LOCKT = 1*1
    Did hold his eyes, lockt in her Christall lookes.   739
    Duk. I, but the doores be lockt, and keyes kept safe,   1180
LODGE = 3
    Shall lodge thee till thy wound be throughly heal'd;   275
    I nightly lodge her in an vpper Towre,   1104
    Himselfe would lodge where (senceles) they are lying.   1213
LODGES = 1
    Host: where Iulia lodges.   2308
LOE = 1
    Loe, here in one line is his name twice writ: 283
LONG = 10*1
    Val. How long hath she beene deform'd?   457
    Luc. Alas, the way is wearisome and long.   983
    By longing for that food so long a time.   992
    (For long agone I haue forgot to court,   1154
    Duk. A cloake as long as thine will serue the turne? | *Val.* I my good
    Lord.   1200
    La. Thou must run to him; for thou hast staid so long,   1438
    She shall not long continue loue to him: 1494
    3.Out. Haue you long soiourn'd there?   1566
    Thu. What? that my leg is too long?   2045
    Leaue not the Mansion so long Tenant-lesse,   2129
    'Twere pitty two such friends should be long foes.   2244
LONGER = 4*1
    That tide will stay me longer then I should,   583
    the Tide, if you tarry any longer.   629
    But if thou linger in my Territories | Longer then swiftest expedition   1233
    Pro. Longer then I proue loyall to your Grace,   1466
    Val. Some sixteene moneths, and longer might haue | (staid,   1567
LONGEST = 1
    Iul. Not so: but it hath bin the longest night   1765
LONGING = 2
    By longing for that food so long a time.   992
    To furnish me vpon my longing iourney: 1060
LONGS = 1
    That longs for euery thing that he can come by.   1194
LOOK = *2
    Ant. Look what thou want'st shalbe sent after thee: 376
    *Why wag: how now? what's the matter? look vp: speak.   2213
LOOKD = 1*1
    Iul. And yet I would I had ore-look'd the Letter;   204
    *when you look'd sadly, it was for want of money: And   424
LOOKE = 14*6
    Looke, here is writ, kinde *Iulia*: vnkinde *Iulia*,   269

LOOKE *cont.*

looke on you, I can hardly thinke you my Master.	426
*no eyes, looke you, wept her selfe blinde at my parting:	605
*for, looke you, she is as white as a lilly, and as	612
To haue a looke of such a worthy a Mistresse.	758
When you haue done, we looke too heare from you.	771
But when I looke on her perfections,	866
Lau. I, and what I do too: looke thee, Ile but leane,	898
Vnlesse I looke on *Siluia* in the day,	1250
There is no day for me to looke vpon.	1251
Launce. I am but a foole, looke you, and yet I haue	1331
*She can milke, looke you, a sweet vertue in a maid with	cleane hands.	1345
Let me not liue, to looke vpon your Grace.	1467
*him (looke you) it goes hard: one that I brought vp of	1823
Sil. I pray thee let me looke on that againe.	1946
Sil. There, hold:	I will not looke vpon your Masters lines:	1948
For I had rather winke, then looke on them.	2055
Vouchsafe me for my meed, but one faire looke:	2144
Would I not vndergoe, for one calme looke:	2163
Pro. Looke to the Boy.	*Val.* Why, Boy?	2211

LOOKES = 2*1

*Sir *Thurio* borrows his wit from your Ladiships lookes,	688
Did hold his eyes, lockt in her Christall lookes.	739
I gaue him gentle lookes, thereby to finde	1100

LOOKING-GLASSE = 1

But since she did neglect her looking-glasse,	1973

LOOKS = *2

*Coy looks, with hart-sore sighes: one fading moments	(mirth,	34
Iul. Oh, know'st y not, his looks are my soules food?	990

LOOSE = 10*6

Made me neglect my Studies, loose my time;	71
*matter? why weep'st thou man? away asse, you'l loose	628
Pant. Tut, man: I meane thou'lt loose the flood, and	634
*in loosing the flood, loose thy voyage, and in loosing thy	635
*voyage, loose thy Master, and in loosing thy Master,	636
*loose thy seruice, and in loosing thy seruice: --- why	637
Laun. For feare thou shouldst loose thy tongue.	639
Panth. Where should I loose my tongue?	640
Laun. Loose the Tide, and the voyage, and the Ma-	ster,	643
Iulia I loose, and *Valentine* I loose,	948
If I keepe them, I needs must loose my selfe:	949
If I loose them, thus finde I by their losse,	950
The loose encounters of lasciuious men:	1016
Dissolues to water, and doth loose his forme.	1454
Val. Then know that I haue little wealth to loose;	1557

LOOSING = 2*4

Loosing his verdure, euen in the prime,	53
And I haue plaid the Sheepe in loosing him.	77
*in loosing the flood, loose thy voyage, and in loosing thy	635
*voyage, loose thy Master, and in loosing thy Master,	636
*loose thy seruice, and in loosing thy seruice: --- why	637

LORD = 23*6

Lu. Lord, Lord: to see what folly raignes in vs.	168
Pro. There is no newes (my Lord) but that he writes	358
Pro. My Lord I cannot be so soone prouided,	374
Val. My Lord, I will be thankfull,	702

LORD *cont.*

Val. I, my good Lord, I know the Gentleman	705
Val. I, my good Lord, a Son, that well deserues	709
Thur. Madam, my Lord your father wold speak with | (you.	767
O gentle *Protheus*, Loue's a mighty Lord,	788
Iul. That fits as well, as tell me (good my Lord)	1025
Pro. My gracious Lord, that which I wold discouer,	1073
Pro. Know (noble Lord) they haue deuis'd a meane	1107
But (good my Lord) doe it so cunningly	1113
Pro. Adiew, my Lord, Sir *Valentine* is comming.	1119
Val. I know it well (my Lord) and sure the Match	1132
Val. It will be light (my Lord) that you may beare it	1198
Duk. A cloake as long as thine will serue the turne? | *Val.* I my good Lord.	1200
Val. Why any cloake will serue the turn (my Lord)	1204
That they should harbour where their Lord should be.	1219
Pro. Gon, my good Lord.	1459
Pro. A little time (my Lord) will kill that griefe.	1461
The match betweene sir *Thurio*, and my daughter? | *Pro.* I doe my Lord.	1469
Pro. She did my Lord, when *Valentine* was here.	1473
Pro. And that (my Lord) I shall be loath to doe:	1485
Pro. You haue preuail'd (my Lord) if I can doe it	1492
Val. Forbeare, forbeare I say: It is my Lord the *Duke*.	2248
And fit for great employment (worthy Lord.)	2284
What thinke you of this Page (my Lord?)	2291
Val. I warrant you (my Lord) more grace, then Boy.	2293

LORDSHIP = 2*2

Pan. He wondred that your Lordship	306
Pan. I thinke your Lordship is not ignorant	327
Pan. 'Twere good, I thinke, your Lordship sent him | (thither,	331
Pro. May't please your Lordship, 'tis a word or two	354

LORDSHIPS = 1

Pro. As one relying on your Lordships will,	363

LOSSE = 2

I haue consider'd well, his losse of time,	321
If I loose them, thus finde I by their losse,	950

LOST = 1*2

If lost, why then a grieuous labour won;	37
*to sigh, like a Schoole-boy that had lost his *A.B.C.* to	417
Laun. It is no matter if the tide were lost, for it is the	630

LOST-MUTTON = 1*1

Sp. I Sir: I (a lost-Mutton) gaue your Letter to her	100
lost-Mutton) nothing for my labour.	102

LOUD = 9*1

Speed. Euer since you lou'd her.	458
Val. I haue lou'd her euer since I saw her,	459
In breaking faith with *Iulia*, whom I lou'd;	1635
He lou'd her out of all nicke.	1697
Thy selfe hast lou'd, and I haue heard thee say	1788
She lou'd me well, deliuer'd it to me.	1892
Iul. It seemes you lou'd not her, not leaue her token:	1893
Iul. Because, me thinkes that she lou'd you as well	1900
When she did thinke my Master lou'd her well;	1971
Thou shalt be worship'd, kiss'd, lou'd, and ador'd;	2019

LOUE = 140*23

To the sweet glaunces of thy honour'd Loue,	7
But since thou lou'st; loue still, and thriue therein,	12

LOUE *cont.*

Euen as I would, when I to loue begin.	13
Pro. Vpon some booke I loue, I'le pray for thee.	23
Val. That's on some shallow Storie of deepe loue,	24
Pro. That's a deepe Storie, of a deeper loue,	26
For he was more then ouer-shooes in loue.	27
Val. 'Tis true; for you are ouer-bootes in loue,	28
Val. To be in loue; where scorne is bought with | (grones:	33
Pro. 'Tis Loue you cauill at, I am not Loue.	42
Val. Loue is your master, for he masters you;	43
The eating Canker dwels; so eating Loue	47
Euen so by Loue, the yong, and tender wit	51
Of thy successe in loue; and what newes else	62
Pro. He after Honour hunts, I after Loue;	67
I loue my selfe, my friends, and all for loue:	69
Would'st thou then counsaile me to fall in loue?	155
In thy opinion which is worthiest loue?	159
Iul. And would'st thou haue me cast my loue on him?	178
Lu. I: if you thought your loue not cast away.	179
Iul. His little speaking, shewes his loue but small.	182
Iul. They doe not loue, that doe not shew their loue.	184
Lu. Oh, they loue least, that let men know their loue.	185
Lu. To plead for loue, deserues more fee, then hate.	201
Fie, fie: how way-ward is this foolish loue;	211
Iul. Some loue of yours, hath writ to you in Rime.	236
Best sing it to the tune of *Light O, Loue.*	240
And here is writ, *Loue wounded Protheus.*	273
Pro. Sweet Loue, sweet lines, sweet life,	347
Here is her oath for loue, her honors paune;	349
Least he should take exceptions to my loue,	383
Hath he excepted most against my loue.	385
Oh, how this spring of loue resembleth	386
Val. Why, how know you that I am in loue?	412
Speed. If you loue her, you cannot see her. | *Val.* Why?	461
Speed. Because Loue is blinde: O that you had mine	463
*for hee beeing in loue, could not see to garter	469
*his hose; and you, beeing in loue, cannot see to put on | your hose.	470
Val. Belike (boy) then you are in loue, for last mor-|(ning	472
Speed. True sir: I was in loue with my bed, I thanke	474
*you, you swing'd me for my loue, which makes mee the	475
*Her self hath taught her Loue himself, to write vnto her | (louer.	558
Speed. I, but hearken sir: though the Cameleon Loue	562
I, so true loue should doe: it cannot speake,	585
Spee. Master, Sir *Thurio* frownes on you. | *Val.* I Boy, it's for loue.	657
He is as worthy for an Empresse loue,	726
Val. Why Lady, Loue hath twenty paire of eyes.	745
Thur. They say that Loue hath not an eye at all.	746
Vpon a homely obiect, Loue can winke.	748
Val. How does your Lady? & how thriues your loue?	777
Pro. My tales of Loue were wont to weary you,	778
I haue done pennance for contemning Loue,	781
For in reuenge of my contempt of loue,	785
Loue hath chas'd sleepe from my enthralled eyes,	786
Now, no discourse, except it be of loue:	792
Vpon the very naked name of Loue.	794
Val. O flatter me: for Loue delights in praises.	801
Except thou wilt except against my Loue.	809

LOUE *cont.*

Because thou seest me doate vpon my loue:	828
For Loue (thou know'st is full of iealousie.)	832
So the remembrance of my former Loue	849
Shee is faire: and so is *Iulia* that I loue,	854
(That I did loue, for now my loue is thaw'd,	855
And that I loue him not as I was wont:	859
O, but I loue his Lady too-too much,	860
And that's the reason I loue him so little.	861
That thus without aduice begin to loue her?	863
If I can checke my erring loue, I will,	868
*himselfe in Loue. If thou wilt goe with me to the Ale-|house:	920
To loue faire *Siluia*; shall I be forsworne?	931
Loue bad mee sweare, and Loue bids me for-sweare;	935
O sweet-suggesting Loue, if thou hast sin'd,	936
I cannot leaue to loue; and yet I doe:	946
But there I leaue to loue, where I should loue.	947
For Loue is still most precious in it selfe,	953
Remembring that my Loue to her is dead.	957
Loue lend me wings, to make my purpose swift	971
And eu'n in kinde loue, I doe coniure thee,	977
Didst thou but know the inly touch of Loue,	993
As seeke to quench the fire of Loue with words.	995
Till the last step haue brought me to my Loue,	1011
With twentie od-conceited true-loue knots:	1021
And instances of infinite of Loue,	1045
His loue sincere, his thoughts immaculate,	1051
Onely deserue my loue, by louing him,	1057
This loue of theirs, my selfe haue often seene,	1093
For, loue of you, not hate vnto my friend,	1115
(Vpon aduice) hath drawne my loue from her,	1142
For scorne at first, makes after-loue the more.	1164
But rather to beget more loue in you.	1166
Duk. This very night; for Loue is like a childe	1193
By heauen, my wrath shall farre exceed the loue	1236
Here, if thou stay, thou canst not see thy loue:	1314
Euen in the milke-white bosome of thy Loue.	1320
*that knowes me to be in loue, yet I am in loue, but a	1334
*'tis I loue: and yet 'tis a woman; but what woman, I	1336
La. I care not for that neither: because I loue crusts.	1403
Sp. Why didst not tell me sooner? 'pox of your loue | Letters.	1440
Du. Sir *Thurio*, feare not, but that she will loue you	1447
Du. This weake impresse of Loue, is as a figure	1452
The loue of *Valentine*, and loue sir *Thurio*?	1476
She shall not long continue loue to him:	1494
But say this weede her loue from *Valentine*,	1495
It followes not that she will loue sir *Thurio*.	1496
Th. Therefore, as you vnwinde her loue from him;	1497
To hate yong *Valentine*, and loue my friend.	1512
Du. This discipline, showes thou hast bin in loue.	1534
Loue thee, as our Commander, and our King.	1613
I haue accesse my owne loue to prefer.	1628
Yet (Spaniel-like) the more she spurnes my loue,	1638
Pro. I gentle *Thurio*, for you know that loue	1643
Th. I, but I hope, Sir, that you loue not here.	1645
Loue doth to her eyes repaire,	1670
Returne, returne, and make thy loue amends:	1723

LOUE *cont.*

Pro. I grant (sweet loue) that I did loue a Lady, | But she is dead.	1729
Assure thy selfe, my loue is buried.	1739
Vouchsafe me yet your Picture for my loue,	1745
And to your shadow, will I make true loue.	1750
As when thy Lady, and thy true-loue dide,	1790
As you doe loue your Lady *Siluia*:	1901
She dreames on him, that has forgot her loue,	1902
You doate on her, that cares not for your loue.	1903
'Tis pitty Loue, should be so contrary:	1904
Because I loue him, I must pitty him.	1917
I am my Masters true confirmed Loue,	1924
Since she respects my Mistris loue so much.	2002
Alas, how loue can trifle with it selfe:	2003
If that be all the difference in his loue,	2010
If this fond Loue, were not a blinded god.	2016
To make my Master out of loue with thee. *Exeunt.*	2025
Pro. But loue will not be spurd to what it loathes.	2048
Thu. But well, when I discourse of loue and peace.	2058
Then for the loue of reck-lesse *Siluia*.	2096
Pro. And I will follow, more for *Siluias* loue	2097
Iul. And I will follow, more to crosse that loue	2099
Then hate for *Siluia*, that is gone for loue. *Exeunt.*	2100
They loue me well: yet I haue much to doe	2137
That would haue forc'd your honour, and your loue,	2143
Loue, lend me patience to forbeare a while.	2148
Oh heauen be iudge how I loue *Valentine*,	2157
Oh 'tis the curse in Loue, and still approu'd	2164
When women cannot loue, where they're belou'd.	2165
*Sil. When *Protheus* cannot loue, where he's belou'd:	2166
Read ouer *Iulia's* heart, (thy first best Loue)	2167
Descended into periury, to loue me,	2170
Pro. In Loue, | Who respects friend?	2175
And loue you 'gainst the nature of Loue: force ye.	2181
*Val. Thou co(m)mon friend, that's without faith or loue,	2187
And that my loue may appeare plaine and free,	2208
Such an immodest rayment; if shame liue | In a disguise of loue?	2232
I dare thee, but to breath vpon my Loue.	2258
And thinke thee worthy of an Empresse loue:	2268

LOUELY = 2

Should censure thus on louely Gentlemen.	172
Were full as louely, as is this of hers;	2006

LOUER = 4*1

*'Tis threefold too little for carrying a letter to your louer	113
***Her self hath taught her Loue himself, to write vnto her | (louer.	558
thou that that my master is become a notable Louer?	910
Spee. I tell thee, my Master is become a hot Louer.	918
For which, the youthfull Louer now is gone,	1110

LOUERS = 5

Alas, this parting strikes poore Louers dumbe. | *Exeunt.*	589
Val. To see such Louers, *Thurio*, as your selfe,	747
Hope is a louers staffe, walke hence with that	1316
The least whereof would quell a louers hope:	1637
She will not faile; for Louers breake not houres,	2031

LOUES = 13

Lu. Yet he, of all the rest, I thinke best loues ye.	181
O that our Fathers would applaud our loues	350

LOUES *cont.*

Speed. Shee that your worship loues?	411
To write some lines to one she loues.	481
Torment me for my Loues forgetfulnesse:	580
O gentle *Protheus*, Loue's a mighty Lord,	788
Pro. But she loues you?	833
Much lesse shall she that hath Loues wings to flie,	986
Luc. I doe not seeke to quench your Loues hot fire,	996
You are already loues firme votary,	1505
Because he loues her, he despiseth me,	1916
His Body, for a Girle that loues him not:	2261
The story of your Loues discouered.	2298

LOUE-AFFAIRES = 1

Of all that may concerne thy Loue-affaires:	1324

LOUE-BOOKE = 1

Val. And on a loue-booke pray for my successe?	22

LOUE-DISCOURSE = 1

I know you ioy not in a Loue-discourse.	779

LOUE-SONG = *1

*Male-content: to rellish a Loue-song, like a *Robin*-red-|breast:	415

LOUING = 4

Valentine. | Cease to perswade, my louing *Protheus*;	3
Oh hatefull hands, to teare such louing words;	265
A iourney to my louing *Protheus*.	982
Onely deserue my loue, by louing him,	1057

LOUST = 5*1

But since thou lou'st; loue still, and thriue therein,	12
Iul. *Lucetta*, as thou lou'st me let me haue	1032
Iul. Now, as thou lou'st me, do him not that wrong,	1055
But as thou lou'st thy life, make speed from hence.	1239
As thou lou'st *Siluia* (though not for thy selfe)	1325
*For thy sweet Mistris sake, because thou lou'st her. Fare-|(well.	1998

LOW = 2

Sil. Too low a Mistres for so high a seruant.	756
I, but her fore-head's low, and mine's as high:	2013

LOWT = 1

For 'tis no trusting to yond foolish Lowt;	1885ʼ

LOYALL = 1

Pro. Longer then I proue loyall to your Grace,	1466

LOYALTY = 1

When I protest true loyalty to her,	1631

LOYTERER = *1

La. Oh illiterate loyterer; it was the sonne of thy	1360

LOYTERING = 1

Where haue you bin these two dayes loytering?	1864

LU = 29*6

LUBBER = *1

Lau. A notable Lubber: as thou reportest him to | bee.	913

LUC = 9*4

LUCETTA *see also Lu., Luc.* = 13

Enter *Iulia and Lucetta*.	153
Iul. But say *Lucetta* (now we are alone)	154
How churlishly, I chid *Lucetta* hence,	214
My pennance is, to call *Lucetta* backe	218
What hoe: *Lucetta*. | *Lu*. What would your Ladiship?	220
Enter *Iulia and* Lucetta.	975
Iul. Counsaile, *Lucetta*, gentle girle assist me,	976

LUCETTA *cont.*

Gentle *Lucetta*, fit me with such weedes	1017
Why eu'n what fashion thou best likes (*Lucetta*.)	1027
Iul. Out, out, (*Lucetta*) that wilbe illfauourd.	1029
Iul. Lucetta, as thou lou'st me let me haue	1032
Iul. That is the least (*Lucetta*) of my feare:	1043
Lucetta: waighting-woman to Iulia.	FINIS.	2315

LUMPISH = 1

For she is lumpish, heauy, mellancholly,	1509

LUSTILY = 1

Let's tune: and too it lustily a while.	1650

LUTE = 1

For *Orpheus* Lute, was strung with Poets sinewes,	1524

LYE = 4*1

Iul. Then let it lye, for those that it concernes.	233
Lu. Madam, it will not lye where it concernes,	234
Goe, get you gone: and let the papers lye:	260
Lu. What, shall these papers lye, like Tel-tales here?	292
Yet here they shall not lye, for catching cold.	295

LYES = 1

Thu. Nay then the wanton lyes: my face is blacke.	2051

LYEST = 1

La. Fie on thee Iolt-head, thou canst not read.	*Sp.* Thou lyest: I can.	1356

LYING = 1

Himselfe would lodge where (senceles) they are lying.	1213

MAD = 1

For why, the fooles are mad, if left alone.	1168

MADAM = 38*9

Luc. I Madam, so you stumble not vnheedfully.	156
Lu. Pardon deare Madam, 'tis a passing shame,	170
Lu. Peruse this paper Madam.	187
Lu. Madam, it will not lye where it concernes,	234
Lu. That I might sing it (Madam) to a tune:	237
Iu. You doe not?	*Lu.* No (Madam) tis too sharpe.	250
Lu. Madam: dinner is ready: and your father staies.	290
Lu. I (Madam) you may say what sights you see;	297
Speed. Madam *Siluia*: Madam *Siluia*.	*Val.* How now Sirha?	403
Val. Goe to, sir, tell me: do you know Madam *Siluia*?	410
Val. Madam & Mistres, a thousand good-morrows.	489
Val. Now trust me (Madam) it came hardly-off	499
Val. No (Madam) so it steed you, I will write	503
Val. Madam, they are for you.	516
Val. If it please me, (Madam?) what then?	523
Val. To doe what?	*Speed.* To be a spokes-man from Madam *Siluia*.	536
Sil. Seruant, you are sad.	*Val.* Indeed, Madam, I seeme so.	662
Val. Giue him leaue, Madam, he is a kind of *Camelion*.	678
Val. 'Tis indeed, Madam, we thank the giuer.	685
Thur. Madam, my Lord your father wold speak with	(you.	767
did thy Master part with Madam *Iulia*?	882
Luc. What fashion (Madam) shall I make your bree-|(ches?	1024
Luc. You must needs haue the(m) with a cod-peece (Ma-|(dam)	1028
Luc. A round hose (Madam) now's not worth a pin	1030
Pro. Madam: good eu'n to your Ladiship.	1708
Pro. Madam: if your heart be so obdurate:	1744
Eg. This is the houre that Madam *Siluia*	1769
Madam, Madam.	*Sil.* Who cals?	1772
Egl. Madam, I pitty much your grieuances,	1807

MADAM *cont.*
*seru'd me, when I tooke my leaue of Madam *Siluia*: did 1854
Deliuer it to Madam *Siluia*; 1891
To bring me where to speake with Madam *Siluia*. 1930
Sil. From whom? | *Iul.* From my Master, Sir *Protheus*, Madam. 1934
Sil. Oh: he sends you for a Picture? | *Iul.* I, Madam. 1936
Iul. Madam, please you peruse this Letter; 1942
Pardon me (Madam) I haue vnaduis'd 1943
Iul. It may not be: good Madam pardon me. 1947
Iul. Madam, he sends your Ladiship this Ring. 1953
Iul. I thanke you Madam, that you tender her: 1961
Iul. She hath bin fairer (Madam) then she is, 1970
And I was trim'd in Madam *Iulias* gowne, 1982
(Madam) 'twas *Ariadne*, passioning 1988
Pro. Madam, this seruice I haue done for you 2140
Pro. Vnhappy were you (Madam) ere I came: 2150
*to Madam *Siluia*: w (out of my neglect) was neuer done. 2215
MADE = 14*2
Made me neglect my Studies, loose my time; 71
*Made Wit with musing, weake; hart sick with thought. 73
When shee hath made you write to your selfe? 544
Made vse, and faire aduantage of his daies: 718
And made them watchers of mine owne hearts sorrow. 787
The Ladder made of Cords, and all the means 837
And *Siluia* (witnesse heauen that made her faire) 954
And when the flight is made to one so deere, 987
My selfe am one made priuy to the plot. 1081
Hath made me publisher of this pretence. 1116
Val. Why then a Ladder quaintly made of Cords 1186
Val. My youthfull trauaile, therein made me happy, 1580
As if the garment had bin made for me: 1984
And at that time I made her weepe a good, 1986
But by my comming, I haue made you happy. 2151
Val. I thank your Grace, y gift hath made me happy: 2275
MAD-CAP = *1
Speed. Come-on you mad-cap: Ile to the Ale-house 879
MAID = 2*7
What 'foole is she, that knowes I am a Maid, 207
And not vpon your Maid. 225
*wayling: my Sister crying: our Maid howling: our 599
*small as a wand: this hat is *Nan* our maid: I am the 613
*will not tell my selfe: and yet 'tis a Milke-maid: yet 'tis 1337
*not a maid: for shee hath had Gossips: yet 'tis a maid, 1338
*for she is her Masters maid, and serues for wages. Shee 1339
*She can milke, looke you, a sweet vertue in a maid with | cleane
hands. 1345
MAIDES = 1
Since Maides, in modesty, say no, to that, 209
MAINTENANCE = 1
What maintenance he from his friends receiues, 370
MAIST *l*.337 1102 = 2
MAKE = 29*4
Sp. Such another proofe will make me cry baa. 97
The execution of it shall make knowne; 338
Speed. Marry sir, so painted to make her faire, that no | man counts of
her beauty. 453
Pro. Why then wee'll make exchange; | Here, take you this. 573

MAKE *cont.*

*Thu. Sir, if you spend word for word with me, I shall | make your wit
bankrupt.   690
Duk. Beshrew me sir, but if he make this good   725
And make rough winter euerlastingly.   817
To her, whose worth, make other worthies nothing;   820
Val. Will you make haste? *Exit.* | *Pro.* I will.   845
Loue lend me wings, to make my purpose swift   971
Luc. Better forbeare, till *Protheus* make returne.   989
And make a pastime of each weary step,   1010
*Luc. What fashion (Madam) shall I make your bree- |(ches?   1024
I feare me it will make me scandaliz'd.   1036
But as thou lou'st thy life, make speed from hence.   1239
And now excesse of it will make me surfet.   1290
Bid him make haste, and meet me at the North-gate.   1328
What might we doe to make the girle forget   1475
Make Tygers tame, and huge *Leuiathans*   1526
If not: we'll make you sit, and rifle you.   1550
To make a vertue of necessity,   1608
Returne, returne, and make thy loue amends: 1723
And to your shadow, will I make true loue.   1750
And make it but a shadow, as I am.   1752
**thou see me heaue vp my leg, and make water against a   1856
But I can make respectiue in my selfe?   2015
To make my Master out of loue with thee. *Exeunt.*   2025
*Thu. Ile weare a Boote, to make it somewhat roun- |(der.   2047
These are my mates, that make their wills their Law,   2135
Oh *Protheus*, let this habit make thee blush.   2230
Let me be blest to make this happy close: 2243
To make such meanes for her, as thou hast done,   2264
With our discourse, to make your Grace to smile.   2290

MAKES = 9*6

*Lu. She makes it stra(n)ge, but she would be best pleas'd   262
**you, you swing'd me for my loue, which makes mee the   475
**Now come I to my sister; marke the moane she makes: 622
That makes me reasonlesse, to reason thus?   853
He makes sweet musicke with th'enameld stones,   1003
For scorne at first, makes after-loue the more.   1164
La. That makes amends for her soure breath.   1391
La. Why that word makes the faults gracious: 1428
Makes me the better to confer with thee.   1465
*lu. I, I would I were deafe: it makes me haue a slow | (heart.   1687
To *Mantua*, where I heare, he makes aboad;   1793
**I did the thing you wot of: he makes me no more adoe,   1847
And thinking on it, makes me cry alas.   1905
Pro. Oh Sir, she makes no doubt of that.   2061
**Fils him with faults: makes him run through all th'sins;   2238

MAKST = *1

*Sil. By thy approach thou mak'st me most vnhappy.   2152

MALADY = 1

**not an eye that sees you, but is a Physician to comment | on your
Malady.   434

MALE-CONTENT = *1

**Male-content: to rellish a Loue-song, like a *Robin*-red- |breast: 415

MALIGNANT = 1

Haue some malignant power vpon my life: 1308

MAN = 21*10

For I will be thy beades-man, *Valentine*.	21
And how he cannot be a perfect man,	322
Speed. Marry sir, so painted to make her faire, that no | man counts of her beauty.	453
Val. To doe what? | *Speed*. To be a spokes-man from Madam *Siluia*.	536
*matter? why weep'st thou man? away asse, you'l loose	628
vnkindest Tide, that euer any man tide.	631
Pant. Tut, man: I meane thou'lt loose the flood, and	634
*and the Seruice, and the tide: why man, if the Riuer	644
Panth. Come: come away man, I was sent to call | thee.	647
Val. Not for the world: why man, she is mine owne,	823
*not welcome. I reckon this alwaies, that a man is neuer	875
And so (vnworthily) disgrace the man	1098
That man that hath a tongue, I say is no man,	1173
That no man hath accesse by day to her.	1178
That no man hath recourse to her by night.	1181
Sp. Why man? how blacke? | *La*. Why, as blacke as Inke.	1353
La. What neede a man care for a stock with a wench,	1372
La. For thee? I, who art thou? he hath staid for a bet-|ter man then thee.	1435
3.Out. I by my beard will we: for he is a proper man.	1556
A man I am, cross'd with aduersitie:	1558
I kil'd a man, whose death I much repent,	1573
A Linguist, and a man of such perfection,	1603
2.*Out*. Indeede because you are a banish'd man,	1605
How doe you, man? the Musicke likes you not.	1679
Ho. I tell you what *Launce* his man told me,	1696
Thou subtile, periur'd, false, disloyall man:	1719
Val. How vse doth breed a habit in a man?	2122
For such is a friend now: treacherous man,	2188
Pro. Then men their minds? tis true: oh heuen, were man	2236
Your Grace is welcome to a man disgrac'd, | Banished *Valentine*.	2249

MANAGE = 1

And manage it, against despairing thoughts:	1317

MANFULLY = 1

But yet I slew him manfully, in fight,	1574

MANNER = 1*1

*nay, Ile shew you the manner of it. This shooe is my fa-|ther:	606
With all the cunning manner of our flight	835

MANNERLY = 1

What thou think'st meet, and is most mannerly.	1033

MANNERS = 1

Speed. Oh, 'giue ye-good-ev'n: heer's a million of | manners.	490

MANS = *2

*As a nose on a mans face, or a Wethercocke on a steeple:	527
Lau. When a mans seruant shall play the Curre with	1822

MANSION = 1

Leaue not the Mansion so long Tenant-lesse,	2129

MANTUA = 3

2.*Out*. And I from *Mantua*, for a Gentleman,	1596
To *Mantua*, where I heare, he makes aboad;	1793
That leads toward *Mantua*, whether they are fled:	2091

MANY = 7*1

Lu. Then thus: of many good, I thinke him best.	174
And so by many winding nookes he straies	1006
With many bitter threats of biding there.	1306

MANY *cont.*

Sp. Item, she hath many namelesse vertues.	1380
That has't deceiu'd so many with thy vowes?	1722
Eg. As many (worthy Lady) to your selfe:	1777
*but whips me out of the chamber: how many Masters	1848
Iul. How many women would doe such a message?	1911

MARIAGE = *1

Val. I, and we are betroathd: nay more, our mariage | (howre,	834

MARKE = *3

*Now come I to my sister; marke the moane she makes:	622
*had not bin there (blesse the marke) a pissing while, but	1839
*not I bid thee still marke me, and doe as I do; when did'st	1855

MARKES = *1

Speed. Marry by these speciall markes: first, you haue	413

MARKET = 1

By the Hangmans boyes in the market place,	1875

MARRE = 1

And marre the concord, with too harsh a descant:	254

MARRIAGE = 1

That done, our day of marriage shall be yours,	2299

MARRY = 7*7

Sp. Marry Sir, the letter very orderly,	125
Speed. Marry by these speciall markes: first, you haue	413
Speed. Marry sir, so painted to make her faire, that no | man counts of her beauty.	453
Lau. Marry after they cloas'd in earnest, they parted | very fairely in iest.	883
Spee. But shall she marry him? | *Lau.* No.	885
Spee. How then? shall he marry her? | *Lau.* No, neither.	887
Lau. Marry thus, when it stands well with him, it | stands well with her.	892
Sp. Marry, the son of my Grand-father.	1359
Iu. Marry (mine *Host*) because I cannot be merry.	1653
Iul. Pray you, where lies Sir *Protheus*? | *Ho.* Marry, at my house:	1762
Nor how my father would enforce me marry	1786
*(quoth I) you meane to whip the dog: I marry doe I	1845
La. Marry Sir, I carried Mistris *Siluia* the dogge you | bad me.	1865
La. Marry she saies your dog was a cur, and tels you	1868

MASKD = 1

But being mask'd, he was not sure of it.	2084

MASQUE = 1

And threw her Sun-expelling Masque away,	1974

MASSE = *1

*feares robbing: to speake puling, like a beggar at Hal- | low-Masse:	420

MASTER = 22*12

Val. Loue is your master, for he masters you;	43
Sp. Sir *Protheus*: 'saue you: saw you my Master?	74
Sp. You conclude that my Master is a Shepheard then, | and I Sheepe? | *Pro.* I doe	80
Pro. True: and thy Master a Shepheard.	87
*Sheepe the Shepheard; but I seeke my Master, and my	91
Master seekes not me: therefore I am no Sheepe.	92
*for wages followest thy Master, thy Master for wages	95
selfe; And so Sir, I'le commend you to my Master.	145
looke on you, I can hardly thinke you my Master.	426
My Master sues to her: and she hath taught her Sutor,	528
That my master being scribe,	531

MASTER *cont.*

Panth. Launce, away, away: a Boord: thy Master is	626
*voyage, loose thy Master, and in loosing thy Master,	636
Laun. Loose the Tide, and the voyage, and the Ma-|ster,	643
Spee. Master, Sir *Thurio* frownes on you. | *Val.* I Boy, it's for loue.	657
did thy Master part with Madam *Iulia?*	882
thou that that my master is become a notable Louer?	910
Lau. Why Foole, I meant not thee, I meant thy | Master.	916
Spee. I tell thee, my Master is become a hot Louer.	918
Oh, could their Master come, and goe as lightly,	1212
Lau. Can nothing speake? Master, shall I strike?	1269
*the wit to thinke my Master is a kinde of knaue: but	1332
La. Why then, will I tell thee, that thy Master staies | for thee at the North gate.	1432
Sp. Master, be one of them:	1585
*to Mistris *Siluia*, from my Master; and I came no	1828
But cannot be true seruant to my Master,	1925
Sil. From whom? | *Iul.* From my Master, Sir *Protheus*, Madam.	1934
Goe, giue your Master this: tell him from me,	1939
Poore Gentlewoman, my Master wrongs her much.	1962
When she did thinke my Master lou'd her well;	1971
To make my Master out of loue with thee. *Exeunt.*	2025
Iul. O good sir, my master charg'd me to deliuer a ring	2214

MASTERS = 4*3

Val. Loue is your master, for he masters you;	43
*for she is her Masters maid, and serues for wages. Shee	1339
*Masters command, hee must carry for a present to his | Lady.	1700
*but whips me out of the chamber: how many Masters	1848
I am my Masters true confirmed Loue,	1924
Sil. There, hold: | I will not looke vpon your Masters lines:	1948
I hope my Masters suit will be but cold,	2001

MASTERSHIP = 2

Speed. How now Signior *Launce*? what newes with | your Mastership?	1347
La. With my Mastership? why, it is at Sea:	1349

MATCH = 5*1

Spee. But tell me true, wil't be a match?	902
To match my friend Sir *Thurio*, to my daughter.	1131
Val. I know it well (my Lord) and sure the Match	1132
*Well, ile haue her: and if it be a match, as nothing is | impossible.	1429
The match betweene sir *Thurio*, and my daughter? | *Pro.* I doe my Lord.	1469
To keepe me from a most vnholy match,	1800

MATES = 2

Bestow thy fawning smiles on equall mates,	1228
These are my mates, that make their wills their Law,	2135

MATTER = 4*6

Pro. Come, come, open the matter in briefe; what | said she.	129
Sp. Open your purse, that the money, and the matter	131
*matter? why weep'st thou man? away asse, you'l loose	628
Laun. It is no matter if the tide were lost, for it is the	630
Spee. Why then, how stands the matter with them?	891
No matter who's displeas'd, when you are gone:	1041
Duk. Nay then no matter: stay with me a while,	1127
La. It's no matter for that; so shee sleepe not in her | talke.	1393
Ther's some great matter she'ld employ me in.	1771
*Why wag: how now? what's the matter? look vp: speak.	2213

MAY *l*.132 202 239 297 341 *399 940 981 1018 1022 1112 1141 1156 1182
1191 1198 1318 1324 *1378 *1388 *1412 *1420 1508 1511 1523 1600
1715 1806 1947 2208 2240 = 26*5
MAYT = *1
  Pro. May't please your Lordship, 'tis a word or two   354
ME *l*.17 30 40 45 58 61 70 71 86 92 97 *109 118 124 127 138 143 155 158
*178 180 197 232 238 249 258 261 302 315 319 326 357 361 371 400
*410 427 429 436 *455 *475 480 494 499 523 542 546 549 577 580 583
*615 649 *690 725 728 738 769 *773 782 789 801 802 819 827 828 839
840 853 858 896 899 902 *907 915 *920 933 934 935 937 971 972 976
980 1008 1011 1017 1025 1032 1034 1036 1042 1046 1055 1058 1060
1063 1072 1074 1076 1077 1078 1092 1094 1101 1116 1127 1129 1137
1140 1148 *1149 1191 1192 1202 1203 1205 1206 1211 1218 1231 1251
1282 1284 1288 1290 1319 1326 1328 *1334 *1335 1355 1358 1362 1434
*1440 1449 1450 1465 1467 1499 1500 1560 1568 1572 1578 1580 1632
1634 *1651 1680 *1687 1696 1724 1740 1745 1756 1764 1770 1771 1780
1786 1800 1804 1810 *1829 *1835 *1837 *1844 *1847 *1848 *1854 *1855
*1856 *1857 1865 1873 1874 1880 1881 1887 1892 1900 1905 1910 1915
1916 1918 1930 1933 1939 1943 1946 1947 1954 1981 1983 1984 2004
2011 2023 2030 2089 2092 2106 2132 2137 2144 2148 *2152 *2153 2156
2158 2161 2170 2190 2191 2198 2199 2210 *2214 2218 2224 2231 2243
*2275 = 207*30
MEANE = 12*2
  Pro. You mistake; I meane the pound, a Pinfold.   111
  There wanteth but a Meane to fill your Song.   255
  Iu. The meane is dround with you vnruly base.   256
  Val. Hast thou obseru'd that? euen she I meane.   438
  Val. I meane that her beauty is exquisite, | But her fauour infinite.   448
  Pant. Tut, man: I meane thou'lt loose the flood, and   634
  Pro. Not so, sweet Lady, but too meane a seruant   757
  To lesson me, and tell me some good meane   980
  Pro. Know (noble Lord) they haue deuis'd a meane   1107
  For, get you gon, she doth not meane away.   1170
  Duk. But she I meane, is promis'd by her friends   1175
  *(quoth I) you meane to whip the dog: I marry doe I   1845
  Gentlewoman, good day: I pray you be my meane   1929
  Duke. What meane you by that saying?   2294
MEANES = 3*1
  Iu. How now? what meanes this passion at his name?   169
  Val. What meanes your Ladiship?   511
  And heere he meanes to spend his time a while,   730
  To make such meanes for her, as thou hast done,   2264
MEANETH = 1
  This night he meaneth with a Corded-ladder   962
MEANING = 1
  Meaning henceforth to trouble you no more.   509
MEANS = 1
  The Ladder made of Cords, and all the means   837
MEANT = *2
  Lau. Why Foole, I meant not thee, I meant thy | Master.   916
MEASURE = 2
  To measure Kingdomes with his feeble steps,   985
  Come not within the measure of my wrath: 2254
MEAT = 1
  That you might kill your stomacke on your meat,   224
MEATE = *1
  *victuals; and would faine haue meate: oh bee not like   564

MEE *l.**101 *475 935 = 1*2
MEED = 2
   Sil. And dutie neuer yet did want his meed.   762
   Vouchsafe me for my meed, but one faire looke: 2144
MEET = 6
   When thou do'st meet good hap; and in thy danger,   18
   He said, that *Protheus,* your sonne, was meet;   314
   As meet to be an Emperors Councellor: 727
   What thou think'st meet, and is most mannerly.   1033
   Bid him make haste, and meet me at the North-gate.   1328
   That *Siluia,* at Fryer *Patricks* Cell should meet me,   2030
MEETE = 3
   Th. Where meete we? | *Pro.* At Saint *Gregories* well. | *Th.* Farewell.   1705
   Eg. Where shall I meete you? | *Sil.* At *Frier Patrickes* Cell,   1814
   But mount you presently, and meete with me   2089
MELLANCHOLLY *see also* allycholly = 1
   For she is lumpish, heauy, mellancholly,   1509
MELLOWED = 1
   His head vn-mellowed, but his Iudgement ripe;   720
MELODIOUS = 1
   Lu. I: and melodious were it, would you sing it,   243
MELT = 1
   A little time will melt her frozen thoughts,   1455
MELTING = 1
   A Sea of melting pearle, which some call teares;   1294
MEMORY = 1
   And leaue no memory of what it was,   2131
MEN = 12*2
   **Lu.* Oh, they loue least, that let men know their loue.   185
   While other men, of slender reputation   308
   Heare sweet discourse, conuerse with Noble-men,   333
   The loose encounters of lasciuious men: 1016
   Luc. All these are seruants to deceitfull men.   1047
   Iul. Base men, that vse them to so base effect;   1048
   And kept seuerely from resort of men,   1177
   Thrust from the company of awfull men.   1592
   Blacke men are Pearles, in beauteous Ladies eyes.   2053
   Sil. All men but *Protheus.*   2177
   Women to change their shapes, then men their minds.   2235
   **Pro.* Then men their minds? tis true: oh heuen, were man   2236
   Val. These banish'd men, that I haue kept withall,   2279
   Are men endu'd with worthy qualities: 2280
MENDED = *1
   **La.* Well: that fault may be mended with a break-|fast: read on.   1388
MENS = 1
   Which serued me as fit, by all mens iudgements,   1983
MERCATIO = 1
   Iu. What think'st thou of the rich *Mercatio?*   165
MERCY = 1
   Iul. Oh, cry you mercy sir, I haue mistooke: 2220
MERIT = 1
   Plead a new state in thy vn-riual'd merit,   2271
MEROPS = 1
   Why *Phaeton* (for thou art *Merops* sonne)   1222
MERRY = 1*1
   Iu. Marry (mine *Host*) because I cannot be merry.   1653
   **Ho.* Come, we'll haue you merry: ile bring you where   1654

MESSAGE = 3
 Your message done, hye home vnto my chamber,   1909
 Iul. How many women would doe such a message?   1911
 To heare me speake the message I am sent on.   1933
MESSENGER = 4*1
 I must goe send some better Messenger,   149
 *Or fearing els some messe(n)ger, y might her mind discouer 557
 To any happy messenger from thence.   703
 Val. Please it your Grace, there is a Messenger   1121
 And now am I (vnhappy Messenger)   1920
MESSENGERS = 1
 His teares, pure messengers, sent from his heart,   1052
MET = 1
 'Tis true: for Frier *Laurence* met them both   2081
METAMORPHISD = 1*1
 Thou *Iulia*, thou hast metamorphis'd me: 70
 *now you are Metamorphis'd with a Mistris, that when I 425
METHINKES *see* thinkes, thinks
MIGHT *l*.224 237 *557 1097 1475 *1567 1667 1992 = 6*2
MIGHTY = 1
 O gentle *Protheus*, Loue's a mighty Lord,   788
MILDE = 1
 A vertuous gentlewoman, milde, and beautifull.   2000
MILDER = 2
 Pro. Oh Sir, I finde her milder then she was,   2043
 Can no way change you to a milder forme;   2179
MILKE = 1*1
 *She can milke, looke you, a sweet vertue in a maid with | cleane
 hands.   1345
 Sp. Inprimis she can milke. | *La*. I that she can.   1364
MILKE-MAID = *1
 *will not tell my selfe: and yet 'tis a Milke-maid: yet 'tis 1337
MILKE-WHITE = 1
 Euen in the milke-white bosome of thy Loue.   1320
MILLAIN = *1
 Pro. But now he parted hence to embarque for *Millain*. 75
MILLAINE = 3
 To *Millaine* let me heare from thee by Letters   61
 Pro. All happinesse bechance to thee in *Millaine*.   65
 1.*Out*. Whence came you? | *Val*. From *Millaine*.   1564
MILLION = *1
 Speed. Oh, 'giue ye-good-ev'n: heer's a million of | manners. 490
MIND = *1
 *Or fearing els some messe(n)ger, y might her mind discouer 557
MINDE = 9*3
 And being so hard to me, that brought your minde;   138
 *I feare she'll proue as hard to you in telling your minde. 139
 Lu. Please you repeat their names, ile shew my minde, 160
 Iul. I would I knew his minde.   186
 Iu. I see you haue a months minde to them.   296
 Thu. That hath more minde to feed on your bloud,   679
 He is compleat in feature, and in minde,   723
 But when I call to minde your gracious fauours   1075
 More then quicke words, doe moue a womans minde.   1160
 And cannot soone reuolt, and change your minde.   1506
 Entreated me to call, and know her minde: 1770
 Feare not: he beares an honourable minde.   2115

MINDS = 1*1
Women to change their shapes, then men their minds. 2235
*Pro. Then men their minds? tis true: oh heuen, were man 2236
MINE l.64 164 *280 384 397 400 *463 716 787 810 *823 851 873 1061
1117 1143 1277 1309 *1416 *1417 1653 1876 1958 2005 2009 2012 2189
2209 2246 2252 = 25*5
MINES = 1
I, but her fore-head's low, and mine's as high: 2013
MINION = 2
Iu. Let's see your Song: | How now Minion? 246
Iu. You (Minion) are too saucie. 252
MINISTER = 1
And I must minister the like to you. 803
MIRTH = 2
*Coy looks, with hart-sore sighes: one fading moments | (mirth, 34
With Triumphes, Mirth, and rare solemnity. 2288
MISCHANCE = 1
The next ensuing howre, some foule mischance 579
MISCHANCES = 1
Sil. A thousand more mischances then this one 2105
MISERABLE = 2
Or else I often had beene often miserable. 1581
Sil. O miserable, vnhappy that I am. 2149
MISTAKE = 2*1
Pro. You mistake; I meane the pound, a Pinfold. 111
*Sp. Well, your old vice still: mistake the word: what | newes then in
your paper? 1350
Iu. You mistake: the Musitian likes me not. 1680
MISTAKST = 1
Spee. Why, thou whorson Asse, thou mistak'st me, 915
MISTOOKE = 3
Sp. You mistooke Sir: I say she did nod; 117
Speed. Your worship sir, or else I mistooke. 407
Iul. Oh, cry you mercy sir, I haue mistooke: 2220
MISTRES = 1*1
*Val. Madam & Mistres, a thousand good-morrows. 489
Sil. Too low a Mistres for so high a seruant. 756
MISTRESSE = 6
your Mistresse, be moued, be moued. Exeunt. 565
Spee. Not of you. | Val. Of my Mistresse then. 659
Had come along with me, but that his Mistresse 738
To haue a looke of such a worthy a Mistresse. 758
Seruant, you are welcome to a worthlesse Mistresse. 763
Pro. Except my Mistresse. 807
MISTRIS = 5*5
*now you are Metamorphis'd with a Mistris, that when I 425
Sil. Seruant. | Val. Mistris. 655
*Val. Welcome, deer Protheus: Mistris, I beseech you 750
Val. Mistris, it is: sweet Lady, entertaine him 754
*to Mistris Siluia, from my Master; and I came no 1828
*La. Marry Sir, I carried Mistris Siluia the dogge you | bad me. 1865
That my poore Mistris moued therewithall, 1991
*For thy sweet Mistris sake, because thou lou'st her. Fare- | (well. 1998
Since she respects my Mistris loue so much. 2002
Ile vse thee kindly, for thy Mistris sake 2022
MOANE = *1
*Now come I to my sister; marke the moane she makes: 622

MODESTY = 4

Iul. Now (by my modesty) a goodly Broker: 194
Since Maides, in modesty, say no, to that,   209
For often haue you writ to her: and she in modesty,   555
It is the lesser blot modesty findes,   2234

MOIST = 1

Moist it againe: and frame some feeling line,   1522

MOMENTS = *1

*Coy looks, with hart-sore sighes: one fading moments | (mirth,   34

MONETHS = *1

Val. Some sixteene moneths, and longer might haue | (staid,   1567

MONEY = *2

Sp. Open your purse, that the money, and the matter   131
*when you look'd sadly, it was for want of money: And   424

MONGST = 1

'Mongst all foes that a friend should be the worst?   2197

MONSTROUS = 1

La. That's monstrous: oh that that were out.   1426

MONTH = 1

Whereon, this month I haue bin hamering.   320

MONTHS = 1

Iu. I see you haue a months minde to them.   296

MOODE = 1

Who, in my moode, I stab'd vnto the heart.   1597

MORE = 37*15

For he was more then ouer-shooes in loue.   27
Once more adieu: my Father at the Road   57
He leaues his friends, to dignifie them more;   68
Or else returne no more into my sight.   200
Lu. To plead for loue, deserues more fee, then hate.   201
To let him spend his time no more at home;   316
No more of stay: to morrow thou must goe;   377
Meaning henceforth to trouble you no more.   509
I would haue had them writ more mouingly: 519
*more pitty in him then a dogge: a Iew would haue wept   603
Thu. That hath more minde to feed on your bloud,   679
Sil. No more, gentlemen, no more: | Here comes my father.   696
Goe with me: once more, new Seruant welcome;   769
Val. I, and we are betroathd: nay more, our mariage | (howre,   834
How shall I doate on her with more aduice,   862
Iul. The more thou dam'st it vp, the more it burnes: 999
More then quicke words, doe moue a womans minde.   1160
For scorne at first, makes after-loue the more.   1164
But rather to beget more loue in you.   1166
And thinke my patience, (more then thy desert)   1229
Thanke me for this, more then for all the fauors   1231
Val. No more: vnles the next word that thou speak'st   1307
*hath more qualities then a Water-Spaniell, which is   1340
*a horse can doe no more; nay, a horse cannot fetch, but   1343
Sp. Item, shee hath more haire then wit, and more   1414
faults then haires, and more wealth then faults.   1415
*mine, twice or thrice in that last Article: rehearse that | once more. 1417
Sp. Item, she hath more haire then wit.   1419
La. More haire then wit: it may be ile proue it: The   1420
*couer of the salt, hides the salt, and therefore it is more   1421
*then the salt; the haire that couers the wit, is more   1422
Sp. And more faults then haires.   1425

113

MORE *cont.*

Sp. And more wealth then faults.	1427
Yet (Spaniel-like) the more she spurnes my loue,	1638
The more it growes, and fawneth on her still;	1639
*things. If I had not had more wit then he, to take a fault	1834
*(quoth he) you doe him the more wrong (quoth I) 'twas	1846
*I did the thing you wot of: he makes me no more adoe,	1847
Sil. The more shame for him, that he sends it me;	1954
Ile after; more to be reueng'd on *Eglamoure*,	2095
Pro. And I will follow, more for *Siluias* loue	2097
Iul. And I will follow, more to crosse that loue	2099
Sil. A thousand more mischances then this one	2105
And full as much (for more there cannot be)	2159
Therefore be gone, sollicit me no more.	2161
I am sorry I must neuer trust thee more,	2194
More fresh in *Iulia's*, with a constant eye?	2241
Duke. The more degenerate and base art thou	2263
Val. I warrant you (my Lord) more grace, then Boy.	2293

MORNE = 1

That wait for execution in the morne.	1759

MORNING = 1*1

Val. Belike (boy) then you are in loue, for last mor-|(ning	472
Send to me in the morning, and ile send it:	And so, good rest.	1756

MORROW = 7*1

Pan. To morrow, may it please you, *Don Alphonso*,	341
To morrow be in readinesse, to goe,	372
No more of stay: to morrow thou must goe;	377
And so good-morrow Seruant. *Exit. Sil.*	525
Ho. Gone to seeke his dog, which to morrow, by his	1699
Sil. Sir *Eglamore*, a thousand times good morrow.	1776
Good morrow (gentle Lady)	1818
Sil. Good morrow, kinde Sir *Eglamoure. Exeunt.*	1819

MORROWS = *1

Val. Madam & Mistres, a thousand good-morrows.	489

MORTALL = 1

She excels each mortall thing	1675

MOST = 9*1

Val. And Writers say; as the most forward Bud	49
Lu. Fire that's closest kept, burnes most of all.	183
Hath he excepted most against my loue.	385
For Loue is still most precious in it selfe,	953
What thou think'st meet, and is most mannerly.	1033
Th. Since his exile she hath despis'd me most,	1449
That ere I watch'd, and the most heauiest.	1766
To keepe me from a most vnholy match,	1800
Sil. By thy approach thou mak'st me most vnhappy.	2152
The priuate wound is deepest: oh time, most accurst.	2196

MOTHER = 1*4

*dogge that liues: My Mother weeping: my Father	598
*shooe is my mother: nay, that cannot bee so neyther:	608
*with the hole in it, is my mother: and this my father:	610
*Now come I to my Mother: Oh that she could speake	619
Grand-mother: this proues that thou canst not read.	1361

MOTHERS = *1

*there 'tis; heere's my mothers breath vp and downe:	621

MOTION = *1

Speed. Oh excellent motion; oh exceeding Puppet:	487

MOUD = 1
Iul. Why he, of all the rest, hath neuer mou'd me.   180
MOUE = 1
More then quicke words, doe moue a womans minde.   1160
MOUED = 3
your Mistresse, be moued, be moued. *Exeunt*.   565
That my poore Mistris moued therewithall,   1991
MOUING = 1
Pro. Nay, if the gentle spirit of mouing words   2178
MOUINGLY = 1
I would haue had them writ more mouingly: 519
MOUNT = 1
But mount you presently, and meete with me   2089
MOUNTAINE = 1
Vpon the rising of the Mountaine foote   2090
MOUTH = 2
dost thou stop my mouth?   638
Sp. Item, she hath a sweet mouth.   1390
MOYSES = 1
But *Moyses* and *Valerius* follow him: 2110
MUCH = 32*7
Val. As much to you at home: and so farewell. *Exit*.   66
Pro. Why? could'st thou perceiue so much from her?   135
No, not so much as take this for thy pains: 137
Sp. No, not so much as take this for thy pains: 142
Ant. Nor need'st thou much importune me to that   319
Which I was much vnwilling to proceed in,   496
Sil. Perchance you think too much of so much pains?   502
(Please you command) a thousand times as much: | And yet---   504
What say you to a Letter from your friends | Of much good newes?   700
Pro. Your frends are wel, & haue the(m) much com(m)ended.   774
O, but I loue his Lady too-too much,   860
Spee. Why? | *Lau*. Because thou hast not so much charity in thee as 923
To wrong my friend, I shall be much forsworne.   932
Much lesse shall she that hath Loues wings to flie,   986
And there Ile rest, as after much turmoile   1012
It would be much vexation to your age.   1085
Duk. Be they of much import?   1124
Which (all too-much) I haue bestowed on thee.   1232
So much of bad already hath possest them.   1276
*much in a bare Christian: Heere is the Cate-log of her   1341
La. That's as much as to say (*Can she so?*)   1370
La. That's as much as to say *Bastard-vertues*: that   1381
Which must be done, by praising me as much   1500
Pro. As much as I can doe, I will effect: 1513
Du. I, much is the force of heauen-bred Poesie.   1518
That all the Trauailers doe feare so much.   1552
I kil'd a man, whose death I much repent,   1573
As we doe in our quality much want.   1604
Egl. Madam, I pitty much your grieuances,   1807
As much, I wish all good befortune you.   1811
Mine shall not doe his *Iulia* so much wrong.   1958
Poore Gentlewoman, my Master wrongs her much.   1962
Since she respects my Mistris loue so much.   2002
Vnlesse I flatter with my selfe too much.   2008
So much they spur their expedition.   2033
They loue me well: yet I haue much to doe   2137

MUCH *cont*.

And full as much (for more there cannot be)	2159
Then plurall faith, which is too much by one:	2173

MURMURE = 1

The Current that with gentle murmure glides	1000

MUSE = 2

Muse not that I thus sodainly proceed;	366
Why muse you sir, 'tis dinner time. | *Val*. I haue dyn'd.	560

MUSICKE = 4

He makes sweet musicke with th'enameld stones,	1003
There is no musicke in the Nightingale.	1249
To sort some Gentlemen, well skil'd in Musicke.	1538
How doe you, man? the Musicke likes you not.	1679

MUSING = *1

*Made Wit with musing, weake; hart sick with thought.	73

MUSIQUE = 5*1

And giue some euening Musique to her eare.	1641
*you shall heare Musique, and see the Gentleman that | you ask'd for.	1655
Iu. That will be Musique. | *Ho*. Harke, harke.	1659
Ho. I perceiue you delight not in Musique.	1688
Ho. Harke, what fine change is in the Musique.	1690
Sil. I thanke you for your Musique (Gentlemen)	1709

MUSITIAN = 2

Enter Protheus, Thurio, Iulia, Host, Musitian, Siluia.	1624
Iu. You mistake: the Musitian likes me not.	1680

MUST = 23*5

Sp. Well, I perceiue I must be faine to beare with you.	123
I must goe send some better Messenger,	149
No more of stay: to morrow thou must goe;	377
Iul. I must where is no remedy.	569
And I must minister the like to you.	803
Is gone with her along, and I must after,	831
Determin'd of: how I must climbe her window,	836
I must vnto the Road, to dis-embarque	842
Some necessaries, that I needs must vse,	843
If I keepe them, I needs must loose my selfe:	949
Luc. Why then your Ladiship must cut your haire.	1019
Luc. You must needs haue the(m) with a cod-peece (Ma- |(dam)	1028
That touch me neere: wherein thou must be secret.	1129
But *Valentine*, if he be tane, must die.	1302
Sp. And must I goe to him?	1437
La. Thou must run to him; for thou hast staid so long,	1438
Therefore it must with circumstance be spoken	1482
Du. Then you must vndertake to slander him.	1484
You must prouide to bottome it on me:	1499
Which must be done, by praising me as much	1500
You must lay Lime, to tangle her desires	1515
And now I must be as vniust to *Thurio*,	1626
But here comes *Thurio*; now must we to her window,	1640
*Masters command, hee must carry for a present to his | Lady.	1700
Because I loue him, I must pitty him.	1917
We must bring you to our Captaine.	2104
*1 *Out*. Come, I must bring you to our Captains caue.	2114
I am sorry I must neuer trust thee more,	2194

MUTTON = 1*3

Sp. I Sir: I (a lost-Mutton) gaue your Letter to her	100
*(a lac'd-Mutton) and she (a lac'd-Mutton) gaue mee (a	101

MUTTON *cont.*
lost-Mutton) nothing for my labour. 102
MUTTONS = 1
Pro. Here's too small a Pasture for such store of | Muttons. 103
MUTUALL = 1
One Feast, one house, one mutuall happinesse. *Exeunt.* 2300
MY *l.*3 20 22 57 58 69 71 74 *80 *83 *91 *98 102 126 145 150 *160 161
*178 194 196 200 208 216 217 218 219 274 303 *358 365 374 382 383
385 392 397 426 436 *440 473 *474 *475 497 517 521 528 531 *563 576
580 581 *595 *597 *598 *599 *604 *605 *606 *607 *608 *610 *611 *615
*616 *618 *619 *621 *622 *624 633 638 640 *645 646 659 672 674 696
702 705 709 712 714 755 761 *767 778 785 786 793 807 809 813 828 829
838 839 849 852 855 858 865 868 869 896 899 *903 910 918 930 932 933
949 951 952 957 960 964 971 978 981 982 *990 1008 1011 1025 1043
1046 1057 1058 1060 1062 1065 *1073 1077 1079 1081 1086 1087 1093
1096 1097 1102 1105 1113 1114 1119 1122 1126 1131 1132 1139
1142 1148 1152 1153 1156 1198 1200 *1204 1208 1210 1214 1217 1218
1229 1233 1236 1237 1241 1242 1252 *1275 1308 1310 1327 1330 *1332
*1337 1349 1359 *1442 1450 1459 1460 1461 1469 1472 1473 1485 1492
1512 1536 1553 *1556 1559 1580 1589 1593 1597 1628 1630 1632 1633
1638 *1651 1681 1684 1704 1717 1727 1739 1745 1761 1762 1786 1787
1797 1798 1799 *1828 *1854 *1856 1867 1870 1878 1879 1884 1887 1907
1909 1919 1924 1925 1926 1929 1934 1938 1962 1964 1971 1972 1978
1985 1990 1991 1996 1997 2001 2002 2008 2015 2021 2025 2042 2045
2049 2051 2056 2060 2063 2066 2076 2127 2128 2135 2144 2151 2158
2182 2189 2198 2208 *2214 *2215 *2222 *2245 *2248 2254 2258 2266
2291 *2293 = 249*53
MYSELFE *see* selfe
NAILE = 1
Or as one naile, by strength driues out another. 848
NAKED = 1
Vpon the very naked name of Loue. 794
NAME = 10*2
Iu. How now? what meanes this passion at his name? 169
Did in your name receiue it: pardon the fault I pray. 193
I throw thy name against the bruzing-stones, 271
Poore wounded name: my bosome, as a bed, 274
*Except mine own name: That, some whirle-winde beare 280
Loe, here in one line is his name twice writ: 283
And yet I will not name it: and yet I care not. 507
Yet hath Sir *Protheus* (for that's his name) 717
Vpon the very naked name of Loue. 794
*if not, thou art an Hebrew, a Iew, and not worth | the name of a
Christian. 921
Pro. Sebastian is thy name: I like thee well, 1859
Doe not name *Siluia* thine: if once againe, 2255
NAMELES = 1
Vnto the secret, nameles friend of yours: 495
NAMELESSE = 1
Sp. Item, she hath many namelesse vertues. 1380
NAMES = 3*1
Lu. Please you repeat their names, ile shew my minde, 160
He couples it, to his complaining Names; 287
*indeede know not their fathers; and therefore haue no | names. 1382
The names of all the Actors. 2301
NAN = *1
*small as a wand: this hat is *Nan* our maid: I am the 613

117

NATURE = 1
And loue you 'gainst the nature of Loue: force ye.   2181
NATURED = *1
*Court: I thinke *Crab* my dog, be the sowrest natured   597
NAUGHT = 1
And naught esteemes my aged eloquence.   1152
NAY = 12*12
  Pro. Ouer the Bootes? nay giue me not the Boots.   30
  Sp. Nay, that I can deny by a circumstance.   88
  Pro. Nay, in that you are astray: 'twere best pound | you.   107
  Sp. Nay Sir, lesse then a pound shall serue me for car-|rying your
Letter.   109
  Lu. Nay, now you are too flat;   253
  lu. Nay, would I were so angred with the same: 264
  Lu. Nay, I was taken vp, for laying them downe.   294
  Speed. Without you? nay, that's certaine: for with-|out   430
But (since vnwillingly) take them againe. | Nay, take them.   514
  Speed. Nay: I was riming: 'tis you y haue the reason.   535
The tide is now; nay, not thy tide of teares,   582
  Launce. Nay, 'twill bee this howre ere I haue done   593
*nay, Ile shew you the manner of it. This shooe is my fa-|ther: 606
*shooe is my mother: nay, that cannot bee so neyther: 608
  Val. Nay sure, I thinke she holds them prisoners stil.   742
  Sil. Nay then he should be blind, and being blind   743
  Val. I, and we are betroathd: nay more, our mariage | (howre,   834
  Iul. Nay, that I will not.   1038
  Duk. Nay then no matter: stay with me a while,   1127
*a horse can doe no more; nay, a horse cannot fetch, but   1343
*would doe this for his Seruant? nay, ile be sworne I haue   1849
*think'st not of this now: nay, I remember the tricke you   1853
  Thu. Nay then the wanton lyes: my face is blacke.   .   2051
  Pro. Nay, if the gentle spirit of mouing words   2178
NEAT = 1
  Lu. As of a Knight, well-spoken, neat, and fine;   163
NECESSARIES = 1
Some necessaries, that I needs must vse,   843
NECESSITY = 1
To make a vertue of necessity,   1608
NECTAR = 1
The water, Nectar, and the Rocks pure gold.   826
NEECE = 1
And heire and Neece, alide vnto the Duke.   1595
NEED = 3
  Val. Why she hath not writ to me? | *Speed.* What need she,   542
For *Valentine*, I need not cite him to it,   735
To take a note of what I stand in need of,   1059
NEEDE = 1*2
  La. What neede a man care for a stock with a wench,   1372
  La. A speciall vertue: for then shee neede not be | wash'd, and
scowr'd.   1375
Partly that I haue neede of such a youth,   1883
NEEDES = *1
  Iul. She needes not, when she knowes it cowardize.   2062
NEEDS = 2*1
Some necessaries, that I needs must vse,   843
If I keepe them, I needs must loose my selfe: 949
  Luc. You must needs haue the(m) with a cod-peece (Ma-|(dam   1028

NEEDST = 1
   Ant. Nor need'st thou much importune me to that   319
NEERE = 3
   Iul. Is't neere dinner time? | *Lu.* I would it were,   222
   That touch me neere: wherein thou must be secret.   1129
   No griefe did euer come so neere thy heart,   1789
NEGLECT = 2*1
   Made me neglect my Studies, loose my time;   71
   But since she did neglect her looking-glasse,   1973
   *to Madam *Siluia*: w (out of my neglect) was neuer done.   2215
NEITHER = 5*1
   Spee. How then? shall he marry her? | *Lau.* No, neither.   887
   Neither regarding that she is my childe,   1139
   Pro. Who then? his Spirit? | *Val.* Neither,   1265
   But neither bended knees, pure hands held vp,   1299
   La. I care not for that neither: because I loue crusts.   1403
   Du. Saw you my daughter? | *Pro.* Neither.   2076
NEPHEW = 1
   Pan. 'Twas of his Nephew *Protheus*, your Sonne.   304
NERE = 3
   Though nere so blacke, say they haue Angells faces,   1172
   1.*Out.* Why nere repent it, if it were done so;   1576
   Or nere returne againe into my sight.   1879
NEUER *see also* nere = 11*4
   And yet you neuer swom the *Hellespont*.   29
   But were I you, he neuer should be mine.   164
   Iul. Why he, of all the rest, hath neuer mou'd me.   180
   Speed. You neuer saw her since she was deform'd.   456
   Sil. And dutie neuer yet did want his meed.   762
   *not welcome. I reckon this alwaies, that a man is neuer   875
   *vndon till hee be hang'd, nor neuer welcome to a place,   876
   Lau. Thou shalt neuer get such a secret from me, but | by a parable.   907
   Lau. I neuer knew him otherwise. | *Spee.* Then how?   911
   Luc. Then neuer dreame on Infamy, but go: 1039
   Duke. Vpon mine Honor, he shall neuer know   1117
   Send her another: neuer giue her ore,   1163
   Your slander neuer can endamage him;   1489
   I am sorry I must neuer trust thee more,   2194
   *to Madam *Siluia*: w (out of my neglect) was neuer done.   2215
NEW = 2
   Goe with me: once more, new Seruant welcome;   769
   Plead a new state in thy vn-riual'd merit,   2271
NEWER = 1
   Is by a newer obiect quite forgotten,   850
NEWES = 8*3
   Of thy successe in loue; and what newes else   62
   Ant. Lend me the Letter: Let me see what newes.   357
   Pro. There is no newes (my Lord) but that he writes   358
   What say you to a Letter from your friends | Of much good newes?   700
   I thinke 'tis no vn-welcome newes to you.   731
   Val. My eares are stopt, & cannot hear good newes,   1275
   What is your newes?   1285
   Pro. That thou art banish'd: oh that's the newes,   1287
   Speed. How now Signior *Launce*? what newes with | your Mastership?   1347
   Sp. Well, your old vice still: mistake the word: what | newes then in
   your paper?   1350
   La. The black'st newes that euer thou heard'st.   1352

NEW-FOUND = 1
And full of new-found oathes, which he will breake   1951
NEXT = 2*2
    The next ensuing howre, some foule mischance   579
    *Val. No more: vnles the next word that thou speak'st   1307
    *then the wit; for the greater hides the lesse: What's | next?   1423
    *Pro. What dangerous action, stood it next to death   2162
NEYTHER = *1
    *shooe is my mother: nay, that cannot bee so neyther: 608
NICE = 1
    Whom I affect: but she is nice, and coy,   1151
NICHOLAS = 1
    La. There: and S.(aint) Nicholas be thy speed.   1363
NICKE = 1
    He lou'd her out of all nicke.   1697
NIGHT = 13
    Val. Last night she enioyn'd me,   480
    This night he meaneth with a Corded-ladder   962
    This night intends to steale away your daughter: 1080
    Val. Why then I would resort to her by night.   1179
    That no man hath recourse to her by night.   1181
    Duk. This very night; for Loue is like a childe   1193
    What's here? Siluia, this night I will enfranchise thee.   1220
    Except I be by Siluia in the night,   1248
    Visit by night your Ladies chamber-window   1529
    Th. And thy aduice, this night, ile put in practise: 1535
    For me (by this pale queene of night I sweare)   1724
    Pro. As wretches haue ore-night   1758
    Iul. Not so: but it hath bin the longest night   1765
NIGHTINGALE = 1
    There is no musicke in the Nightingale.   1249
NIGHTINGALES = 1
    And to the Nightingales complaining Notes   2126
NIGHTLY = 3
    With nightly teares, and daily hart-sore sighes,   784
    I nightly lodge her in an vpper Towre,   1104
    My thoughts do harbour with my Siluia nightly,   1210
NIGHTS = 2
    With twenty watchfull, weary, tedious nights;   35
    Tune a deploring dumpe: the nights dead silence   1531
NIMBLE = 1
    3 Out. Being nimble footed, he hath out-run vs.   2109
NIMPH = 1
    Thou gentle Nimph, cherish thy for-lorne swaine.   2133
NO l.31 *60 92 122 137 140 142 175 200 209 250 316 318 *358 377 393
    *453 485 503 509 546 547 553 569 *602 *605 *607 *614 *630 693 696
    731 790 791 792 798 857 867 885 887 890 *904 1020 1041 1078 1127
    1137 1169 1173 1178 1181 1249 1251 1263 1279 1281 1282 1284 *1307
    *1343 *1382 *1393 1402 1405 1617 1619 1789 *1828 *1847 1870 1885
    2046 2061 2131 2161 2171 2179 = 64*17
NOBLE = 1
    Pro. Know (noble Lord) they haue deuis'd a meané   1107
NOBLENESSE = 1
    Worthy his youth, and noblenesse of birth.   335
NOBLE-MEN = 1
    Heare sweet discourse, conuerse with Noble-men,   333

NOD = 2
 Sp. You mistooke Sir: I say she did nod;   117
 And you aske me if she did nod, and I say I.   118
NODDY = 3
 Pro. Nod-I, why that's noddy.   116
 Pro. And that set together is noddy.   119
 Hauing nothing but the word noddy for my paines.   126
NOD-I = 1
 Pro. Nod-I, why that's noddy.   116
NONE = 5*1
 *you were so simple, none else would: but you are   431
 But I will none of them: they are for you: 518
 Val. She gaue me none, except an angry word.   549
 Least it should rauell, and be good to none,   1498
 And that's farre worse then none: better haue none 2172
NOOKES = 1
 And so by many winding nookes he straies   1006
NOR *l*.319 *611 *623 791 *876 1140 1300 *1335 1786 2074 2206 = 8*4
NORTH = 1
 La. Why then, will I tell thee, that thy Master staies | for thee at the
 North gate.   1432
NORTH-GATE = 1
 Bid him make haste, and meet me at the North-gate. 1328
NOSE = *1
 *As a nose on a mans face, or a Wethercocke on a steeple: 527
NOT *l*.6 30 31 42 45 *90 92 *94 96 137 142 150 156 173 179 *184 208 225
 234 244 249 250 258 278 286 295 323 327 364 366 373 397 405 *434 439
 440 442 443 *446 *469 473 484 507 512 522 542 545 556 *564 571 578
 581 582 *601 *617 *623 659 664 668 707 708 735 746 757 779 797 799
 804 808 810 *823 827 859 869 *874 *875 894 895 *916 *919 *921 *923
 984 *990 996 1002 1008 1015 1030 *1037 1038 1055 1064 1114 1115
 1130 1148 1158 1165 1167 1170 1238 *1240 1244 1245 1253 1255 1262
 1311 1314 1321 1325 *1333 *1335 *1337 *1338 1356 1361 *1375 *1382
 *1386 *1393 *1403 *1407 *1411 *1416 *1440 1447 1462 1467 1471 1494
 1496 1514 *1548 1550 1553 1568 *1615 1645 1679 1680 1684 1688 1689
 1703 1732 1735 1743 1765 1782 1784 1797 1805 1817 *1834 *1839 *1853
 *1855 1870 1887 *1893 1894 1903 1921 1928 1944 1947 1948 1958 1969
 1993 2016 2031 2038 2048 *2062 2074 2084 2086 2088 2115 2116 2129
 2141 2163 2190 2205 2254 2255 2256 2259 2261 2262 = 158*44
NOTABLE = 1*1
 thou that that my master is become a notable Louer? 910
 Lau. A notable Lubber: as thou reportest him to | bee. 913
NOTE = 2
 Giue me a Note, your Ladiship can set   238
 To take a note of what I stand in need of,   1059
NOTES = 1
 And to the Nightingales complaining Notes   2126
NOTE-WORTHY = 1
 Some rare note-worthy obiect in thy trauaile.   16
NOTHING = 16*2
 lost-Mutton) nothing for my labour.   102
 Hauing nothing but the word noddy for my paines. 126
 Sp. Sir, I could perceiue nothing at all from her; 136
 Pro. What said she, nothing?   141
 Lu. Nothing. | *Iu*. Why didst thou stoope then? 228
 Iul. And is that paper nothing?   231
 Lu. Nothing concerning me.   232

NOTHING *cont.*

Pro. My dutie will I boast of, nothing else.	761
Val. Pardon me (*Protheus*) all I can is nothing,	819
To her, whose worth, make other worthies nothing;	820
*no, it will: if hee shake his taile, and say nothing, it | will.	904
Pro. What then? | *Val.* Nothing.	1267
Lau. Can nothing speake? Master, shall I strike?	1269
Pro. Who wouldst thou strike? | *Lau.* Nothing.	1270
Lau. Why Sir, Ile strike nothing: I pray you.	1273
*Well, ile haue her: and if it be a match, as nothing is | impossible.	1429
This, or else nothing, will inherit her.	1533
Val. Nothing but my fortune.	1589

NOTICE = 1

Now presently Ile giue her father notice	965

NOTWITHSTANDING = 1

And notwithstanding all her sodaine quips,	1636

NOUGHT = 2

Warre with good counsaile; set the world at nought;	72
Thou hast beguil'd my hopes; nought but mine eye	2189

NOURISHD = *1

*can feed on the ayre, I am one that am nourish'd by my	563

NOW = 50*24

Val. Sweet *Protheus*, no: Now let vs take our leaue:	60
Pro. But now he parted hence to embarque for *Millain*.	75
Sp. Now you haue taken the paines to set it toge-|ther, take it for	
your paines.	120
Iul. But say *Lucetta* (now we are alone)	154
Iu. How now? what meanes this passion at his name?	169
Iul. Now (by my modesty) a goodly Broker:	194
Now trust me, 'tis an office of great worth,	197
Iu. Let's see your Song: | How now Minion?	246
Lu. Nay, now you are too flat;	253
Now kisse, embrace, contend, doe what you will.	289
And in good time: now will we breake with him.	346
Ant. How now? What Letter are you reading there?	353
Which now shewes all the beauty of the Sun,	388
Speed. Madam *Siluia*: Madam *Siluia*. | *Val.* How now Sirha?	403
*now you are Metamorphis'd with a Mistris, that when I	425
Now will he interpret to her.	488
Val. Now trust me (Madam) it came hardly-off	499
Val. How now Sir? | What are you reasoning with your selfe?	533
The tide is now; nay, not thy tide of teares,	582
*oh, the dogge is me, and I am my selfe: I; so, so: now	615
*come I to my Father; Father, your blessing: now	616
*now should I kisse my Father; well, hee weeps on:	618
*Now come I to my Mother: Oh that she could speake	619
*now, like a would-woman: well, I kisse her: why	620
*Now come I to my sister; marke the moane she makes:	622
*now the dogge all this while sheds not a teare: nor	623
Duk. Now, daughter *Siluia*, you are hard beset.	698
Comes all the praises that I now bestow.)	722
Sil. Be-like that now she hath enfranchis'd them	740
Val. Now tell me: how do al from whence you came?	773
Val. I *Protheus*, but that life is alter'd now,	780
Now, no discourse, except it be of loue:	792
Now can I breake my fast, dine, sup, and sleepe,	793
(That I did loue, for now my loue is thaw'd,	855

NOW *cont.*

But now I worship a celestiall Sunne:	939
I cannot now proue constant to my selfe,	960
Now presently Ile giue her father notice	965
Iul. Now, as thou lou'st me, do him not that wrong,	1055
Now tell me *Protheus*, what's your will with me?	1072
That which thy selfe hast now disclos'd to me.	1101
For which, the youthfull Louer now is gone,	1110
I now am full resolu'd to take a wife,	1145
Now therefore would I haue thee to my Tutor	1153
Duk. Now as thou art a Gentleman of blood	1190
And now excesse of it will make me surfet.	1290
As if but now they waxed pale for woe:	1298
The time now serues not to expostulate,	1321
*that's all one, if he be but one knaue: He liues not now	1333
Speed. How now Signior *Launce*? what newes with | your Mastership?	1347
*keepe shut: Now, of another thing shee may, and that | cannot I helpe.	
Well, proceede.	1412
La. Now will he be swing'd for reading my Letter;	1442
Now *Valentine* is banish'd from her sight.	1448
How now sir *Protheus*, is your countriman	1457
Du. Euen now about it, I will pardon you. *Exeunt.*	1544
Val. For that which now torments me to rehearse;	1572
And now I must be as vniust to *Thurio*,	1626
But here comes *Thurio*; now must we to her window,	1640
Th. How now, sir *Protheus*, are you crept before vs?	1642
Th. I thanke you for your owne: Now Gentlemen	1649
Ho. Now, my yong guest; me thinks your' allycholly;	1651
Ho. How now? are you sadder then you were before;	1678
*think'st not of this now: nay, I remember the tricke you	1853
How now you whor-son pezant,	1863
And now am I (vnhappy Messenger)	1920
That now she is become as blacke as I.	1977
And now it is about the very houre	2029
Du. How now sir *Protheus*; how now *Thurio*?	2072
Thou hast no faith left now, vnlesse thou'dst two,	2171
For such is a friend now: treacherous man,	2188
Could haue perswaded me: now I dare not say	2190
*Why wag: how now? what's the matter? look vp: speak.	2213
Now, by the honor of my Ancestry,	2266
I now beseech you (for your daughters sake)	2276

NOWS = 1

Luc. A round hose (Madam) now's not worth a pin	1030

NURSE = 2

That (like a testie Babe) will scratch the Nurse,	212
Time is the Nurse, and breeder of all good;	1313

O *l*.350 *463 788 801 860 936 *1830 2018 2117 2128 2149 *2214 = 9*3, 1

Best sing it to the tune of *Light O, Loue*.	240

OARES = *1

*ship'd, and thou art to post after with oares; what's the	627

OATH = 2

Here is her oath for loue, her honors paune;	349
And ev'n that Powre which gaue me first my oath	933

OATHES = 7

With twenty thousand soule-confirming oathes.	945
A thousand oathes, an Ocean of his teares,	1044
His words are bonds, his oathes are oracles,	1050

OATHES *cont*.

And full of new-found oathes, which he will breake	1951
Into a thousand oathes; and all those oathes,	2169
Iul. Behold her, that gaue ayme to all thy oathes,	2227

OBDURATE = 1

Pro. Madam: if your heart be so obdurate:	1744

OBIECT = 3

Some rare note-worthy obiect in thy trauaile.	16
Vpon a homely obiect, Loue can winke.	748
Is by a newer obiect quite forgotten,	850

OBSERUD = 1

Val. Hast thou obseru'd that? euen she I meane.	438

OBTAINE = 1

To plead for that, which I would not obtaine;	1921

OBTAINING = 1

That I am desperate of obtaining her.	1451

OCEAN = 2

With willing sport to the wilde Ocean.	1007
A thousand oathes, an Ocean of his teares,	1044

OCLOCK *see* clock

OD-CONCEITED = 1

With twentie od-conceited true-loue knots:	1021

OF *see also* a, o' = 192*38

OFF *see also* falls-off, hardly-off *l*.499 *684 759 2038 2239 = 4*1

OFFENCE = 2

Val. I was. | 2.*Out*. For what offence?	1570
Be a sufficient Ransome for offence,	2200

OFFER = 2

Val. I take your offer, and will liue with you,	1616
Pro. What, didst thou offer her this from me?	1873

OFFERD = 1*1

*2.*Out*. Thou shalt not liue, to brag what we haue of-|(fer'd.	1615
And then I offer'd her mine owne, who is a dog	1876

OFFERED = 1

Pro. I, I: and she hath offered to the doome	1292

OFFICE = 3

Now trust me, 'tis an office of great worth,	197
'Tis an ill office for a Gentleman,	1486
Therefore the office is indifferent,	1490

OFFICER = 1

And you an officer fit for the place:	198

OFT = 3

If this be he you oft haue wish'd to heare from.	753
Whose soueraignty so oft thou hast preferd,	944
How oft hast thou with periury cleft the roote?	2229

OFTEN = 8

Pro. Indeede a Sheepe doth very often stray,	78
For often haue you writ to her: and she in modesty,	555
This loue of theirs, my selfe haue often seene,	1093
Dumbe Iewels often in their silent kinde	1159
Sp. Item, she will often praise her liquor.	1406
Or else I often had beene often miserable.	1581
Often resort vnto this Gentlewoman?	1695

OFTENTIMES = 1

And oftentimes haue purpos'd to forbid	1095

OH *see also* O *l.**185 265 352 386 *487 *490 526 530 *564 *615 *619 *990
   1212 1287 1289 1330 *1360 *1396 1426 1781 1936 2043 2061 2067 2157
   2164 2182 2196 2210 2220 2230 *2236 = 22*11
OLD = 2*1

His yeares but yong, but his experience old:	719
*Sp. Well, your old vice still: mistake the word: what | newes then in	
your paper?	1350
Pro. But Pearles are faire; and the old saying is,	2052

OMITTING = 1

Omitting the sweet benefit of time	715

ON *see also* come-on = 53*13
ONCE = 7

Once more adieu: my Father at the Road	57
may be both at once deliuered.	132
Goe with me: once more, new Seruant welcome;	769
Ile be so bold to breake the seale for once.	1209
*mine, twice or thrice in that last Article: rehearse that | once more.	1417
And once againe, I doe receiue thee honest;	2204
Doe not name *Siluia* thine: if once againe,	2255

ONE = 31*19

*Coy looks, with hart-sore sighes: one fading moments | (mirth,	34
Sp. Twenty to one then, he is ship'd already,	76
Loe, here in one line is his name twice writ:	283
Thus will I fold them, one vpon another;	288
Pro. As one relying on your Lordships will,	363
*Sp. Why then this may be yours: for this is but one.	399
*to walke alone like one that had the pestilence:	416
*to fast, like one that takes diet: to watch, like one that	419
*like a cocke; when you walk'd, to walke like one of the	422
*Speed. That's because the one is painted, and the o-|ther out of all	
count.	450
To write some lines to one she loues.	481
*can feed on the ayre, I am one that am nourish'd by my	563
*one teare: he is a stone, a very pibble stone, and has no	602
Euen as one heate, another heate expels,	847
Or as one naile, by strength driues out another.	848
*with you presently; where, for one shot of fiue pence,	880
Lau. Why, stand-vnder: and vnder-stand is all one.	901
And when the flight is made to one so deere,	987
My selfe am one made priuy to the plot.	1081
Val. What letts but one may enter at her window?	1182
And built so sheluing, that one cannot climbe it	1184
Ile get me one of such another length.	1203
*that's all one, if he be but one knaue: He liues not now	1333
By one, whom she esteemeth as his friend.	1483
Sp. Master, be one of them:	1585
*Ho. You would haue them alwaies play but one thing.	1692
Iu. I would alwaies haue one play but one thing.	1693
Pro. One (Lady) if you knew his pure hearts truth,	1711
One that attends your Ladiships command.	1775
*him (looke you) it goes hard: one that I brought vp of	1823
*a puppy: one that I sau'd from drowning, when three or	1824
*taught him (euen as one would say precisely, thus I	1826
*I would haue (as one should say) one that takes vp-|on	1832
*all the chamber smelt him: out with the dog (saies one)	1840
One *Iulia*, that his changing thoughts forget	1940
Pro. She saies it is a faire one.	2050

ONE *cont.*

Sil. A thousand more mischances then this one	2105
Vouchsafe me for my meed, but one faire looke:	2144
Would I not vndergoe, for one calme looke:	2163
Then plurall faith, which is too much by one:	2173
I haue one friend aliue; thou wouldst disproue me:	2191
But Constant, he were perfect; that one error	2237
To grant one Boone that I shall aske of you.	2277
One Feast, one house, one mutuall happinesse. *Exeunt.*	2300

ONELY = 4*1

(Onely for his possessions are so huge)	830
Onely deserue my loue, by louing him,	1057
Onely, in lieu thereof, dispatch me hence:	1063
*onely carry, therefore is shee better then a Iade. *Item.*	1344
To be slow in words, is a womans onely vertue:	1397

ONES = 1

Who should be trusted, when ones right hand	2192

ONS = 1

There's not a haire on's head, but 'tis a *Valentine*.	1262

ONT = *1

*a veng'ance on't, there 'tis: Nor sir, this staffe is my si-|ster:	611

ON-SET = 1

To giue the on-set to thy good aduise.	1540

OPEN = *2

**Pro.* Come, come, open the matter in briefe; what | said she.	129
**Sp.* Open your purse, that the money, and the matter	131

OPINION = 2

In thy opinion which is worthiest loue?	159
To beare a hard opinion of his truth:	1056

OPPOSES = 1

How she opposes her against my will?	1472

OR *l.*39 83 200 277 313 *354 375 407 *464 *527 556 *557 848 851 852 1237 *1417 1533 1575 1581 1617 1646 1742 *1824 *1837 1879 2023 *2187 2253 = 21*8

ORACLES = 1

His words are bonds, his oathes are oracles,	1050

ORDERLY = 1

Sp. Marry Sir, the letter very orderly,	125

ORE = 1

Send her another: neuer giue her ore,	1163

ORE-LOOKD = 1

Iul. And yet I would I had ore-look'd the Letter;	204

ORE-NIGHT = 1

Pro. As wretches haue ore-night	1758

ORE-SLIPS = 1

And when that howre ore-slips me in the day,	577

ORNAMENT = 1

Sweet Ornament, that deckes a thing diuine, | Ah *Siluia, Siluia.*	401

ORPHEUS = 1

For *Orpheus* Lute, was strung with Poets sinewes,	1524

OTHER = 7*1

Iul. Your reason? | *Lu.* I haue no other but a womans reason:	175
While other men, of slender reputation	308
With other Gentlemen of good esteeme	342
**Speed.* That's because the one is painted, and the o-|ther out of all count.	450
And I thinke, no other treasure to giue your followers:	693

OTHER *cont.*
Vpon some other pawne for fealty.	741
To her, whose worth, make other worthies nothing;	820
La. I Sir, the other Squirrill was stolne from me	1874

OTHERWISE = 1*2
Lau. I neuer knew him otherwise. | *Spee.* Then how?	911
*sat in the stockes, for puddings he hath stolne, otherwise	1850
*Geese he hath kil'd, otherwise he had sufferd for't: thou	1852

OUER *see also* ore = 5
Pro. Ouer the Bootes? nay giue me not the Boots.	30
Sp. From a pound to a pin? fold it ouer and ouer,	112
Sil. And when it's writ: for my sake read it ouer,	521
Read ouer *Iulia's* heart, (thy first best Loue)	2167

OUER-BOOTES = 1
Val. 'Tis true; for you are ouer-bootes in loue,	28

OUER-CHARGD = *1
Sp. If the ground be ouer-charg'd, you were best | sticke her.	105

OUER-SHOOES = 1
For he was more then ouer-shooes in loue.	27

OUER-TAKE = 1
Sp. And yet it cannot ouer-take your slow purse.	128

OUER-TAKETH = 1
He ouer-taketh in his pilgrimage.	1005

OUER-WEENING = 1
Goe base Intruder, ouer-weening Slaue,	1227

OUGHT = 1
By ought that I can speake in his dispraise,	1493

OUR *l.*60 350 351 *599 *600 *604 *613 712 713 *834 835 1235 1458 1543 1583 1599 1600 1604 1607 *1610 1613 1614 1620 1622 1664 1980 1981 2104 2112 *2114 2290 2299 = 26*9

OURSELUES *see* selues

OUT
*l.*11 248 309 *450 452 744 848 1029 1146 1258 1329 *1398 1399 1426 1683 1697 *1840 *1841 *1848 2024 2025 2036 2054 2070 *2215 = 3*1 = 20*6

OUTRAGES = 2
Prouided that you do no outrages | On silly women, or poore passengers.	1617
To keepe them from vnciuill outrages.	2138

OUT-L = 1
Iul. And I mine. | *Out-l.* A prize: a prize: a prize.	2246

OUT-LAWES *see also* Out., Out-l., 1. Out., 1. Out-l., 2. Out., 3. Out. = 4
Enter Valentine, Speed, and certaine Out-lawes.	1546
Siluia, Out-lawes.	2102
Enter Valentine, Protheus, Siluia, Iulia, Duke, Thurio, | Out-lawes.	2120
Out-lawes with Valentine.	2309

OUT-RUN = 1
3 *Out.* Being nimble footed, he hath out-run vs.	2109

OWE = 1
Thu. Wherefore? | *Iul.* That such an Asse should owe them.	2068

OWN = *1
*Except mine own name: That, some whirle-winde beare	280

OWNE = 7*4
And with the vantage of mine owne excuse	384
*eyes, or your owne eyes had the lights they were wont	464
Speed. Your owne present folly, and her passing de-|formitie:	468
And made them watchers of mine owne hearts sorrow.	787

OWNE *cont.*

Pro. Haue I not reason to prefer mine owne?	810
*Val. Not for the world: why man, she is mine owne,	823
With goodly shape; and by your owne report,	1602
I haue accesse my owne loue to prefer.	1628
*Th. I thanke you for your owne: Now Gentlemen	1649
And then I offer'd her mine owne, who is a dog	1876
Duke. I grant it (for thine owne) what ere it be.	2278

PACK = 1

A pack of sorrowes, which would presse you downe	1089

PADUA = 1

Speed. Launce, by mine honesty welcome to *Padua.*	873

PAGE = 2*1

*Lu. Sir *Valentines* page: & sent I think from *Protheus*;	191
As may beseeme some well reputed Page.	1018
What thinke you of this Page (my Lord?)	2291

PAGEANTS = 1

When all our Pageants of delight were plaid,	1980

PAID = 1*1

**till some certaine shot be paid, and the Hostesse say wel-|come.	877
Val. Then I am paid:	2203

PAINES = 1*3

*Sp. Now you haue taken the paines to set it toge-|ther, take it for	
your paines.	120
Hauing nothing but the word noddy for my paines.	126
*Pro. Well Sir: here is for your paines: what said she?	133

PAINS = 1*1

Sp. No, not so much as take this for thy pains:	142
*Sil. Perchance you think too much of so much pains?	502

PAINTED = 1*2

*Speed. That's because the one is painted, and the o-|ther out of all	
count.	450
Val. How painted? and how out of count?	452
*Speed. Marry sir, so painted to make her faire, that no | man counts of	
her beauty.	453

PAINTER = 1

And yet the Painter flatter'd her a little,	2007

PAIRE = 2

Val. Why Lady, Loue hath twenty paire of eyes.	745
To cast vp, with a paire of anchoring hookes,	1187

PALE = 2

As if but now they waxed pale for woe:	1298
For me (by this pale queene of night I sweare)	1724

PAN = 5*1

PANT = 1*1

PANTH = 4*2

PANTHINO see also Pan., Pant., Panth., Panthion = 3

Enter Antonio and Panthino. *Protheus.*	301
Ant. Tell me *Panthino,* what sad talke was that,	302
Come on *Panthino*; you shall be imployd,	378

PANTHION = 3

Enter Protheus, *Iulia, Panthion.*	567
Enter Launce, *Panthion.*	592
Panthion: seruant to Antonio.	2312

PAPER = 9

Lu. Peruse this paper Madam.	187
There: take the paper: see it be return'd,	199

PAPER *cont.*
Lu. To take a paper vp, that I let fall.	230
Iul. And is that paper nothing?	231
Ile kisse each seuerall paper, for amends:	268
*Sp. Well, your old vice still: mistake the word: what | newes then in your paper?	1350
Sp. Come foole, come: try me in thy paper.	1362
Deliuer'd you a paper that I should not;	1944
As easily as I doe teare his paper.	1952

PAPERS = 1*1
Goe, get you gone: and let the papers lye:	260
*Lu. What, shall these papers lye, like Tel-tales here?	292

PARABLE = 1
*Lau. Thou shalt neuer get such a secret from me, but | by a parable.	907

PARAGON = 1
Pro. No; But she is an earthly Paragon.	798

PARDON = 6*1
Lu. Pardon deare Madam, 'tis a passing shame,	170
Did in your name receiue it: pardon the fault I pray.	193
Val. Pardon me (*Protheus*) all I can is nothing,	819
*Du. Euen now about it, I will pardon you. *Exeunt.*	1544
Pardon me (Madam) I haue vnaduis'd	1943
Iul. It may not be: good Madam pardon me.	1947
Duke. Thou hast preuaild, I pardon them and thee:	2285

PARLE = 1
That euery day with par'le encounter me,	158

PARLEY = 1
Therefore, aboue the rest, we parley to you:	1606

PART = 4
did thy Master part with Madam *Iulia*?	882
And ere I part with thee, confer at large	1323
Our youth got me to play the womans part,	1981
For I did play a lamentable part.	1987

PARTAKER = 1
Wish me partaker in thy happinesse,	17

PARTED = 1*2
*Pro. But now he parted hence to embarque for *Millain*.	75
*Lau. Marry after they cloas'd in earnest, they parted | very fairely in iest.	883
This Ring I gaue him, when he parted from me,	1918

PARTING = 1*2
Alas, this parting strikes poore Louers dumbe. | *Exeunt.*	589
*to haue seene our parting: why my Grandam hauing	604
*no eyes, looke you, wept her selfe blinde at my parting:	605

PARTLY = 2
And partly seeing you are beautifide	1601
Partly that I haue neede of such a youth,	1883

PARTNER = 1
Wishing me with him, partner of his fortune.	361

PARTS = 1
Iu. Peace, stand aside, the company parts.	1702

PASSE = 2
And for the waies are dangerous to passe,	1794
Val. Please you, Ile tell you, as we passe along,	2295

PASSENGER = 2
1.*Out-I.* Fellowes, stand fast: I see a passenger.	1547
Haue some vnhappy passenger in chace;	2136

PASSENGERS = 1
Prouided that you do no outrages | On silly women, or poore
passengers.   1617
PASSING = 2*1
Lu. Pardon deare Madam, 'tis a passing shame,   170
*Speed. Your owne present folly, and her passing de-|formitie: 468
Sil. Is she not passing faire?   1969
PASSION = *1
*Iu. How now? what meanes this passion at his name?   169
PASSIONATE = 1
Poore forlorne Protheus, passionate Protheus: 284
PASSIONING = 1
(Madam) 'twas *Ariadne*, passioning   1988
PAST = 1
And aske remission, for my folly past.   219
PASTIME = 1
And make a pastime of each weary step,   1010
PASTURE = *1
*Pro. Here's too small a Pasture for such store of | Muttons.   103
PATIENCE = 4
Pro. Haue patience, gentle *Iulia*:   568
And thinke my patience, (more then thy desert)   1229
Iul. If you be she, I doe intreat your patience   1932
Loue, lend me patience to forbeare a while.   2148
PATIENT = 2
Ile be as patient as a gentle streame,   1009
1.*Out.* Come, come be patient: 2103
PATIENTLY = 1
Haue learn'd me how to brooke this patiently.   2106
PATRICKES = 1
Eg. Where shall I meete you? | *Sil.* At *Frier Patrickes* Cell,   1814
PATRICKS = 2
That *Siluia*, at Fryer *Patricks* Cell should meet me,   2030
At *Patricks* Cell this euen, and there she was not.   2086
PAUNE = 1
Here is her oath for loue, her honors paune;   349
PAWNE = 1
Vpon some other pawne for fealty.   741
PEACE = 7
Peace, here she comes.   486
2.*Out.* Peace: we'll heare him.   1555
Val. Peace villaine.   1587
Iu. Is he among these? | *Ho.* I: but peace, let's heare'm.   1661
Iu. Peace, stand aside, the company parts.   1702
Thu. But well, when I discourse of loue and peace.   2058
Iul. But better indeede, when you hold you peace.   2059
PEARLE = 2
As twenty Seas, if all their sand were pearle,   825
A Sea of melting pearle, which some call teares;   1294
PEARLES = 3
Pro. But Pearles are faire; and the old saying is,   2052
Blacke men are Pearles, in beauteous Ladies eyes.   2053
Thu. 'Tis true, such Pearles as put out Ladies eyes,   2054
PEECE = 1*1
*Luc. You must needs haue the(m) with a cod-peece (Ma-|(dam)   1028
Vnlesse you haue a cod-peece to stick pins on.   1031

PEEUISH = 2
   Duk. No, trust me, She is peeuish, sullen, froward,   1137
   Thu. Why this it is, to be a peeuish Girle,   2093
PENCE = *1
   *with you presently; where, for one shot of fiue pence,   880
PENETRATE = 1
   Could penetrate her vncompassionate Sire;   1301
PENITENCE = 1
   By Penitence th'Eternalls wrath's appeas'd: 2207
PENITENTIALL = 1
   With bitter fasts, with penitentiall grones,   783
PENNANCE = 4
   My pennance is, to call *Lucetta* backe   218
   I haue done pennance for contemning Loue,   781
   As he, in pennance wander'd through the Forrest: 2082
   Come *Protheus*, 'tis your pennance, but to heare   2297
PENTECOST = 1
   Sil. How tall was she? | *Iul*. About my stature: for at *Pentecost*,   1978
PEOPLED = 1
   I better brooke then flourishing peopled Townes: 2124
PERCEIUD = 2
   Val. Are all these things perceiu'd in me?   427
   Speed. They are all perceiu'd without ye.   428
PERCEIUE = 6*2
   Sp. Well, I perceiue I must be faine to beare with you.   123
   Pro. Why? could'st thou perceiue so much from her?   135
   Sp. Sir, I could perceiue nothing at all from her;   136
   And that thou maist perceiue how well I like it,   337
   Why, doe you not perceiue the iest?   545
   But did you perceiue her earnest?   548
   And that thou maist perceiue my feare of this,   1102
   Ho. I perceiue you delight not in Musique.   1688
PERCHANCE = *1
   Sil. Perchance you think too much of so much pains?   502
PEREMPTORY = 1
   Excuse it not: for I am peremptory.   373
PERFECT = 4
   And how he cannot be a perfect man,   322
   For since the substance of your perfect selfe   1748
   Her haire is *Aburne*, mine is perfect *Yellow*;   2009
   But Constant, he were perfect; that one error   2237
PERFECTED = 1
   And perfected by the swift course of time: 325
PERFECTION = 5
   To cloath mine age with Angel-like perfection: 716
   Her true perfection, or my false transgression?   852
   Of such diuine perfection as Sir *Protheus*.   988
   And feed vpon the shadow of perfection.   1247
   A Linguist, and a man of such perfection,   1603
PERFECTIONS = 1
   But when I looke on her perfections,   866
PERHAPS = 1
   If hap'ly won, perhaps a haplesse gaine;   36
PERIOD = 1
   Sil. A pretty period: well: I ghesse the sequell;   506
PERISH = 1
   Which cannot perish hauing thee aboarde,   147

PERIURD = 2
  Thou subtile, periur'd, false, disloyall man: 1719
  I doe detest false periur'd *Protheus*:   2160
PERIURED = 1
  Is periured to the bosome? *Protheus*   2193
PERIURIE = 1
  Prouokes me to this three-fold periurie.   934
PERIURY = 3
  For *Thesus* periury, and vniust flight;   1989
  Descended into periury, to loue me,   2170
  How oft hast thou with periury cleft the roote?   2229
PERPLEXITIE = *1
  *perplexitie, yet did not this cruell-hearted Curre shedde   601
PERRYWIG = 1
  Ile get me such a coulour'd Perrywig: 2011
PERSEUERS = 1
  Du. I, and peruersly, she perseuers so: 1474
PERSON = 1
  And yet she takes exceptions at your person.   2044
PERSWADE = 1
  Valentine. | Cease to perswade, my louing *Protheus*;   3
PERSWADED = 1
  Could haue perswaded me: now I dare not say   2190
PERSWASION = 1
  Where you may temper her, by your perswasion,   1511
PERUERSLY = 1
  Du. I, and peruersly, she perseuers so: 1474
PERUSE = 2
  Lu. Peruse this paper Madam.   187
  Iul. Madam, please you peruse this Letter;   1942
PESTILENCE = *1
  *to walke alone like one that had the pestilence: 416
PETTY = 1
  1.*Out.* And I, for such like petty crimes as these.   1598
PEZANT = 2
  How now you whor-son pezant,   1863
  Du. Why then | She's fled vnto that pezant, *Valentine*;   2078
PHAETON = 1
  Why *Phaeton* (for thou art *Merops* sonne)   1222
PHYSICIAN = *1
  *not an eye that sees you, but is a Physician to comment | on your
  Malady.   434
PIBBLE = *1
  *one teare: he is a stone, a very pibble stone, and has no   602
PICTURE = 7
  'Tis but her picture I haue yet beheld,   864
  Vouchsafe me yet your Picture for my loue,   1745
  The Picture that is hanging in your chamber: 1746
  I claime the promise for her heauenly Picture: 1908
  Sil. Oh: he sends you for a Picture? | *Iul.* I, Madam.   1936
  Sil. Vrsula, bring my Picture there,   1938
  Here is her Picture: let me see, I thinke   2004
PILGRIMAGE = 1
  He ouer-taketh in his pilgrimage.   1005
PILGRIME = 1
  Iul. A true-deuoted Pilgrime is not weary   984

PILLORIE = *1
  *he had bin executed: I haue stood on the Pillorie for   1851
PILS = 1
  Pro. When I was sick, you gaue me bitter pils,   802
PIN = 2
  Sp. From a pound to a pin? fold it ouer and ouer,   112
  Luc. A round hose (Madam) now's not worth a pin   1030
PINCHD = 1
  And pinch'd the lilly-tincture of her face,   1976
PINED = 1
  Pitty the dearth that I haue pined in,   991
PINFOLD = 1
  Pro. You mistake; I meane the pound, a Pinfold.   111
PINS = 1
  Vnlesse you haue a cod-peece to stick pins on.   1031
PISSING = *1
  *had not bin there (blesse the marke) a pissing while, but   1839
PITTIES = 1
  Pro. Oh, I: and pitties them.   2067
PITTY = 8*1
  *more pitty in him then a dogge: a Iew would haue wept   603
  Pitty the dearth that I haue pined in,   991
  Egl. Madam, I pitty much your grieuances,   1807
  Iul. I cannot choose but pitty her.   1898
  Pro. Wherefore should'st thou pitty her?   1899
  'Tis pitty Loue, should be so contrary: 1904
  Alas, poore foole, why doe I pitty him   1914
  Because I loue him, I must pitty him.   1917
  'Twere pitty two such friends should be long foes.   2244
PLACD = 1
  Which, since I know they vertuously are plac'd,   1808
PLACE = 2*2
  And you an officer fit for the place: 198
  *vndon till hee be hang'd, nor neuer welcome to a place,   876
  *I pray thee out with't, and place it for her chiefe vertue.   1398
  By the Hangmans boyes in the market place,   1875
PLAGUES = 1
  Which heauen and fortune still rewards with plagues.   1801
PLAID = 2
  And I haue plaid the Sheepe in loosing him.   77
  When all our Pageants of delight were plaid,   1980
PLAIES = 1
  Ho. Why, my pretty youth? | *Iu.* He plaies false (father.)   1681
PLAINE = 1
  And that my loue may appeare plaine and free,   2208
PLAY = 3*2
  Ho. You would haue them alwaies play but one thing.   1692
  Iu. I would alwaies haue one play but one thing.   1693
  Lau. When a mans seruant shall play the Curre with   1822
  Our youth got me to play the womans part,   1981
  For I did play a lamentable part.   1987
PLEAD = 3
  Lu. To plead for loue, deserues more fee, then hate.   201
  To plead for that, which I would not obtaine;   1921
  Plead a new state in thy vn-riual'd merit,   2271
PLEADE = 1
  Pro. Sir *Thurio*, feare not you, I will so pleade,   1703

PLEASD = 2*1
*Lu. She makes it stra(n)ge, but she would be best pleas'd   262
I feare me he will scarce be pleas'd with all.   1042
Is nor of heauen, nor earth; for these are pleas'd: 2206
PLEASE = 13*2
*Lu. Please you repeat their names, ile shew my minde,   160
Iu. Come, come, wilt please you goe. Exeunt.   299
Pan. To morrow, may it please you, Don Alphonso,   341
*Pro. May't please your Lordship, 'tis a word or two   354
Please you deliberate a day or two.   375
(Please you command) a thousand times as much: | And yet---   504
Val. Please you, Ile write your Ladiship another.   520
And if it please you, so: if not: why so: 522
Val. If it please me, (Madam?) what then?   523
Sil. Why if it please you, take it for your labour;   524
Where (if it please you) you may intercept him.   1112
Val. Please it your Grace, there is a Messenger   1121
Iu. In what you please, ile doe what I can.   1861
Iul. Madam, please you peruse this Letter;   1942
Val. Please you, Ile tell you, as we passe along,   2295
PLEASURE = 2
Sil. I wait vpon his pleasure: Come Sir Thurio,   768
It is your pleasure to command me in.   1780
PLOT = 2
As thou hast lent me wit, to plot this drift. | Exit.   972
My selfe am one made priuy to the plot.   1081
PLOTTED = 1
Plotted, and 'greed on for my happinesse.   838
PLUCKE = *1
*Teeme of horse shall not plucke that from me: nor who   1335
PLURALL = 1
Then piurall faith, which is too much by one: 2173
POESIE = 1
Du. I, much is the force of heauen-bred Poesie.   1518
POETS = 1
For Orpheus Lute, was strung with Poets sinewes,   1524
POORE = 11
Poore wounded name: my bosome, as a bed,   274
Poore forlorne Protheus, passionate Protheus: 284
Alas, this parting strikes poore Louers dumbe. | Exeunt.   589
With falsehood, cowardize, and poore discent: 1478
My riches, are these poore habiliments,   1559
Prouided that you do no outrages | On silly women, or poore
passengers.   1617
Alas poore Protheus, thou hast entertain'd   1912
Alas, poore foole, why doe I pitty him   1914
Poore Gentlewoman, my Master wrongs her much.   1962
That my poore Mistris moued therewithall,   1991
Alas (poore Lady) desolate, and left;   1995
POSSESSION = 1
Take but possession of her, with a Touch: 2257
POSSESSIONS = 3
(Onely for his possessions are so huge)   830
For me, and my possessions she esteemes not.   1148
Thu. Considers she my Possessions?   2066
POSSEST = 1
So much of bad already hath possest them.   1276

POSSIBLE = 1
   Iul. As little by such toyes, as may be possible: 239
POSSIBLY = 1
   Pro. When possibly I can, I will returne.   570
POST = 1*1
   Receiuing them from such a worthlesse post. *Exit*.   151
   *ship'd, and thou art to post after with oares; what's the   627
POSTERNE = 1
   Out at the Posterne by the Abbey wall;   2036
POTENTATES = 1
   With Commendation from great Potentates,   729
POUND = 2*2
   Pro. Nay, in that you are astray: 'twere best pound | you.   107
   Sp. Nay Sir, lesse then a pound shall serue me for car-|rying your
   Letter.   109
   Pro. You mistake; I meane the pound, a Pinfold.   111
   Sp. From a pound to a pin? fold it ouer and ouer,   112
POWER = 1
   Haue some malignant power vpon my life: 1308
POWRE = 1
   And ev'n that Powre which gaue me first my oath   933
POX = *1
   Sp. Why didst not tell me sooner? 'pox of your loue | Letters.   1440
PRACTISE = 2
   There shall he practise Tilts, and Turnaments;   332
   Th. And thy aduice, this night, ile put in practise: 1535
PRACTISES = 1
   3.Out. No, we detest such vile base practises.   1619
PRACTISING = 1
   For practising to steale away a Lady,   1594
PRAISE = 4
   It is mine, or *Valentines* praise?   851
   Flatter, and praise, commend, extoll their graces: 1171
   Sp. Item, she will often praise her liquor.   1406
   To praise his faith, which I would haue disprais'd.   1923
PRAISED = 1
   I will; for good things should be praised.   ·1408
PRAISES = 2
   Comes all the praises that I now bestow.)   722
   Val. O flatter me: for Loue delights in praises.   801
PRAISING = 1
   Which must be done, by praising me as much   1500
PRAY = 16*2
   Val. And on a loue-booke pray for my successe?   22
   Pro. Vpon some booke I loue, I'le pray for thee.   23
   Did in your name receiue it: pardon the fault I pray.   193
   And pray her to a fault, for which I chid her.   206
   He is in hast, therefore I pray you go.   391
   Luc. Pray heau'n he proue so when you come to him.   1054
   Duke. Sir *Thurio*, giue vs leaue (I pray) a while,   1070
   Val. When would you vse it? pray sir, tell me that.   1192
   I pray thee let me feele thy cloake vpon me.   1206
   Lau. Why Sir, Ile strike nothing: I pray you.   1273
   If so: I pray thee breath it in mine eare,   1309
   Val. I pray thee *Launce*, and if thou seest my Boy   1327
   *I pray thee out with't, and place it for her chiefe vertue.   1398
   I pray you why is it?   1652

PRAY *cont.*

Iul. Pray you, where lies Sir *Protheus?* | *Ho.* Marry, at my house:	1762
Gentlewoman, good day: I pray you be my meane	1929
Sil. I pray thee let me looke on that againe.	1946
Therefore I pray you stand, not to discourse,	2088

PRAYERS = 1

Commend thy grieuance to my holy prayers,	20

PRECIOUS = 1

For Loue is still most precious in it selfe,	953

PRECISELY = *1

*taught him (euen as one would say precisely, thus I	1826

PREFER = 3

Pro. Haue I not reason to prefer mine owne?	810
Val. And I will help thee to prefer her to:	811
I haue accesse my owne loue to prefer.	1628

PREFERD = 1

Whose soueraignty so oft thou hast preferd,	944

PREFERMENT = 1

Put forth their Sonnes, to seeke preferment out.	309

PRESENCE = 1*1

Repaire me, with thy presence, *Siluia*:	2132
Iul. And me, when he approcheth to your presence.	2153

PRESENT = 2*3

Speed. Your owne present folly, and her passing de-|formitie:	468
Duk. But she did scorne a present that I sent her,	1161
*Masters command, hee must carry for a present to his | Lady.	1700
*would teach a dog) I was sent to deliuer him, as a pre-|sent	1827
currish thanks is good enough for such a present.	1869

PRESENTLY = 12*2

And presently, all humbled kisse the Rod?	213
*Lions: when you fasted, it was presently after dinner:	423
I will send him hither to you presently.	736
And then Ile presently attend you.	844
*with you presently; where, for one shot of fiue pence,	880
Now presently Ile giue her father notice	965
And presently goe with me to my chamber	1058
Come; answere not: but to it presently,	1064
And this way comes he with it presently.	1111
Let vs into the City presently	1537
That presently you hie you home to bed:	1718
And will imploy thee in some seruice presently.	1860
Go presently, and take this Ring with thee,	1890
But mount you presently, and meete with me	2089

PRESSE = 1

A pack of sorrowes, which would presse you downe	1089

PRESUME = 1

Dare you presume to harbour wanton lines?	195

PRETENCE = 1

Hath made me publisher of this pretence.	1116

PRETENDED = 1

Of their disguising and pretended flight:	966

PRETTILY = 1

And yet I will not, sith so prettily	286

PRETTY = 2

Sil. A pretty period: well: I ghesse the sequell;	506
Ho. Why, my pretty youth? | *Iu.* He plaies false (father.)	1681

PREUAILD = 2
Pro. You haue preuail'd (my Lord) if I can doe it   1492
Duke. Thou hast preuaild, I pardon them and thee: 2285
PREUENT = 1
Iul. Not like a woman, for I would preuent   1015
PRICKS = 1
My dutie pricks me on to vtter that   1077
PRIDE = 1
And may I say to thee, this pride of hers   1141
PRIMA *l.*1 395 1067 1545 2026 = 5
PRIME = 1
Loosing his verdure, euen in the prime,   53
PRIMUS *l.*1 = 1
PRINCE = 1
Know (worthy Prince) Sir *Valentine* my friend   1079
PRINCIPALITIE = 1
Yet let her be a principalitie,   805
PRINT = 2
All this I speak in print, for in print I found it.   559
PRISON = 1
That to close prison he commanded her,   1305
PRISONERS = *1
*Val. Nay sure, I thinke she holds them prisoners stil.   742
PRIUATE = 1
The priuate wound is deepest: oh time, most accurst.   2196
PRIUILEDGE = 1
Is priuiledge for thy departure hence.   1230
PRIUY = 1
My selfe am one made priuy to the plot.   1081
PRIZE = 3
Iul. And I mine. | *Out-l*. A prize: a prize: a prize.   2246
PRO = 131*18
PROCEED = 2
Muse not that I thus sodainly proceed;   366
Which I was much vnwilling to proceed in,   496
PROCEEDE = 1
**keepe shut: Now, of another thing shee may, and that | cannot I helpe.
Well, proceede.   1412
PROCEEDING = 2
By some slie tricke, blunt *Thurio's* dull proceeding.   970
And heere an Engine fit for my proceeding,   1208
PROCEEDINGS = 1
And afterward determine our proceedings.   1543
PROCLAMATION = 1*1
*Lau. Sir, there is a proclamation, y you are vanished.   1286
(According to our Proclamation) gon?   1458
PRODIGIOUS = *1
**fault: I haue receiu'd my proportion, like the prodigious   595
PROFFERER = 1
Which they would haue the profferer construe, I.   210
PROMISD = 1
Duk. But she I meane, is promis'd by her friends   1175
PROMISE = 1
I claime the promise for her heauenly Picture: 1908
PROOFE = 1
Sp. Such another proofe will make me cry baa.   97

PROPER = *1
*3.*Out*. I by my beard will we: for he is a proper man.   1556
PROPHAND = 1
Though his false finger haue prophan'd the Ring,   1957
PROPORTION = *1
*fault: I haue receiu'd my proportion, like the prodigious   595
PROTEST = 2
When I protest true loyalty to her,   1631
To thinke vpon her woes, I doe protest   1965
PROTESTATION = 1
Here is a coile with protestation: 259
PROTESTATIONS = 1
I know they are stuft with protestations,   1950
PROTHEUS see also Pro. = 60*10
Valentine: Protheus, and Speed.   2
Valentine. | Cease to perswade, my louing *Protheus*;   3
Thinke on thy *Protheus*, when thou (hap'ly) seest   15
Val. Sweet *Protheus*, no: Now let vs take our leaue: 60
Sp. Sir *Protheus:* 'saue you: saw you my Master?   74
Iu. What think'st thou of the gentle *Protheus*?   167
Iu. Why not on *Protheus*, as of all the rest?   173
Lu. Sir *Valentines* page: & sent I think from *Protheus*;   191
Lu. Indeede I bid the base for *Protheus*.   257
And here is writ, *Loue wounded Protheus*.   273
But twice, or thrice, was *Protheus* written downe: 277
Poore forlorne Protheus, passionate Protheus: 284
Enter Antonio and Panthino. Protheus.   301
Pan. 'Twas of his Nephew *Protheus*, your Sonne.   304
He said, that *Protheus*, your sonne, was meet;   314
Ant. Good company: with them shall *Protheus* go: 345
Pan. Sir *Protheus*, your Fathers call's for you,   390
*learn'd (like Sir *Protheus*) to wreath your Armes like a   414
*to haue, when you chidde at Sir *Protheus*, for going vn- | garter'd.   465
Enter Protheus, Iulia, Panthion.   567
Panth. Sir *Protheus*: you are staid for.   587
*Sonne, and am going with Sir *Protheus* to the Imperialls   596
Enter Valentine, Siluia, Thurio, Speed, Duke, Protheus.   654
Yet hath Sir *Protheus* (for that's his name)   717
Val. Welcome, deer *Protheus*: Mistris, I beseech you   750
Val. I *Protheus*, but that life is alter'd now,   780
O gentle *Protheus*, Loue's a mighty Lord,   788
Val. Pardon me (*Protheus*) all I can is nothing,   819
Good *Protheus* goe with me to my chamber,   839
Enter Protheus *solus.*   929
A iourney to my louing *Protheus*.   982
Of such diuine perfection as Sir *Protheus*.   988
Luc. Better forbeare, till *Protheus* make returne.   989
If *Protheus* like your iourney, when you come,   1040
Warrant me welcome to my *Protheus*.   1046
But truer starres did gouerne *Protheus* birth,   1049
Enter Duke, Thurio, Protheus, Valentine, | *Launce, Speed.*   1068
Now tell me *Protheus*, what's your will with me?   1072
Duke. Protheus, I thank thee for thine honest care,   1091
Enter Duke, Thurio, Protheus.   1446
How now sir *Protheus*, is your countriman   1457
Protheus, the good conceit I hold of thee,   1463
Du. And *Protheus*, we dare trust you in this kinde,   1502

PROTHEUS *cont*.

Therefore, sweet *Protheus*, my direction-giuer,	1536
Enter Protheus, Thurio, Iulia, Host, Musitian, Siluia.	1624
Th. How now, sir *Protheus*, are you crept before vs?	1642
But Host, doth this Sir *Protheus*, that we talke on,	1694
Sil. Sir *Protheus*, as I take it.	1713
Pro. Sir *Protheus* (gentle Lady) and your Seruant.	1714
Iul. Pray you, where lies Sir *Protheus*? | *Ho*. Marry, at my house:	1762
Enter Launce, Protheus, Iulia, Siluia.	1821
Alas poore *Protheus*, thou hast entertain'd	1912
Sil. From whom? | *Iul*. From my Master, Sir *Protheus*, Madam.	1934
Sil. Belike she thinks that *Protheus* hath forsook her?	1967
Enter Thurio, Protheus, Iulia, Duke.	2041
Th. Sir *Protheus*, what saies *Siluia* to my suit?	2042
Du. How now sir *Protheus*; how now *Thurio*?	2072
Enter Valentine, Protheus, Siluia, Iulia, Duke, Thurio, | Out-lawes.	2120
Rather then haue false *Protheus* reskue me:	2156
I doe detest false periur'd *Protheus*:	2160
Sil. When *Protheus* cannot loue, where he's belou'd:	2166
Sil. All men but *Protheus*.	2177
Is periured to the bosome? *Protheus*	2193
Oh *Protheus*, let this habit make thee blush.	2230
Come *Protheus*, 'tis your pennance, but to heare	2297
Valentine. | *Protheus. the two Gentlemen*.	2303
Anthonio: father to Protheus.	2305
Launce: the like to Protheus.	2311
Iulia: beloued of Protheus.	2313

PROUD = 2

And of so great a fauor growing proud,	815
Sp. Item, she is proud. | *La*. Out with that too:	1399

PROUE = 5*3

Val. So, by your circumstance, I feare you'll proue.	41
Pro. It shall goe hard but ile proue it by another.	89
*I feare she'll proue as hard to you in telling your minde.	139
I cannot now proue constant to my selfe,	960
Luc. Pray heau'n he proue so when you come to him.	1054
La. More haire then wit: it may be ile proue it: The	1420
Pro. Longer then I proue loyall to your Grace,	1466
Vnlesse I proue false traitor to my selfe.	1926

PROUERBE = *1

La. And thereof comes the prouerbe: (*Blessing of | your heart, you brew good Ale*.)	1367

PROUES = 2

Sp. This proues me still a Sheepe.	86
Grand-mother: this proues that thou canst not read.	1361

PROUIDE = 1

You must prouide to bottome it on me:	1499

PROUIDED = 2

Pro. My Lord I cannot be so soone prouided,	374
Prouided that you do no outrages | On silly women, or poore passengers.	1617

PROUOKES = 1

Prouokes me to this three-fold periurie.	934

PROWD = 1

Prowd, disobedient, stubborne, lacking duty,	1138

PUBLISHER = 1

Hath made me publisher of this pretence.	1116

PUDDINGS = *1
*sat in the stockes, for puddings he hath stolne, otherwise 1850
PULING = *1
*feares robbing: to speake puling, like a beggar at Hal-|low-Masse: 420
PUNISHD = 1
Whose high emperious thoughts haue punish'd me 782
PUPILL = 1
He being her Pupill, to become her Tutor. 529
PUPPET = *1
*Speed. Oh excellent motion; oh exceeding Puppet: 487
PUPPY = *1
*a puppy: one that I sau'd from drowning, when three or 1824
PURE = 6
The water, Nectar, and the Rocks pure gold. 826
His teares, pure messengers, sent from his heart, 1052
My Herald Thoughts, in thy pure bosome rest-them, 1214
But neither bended knees, pure hands held vp, 1299
Pro. One (Lady) if you knew his pure hearts truth, 1711
Vpon whose Graue thou vow'dst pure chastitie: 1791
PURPOSD = 1
And oftentimes haue purpos'd to forbid 1095
PURPOSE = 3
Loue lend me wings, to make my purpose swift 971
'Tis so: and heere's the Ladder for the purpose. 1221
But to the purpose: for we cite our faults, 1599
PURSE = 2*2
Sp. And yet it cannot ouer-take your slow purse. 128
*Sp. Open your purse, that the money, and the matter 131
*she is slow of: of her purse, shee shall not, for that ile 1411
Here youth: there is my purse; I giue thee this 1997
PUT = 3*1
Put forth their Sonnes, to seeke preferment out. 309
*his hose; and you, beeing in loue, cannot see to put on | your hose. 470
Th. And thy aduice, this night, ile put in practise: 1535
Thu. 'Tis true, such Pearles as put out Ladies eyes, 2054
QUAINTLY see also queintly = 1
Val. Why then a Ladder quaintly made of Cords 1186
QUALIFIE = 1
But qualifie the fires extreame rage, 997
QUALITIES = 2*1
Is full of Vertue, Bounty, Worth, and Qualities 1134
*hath more qualities then a Water-Spaniell, which is 1340
Are men endu'd with worthy qualities: 2280
QUALITY = 1
As we doe in our quality much want. 1604
QUARTA l.653 1820 2119 = 3
QUARTUS l.1545 = 1
QUEENE = 1
For me (by this pale queene of night I sweare) 1724
QUEINTLY = 1
Sil. Yes, yes: the lines are very queintly writ, 513
QUELL = 1
The least whereof would quell a louers hope: 1637
QUENCH = 2
As seeke to quench the fire of Loue with words. 995
Luc. I doe not seeke to quench your Loues hot fire, 996

QUICKE = 3
   Pro. Beshrew me, but you haue a quicke wit.   127
   More then quicke words, doe moue a womans minde.   1160
   Ho. You haue a quicke eare.   1686
QUICKELY = 1
   But *Valentine* being gon, Ile quickely crosse   969
QUICKLY = 1*1
   Sil. A fine volly of words, gentleme(n), & quickly shot off   684
   You would quickly learne to know him by his voice.   1712
QUINTA *l.*871 = 1
QUINTUS *l.*2026 = 1
QUIPS = 1
   And notwithstanding all her sodaine quips,   1636
QUITE = 1
   Is by a newer obiect quite forgotten,   850
QUOAT = 2
   Thu. And how quoat you my folly?   672
   Val. I quoat it in your Ierkin.   673
QUOTH = *3
   *(quoth I) you meane to whip the dog: I marry doe I   1845
   *(quoth he) you doe him the more wrong (quoth I) 'twas   1846
RAGE = 2
   But qualifie the fires extreame rage,   997
   (Thou know'st) being stop'd, impatiently doth rage: 1001
RAGGED = 1
   Vnto a ragged, fearefull, hanging Rocke,   281
RAGING = 1
   And throw it thence into the raging Sea.   282
RAIGNES = 1
   Lu. Lord, Lord: to see what folly raignes in vs.   168
RAILD = 1
   Forsworne my company, and rail'd at me,   1450
RAKE = 1
   Pro. Sweet Lady, let me rake it from the earth.   1740
RANDOME = 1
   I writ at randome, very doubtfully.   501
RANSOME = 1
   Be a sufficient Ransome for offence,   2200
RARE = 2
   Some rare note-worthy obiect in thy trauaile.   16
   With Triumphes, Mirth, and rare solemnity.   2288
RASHNESSE = 1
   (A rashnesse that I euer yet haue shun'd)   1099
RATHER = 5*1
   I rather would entreat thy company,   8
   Thus (for my duties sake) I rather chose   1086
   But rather to beget more loue in you.   1166
   Val. And why not death, rather then liuing torment?   1240
   For I had rather winke, then looke on them.   2055
   Rather then haue false *Protheus* reskue me: 2156
RAUELL = 1
   Least it should rauell, and be good to none,   1498
RAYMENT = 1
   Such an immodest rayment; if shame liue | In a disguise of loue?   2232
REACH = 2
   Iu. And why not you? | *Lu.* I cannot reach so high.   244
   Wilt thou reach stars, because they shine on thee?   1225

READ = 6*1
Sil. And when it's writ: for my sake read it ouer,	521
Pro. Enough; I read your fortune in your eye:	795
Sp. Let me read them?	1355
La. Fie on thee Iolt-head, thou canst not read. | *Sp.* Thou lyest: I can.	1356
Grand-mother: this proues that thou canst not read.	1361
La. Well: that fault may be mended with a break-|fast: read on.	1388
Read ouer *Iulia's* heart, (thy first best Loue)	2167

READINESSE = 1
To morrow be in readinesse, to goe,	372

READING = *2
Ant. How now? What Letter are you reading there?	353
La. Now will he be swing'd for reading my Letter;	1442

READY = *1
Lu. Madam: dinner is ready: and your father staies.	290

REASON = 7*1
Iul. Your reason? | *Lu.* I haue no other but a womans reason:	175
Speed. Nay: I was riming: 'tis you y haue the reason.	535
Pro. Haue I not reason to prefer mine owne?	810
That makes me reasonlesse, to reason thus?	853
And that's the reason I loue him so little.	861
There is no reason, but I shall be blinde.	867
Lest it should burne aboue the bounds of reason.	998

REASONING = 1
Val. How now Sir? | What are you reasoning with your selfe?	533

REASONLESSE = 1
That makes me reasonlesse, to reason thus?	853

REASONS = 1
And that hath dazel'd my reasons light:	865

RECALLD = 1
And let them be recall'd from their Exile:	2282

RECEIUD = 1*1
*fault: I haue receiu'd my proportion, like the prodigious	595
Pro. But she receiu'd my dog? | *La.* No indeede did she not:	1870

RECEIUE = 2
Did in your name receiue it: pardon the fault I pray.	193
And once againe, I doe receiue thee honest;	2204

RECEIUES = 1
What maintenance he from his friends receiues,	370

RECEIUING = 1
Receiuing them from such a worthlesse post. *Exit.*	151

RECKON = *1
*not welcome. I reckon this alwaies, that a man is neuer	875

RECK-LESSE = 1
Then for the loue of reck-lesse *Siluia.*	2096

RECORD = 1
Tune my distresses, and record my woes.	2127

RECOUER = 1
If we recouer that, we are sure enough. *Exeunt.*	2039

RECOURSE = 1
That no man hath recourse to her by night.	1181

RED = *1
*Male-content: to rellish a Loue-song, like a *Robin*-red-|breast:	415

REFORMED = 1
They are reformed, ciuill, full of good,	2283

REFUSD = 1
To carry that, which I would haue refus'd;	1922

REGARD = 2
The honor, and regard of such a father.   710
Regard thy danger, and along with me.   1326
REGARDED = 1
To be regarded in her sun-bright eye.   1157
REGARDING = 1
Neither regarding that she is my childe,   1139
REHEARSE = 1*1
*mine, twice or thrice in that last Article: rehearse that | once more.   1417
Val. For that which now torments me to rehearse;   1572
REIOYCE = *1
*Ile after, to reioyce in the boyes correctio(n). *Exeunt.*   1444
RELLISH = *1
*Male-content: to rellish a Loue-song, like a *Robin*-red- | breast: 415
RELYING = 1
Pro. As one relying on your Lordships will,   363
REMEDY = 1
Iul. I must where is no remedy.   569
REMEMBER = 1*1
*think'st not of this now: nay, I remember the tricke you   1853
To binde him to remember my good will: 1919
REMEMBRANCE = 2
Keepe this remembrance for thy *Iulia's* sake.   572
So the remembrance of my former Loue   849
REMEMBRING = 1
Remembring that my Loue to her is dead.   957
REMISSION = 1
And aske remission, for my folly past.   219
REMNANT = 1
And where I thought the remnant of mine age   1143
REMORSE-FULL = 1
Valiant, wise, remorse-full, well accomplish'd.   1783
REND = 1
For whose deare sake, thou didst then rend thy faith   2168
REPAIRE = 2
Loue doth to her eyes repaire,   1670
Repaire me, with thy presence, *Siluia*:   2132
REPEALE = 2
When she for thy repeale was suppliant,   1304
Cancell all grudge, repeale thee home againe,   2270
REPEAT = *1
Lu. Please you repeat their names, ile shew my minde,   160
REPENT = 2
I kil'd a man, whose death I much repent,   1573
1.*Out*. Why nere repent it, if it were done so;   1576
REPENTANCE = 1
Who by Repentance is not satisfied,   2205
REPLY = 1
Or else for want of idle time, could not againe reply,   556
REPORT = 2
Because we know (on *Valentines* report)   1504
With goodly shape; and by your owne report,   1602
REPORTEST = *1
Lau. A notable Lubber: as thou reportest him to | bee.   913
REPOSE = 1
Vpon whose faith and honor, I repose.   1796

REPULSE = 1
Take no repulse, what euer she doth say,   1169
REPUTATION = 2
    While other men, of slender reputation   308
    My goods, my Lands, my reputation,   1062
REPUTE = 1
    But tell me (wench) how will the world repute me   1034
REPUTED = 2
    And not without desert so well reputed.   707
    As may beseeme some well reputed Page.   1018
REQUEST = 3
    And did request me, to importune you   315
    Silu. I, I: you writ them Sir, at my request,   517
    I am so farre from granting thy request,   1725
REQUITAL = *1
    *In requital whereof, henceforth, carry your letters your   144
REQUITE = 1
    Which to requite, command me while I liue.   1092
RESEMBLETH = 1
    Oh, how this spring of loue resembleth   386
RESKEW = 1
    To hazard life, and reskew you from him,   2142
RESKUE = 1
    Rather then haue false *Protheus* reskue me: 2156
RESOLUD = 2
    I am resolu'd, that thou shalt spend some time   368
    I now am full resolu'd to take a wife,   1145
RESOLUED = 1
    And he wants wit, that wants resolued will,   941
RESORT = 4
    Iul. Of all the faire resort of Gentlemen,   157
    And kept seuerely from resort of men,   1177
    Val. Why then I would resort to her by night.   1179
    Often resort vnto this Gentlewoman?   1695
RESPECT = 3*1
    Iu. If you respect them; best to take them vp.   293
    Val. Win her with gifts, if she respect not words,   1158
    Sp. Item, shee is not to be fasting in respect of her | breath.   1386
    (Though you respect not aught your seruant doth)   2141
RESPECTIUE = 1
    But I can make respectiue in my selfe?   2015
RESPECTS = 3
    Since she respects my Mistris loue so much.   2002
    What should it be that he respects in her,   2014
    Pro. In Loue, | Who respects friend?   2175
REST = 7
    Iu. Why not on *Protheus*, as of all the rest?   173
    Iul. Why he, of all the rest, hath neuer mou'd me.   180
    Lu. Yet he, of all the rest, I thinke best loues ye.   181
    And there Ile rest, as after much turmoile   1012
    Therefore, aboue the rest, we parley to you: 1606
    Which, with our selues, all rest at thy dispose. *Exeunt.*   1622
    Send to me in the morning, and ile send it: | And so, good rest.   1756
REST-THEM = 1
    My Herald Thoughts, in thy pure bosome rest-them,   1214
RETURN = 1
    Iul. If you turne not: you will return the sooner: 571

RETURND = 1
There: take the paper: see it be return'd,   199
RETURNE = 6
Or else returne no more into my sight.   200
Pro. When possibly I can, I will returne.   570
Luc. Better forbeare, till *Protheus* make returne.   989
Returne, returne, and make thy loue amends: 1723
Or nere returne againe into my sight.   1879
REUENGD = 1
Ile after; more to be reueng'd on *Eglamoure*,   2095
REUENGE = 2
As in reuenge of thy ingratitude,   270
For in reuenge of my contempt of loue,   785
REUERST = 1
(Which vn-reuerst stands in effectuall force)   1293
REUOLT = 1
And cannot soone reuolt, and change your minde.   1506
REWARDS = 1
Which heauen and fortune still rewards with plagues.   1801
RICH = 3
Iu. What think'st thou of the rich *Mercatio*?   .   165
And I as rich in hauing such a Iewell   824
Were rich and honourable: besides, the gentleman   1133
RICHES = 1
My riches, are these poore habiliments,   1559
RIFLE = 1
If not: we'll make you sit, and rifle you.   1550
RIGHT = 1
Who should be trusted, when ones right hand   2192
RIME = 1
Iul. Some loue of yours, hath writ to you in Rime.   236
RIMES = 1
By walefull Sonnets, whose composed Rimes   1516
RIMING = *1
Speed. Nay: I was riming: 'tis you y haue the reason.   535
RING = 8*2
Go presently, and take this Ring with thee,   1890
Pro. Well: giue her that Ring, and therewithall   1906
This Ring I gaue him, when he parted from me,   1918
Iul. Madam, he sends your Ladiship this Ring.   1953
Though his false finger haue prophan'd the Ring,   1957
Iul. O good sir, my master charg'd me to deliuer a ring   2214
Pro. Where is that ring? boy? | *Iul.* Heere 'tis: this is it.   2216
Pro. How? let me see. | Why this is the ring I gaue to *Iulia*.   2218
This is the ring you sent to *Siluia*.   2221
Pro. But how cam'st thou by this ring? at my depart | I gaue this vnto
Iulia.   2222
RIPE = 1
His head vn-mellowed, but his Iudgement ripe;   720
RISING = 1
Vpon the rising of the Mountaine foote   2090
RIUALD = 1
Plead a new state in thy vn-riual'd merit,   2271
RIUALL = 3
My foolish Riuall that her Father likes   829
For 'tis thy riuall: O thou sencelesse forme,   2018
Thurio: a foolish riuall to Valentine.   2306

RIUER = *1
*and the Seruice, and the tide: why man, if the Riuer   644
ROAD = 2
Once more adieu: my Father at the Road   57
I must vnto the Road, to dis-embarque   842
ROBBING = *1
*feares robbing: to speake puling, like a' beggar at Hal-|low-Masse: 420
ROBIN = 1
3.*Out.* By the bare scalpe of *Robin Hoods* fat Fryer,   1582
ROBIN-REDBREAST = *1
*Male-content: to rellish a Loue-song, like a *Robin*-red-|breast: 415
ROCKE = 1
Vnto a ragged, fearefull, hanging Rocke,   281
ROCKS = 1
The water, Nectar, and the Rocks pure gold.   826
ROD = 1
And presently, all humbled kisse the Rod?   213
ROOTE = 2
Disdaine to roote the Sommer-swelling flowre,   816
How oft hast thou with periury cleft the roote?   2229
ROSES = 1
The ayre hath staru'd the roses in her cheekes,   1975
ROUGH = 1
And make rough winter euerlastingly.   817
ROUND = 1
Luc. A round hose (Madam) now's not worth a pin   1030
ROUNDER = *1
Thu. Ile weare a Boote, to make it somewhat roun-|(der.   2047
ROYALL = 2
Attends the Emperour in his royall Court.   329
Will giue thee time to leaue our royall Court,   1235
RUDE = 1
Val. Ruffian: let goe that rude vnciuill touch,   2184
RUFFIAN = 1
Val. Ruffian: let goe that rude vnciuill touch,   2184
RUINOUS = 1
Lest growing ruinous, the building fall,   2130
RULD = 1
We'll doe thee homage, and be rul'd by thee,   1612
RUMINATE = 1
Iul. Will ye be gon? | *Lu.* That you may ruminate. *Exit.*   202
RUN = 4*2
Pro. Run (boy) run, run, and seeke him out.   1258
La. Thou must run to him; for thou hast staid so long,   1438
3 *Out.* Being nimble footed, he hath out-run vs.   2109
*Fils him with faults: makes him run through all th'sins;   2238
SACRED = 1
Val. No *Valentine* indeed, for sacred *Siluia,*   1281
SACRIFICE = 1
You sacrifice your teares, your sighes, your heart: 1520
SAD = 4
Ant. Tell me *Panthino*, what sad talke was that,   302
Sil. Seruant, you are sad. | *Val.* Indeed, Madam, I seeme so.   662
Sad sighes, deepe grones, nor siluer-shedding teares   1300
Where thou shalt finde me sad, and solitarie.   1910
SADDER = *1
Ho. How now? are you sadder then you were before;   1678

146

SADLY = *1
*when you look'd sadly, it was for want of money: And   424
SAFE = *1
*Duk. I, but the doores be lockt, and keyes kept safe,   1180
SAID = 6*1
   Pro. But what said she? | Sp. I.   114
   *Pro. Come, come, open the matter in briefe; what | said she.   129
   *Pro. Well Sir: here is for your paines: what said she?   133
   Pro. What said she, nothing?   141
   He said, that Protheus, your sonne, was meet;   314
   Val. You haue said Sir. | Thu. I Sir, and done too for this time. 681
   If not, to hide what I haue said to thee,   1805
SAIES = 6*5
   Pro. Ile die on him that saies so but your selfe.   764
   *all the chamber smelt him: out with the dog (saies one)   1840
   *what cur is that (saies another) whip him out (saies the   1841
   *third) hang him vp (saies the Duke.) I hauing bin ac- |quainted   1842
   Pro. And what saies she to my little Iewell?   1867
   *La. Marry she saies your dog was a cur, and tels you   1868
   Th. Sir Protheus, what saies Siluia to my suit?   2042
   Thu. What saies she to my face?   2049
   Pro. She saies it is a faire one.   2050
   Thu. What saies she to my birth?   2063
SAINT = 3
   Val. Euen She; and is she not a heauenly Saint?   797
   La. There: and S.(aint) Nicholas be thy speed.   1363
   Th. Where meete we? | Pro. At Saint Gregories well. | Th. Farewell. 1705
SAIST = 2*2
   My staffe vnderstands me? | Spee. What thou saist?   896
   *Spee. 'Tis well that I get it so: but Launce, how saist   909
   *3.Out. What saist thou? wilt thou be of our consort?   1610
   Iul. She thankes you. | Sil. What sai'st thou?   1959
SAKE = 10*1
   Sil. And when it's writ: for my sake read it ouer,   521
   Keepe this remembrance for thy Iulia's sake.   572
   Wherein I sigh not (Iulia) for thy sake,   578
   Thus (for my duties sake) I rather chose   1086
   And (for your friends sake) will be glad of you;   1510
   Th. Who, Siluia? | Pro. I, Siluia, for your sake.   1647
   *For thy sweet Mistris sake, because thou lou'st her. Fare- |(well. 1998
   Ile vse thee kindly, for thy Mistris sake   2022
   For whose deare sake, thou didst then rend thy faith   2168
   But count the world a stranger for thy sake: 2195
   I now beseech you (for your daughters sake)   2276
SALT = *3
   *couer of the salt, hides the salt, and therefore it is more   1421
   *then the salt; the haire that couers the wit, is more   1422
SALUTE = 1
   Are iournying, to salute the Emperor,   343
SAME = 2
   Iu. Nay, would I were so angred with the same: 264
   What Letter is this same? what's here? to Siluia?   1207
SAND = 1
   As twenty Seas, if all their sand were pearle,   825
SANDS = 2
   Forsake vnsounded deepes, to dance on Sands.   1527
   As full of sorrowes, as the Sea of sands,   1803

SAT = *1
  *sat in the stockes, for puddings he hath stolne, otherwise   1850
SATISFIED = 1
  Who by Repentance is not satisfied,   2205
SAUCIE = 1
  Iu. You (Minion) are too saucie.   252
SAUD = *1
  *a puppy: one that I sau'd from drowning, when three or   1824
SAUE = 1*1
  Sp. Sir *Protheus:* 'saue you: saw you my Master?   74
  **Pro*. Go, go, be gone, to saue your Ship from wrack,   146
SAW = 5
  Sp. Sir *Protheus:* 'saue you: saw you my Master?   74
  Speed. You neuer saw her since she was deform'd.   456
  Val. I haue lou'd her euer since I saw her,   459
  Which of you saw *Eglamoure* of late?   2073
  Du. Saw you my daughter? | *Pro*. Neither.   2076
SAY = 28*8
  Pro. Yet Writers say; as in the sweetest Bud,   46
  Val. And Writers say; as the most forward Bud   49
  Sp. You mistooke Sir: I say she did nod;   117
  And you aske me if she did nod, and I say I.   118
  Iul. But say *Lucetta* (now we are alone)   154
  Iul. To *Iulia:* say, from whom?   188
  Iul. Say, say: who gaue it thee?   190
  Since Maides, in modesty, say no, to that,   209
  Lu. I (Madam) you may say what sights you see;   297
  Val. What figure? | *Speed*. By a Letter, I should say.   540
  What say you to a Letter from your friends | Of much good newes?   700
  Thur. They say that Loue hath not an eye at all.   746
  *till some certaine shot be paid, and the Hostesse say wel-|come.   877
  **Lau*. Aske my dogge, if he say I, it will: if hee say   903
  *no, it will: if hee shake his taile, and say nothing, it | will.   904
  And may I say to thee, this pride of hers   1141
  Take no repulse, what euer she doth say,   1169
  Though nere so blacke, say they haue Angells faces,   1172
  That man that hath a tongue, I say is no man,   1173
  Pro. Sirha, I say forbeare: friend *Valentine*, a word.   1274
  La. That's as much as to say (*Can she so?*)   1370
  **La*. That's as much as to say *Bastard-vertues*: that   1381
  But say this weede her loue from *Valentine*,   1495
  Pro. Say that vpon the altar of her beauty   1519
  Say I, and be the captaine of vs all: 1611
  That you shall say, my cunning drift excels.   1704
  Sil. Say that she be: yet *Valentine* thy friend   1733
  Thy selfe hast lou'd, and I haue heard thee say   1788
  *taught him (euen as one would say precisely, thus I   1826
  *I would haue (as one should say) one that takes vp-|on   1832
  Away, I say: stayest thou to vexe me here;   1880
  For I haue heard him say a thousand times,   1955
  Could haue perswaded me: now I dare not say   2190
  **Val*. Forbeare, forbeare I say: It is my Lord the *Duke*.   2248
SAYES = 1
  Thu. What sayes she to my valour?   2060
SAYING = 2
  Pro. But Pearles are faire; and the old saying is,   2052
  Duke. What meane you by that saying?   2294

SCALE = 1
  Would serue to scale another *Hero's* towre,   1188
SCALPE = 1
  3.*Out*. By the bare scalpe of *Robin Hoods* fat Fryer,   1582
SCANDALIZD = 1
  I feare me it will make me scandaliz'd.   1036
SCAPE = 1
  The Thicket is beset, he cannot scape.   2113
SCARCE = 2
  I feare me he will scarce be pleas'd with all.   1042
  that going will scarce serue the turne.   1439
SCENA *l*.1 653 871 1067 1445 1820 2101 = 7
SCHOOLE-BOY = *1
  *to sigh, like a Schoole-boy that had lost his *A.B.C.* to   417
SCOENA *l*.152 300 395 566 591 928 974 1545 1623 1767 2026 2040
  2119 = 13
SCORNE = 3*1
  Val. To be in loue; where scorne is bought with | (grones: 33
  Duk. But she did scorne a present that I sent her,   1161
  For scorne at first, makes after-loue the more.   1164
  1.*Out*. But if thou scorne our curtesie, thou dyest.   1614
SCORNS = *1
  Val. A woman somtime scorns what best co(n)tents her.   1162
SCOURE = 1
  Sp. Item, she can wash and scoure.   1374
SCOWRD = 1
  La. A speciall vertue: for then shee neede not be | wash'd, and
  scowr'd.   1375
SCRATCH = 1
  That (like a testie Babe) will scratch the Nurse,   212
SCRATCHD = 1
  I should haue scratch'd out your vnseeing eyes,   2024
SCRIBE = 1
  That my master being scribe,   531
SEA = 5
  And throw it thence into the raging Sea.   282
  And drench'd me in the sea, where I am drown'd.   381
  A Sea of melting pearle, which some call teares;   1294
  La. With my Mastership? why, it is at Sea: 1349
  As full of sorrowes, as the Sea of sands,   1803
SEALE = 3
  To seale our happinesse with their consents.   351
  Iul. And seale the bargaine with a holy kisse.   575
  Ile be so bold to breake the seale for once.   1209
SEARCH = 1
  And thus I search it with a soueraigne kisse.   276
SEAS = 1
  As twenty Seas, if all their sand were pearle,   825
SEAUEN = 1
  Val. By seauen a clock, ile get you such a Ladder.   1195
SEBASTIAN = 2
  Pro. Sebastian is thy name: I like thee well,   1859
  Sebastian, I haue entertained thee,   1882
SECRET = 2*1
  Vnto the secret, nameles friend of yours: 495
  Lau. Thou shalt neuer get such a secret from me, but | by a parable.   907
  That touch me neere: wherein thou must be secret.   1129

SECRETS = 1*1

We haue some secrets to confer about.	1071
*An vnmannerly slaue, that will thrust himselfe into se- | crets:	1443

SECUNDA *l.*152 566 1445 1623 2040 = 5
SECUNDUS *l.*395 = 1
SEDGE = 1

Giuing a gentle kisse to euery sedge	1004

SEDUCED = 1

To be seduced by thy flattery,	1721

SEE = 23*6

To see the wonders of the world abroad,	9
Expects my comming, there to see me ship'd.	58
Lu. Lord, Lord: to see what folly raignes in vs.	168
There: take the paper: see it be return'd,	199
Iu. Let's see your Song: | How now Minion?	246
Iu. I see you haue a months minde to them.	296
Lu. I (Madam) you may say what sights you see;	297
I see things too, although you iudge I winke.	298
Ant. Lend me the Letter: Let me see what newes.	357
Val. Ha? Let me see: I, giue it me, it's mine:	400
And still I see her beautifull.	460
Speed. If you loue her, you cannot see her. | *Val.* Why?	461
Val. What should I see then?	467
*for hee beeing in loue, could not see to garter	469
*his hose; and you, beeing in loue, cannot see to put on | your hose.	470
You could not see to wipe my shooes.	473
*speakes a word: but see how I lay the dust with my | teares.	624
How could he see his way to seeke out you?	744
Val. To see such Louers, *Thurio,* as your selfe,	747
Duk. Then let me see thy cloake,	1202
Here, if thou stay, thou canst not see thy loue:	1314
1.Out-l. Fellowes, stand fast: I see a passenger.	1547
*you shall heare Musique, and see the Gentleman that | you ask'd for.	1655
*thou see me heaue vp my leg, and make water against a	1856
*Gentlewomans farthingale? did'st thou euer see me doe | such a tricke?	1857
Here is her Picture: let me see, I thinke	2004
See where she comes: Lady a happy euening.	2034
Val. How like a dreame is this? I see, and heare:	2147
Pro. How? let me see. | Why this is the ring I gaue to *Iulia.*	2218

SEEING = 1

And partly seeing you are beautifide	1601

SEEKE = 5*2

*Sheepe the Shepheard; but I seeke my Master, and my	91
Put forth their Sonnes, to seeke preferment out.	309
How could he see his way to seeke out you?	744
As seeke to quench the fire of Loue with words.	995
Luc. I doe not seeke to quench your Loues hot fire,	996
Pro. Run (boy) run, run, and seeke him out.	1258
Ho. Gone to seeke his dog, which to morrow, by his	1699

SEEKES = 1*1

Sp. The Shepheard seekes the Sheepe, and not the	90
Master seekes not me: therefore I am no Sheepe.	92

SEEME = 3

Sil. Seruant, you are sad. | *Val.* Indeed, Madam, I seeme so.	662
Thu. Seeme you that you are not? | *Val.* Hap'ly I doe.	664
Thu. What seeme I that I am not? | *Val.* Wise.	668

SEEMES = *1
   Iul. It seemes you lou'd not her, not leaue her token: 1893
SEENE = 3*1
   *to haue seene our parting: why my Grandam hauing   604
   This loue of theirs, my selfe haue often seene,   1093
   What light, is light, if *Siluia* be not seene?   1244
   Here can I sit alone, vn-seene of any,   2125
SEES = *1
   *not an eye that sees you, but is a Physician to comment | on your
   Malady.   434
SEEST = 4
   Thinke on thy *Protheus*, when thou (hap'ly) seest   15
   Because thou seest me doate vpon my loue: 828
   Pro. What seest thou? | *Lau*. Him we goe to finde,   1260
   Val. I pray thee *Launce*, and if thou seest my Boy   1327
SEIZED *see* ceazed
SELF = *1
   *Her self hath taught her Loue himself, to write vnto her | (louer. 558
SELFE = 44*5
   I loue my selfe, my friends, and all for loue: 69
   selfe; And so Sir, I'le commend you to my Master.   145
   Val. How now Sir? | What are you reasoning with your selfe? 533
   Val. To whom? | *Speed*. To your selfe: why, she woes you by a figure. 538
   When shee hath made you write to your selfe?   544
   *no eyes, looke you, wept her selfe blinde at my parting: 605
   *oh, the dogge is me, and I am my selfe: I; so, so: now   615
   Val. Your selfe (sweet Lady) for you gaue the fire,   687
   Val. I knew him as my selfe: for from our Infancie   712
   And though my selfe haue beene an idle Trewant,   714
   Val. To see such Louers, *Thurio*, as your selfe,   747
   Pro. Ile die on him that saies so but your selfe.   764
   Laun. Forsweare not thy selfe, sweet youth, for I am   874
   If I keepe them, I needs must loose my selfe: 949
   For *Valentine*, my selfe: for *Iulia*, *Siluia*.   951
   I to my selfe am deerer then a friend,   952
   For Loue is still most precious in it selfe,   953
   I cannot now proue constant to my selfe,   960
   My selfe in counsaile his competitor.   964
   My selfe am one made priuy to the plot.   1081
   This loue of theirs, my selfe haue often seene,   1093
   That which thy selfe hast now disclos'd to me.   1101
   The key whereof, my selfe haue euer kept: 1105
   How, and which way I may bestow my selfe   1156
   Because my selfe doe want my seruants fortune.   1217
   I curse my selfe, for they are sent by me,   1218
   I euer bore my daughter, or thy selfe.   1237
   To die, is to be banisht from my selfe,   1241
   And *Siluia* is my selfe: banish'd from her   1242
   Is selfe from selfe. A deadly banishment: 1243
   With them vpon her knees, her humble selfe,   1296
   As thou lou'st *Siluia* (though not for thy selfe)   1325
   *will not tell my selfe: and yet 'tis a Milke-maid: yet 'tis 1337
   My selfe was from *Verona* banished,   1593
   And by and by intend to chide my selfe,   1727
   Suruiues; to whom (thy selfe art witnesse)   1734
   Assure thy selfe, my loue is buried.   1739
   For since the substance of your perfect selfe   1748

SELFE *cont.*

Eg. As many (worthy Lady) to your selfe:	1777
Thy selfe hast lou'd, and I haue heard thee say	1788
Vnlesse I proue false traitor to my selfe.	1926
Iul. Almost as well as I doe know my selfe.	1964
I weepe my selfe to thinke vpon thy words:	1996
Alas, how loue can trifle with it selfe:	2003
Vnlesse I flatter with my selfe too much.	2008
But I can make respectiue in my selfe?	2015
Iul. And *Iulia* her selfe did giue it me,	2224
And *Iulia* her selfe hath brought it hither. | *Pro.* How? *Iulia?*	2225

SELUES = 1

Which, with our selues, all rest at thy dispose. *Exeunt.*	1622

SENCE = 1

And were there sence in his Idolatry,	2020

SENCELES = 1

Himselfe would lodge where (senceles) they are lying.	1213

SENCELESSE = 1

For 'tis thy riuall: O thou sencelesse forme,	2018

SEND = 7

I must goe send some better Messenger,	149
Then tell me, whether were I best to send him?	326
I will send him hither to you presently.	736
Send her another: neuer giue her ore,	1163
And slaues they are to me, that send them flying.	1211
Send to me in the morning, and ile send it: | And so, good rest.	1756

SENDS = 3

Sil. Oh: he sends you for a Picture? | *Iul.* I, Madam.	1936
Iul. Madam, he sends your Ladiship this Ring.	1953
Sil. The more shame for him, that he sends it me;	1954

SENT = 6*5

*Lu. Sir *Valentines* page: & sent I think from *Protheus;*	191
*Pan. 'Twere good, I thinke, your Lordship sent him | (thither,	331
Of commendations sent from *Valentine;*	355
*Ant. Look what thou want'st shalbe sent after thee:	376
*Panth. Come: come away man, I was sent to call | thee.	647
His teares, pure messengers, sent from his heart,	1052
Duk. But she did scorne a present that I sent her,	1161
I curse my selfe, for they are sent by me,	1218
**would teach a dog) I was sent to deliuer him, as a pre-|sent	1827
To heare me speake the message I am sent on.	1933
This is the ring you sent to *Siluia.*	2221

SEPTIMA *l.*974 = 1

SEPULCHER = 1

Or at the least, in hers, sepulcher thine.	1742

SEQUELL = 1

Sil. A pretty period: well: I ghesse the sequell;	506

SERUANT = 17*3

Sil. Sir *Valentine,* and seruant, to you two thousand.	492
*Sil. I thanke you (gentle Seruant) 'tis very Clerkly-|(done.	498
And so good-morrow Seruant. *Exit. Sil.*	525
Sil. Seruant. | *Val.* Mistris.	655
Sil. Seruant, you are sad. | *Val.* Indeed, Madam, I seeme so.	662
Sil. Who is that Seruant?	686
To be my fellow-seruant to your Ladiship.	755
Sil. Too low a Mistres for so high a seruant.	756
Pro. Not so, sweet Lady, but too meane a seruant	757

SERUANT *cont.*

Sweet Lady, entertaine him for your Seruant.	760
Seruant, you are welcome to a worthlesse Mistresse.	763
Goe with me: once more, new Seruant welcome;	769
Pro. Sir *Protheus* (gentle Lady) and your Seruant.	1714
Eg. Your seruant, and your friend;	1774
Lau. When a mans seruant shall play the Curre with	1822
*would doe this for his Seruant? nay, ile be sworne I haue	1849
But cannot be true seruant to my Master,	1925
(Though you respect not aught your seruant doth)	2141
Speed: a clownish seruant to Valentine.	2310
Panthion: seruant to Antonio.	2312

SERUANTS = 2

Luc. All these are seruants to deceitfull men.	1047
Because my selfe doe want my seruants fortune.	1217

SERUD = *1

*seru'd me, when I tooke my leaue of Madam *Siluia*: did	1854

SERUE = 4*2

Sp. Nay Sir, lesse then a pound shall serue me for car-|rying your Letter.	109
Would serue to scale another *Hero's* towre,	1188
Duk. A cloake as long as thine will serue the turne? | *Val.* I my good Lord.	1200
Val. Why any cloake will serue the turn (my Lord)	1204
that going will scarce serue the turne.	1439
I haue a Sonnet, that will serue the turne	1539

SERUED = 1

Which serued me as fit, by all mens iudgements,	1983

SERUES = 1*1

The time now serues not to expostulate,	1321
*for she is her Masters maid, and serues for wages. Shee	1339

SERUICE = 7*3

And to commend their seruice to his will.	344
*loose thy seruice, and in loosing thy seruice: --- why	637
*and the Seruice, and the tide: why man, if the Riuer	644
Nor to his Seruice, no such ioy on earth:	791
Spee. At thy seruice. | *Exeunt.*	926
Will creepe in seruice, where it cannot goe.	1644
I am thus early come, to know what seruice	1779
And will imploy thee in some seruice presently.	1860
Pro. Madam, this seruice I haue done for you	2140

SERUICEABLE = 1

Should be full fraught with seruiceable vowes.	1517

SET = 4*4

Warre with good counsaile; set the world at nought;	72
Pro. And that set together is noddy.	119
Sp. Now you haue taken the paines to set it toge-|ther, take it for your paines.	120
Giue me a Note, your Ladiship can set	238
Speed. I would you were set, so your affection would | cease.	478
La. Then may I set the world on wheeles, when she | can spin for her liuing.	1378
La. Oh villaine, that set this downe among her vices;	1396
To giue the on-set to thy good aduise.	1540

SEUERALL = 2

Ile kisse each seuerall paper, for amends:	268
That I haue wept a hundred seuerall times.	1966

SEUERELY = 1
  And kept seuerely from resort of men,   1177
SEXTA *l.*928 = 1
SHADOW = 7
  And feed vpon the shadow of perfection.   1247
  Is else deuoted, I am but a shadow;   1749
  And to your shadow, will I make true loue.   1750
  And make it but a shadow, as I am.   1752
  Would better fit his Chamber, then this Shadow.   1941
  Come shadow, come, and take this shadow vp,   2017
SHADOWES = 1
  To worship shadowes, and adore false shapes,   1755
SHADOWY = 1
  This shadowy desert, vnfrequented woods   2123
SHAKE = *1
  *no, it will: if hee shake his taile, and say nothing, it | will.   904
SHALBE = *1
  *Ant. Look what thou want'st shalbe sent after thee: 376
SHALL *l.*89 *109 122 258 275 *292 295 332 338 *345 378 *690 812 841
  862 867 885 887 930 931 932 968 986 1023 *1024 1117 1197 1205 1236
  1269 1319 *1335 *1407 *1411 1456 1485 1494 1507 *1655 1657 1704
  1754 1814 *1822 *1836 1958 *1999 2256 2277 2299 = 39*12
SHALLOW = 3
  Val. That's on some shallow Storie of deepe loue,   24
  According to my shallow simple skill.   161
  Think'st thou I am so shallow, so conceitlesse,   1720
SHALT *l.*368 371 *881 *907 *1615 1910 2019 = 4*3
SHAME = 6
  Lu. Pardon deare Madam, 'tis a passing shame,   170
  It were a shame to call her backe againe,   205
  A Slaue, that still an end, turnes me to shame: 1881
  Sil. The more shame for him, that he sends it me;   1954
  Pro. My shame and guilt confounds me: 2198
  Such an immodest rayment; if shame liue | In a disguise of loue?   2232
SHAPE = 1
  With goodly shape; and by your owne report,   1602
SHAPELESSE = 1
  Weare out thy youth with shapelesse idlenesse.   11
SHAPES = 2
  To worship shadowes, and adore false shapes,   1755
  Women to change their shapes, then men their minds.   2235
SHARPE = 2
  Iu. You doe not? | *Lu.* No (Madam) tis too sharpe.   250
  But you sir *Thurio*, are not sharpe enough: 1514
SHE = 123*27
SHEDDE = *1
  *perplexitie, yet did not this cruell-hearted Curre shedde   601
SHEDDING = 1
  Sad sighes, deepe grones, nor siluer-shedding teares   1300
SHEDS = *1
  *now the dogge all this while sheds not a teare: nor   623
SHEE *l.*405 411 *437 *446 544 812 821 854 1252 *1338 *1339 *1342 *1344
  *1375 *1386 *1393 *1411 *1412 *1414 = 7*12
SHEEPE = 7*4
  And I haue plaid the Sheepe in loosing him.   77
  Pro. Indeede a Sheepe doth very often stray,   78

SHEEPE *cont.*
*Sp. You conclude that my Master is a Shepheard then, | and I	
Sheepe? | *Pro.* I doe	80
Pro. A silly answere, and fitting well a Sheepe.	85
Sp. This proues me still a Sheepe.	86
*Sp. The Shepheard seekes the Sheepe, and not the	90
**Sheepe the Shepheard; but I seeke my Master, and my	91
Master seekes not me: therefore I am no Sheepe.	92
* Pro. The Sheepe for fodder follow the Shepheard,	93
**the Shepheard for foode followes not the Sheepe: thou	94
followes not thee: therefore thou art a Sheepe.	96

SHELD = 1
Ther's some great matter she'ld employ me in.	1771

SHELL = 1 *1
**I feare she'll proue as hard to you in telling your minde.	139
Du. I, but she'll thinke, that it is spoke in hate.	1480

SHELUING = 1
And built so sheluing, that one cannot climbe it	1184

SHEPHEARD = 3 *5
And if the Shepheard be awhile away.	79
*Sp. You conclude that my Master is a Shepheard then, | and I	
Sheepe? | *Pro.* I doe	80
Pro. True: and thy Master a Shepheard.	87
*Sp. The Shepheard seekes the Sheepe, and not the	90
**Sheepe the Shepheard; but I seeke my Master, and my	91
* Pro. The Sheepe for fodder follow the Shepheard,	93
**the Shepheard for foode followes not the Sheepe: thou	94
A Foxe, to be the Shepheard of thy Lambs;	1913

SHES = 2
Giue her no token but stones, for she's as hard as steele.	140
Du. Why then | She's fled vnto that pezant, *Valentine*;	2078

SHEW = 3 *3
*Lu. Please you repeat their names, ile shew my minde,	160
*Iul. They doe not loue, that doe not shew their loue.	184
Lu. That the Contents will shew.	189
I fear'd to shew my Father *Iulias* Letter,	382
**nay, Ile shew you the manner of it. This shooe is my fa- | ther:	606
Of greater time then I shall shew to be.	1023

SHEWES = 3
Iul. His little speaking, shewes his loue but small.	182
Which now shewes all the beauty of the Sun,	388
Shewes *Iulia* but a swarthy Ethiope.	955

SHINE = 1 *1
**and shine through you like the water in an Vrinall: that	433
Wilt thou reach stars, because they shine on thee?	1225

SHIP = *1
* Pro. Go, go, be gone, to saue your Ship from wrack,	146

SHIPD = 2 *1
Expects my comming, there to see me ship'd.	58
Sp. Twenty to one then, he is ship'd already,	76
**ship'd, and thou art to post after with oares; what's the	627

SHOOE = *5
**nay, Ile shew you the manner of it. This shooe is my fa- | ther:	606
**no, this left shooe is my father; no, no, this left	607
**shooe is my mother: nay, that cannot bee so neyther:	608
**yes; it is so, it is so: it hath the worser sole: this shooe	609
**should not the shooe speake a word for weeping:	617

SHOOES = 2
  For he was more then ouer-shooes in loue.   27
  You could not see to wipe my shooes.   473
SHORE = 1
  Being destin'd to a drier death on shore: 148
SHOT = *3
  *Sil. A fine volly of words, gentleme(n), & quickly shot off   684
  *till some certaine shot be paid, and the Hostesse say wel-|come.   877
  *with you presently; where, for one shot of fiue pence,   880
SHOULD *l*.45 164 172 383 467 *493 532 540 583 585 *617 *618 640 732
  743 814 947 998 1078 1084 1144 1219 1408 1498 1517 1560 1731 *1832
  1904 1944 2014 2021 2024 2030 2068 2192 2197 2244 = 35*4
SHOULDST *l*.639 1899 = 2
SHOW = 1
  And show thee all the Treasure we haue got;   1621
SHOWES = 1
  Du. This discipline, showes thou hast bin in loue.   1534
SHOWNE = 1
  (For thou hast showne some signe of good desert)   1464
SHRINKE = *1
  *2.Out. If there be ten, shrinke not, but down with'em.   1548
SHUND = 1*1
  *Pro. Thus haue I shund the fire, for feare of burning,   380
  (A rashnesse that I euer yet haue shun'd)   1099
SHUT = *1
  *keepe shut: Now, of another thing shee may, and that | cannot I helpe.
  Well, proceede.   1412
SICK = 1*1
  *Made Wit with musing, weake; hart sick with thought.   73
  Pro. When I was sick, you gaue me bitter pils,   802
SIGH = 2*1
  *to sigh, like a Schoole-boy that had lost his A.B.C. to   417
  Wherein I sigh not (Iulia) for thy sake,   578
  To that ile speake, to that ile sigh and weepe: 1747
SIGHES = 4*1
  *Coy looks, with hart-sore sighes: one fading moments | (mirth,   34
  were downe, I could driue the boate with my sighes.   646
  With nightly teares, and daily hart-sore sighes,   784
  Sad sighes, deepe grones, nor siluer-shedding teares   1300
  You sacrifice your teares, your sighes, your heart: 1520
SIGHT = 3
  Or else returne no more into my sight.   200
  Now Valentine is banish'd from her sight.   1448
  Or nere returne againe into my sight.   1879
SIGHTS = 1
  Lu. I (Madam) you may say what sights you see;   297
SIGNE = 1
  (For thou hast showne some signe of good desert)   1464
SIGNIFIE = 1
  Val. The tenure of them doth but signifie   1125
SIGNIOR = *1
  *Speed. How now Signior Launce? what newes with | your Mastership?   1347
SIL = 50*7, 1
  And so good-morrow Seruant. Exit. Sil.   525
SILENCE = 2
  Pro. Then in dumbe silence will I bury mine,   1277
  Tune a deploring dumpe: the nights dead silence   1531

SILENT = 1
Dumbe Iewels often in their silent kinde | 1159
SILKEN = 1
Iul. No girle, Ile knit it vp in silken strings, | 1020
SILLY = 2
Pro. A silly answere, and fitting well a Sheepe. | 85
Prouided that you do no outrages | On silly women, or poore passengers. | 1617
SILU = 1
SILUER-SHEDDING = 1
Sad sighes, deepe grones, nor siluer-shedding teares | 1300
*SILUIA see also Sil., Silu. = 58*6
Enter Valentine, Speed, Siluia. | 396
Sweet Ornament, that deckes a thing diuine, | Ah *Siluia, Siluia.* | 401
Speed. Madam *Siluia*: Madam *Siluia.* | *Val.* How now Sirha? | 403
*Val. Goe to, sir, tell me: do you know Madam *Siluia*? | 410
Val. But tell me: do'st thou know my Lady *Siluia*? | 436
Val. To doe what? | *Speed.* To be a spokes-man from Madam *Siluia.* | 536
Enter Valentine, Siluia, Thurio, Speed, Duke, Protheus. | 654
Duk. Now, daughter *Siluia*, you are hard beset. | 698
Siluia, I speake to you, and you Sir *Thurio*, | 734
To loue faire *Siluia*; shall I be forsworne? | 931
For *Valentine*, my selfe: for *Iulia, Siluia.* | 951
And *Siluia* (witnesse heauen that made her faire) | 954
Ayming at *Siluia* as a sweeter friend. | 959
What Letter is this same? what's here? to *Siluia*? | 1207
My thoughts do harbour with my Siluia *nightly,* | 1210
What's here? *Siluia, this night I will enfranchise thee.* | 1220
And *Siluia* is my selfe: banish'd from her | 1242
What light, is light, if *Siluia* be not seene? | 1244
What ioy is ioy, if *Siluia* be not by? | 1245
Except I be by *Siluia* in the night, | 1248
Vnlesse I looke on *Siluia* in the day, | 1250
Val. Is *Siluia* dead? | *Pro.* No, *Valentine.* | 1279
Val. No *Valentine* indeed, for sacred *Siluia*, | 1281
Val. No *Valentine*, if *Siluia* haue forsworne me. | 1284
From hence, from *Siluia*, and from me thy friend. | 1288
Doth *Siluia* know that I am banish'd? | 1291
As thou lou'st *Siluia* (though not for thy selfe) | 1325
Val. Oh my deere *Siluia*; haplesse *Valentine.* | 1330
Where you, with *Siluia*, may conferre at large. | 1508
Enter Protheus, Thurio, Iulia, Host, Musitian, Siluia. | 1624
But *Siluia* is too faire, too true, too holy, | 1629
Th. Who, *Siluia*? | *Pro.* I, *Siluia*, for your sake. | 1647
Song. Who is Siluia? what is she? | 1663
Then to Siluia, let vs sing, | 1673
That Siluia is excelling; | 1674
Enter Eglamore, Siluia. | 1768
Eg. This is the houre that Madam *Siluia* | 1769
Enter Launce, Protheus, Iulia, Siluia. | 1821
**to Mistris *Siluia*, from my Master; and I came no | 1828
**seru'd me, when I tooke my leaue of Madam *Siluia*: did | 1854
*La. Marry Sir, I carried Mistris *Siluia* the dogge you | bad me. | 1865
Deliuer it to Madam *Siluia*; | 1891
As you doe loue your Lady *Siluia*: | 1901
To bring me where to speake with Madam *Siluia.* | 1930
Enter Eglamoure, Siluia. | 2027

SILUIA cont.

That *Siluia*, at Fryer *Patricks* Cell should meet me,	2030
Th. Sir *Protheus*, what saies *Siluia* to my suit?	2042
Then for the loue of reck-lesse *Siluia*.	2096
Then hate for *Siluia*, that is gone for loue. *Exeunt*.	2100
Siluia, Out-lawes.	2102
*Enter Valentine, Protheus, Siluia, Iulia, Duke, Thurio, | Out-lawes.	2120
Repaire me, with thy presence, *Siluia*:	2132
All that was mine, in *Siluia*, I giue thee.	2209
*to Madam Siluia: w (out of my neglect) was neuer done.	2215
This is the ring you sent to *Siluia*.	2221
Thu. Yonder is *Siluia*: and *Siluia*'s mine.	2252
Doe not name *Siluia* thine: if once againe,	2255
Take thou thy *Siluia*, for thou hast deseru'd her.	2274
Duke: Father to Siluia.	2302
Eglamoure: Agent for Siluia in her escape.	2307
Siluia: beloued of Valentine.	2314

SILUIAS = 4

To climbe celestiall *Siluia's* chamber window,	963
Pro. And I will follow, more for *Siluias* loue	2097
What is in *Siluia's* face, but I may spie	2240
Thu. Yonder is *Siluia*: and *Siluia*'s mine.	2252

SIMPLE = 1*1

According to my shallow simple skill.	161
*you were so simple, none else would: but you are	431

SINCE = 12

But since thou lou'st; loue still, and thriue therein,	12
Since Maides, in modesty, say no, to that,	209
Speed. You neuer saw her since she was deform'd.	456
Speed. Euer since you lou'd her.	458
Val. I haue lou'd her euer since I saw her,	459
But (since vnwillingly) take them againe. | Nay, take them.	514
Th. Since this exile she hath despis'd me most,	1449
For since the substance of your perfect selfe	1748
But, since your falsehood shall become you well	1754
Which, since I know they vertuously are plac'd,	1808
But since she did neglect her looking-glasse,	1973
Since she respects my Mistris loue so much.	2002

SINCERE = 1

His loue sincere, his thoughts immaculate,	1051

SIND = 1

O sweet-suggesting Loue, if thou hast sin'd,	936

SINEWES = 1

For *Orpheus* Lute, was strung with Poets sinewes,	1524

SING = 5

Lu. That I might sing it (Madam) to a tune:	237
Best sing it to the tune of *Light O, Loue*.	240
Lu. I: and melodious were it, would you sing it,	243
Lu. Keepe tune there still; so you will sing it out:	248
Then to Siluia, let vs sing,	1673

SINS = *1

*Fils him with faults: makes him run through all th'sins;	2238

SIR *l*.74 *100 *109 117 124 125 *133 134 136 145 162 *191 390 397 405
406 407 *410 *414 439 442 444 *453 *465 *474 492 517 533 547 560
*562 587 *596 *611 649 657 677 681 *683 *688 *690 *692 699 717 725
728 734 768 988 1070 1079 1096 1119 1120 1131 1192 1273 *1286 1447
1457 1469 1476 1496 1501 1514 *1549 1551 1553 1642 1645 1646 1694

SIR *cont.*
  1703 1713 1714 1753 1762 1776 1792 1819 *1865 1874 1934 2042 2043
  2061 2072 *2214 2220 2251 2259 2272 = 73*20
SIRE = 1
  Could penetrate her vncompassionate Sire;   1301
SIRHA = 3*1
  Speed. Madam *Siluia*: Madam *Siluia*. | *Val*. How now Sirha?   403
  *thou shalt haue fiue thousand welcomes: But sirha, how   881
  Pro. Sirha, I say forbeare: friend *Valentine*, a word.   1274
  Pro. Goe sirha, finde him out: Come *Valentine*.   1329
SIRS = 1
  1.*Out*. We'll haue him: Sirs, a word.   1584
SISTER = *3
  *wayling: my Sister crying: our Maid howling: our   599
  *a veng'ance on't, there 'tis: Nor sir, this staffe is my si-|ster: 611
  *Now come I to my sister; marke the moane she makes: 622
SISTERS = *1
  *foure of his blinde brothers and sisters went to it: I haue   1825
SIT = 2
  If not: we'll make you sit, and rifle you.   1550
  Here can I sit alone, vn-seene of any,   2125
SITH = 1
  And yet I will not, sith so prettily   286
SITS = *1
  Speed. Shee that you gaze on so, as she sits at supper?   437
SIXTEENE = *1
  Val. Some sixteene moneths, and longer might haue | (staid, 1567
SKIE = 1
  Egl. The Sun begins to guild the westerne skie,   2028
SKILD = 1
  To sort some Gentlemen, well skil'd in Musicke.   1538
SKILL = 2
  According to my shallow simple skill.   161
  If not, to compasse her Ile vse my skill. | *Exeunt*.   869
SLANDER = 3
  Pro. The best way is, to slander *Valentine*,   1477
  Du. Then you must vndertake to slander him.   1484
  Your slander neuer can endamage him;   1489
SLAUE = 2*1
  Goe base Intruder, ouer-weening Slaue,   1227
  *An vnmannerly slaue, that will thrust himselfe into se-|crets: 1443
  A Slaue, that still an end, turnes me to shame: 1881
SLAUES = 1
  And slaues they are to me, that send them flying.   1211
SLEEPE = 4*1
  Sp. Why then my hornes are his hornes, whether I | wake or sleepe. 83
  Loue hath chas'd sleepe from my enthralled eyes,   786
  Now can I breake my fast, dine, sup, and sleepe,   793
  Sp. Item, she doth talke in her sleepe.   1392
  La. It's no matter for that; so shee sleepe not in her | talke. 1393
SLENDER = 1
  While other men, of slender reputation   308
SLEW = 1
  But yet I slew him manfully, in fight,   1574
SLIE = 1
  By some slie tricke, blunt *Thurio's* dull proceeding.   970

SLIGHT = 1
And leaue her on such slight conditions.   2265
SLIPS = 1
And when that howre ore-slips me in the day,   577
SLOW = 3*3
Sp. And yet it cannot ouer-take your slow purse.   128
**Speed*. And yet I was last chidden for being too slow.   409
Sp. Item, she is slow in words.   1395
To be slow in words, is a womans onely vertue: 1397
*she is slow of: of her purse, shee shall not, for that ile   1411
**Iu*. I, I would I were deafe: it makes me haue a slow | (heart.   1687
SLUGGARDIZD = 1
Then (liuing dully sluggardiz'd at home)   10
SMALL = 2*2
**Pro*. Here's too small a Pasture for such store of | Muttons.   103
Iul. His little speaking, shewes his loue but small.   182
*small as a wand: this hat is *Nan* our maid: I am the   613
But were you banisht for so small a fault?   1577
SMALLER = 1
(A smaller boone then this I cannot beg,   2145
SMELL = *1
*with the smell before, knew it was Crab; and   1843
SMELT = *1
*all the chamber smelt him: out with the dog (saies one)   1840
SMILE = 2
When inward ioy enforc'd my heart to smile?   217
With our discourse, to make your Grace to smile.   2290
SMILES = 1
Bestow thy fawning smiles on equall mates,   1228
SNOW = 1
Thou wouldst as soone goe kindle fire with snow   994
SO *l*.40 41 44 47 51 66 *135 137 138 142 145 156 166 177 226 241 244 248
   263 264 286 374 *431 *432 *437 443 *446 *453 *478 *502 503 522 525
   585 *608 *609 *615 662 666 707 756 757 764 789 796 815 830 849 854
   861 *909 *923 944 987 992 1006 1035 *1037 1048 *1054 1098 1113 1120
   1172 1184 1189 1209 1221 1276 *1297 1303 1309 1370 *1393 *1438 1462
   1474 1552 1553 1576 1577 1684 1689 1703 1720 1722 1725 1738 1744
   1756 1765 1789 1894 1904 1927 1958 1990 2002 2012 2023 2033
   2129 = 91*20
SOA = 1
Lau. So-hough, Soa hough---   1259
SODAINE = 1
And notwithstanding all her sodaine quips,   1636
SODAINLY = 1
Muse not that I thus sodainly proceed;   366
SOFTEN = 1
Whose golden touch could soften steele and stones;   1525
SOIOURND = 1
3.*Out*. Haue you long soiourn'd there?   1566
SOLE = *1
*yes; it is so, it is so: it hath the worser sole: this shooe   609
SOLEMNITY = 1
With Triumphes, Mirth, and rare solemnity.   2288
SOLITARIE = 1
Where thou shalt finde me sad, and solitarie.   1910
SOLLICIT = 1
Therefore be gone, sollicit me no more.   2161

SOLUS = 1
Enter Protheus *solus.* 929
SOME = 34*4
Some rare note-worthy obiect in thy trauaile. 16
Pro. Vpon some booke I loue, I'le pray for thee. 23
Val. That's on some shallow Storie of deepe loue, 24
I must goe send some better Messenger, 149
Iul. Some loue of yours, hath writ to you in Rime. 236
Iu. Heauy? belike it hath some burden then? 242
*Except mine own name: That, some whirle-winde beare 280
Some to the warres, to try their fortune there; 310
Some, to discouer Islands farre away: 311
Some, to the studious Vniuersities; 312
I am resolu'd, that thou shalt spend some time 368
To write some lines to one she loues. 481
*Or fearing els some messe(n)ger, y might her mind discouer 557
The next ensuing howre, some foule mischance 579
Vpon some other pawne for fealty. 741
Confirme his welcome, with some speciall fauor. 751
Some necessaries, that I needs must vse, 843
*till some certaine shot be paid, and the Hostesse say wel-|come. 877
Without some treachery vs'd to *Valentine.* 961
By some slie tricke, blunt *Thurio's* dull proceeding. 970
To lesson me, and tell me some good meane 980
As may beseeme some well reputed Page. 1018
We haue some secrets to confer about. 1071
I am to breake with thee of some affaires 1128
A Sea of melting pearle, which some call teares; 1294
Haue some malignant power vpon my life: 1308
(For thou hast showne some signe of good desert) 1464
Moist it againe: and frame some feeling line, 1522
With some sweet Consort; To their Instruments 1530
To sort some Gentlemen, well skil'd in Musicke. 1538
Val. Some sixteene moneths, and longer might haue | (staid, 1567
3.*Out.* Know then, that some of vs are Gentlemen, 1590
And giue some euening Musique to her eare. 1641
Ther's some great matter she'ld employ me in. 1771
And will imploy thee in some seruice presently. 1860
That can with some discretion doe my businesse: 1884
I feare I am attended by some Spies. 2037
Haue some vnhappy passenger in chace; 2136
SOMETHING = 1
Ant. My will is something sorted with his wish: 365
SOMEWHAT = *1
Thu. Ile weare a Boote, to make it somewhat roun-|(der. 2047
SOMMER-SWELLING = 1
Disdaine to roote the Sommer-swelling flowre, 816
SOMTIME = *1
Val. A woman somtime scorns what best co(n)tents her. 1162
SON = 2
Val. I, my good Lord, a Son, that well deserues 709
Sp. Marry, the son of my Grand-father. 1359
SONG = 3*1
Iu. Let's see your Song: | How now Minion? 246
There wanteth but a Meane to fill your Song. 255
*Male-content: to rellish a Loue-song, like a *Robin*-red-|breast: 415
Song. Who is Siluia? what is she? 1663

SONNE = 4*2

Pan. 'Twas of his Nephew *Protheus*, your Sonne.   304

He said, that *Protheus*, your sonne, was meet;   314

*Sonne, and am going with Sir *Protheus* to the Imperialls   596

Duk. Hath he not a Sonne?   708

Why *Phaeton* (for thou art *Merops* sonne)   1222

La. Oh illiterate loyterer; it was the sonne of thy   1360

SONNES = 1

Put forth their Sonnes, to seeke preferment out.   309

SONNET = 1

I haue a Sonnet, that will serue the turne   1539

SONNETS = 1

By walefull Sonnets, whose composed Rimes   1516

SOONE = 4

Pro. My Lord I cannot be so soone prouided,   374

Thou wouldst as soone goe kindle fire with snow   994

Knowing that tender youth is soone suggested,   1103

And cannot soone reuolt, and change your minde.   1506

SOONER = 1*2

Iul. If you turne not: you will return the sooner: 571

Sp. Why didst not tell me sooner? 'pox of your loue | Letters.   1440

*sooner into the dyning-chamber, but he steps me to her   1829

SORE = 1*1

*Coy looks, with hart-sore sighes: one fading moments | (mirth,   34

With nightly teares, and daily hart-sore sighes,   784

SORROW = 3*1

And made them watchers of mine owne hearts sorrow.   787

Iul. I thinke she doth: and that's her cause of sorrow.   1968

If I in thought felt not her very sorrow.   1993

Forgiue me *Valentine*: if hearty sorrow   2199

SORROWES = 2

A pack of sorrowes, which would presse you downe   1089

As full of sorrowes, as the Sea of sands,   1803

SORRY = 1

I am sorry I must neuer trust thee more,   2194

SORT = 1

To sort some Gentlemen, well skil'd in Musicke.   1538

SORTED = 1

Ant. My will is something sorted with his wish: 365

SOUERAIGNE = 2

And thus I search it with a soueraigne kisse.   276

Soueraigne to all the Creatures on the earth.   806

SOUERAIGNTY = 1

Whose soueraignty so oft thou hast preferd,   944

SOUGHT = 1

'Tis not vnknown to thee, that I haue sought   1130

SOULDIER = 1

Ile wooe you like a Souldier, at armes end,   2180

SOULE = 3

A blessed soule doth in *Elizium*.   1013

Vaine *Thurio* (whom my very soule abhor'd.)   1787

Whose life's as tender to me as my soule,   2158

SOULES = *1

Iul. Oh, know'st y not, his looks are my soules food?   990

SOULE-CONFIRMING = 1

With twenty thousand soule-confirming oathes.   945

SOURE = 1
   La. That makes amends for her soure breath.   1391
SOWE = 1
   Sp. Item, she can sowe.   1369
SOWREST = *1
   *Court: I thinke *Crab* my dog, be the sowrest natured   597
SO-HOUGH = 1
   Lau. So-hough, Soa hough---   1259
SP = 42*14
SPAKE = 1
   Who is that that spake?   1710
SPANIELL = *1
   *hath more qualities then a Water-Spaniell, which is   1340
SPANIEL-LIKE = 1
   Yet (Spaniel-like) the more she spurnes my loue,   1638
SPEAK = 1*2
   All this I speak in print, for in print I found it.   559
   Thur. Madam, my Lord your father wold speak with | (you.   767
   *Why wag: how now? what's the matter? look vp: speak.   2213
SPEAKE = 10*3
   *feares robbing: to speake puling, like a beggar at Hal-|low-Masse: 420
   I, so true loue should doe: it cannot speake,   585
   *should not the shooe speake a word for weeping: 617
   *Now come I to my Mother: Oh that she could speake   619
   Siluia, I speake to you, and you Sir *Thurio*,   734
   Val. Then speake the truth by her; if not diuine,   804
   Lau. Can nothing speake? Master, shall I strike?   1269
   By ought that I can speake in his dispraise,   1493
   Iu. But shall I heare him speake. | *Ho*. I that you shall.   1657
   Iu. 'Twere false, if I should speake it;   1731
   To that ile speake, to that ile sigh and weepe: 1747
   To bring me where to speake with Madam *Siluia*.   1930
   To heare me speake the message I am sent on.   1933
SPEAKES = *1
   *speakes a word: but see how I lay the dust with my | teares.   624
SPEAKING = 1
   Iul. His little speaking, shewes his loue but small.   182
SPEAKST = *1
   Val. No more: vnles the next word that thou speak'st   1307
SPECIALL = 1*2
   Speed. Marry by these speciall markes: first, you haue   413
   Confirme his welcome, with some speciall fauor.   751
   La. A speciall vertue: for then shee neede not be | wash'd, and
   scowr'd.   1375
SPEE = 17*1
SPEED see also Sp., Spe., Spee. = 23*20, 10
   Valentine: Protheus, and *Speed*.   2
   Enter Valentine, Speed, Siluia.   396
   Enter Valentine, Siluia, Thurio, Speed, Duke, Protheus.   654
   Enter Speed and Launce.   872
   Enter Duke, Thurio, Protheus, Valentine, | Launce, Speed.   1068
   But as thou lou'st thy life, make speed from hence.   1239
   La. There: and S.(aint) *Nicholas* be thy speed.   1363
   Enter Valentine, Speed, and certaine Out-lawes.   1546
   As (heauen it knowes) I would not haue him speed.   1928
   Speed: a clownish seruant to Valentine.   2310

SPEEDIEST = 1
  Euen with the speediest expedition,   339
SPEND = 5*1
  Would suffer him, to spend his youth at home,   307
  To let him spend his time no more at home;   316
  I am resolu'd, that thou shalt spend some time   368
  *Thu. Sir, if you spend word for word with me, I shall | make your wit
  bankrupt.   690
  And heere he meanes to spend his time a while,   730
  Euen for this time I spend in talking to thee.   1728
SPENDS = *1
  *And spends what he borrowes kindly in your company.   689
SPENT = 1
  We haue conuerst, and spent our howres together,   713
SPIE = 1
  What is in Siluia's face, but I may spie   2240
SPIES = 1
  I feare I am attended by some Spies.   2037
SPIGHT = 1
  Iu. I: that change is the spight.   1691
SPIN = 2
  Sp. Item, she can spin.   1377
  *La. Then may I set the world on wheeles, when she | can spin for her
  liuing.   1378
SPIRIT = 3
  Pro. Who then? his Spirit? | Val. Neither,   1265
  Pro. Nay, if the gentle spirit of mouing words   2178
  I doe applaud thy spirit, Valentine,   2267
SPOKE = 1
  Du. I, but she'll thinke, that it is spoke in hate.   1480
SPOKEN = 2
  Lu. As of a Knight, well-spoken, neat, and fine;   163
  Therefore it must with circumstance be spoken   1482
SPOKES-MAN = 1
  Val. To doe what? | Speed. To be a spokes-man from Madam Siluia.   536
SPORT = 1
  With willing sport to the wilde Ocean.   1007
SPRING = 1
  Oh, how this spring of loue resembleth   386
SPUR = 1
  So much they spur their expedition.   2033
SPURD = 1
  Pro. But loue will not be spurd to what it loathes.   2048
SPURNES = 1
  Yet (Spaniel-like) the more she spurnes my loue,   1638
SQUIRRILL = 1
  La. I Sir, the other Squirrill was stolne from me   1874
STABD = 1
  Who, in my moode, I stab'd vnto the heart.   1597
STAFFE = 3*1
  *a veng'ance on't, there 'tis: Nor sir, this staffe is my si-|ster: 611
  My staffe vnderstands me? | Spee. What thou saist?   896
  and my staffe vnderstands me.   899
  Hope is a louers staffe, walke hence with that   1316
STAID = 2*2
  Panth. Sir Protheus: you are staid for.   587

STAID *cont.*

  La. For thee? I, who art thou? he hath staid for a bet-|ter man then
    thee.   1435
  La. Thou must run to him; for thou hast staid so long,   1438
  Val. Some sixteene moneths, and longer might haue | (staid,   1567
STAIES = 1 *2
  Lu. Madam: dinner is ready: and your father staies.   290
  My father staies my comming: answere not: 581
  La. Why then, will I tell thee, that thy Master staies | for thee at the
    North gate.   1432
STAND = 7*1
  Ant. And how stand you affected to his wish?   362
  Val. In conclusion, I stand affected to her.   477
  Lau. Why, stand-vnder: and vnder-stand is all one.   901
  To take a note of what I stand in need of,   1059
  1.*Out-l.* Fellowes, stand fast: I see a passenger.   1547
  3.Out. Stand sir, and throw vs that you haue about'ye.   1549
  Iu. Peace, stand aside, the company parts.   1702
  Therefore I pray you stand, not to discourse,   2088
STANDS = 5*1
  Spee. Why then, how stands the matter with them?   891
  Lau. Marry thus, when it stands well with him, it | stands well with
    her.   892
  Spee. It stands vnder thee indeed.   900
  (Which vn-reuerst stands in effectuall force)   1293
  Verona shall not hold thee: heere she stands,   2256
STAND-VNDER = 1
  Lau. Why, stand-vnder: and vnder-stand is all one.   901
STARRE = 1
  At first I did adore a twinkling Starre,   938
STARRES = 1
  But truer starres did gouerne *Protheus* birth,   1049
STARS = 1
  Wilt thou reach stars, because they shine on thee?   1225
STARUD = 1
  The ayre hath staru'd the roses in her cheekes,   1975
STATE = 1
  Plead a new state in thy vn-riual'd merit,   2271
STATUE = 1
  My substance should be statue in thy stead.   2021
STATURE = 1
  Sil. How tall was she? | *Iul.* About my stature: for at *Pentecost,*   1978
STAY = 4*1
  No more of stay: to morrow thou must goe;   377
  That tide will stay me longer then I should,   583
  Luc. If you thinke so, then stay at home, and go not.   1037
  Duk. Nay then no matter: stay with me a while,   1127
  Here, if thou stay, thou canst not see thy loue: 1314
STAYES = 1
  That stayes to beare my Letters to my friends,   1122
STAYEST = 1
  Away, I say: stayest thou to vexe me here;   1880
STAYING = 1
  Besides, thy staying will abridge thy life: 1315
STEAD = 1
  My substance should be statue in thy stead.   2021

STEALE = 3
  Should from her vesture chance to steale a kisse,   814
  This night intends to steale away your daughter: 1080
  For practising to steale away a Lady,   1594
STEALES = *1
  *Trencher, and steales her Capons-leg: O, 'tis a foule   1830
STEED = 1
  Val. No (Madam) so it steed you, I will write   503
STEELE = 2
  Giue her no token but stones, for she's as hard as steele.   140
  Whose golden touch could soften steele and stones;   1525
STEEPLE = *1
  *As a nose on a mans face, or a Wethercocke on a steeple: 527
STEP = 2
  And make a pastime of each weary step,   1010
  Till the last step haue brought me to my Loue,   1011
STEPS = 1*1
  To measure Kingdomes with his feeble steps,   985
  *sooner into the dyning-chamber, but he steps me to her   1829
STICK = 1
  Vnlesse you haue a cod-peece to stick pins on.   1031
STICKE = 1
  Sp. If the ground be ouer-charg'd, you were best | sticke her.   105
STIL = *1
  Val. Nay sure, I thinke she holds them prisoners stil.   742
STILL = 10*2
  But since thou lou'st; loue still, and thriue therein,   12
  Sp. This proues me still a Sheepe.   86
  Lu. Keepe tune there still; so you will sing it out: 248
  Val. Well: you'll still be too forward.   408
  And still I see her beautifull.   460
  For Loue is still most precious in it selfe,   953
  Sp. Well, your old vice still: mistake the word: what | newes then in
  your paper?   1350
  The more it growes, and fawneth on her still;   1639
  Which heauen and fortune still rewards with plagues.   1801
  *not I bid thee still marke me, and doe as I do; when did'st   1855
  A Slaue, that still an end, turnes me to shame: 1881
  Oh 'tis the curse in Loue, and still approu'd   2164
STINGS = 1
  And kill the Bees that yeelde it, with your stings;   267
STIR = 1
  What hallowing, and what stir is this to day?   2134
STOCK = *1
  La. What neede a man care for a stock with a wench,   1372
STOCKE = 1
  When she can knit him a stocke?   1373
STOCKES = *1
  *sat in the stockes, for puddings he hath stolne, otherwise   1850
STOLNE = 2*1
  And should she thus be stolne away from you,   1084
  *sat in the stockes, for puddings he hath stolne, otherwise   1850
  La. I Sir, the other Squirrill was stolne from me   1874
STOMACKE = 1
  That you might kill your stomacke on your meat,   224
STONE = *2
  *one teare: he is a stone, a very pibble stone, and has no   602

STONES = 4
  Giue her no token but stones, for she's as hard as steele.   140
  I throw thy name against the bruzing-stones,   271
  He makes sweet musicke with th'enameld stones,   1003
  Whose golden touch could soften steele and stones;   1525
STOOD = *2
  *he had bin executed: I haue stood on the Pillorie for   1851
  *Pro. What dangerous action, stood it next to death   2162
STOOPE = 1
  Lu. Nothing. | Iu. Why didst thou stoope then?   228
STOP = 1*1
  dost thou stop my mouth?   638
  *La. Stop there: Ile haue her: she was mine, and not   1416
STOPD = 1
  (Thou know'st) being stop'd, impatiently doth rage: 1001
STOPT = *1
  *Val. My eares are stopt, & cannot hear good newes,   1275
STORE = *1
  *Pro. Here's too small a Pasture for such store of | Muttons.   103
STORIE = 2
  Val. That's on some shallow Storie of deepe loue,   24
  Pro. That's a deepe Storie, of a deeper loue,   26
STORY = 1
  The story of your Loues discouered.   2298
STRAIES = 1
  And so by many winding nookes he straies   1006
STRANGE = *1
  *Lu. She makes it stra(n)ge, but she would be best pleas'd   262
STRANGER = 1
  But count the world a stranger for thy sake: 2195
STRAY = 1
  Pro. Indeede a Sheepe doth very often stray,   78
STREAME = 1
  Ile be as patient as a gentle streame,   1009
STRENGTH = 1
  Or as one naile, by strength driues out another.   848
STRIKE = 3
  Lau. Can nothing speake? Master, shall I strike?   1269
  Pro. Who wouldst thou strike? | Lau. Nothing.   1270
  Lau. Why Sir, Ile strike nothing: I pray you.   1273
STRIKES = 1
  Alas, this parting strikes poore Louers dumbe. | Exeunt.   589
STRINGS = 3
  Iul. No girle, Ile knit it vp in silken strings,   1020
  Ho. How, out of tune on the strings.   1683
  Iu. Not so: but yet | So false that he grieues my very heart-strings.   1684
STRUNG = 1
  For Orpheus Lute, was strung with Poets sinewes,   1524
STUBBORNE = 1
  Prowd, disobedient, stubborne, lacking duty,   1138
STUDIES = 1
  Made me neglect my Studies, loose my time;   71
STUDIOUS = 1
  Some, to the studious Vniuersities;   312
STUDY = 1
  And study helpe for that which thou lament'st,   1312

STUFT = 1
I know they are stuft with protestations,   1950
STUMBLE = 1
Luc. I Madam, so you stumble not vnheedfully.   156
SUBIECT = 1
Teach me (thy tempted subiect) to excuse it.   937
SUBSCRIBE = 1
To which I thus subscribe: Sir *Valentine*,   2272
SUBSTANCE = 3*1
You take the sum and substance that I haue.   1561
For since the substance of your perfect selfe   1748
Iul. If 'twere a substance you would sure deceiue it,   1751
My substance should be statue in thy stead.   2021
SUBTILE = 1
Thou subtile, periur'd, false, disloyall man: 1719
SUCCESSE = 2
Val. And on a loue-booke pray for my successe?   22
Of thy successe in loue; and what newes else   62
SUCH = 38*2
Sp. Such another proofe will make me cry baa.   97
**Pro.* Here's too small a Pasture for such store of | Muttons.   103
Receiuing them from such a worthlesse post. *Exit.*   151
Iul. As little by such toyes, as may be possible: 239
Oh hatefull hands, to teare such louing words;   265
Iniurious Waspes, to feede on such sweet hony,   266
The honor, and regard of such a father.   710
Val. To see such Louers, *Thurio*, as your selfe,   747
To haue a looke of such a worthy a Mistresse.   758
Nor to his Seruice, no such ioy on earth: 791
And I as rich in hauing such a Iewell   824
**Lau.* Thou shalt neuer get such a secret from me, but | by a parable.   907
Of such diuine perfection as Sir *Protheus*.   988
Gentle *Lucetta*, fit me with such weedes   1017
Beseeming such a Wife, as your faire daughter: 1135
Aduise me, where I may haue such a Ladder.   1191
Val. By seauen a clock, ile get you such a Ladder.   1195
Ile get me one of such another length.   1203
Doe curse the grace, that with such grace hath blest them,   1216
That may discouer such integrity: 1523
Will well become such sweet complaining grieuance: 1532
Val. I was, and held me glad of such a doome.   1578
Such as the fury of vngouern'd youth   1591
1.*Out.* And I, for such like petty crimes as these.   1598
A Linguist, and a man of such perfection,   1603
3.*Out.* No, we detest such vile base practises.   1619
The heauen such grace did lend her,   1666
**Gentlewomans farthingale? did'st thou euer see me doe | such a tricke?   1857
currish thanks is good enough for such a present.   1869
Partly that I haue neede of such a youth,   1883
Iul. How many women would doe such a message?   1911
If I had such a Tyre, this face of mine   2005
Ile get me such a coulour'd Perrywig.   2011
Thu. 'Tis true, such Pearles as put out Ladies eyes,   2054
Thu. Wherefore? | *Iul.* That such an Asse should owe them.   2068
For such is a friend now: treacherous man,   2188
Such an immodest rayment; if shame liue | In a disguise of loue?   2232
'Twere pitty two such friends should be long foes.   2244

SUCH *cont.*
To make such meanes for her, as thou hast done,	2264
And leaue her on such slight conditions.	2265

SUES = 1
My Master sues to her: and she hath taught her Sutor,	528

SUFFER = 2
Would suffer him, to spend his youth at home,	307
I tender't heere: I doe as truely suffer, | As ere I did commit.	2201

SUFFERD = *2
*for't: sure as I liue he had suffer'd for't: you shall iudge:	1836
*Geese he hath kil'd, otherwise he had sufferd for't: thou	1852

SUFFICIENT = 1
Be a sufficient Ransome for offence,	2200

SUGGESTED = 1
Knowing that tender youth is soone suggested,	1103

SUGGESTING = 1
O sweet-suggesting Loue, if thou hast sin'd,	936

SUIT = 2
I hope my Masters suit will be but cold,	2001
Th. Sir *Protheus*, what saies *Siluia* to my suit?	2042

SUITE = 1
That I despise thee, for thy wrongfull suite;	1726

SULLEN = 1
Duk. No, trust me, She is peeuish, sullen, froward,	1137

SUM = 1
You take the sum and substance that I haue.	1561

SUN = 2
Which now shewes all the beauty of the Sun,	388
Egl. The Sun begins to guild the westerne skie,	2028

SUNNE = 1
But now I worship a celestiall Sunne:	939

SUN-BRIGHT = 1
To be regarded in her sun-bright eye.	1157

SUN-EXPELLING = 1
And threw her Sun-expelling Masque away,	1974

SUP = 1
Now can I breake my fast, dine, sup, and sleepe,	793

SUPPER = 1*1
Speed. Shee that you gaze on so, as she sits at supper?	437
Pro. We'll wait vpon your Grace, till after Supper,	1542

SUPPLIANT = 1
When she for thy repeale was suppliant,	1304

SUPPOSE = 1
Sil. And so suppose am I; for in her graue	1738

SURE = 5*3
Val. Nay sure, I thinke she holds them prisoners stil.	742
Val. I know it well (my Lord) and sure the Match	1132
For I am sure she is not buried.	1732
Iul. If 'twere a substance you would sure deceiue it,	1751
*for't: sure as I liue he had suffer'd for't: you shall iudge:	1836
If we recouer that, we are sure enough. *Exeunt.*	2039
But being mask'd, he was not sure of it.	2084
And lesse then this, I am sure you cannot giue.)	2146

SURFET = 1
And now excesse of it will make me surfet.	1290

SURUIUES = 1
Suruiues; to whom (thy selfe art witnesse)	1734

SUTOR = 1
My Master sues to her: and she hath taught her Sutor,   528
SWAINE = 1
Thou gentle Nimph, cherish thy for-lorne swaine.   2133
SWAINES = 1
That all our Swaines commend her?   1664
SWARTHY = 1
Shewes *Iulia* but a swarthy Ethiope.   955
SWEARE = 4
Loue bad mee sweare, and Loue bids me for-sweare;   935
For me (by this pale queene of night I sweare)   1724
Thinke not I flatter (for I sweare I doe not)   1782
SWEET = 23*4
To the sweet glaunces of thy honour'd Loue,   7
Pro. Wilt thou be gone? Sweet *Valentine* adew,   14
*Val. Sweet *Protheus*, no: Now let vs take our leaue: 60
Iniurious Waspes, to feede on such sweet hony,   266
To the sweet Iulia: that ile teare away: 285
Heare sweet discourse, conuerse with Noble-men,   333
Pro. Sweet Loue, sweet lines, sweet life,   347
Sweet Ornament, that deckes a thing diuine, | Ah *Siluia, Siluia*.   401
Val. Your selfe (sweet Lady) for you gaue the fire,   687
Omitting the sweet benefit of time   715
Val. Mistris, it is: sweet Lady, entertaine him   754
Pro. Not so, sweet Lady, but too meane a seruant   757
Sweet Lady, entertaine him for your Seruant.   760
Val. Sweet: except not any,   808
*Laun. Forsweare not thy selfe, sweet youth, for I am   874
He makes sweet musicke with th'enameld stones,   1003
**She can milke, looke you, a sweet vertue in a maid with | cleane
hands.   1345
Sp. Item, she hath a sweet mouth.   1390
With some sweet Consort; To their Instruments   1530
Will well become such sweet complaining grieuance: 1532
Therefore, sweet *Protheus*, my direction-giuer,   1536
Pro. I grant (sweet loue) that I did loue a Lady, | But she is dead.   1729
Pro. Sweet Lady, let me rake it from the earth.   1740
**For thy sweet Mistris sake, because thou lou'st her. Fare- |(well.   1998
Dispatch (sweet Gentlemen) and follow me.   2092
SWEETER = 1
Ayming at *Siluia* as a sweeter friend.   959
SWEETEST = 1
Pro. Yet Writers say; as in the sweetest Bud,   46
SWEET-SUGGESTING = 1
O sweet-suggesting Loue, if thou hast sin'd,   936
SWELLING = 1
Disdaine to roote the Sommer-swelling flowre,   816
SWIFT = 2
And perfected by the swift course of time: 325
Loue lend me wings, to make my purpose swift   971
SWIFTEST = 1
But if thou linger in my Territories | Longer then swiftest expedition   1233
SWINGD = *2
**you, you swing'd me for my loue, which makes mee the   475
*La. Now will he be swing'd for reading my Letter;   1442
SWOM = 1
And yet you neuer swom the *Hellespont*.   29

SWORNE = *1
    *would doe this for his Seruant? nay, ile be sworne I haue   1849
T = 1
    To learne his wit, t'exchange the bad for better;   942
TABLE = 1*1
    Who art the Table wherein all my thoughts   978
    *foure gentleman-like-dogs, vnder the Dukes table: hee   1838
TAILE = 1*1
    Laun. In thy Tale.| *Panth*. In thy Taile.   641
    *no, it will: if hee shake his taile, and say nothing, it | will.   904
TAKE = 23*3
    Val. Sweet *Protheus*, no: Now let vs take our leaue: 60
    Sp. Now you haue taken the paines to set it toge-|ther, take it for
      your paines.   120
    Sp. And yet it cannot ouer-take your slow purse.   128
    Sp. No, not so much as take this for thy pains: 142
    There: take the paper: see it be return'd,   199
    Lu. To take a paper vp, that I let fall.   230
    Iu. If you respect them; best to take them vp.   293
    Least he should take exceptions to my loue,   383
    And yet, take this againe: and yet I thanke you: 508
    But (since vnwillingly) take them againe. | Nay, take them.   514
    Sil. Why if it please you, take it for your labour;   524
    Pro. Why then wee'll make exchange; | Here, take you this.   573
    To take a note of what I stand in need of,   1059
    I now am full resolu'd to take a wife,   1145
    And turne her out, to who will take her in: 1146
    Take no repulse, what euer she doth say,   1169
    You take the sum and substance that I haue.   1561
    2.*Out*. Tell vs this: haue you any thing to take to?   1588
    Val. I take your offer, and will liue with you,   1616
    Sil. Sir *Protheus*, as I take it.   1713
    *things. If I had not had more wit then he, to take a fault   1834
    Go presently, and take this Ring with thee,   1890
    Come shadow, come, and take this shadow vp,   2017
    Take but possession of her, with a Touch: 2257
    Take thou thy *Siluia*, for thou hast deseru'd her.   2274
TAKEN *see also* tane = 1*1
    Sp. Now you haue taken the paines to set it toge-|ther, take it for
      your paines.   120
    Lu. Nay, I was taken vp, for laying them downe.   294
TAKES = 3*2
    And by and by a clowd takes all away.   389
    *to fast, like one that takes diet: to watch, like one that   419
    Du. My daughter takes his going grieuously?   1460
    *I would haue (as one should say) one that takes vp-|on   1832
    And yet she takes exceptions at your person.   2044
TAKETH = 1
    He ouer-taketh in his pilgrimage.   1005
TALE = 1
    Laun. In thy Tale.| *Panth*. In thy Taile.   641
TALES = 1*1
    Lu. What, shall these papers lye, like Tel-tales here?   292
    Pro. My tales of Loue were wont to weary you,   778
TALKE = 5
    Ant. Tell me *Panthino*, what sad talke was that,   302
    Sp. Item, she doth talke in her sleepe.   1392

TALKE *cont.*
La. It's no matter for that; so shee sleepe not in her	talke.	1393
But Host, doth this Sir *Protheus*, that we talke on,	1694
Pro. Ill, when you talke of war.	2057

TALKING = 1
Euen for this time I spend in talking to thee.	1728

TALL = 1
Sil. How tall was she?	*Iul*. About my stature: for at *Pentecost*,	1978

TAME = 1
Make Tygers tame, and huge *Leuiathans*	1526

TANE = 2
But *Valentine*, if he be tane, must die.	1302
It was *Eues* legacie, and cannot be t'ane from her.	1401

TANGLE = 1
You must lay Lime, to tangle her desires	1515

TARRIANCE = 1
I am impatient of my tarriance.	*Exeunt*.	1065

TARRY = 2
the Tide, if you tarry any longer.	629
Tarry I heere, I but attend on death,	1256

TAUGHT = 2*2
How angerly I taught my brow to frowne,	216
My Master sues to her: and she hath taught her Sutor,	528
*Her self hath taught her Loue himself, to write vnto her	(louer.	558
*taught him (euen as one would say precisely, thus I	1826

TEACH = 1*1
Teach me (thy tempted subiect) to excuse it.	937
*would teach a dog) I was sent to deliuer him, as a pre-	sent	1827

TEARE = 3*2
Oh hatefull hands, to teare such louing words;	265
To the sweet Iulia: that ile teare away:	285
*one teare: he is a stone, a very pibble stone, and has no	602
*now the dogge all this while sheds not a teare: nor	623
As easily as I doe teare his paper.	1952

TEARES = 10*1
The tide is now; nay, not thy tide of teares,	582
*speakes a word: but see how I lay the dust with my	teares.	624
*were drie, I am able to fill it with my teares: if the winde	645
With nightly teares, and daily hart-sore sighes,	784
A thousand oathes, an Ocean of his teares,	1044
His teares, pure messengers, sent from his heart,	1052
A Sea of melting pearle, which some call teares;	1294
Sad sighes, deepe grones, nor siluer-shedding teares	1300
You sacrifice your teares, your sighes, your heart:	1520
Write till your inke be dry: and with your teares	1521
Which I so liuely acted with my teares:	1990

TEDIOUS = 1
With twenty watchfull, weary, tedious nights;	35

TEEME = *1
*Teeme of horse shall not plucke that from me: nor who	1335

TEETH = 2
Sp. Item, she hath no teeth.	1402
La. Well: the best is, she hath no teeth to bite.	1405

TELL = 16*6
Ant. Tell me *Panthino*, what sad talke was that,	302
Then tell me, whether were I best to send him?	326
Val. Goe to, sir, tell me: do you know Madam *Siluia*?	410

TELL *cont.*

Val. But tell me: do'st thou know my Lady *Siluia?*	436
*Val. Now tell me: how do al from whence you came?	773
Spee. But tell me true, wil't be a match?	902
Spee. I tell thee, my Master is become a hot Louer.	918
*Lau. Why, I tell thee, I care not, though hee burne	919
To lesson me, and tell me some good meane	980
Iul. That fits as well, as tell me (good my Lord)	1025
But tell me (wench) how will the world repute me	1034
Now tell me *Protheus*, what's your will with me?	1072
Val. When would you vse it? pray sir, tell me that.	1192
*will not tell my selfe: and yet 'tis a Milke-maid: yet 'tis	1337
La. I will try thee: tell me this: who begot thee?	1358
*La. Why then, will I tell thee, that thy Master staies | for thee at the	
North gate.	1432
*Sp. Why didst not tell me sooner? 'pox of your loue | Letters.	1440
2.*Out*. Tell vs this: haue you any thing to take to?	1588
Ho. I tell you what *Launce* his man told me,	1696
This Letter: that's her chamber: Tell my Lady,	1907
Goe, giue your Master this: tell him from me,	1939
Val. Please you, Ile tell you, as we passe along,	2295

TELLING = *1

*I feare she'll proue as hard to you in telling your minde.	139

TELS = *1

*La. Marry she saies your dog was a cur, and tels you	1868

TEL-TALES = *1

*Lu. What, shall these papers lye, like Tel-tales here?	292

TEMPER = 1

Where you may temper her, by your perswasion,	1511

TEMPTED = 1

Teach me (thy tempted subiect) to excuse it.	937

TEN = *2

*2.*Out*. If there be ten, shrinke not, but down with'em.	1548
*As big as ten of yours, & therefore the guift the greater.	1877

TENANT-LESSE = 1

Leaue not the Mansion so long Tenant-lesse,	2129

TENDER = 5

Wer't not affection chaines thy tender dayes	6
Euen so by Loue, the yong, and tender wit	51
Knowing that tender youth is soone suggested,	1103
Iul. I thanke you Madam, that you tender her:	1961
Whose life's as tender to me as my soule,	2158

TENDERD = 1

Those at her fathers churlish feete she tenderd,	1295

TENDERT = 1

I tender't heere: I doe as truely suffer, | As ere I did commit.	2201

TENURE = 1

Val. The tenure of them doth but signifie	1125

TERRITORIES = 1

But if thou linger in my Territories | Longer then swiftest expedition	1233

TERTIA *l*.300 591 1767 2101 = 4
TERTIUS *l*.1067 = 1
TESTIE = 1

That (like a testie Babe) will scratch the Nurse,	212

TESTIFIE = *1

*To testifie your bounty, I thank you, you haue cestern'd | (me;	143

TH = 9*1, 2*1

He makes sweet musicke with th'enameld stones,	1003
By Penitence th'Eternalls wrath's appeas'd:	2207
*Fils him with faults: makes him run through all th'sins;	2238

THAN *see* then

THANK = 2*2

*To testifie your bounty, I thank you, you haue cestern'd | (me;	143
Val. 'Tis indeed, Madam, we thank the giuer.	685
Duke. Protheus, I thank thee for thine honest care,	1091
Val. I thank your Grace, y gift hath made me happy:	2275

THANKE = 4*4

Speed. True sir: I was in loue with my bed, I thanke	474
Sil. I thanke you (gentle Seruant) 'tis very Clerkly- |(done.	498
And yet, take this againe: and yet I thanke you:	508
Thanke me for this, more then for all the fauors	1231
Th. I thanke you for your owne: Now Gentlemen	1649
Sil. I thanke you for your Musique (Gentlemen)	1709
Iul. I thanke you Madam, that you tender her:	1961
Iul. And she shall thanke you for't, if ere you know | (her.	1999

THANKES = 1

Iul. She thankes you. | *Sil.* What sai'st thou?	1959

THANKFULL = 1

Val. My Lord, I will be thankfull,	702

THANKS = 1

currish thanks is good enough for such a present.	1869

THAT *see also* y *l.*44 56 *80 88 *107 119 *131 138 158 171 *184 *185 189 202 207 209 212 224 226 230 231 233 237 267 *280 285 302 306 314 319 337 350 356 *358 366 368 401 411 412 *416 *417 *418 *419 *425 *432 *433 *434 *437 438 444 *446 448 *453 *463 531 *563 577 583 *598 *608 *619 631 664 668 *679 686 695 709 722 738 740 746 764 765 766 780 796 827 829 843 853 854 855 859 863 865 *875 895 906 *909 910 933 941 954 956 957 986 991 992 1000 1025 1029 1038 1043 1048 1055 1061 *1073 1077 1099 1101 1102 1103 1114 1118 1122 1129 1130 1139 1161 1173 1178 1181 1184 1192 1194 1198 1199 1211 1215 1216 1219 1246 1287 1291 1305 *1307 1311 1312 1316 1324 *1334 *1335 1352 1361 1364 *1381 *1388 1391 *1393 *1396 1399 *1403 *1411 *1412 *1417 *1422 1426 1428 *1432 1439 *1443 1447 1451 1461 1479 1480 1485 1493 1496 1519 1523 1539 *1549 1552 1557 1561 1572 1590 1600 1617 1643 1645 *1655 1657 1659 1664 1667 1674 1684 1691 1694 1704 1710 1715 1718 1722 1726 1729 1733 1737 1743 1746 1747 1759 1766 1769 1775 1806 *1823 *1824 *1832 *1835 *1841 *1844 1881 1883 1884 1900 1902 1903 1906 1915 1921 1922 1931 1940 1944 1946 1954 1961 1966 *1967 1977 1986 1991 2010 2014 2023 2030 2039 2045 2046 2061 2064 2068 2070 2078 2083 2091 2094 2098 2099 2100 2108 2128 2135 2143 2149 2184 2197 2208 2209 2216 2227 2231 2237 2260 2261 2277 2279 2294 2296 2299 = 230*52

THATS = 15*7

Val. That's on some shallow Storie of deepe loue,	24
Pro. That's a deepe Storie, of a deeper loue,	26
Pro. Nod-I, why that's noddy.	116
Lu. Fire that's closest kept, burnes most of all.	183
Speed. Without you? nay, that's certaine: for with- |out	430
Speed. That's because the one is painted, and the o- |ther out of all count.	450
Val. That's the Letter I writ to her friend.	551
Lau. Why, he that's tide here, *Crab* my dog.	633
Yet hath Sir *Protheus* (for that's his name)	717

THATS *cont.*

 And that's the reason I loue him so little.   861
 Pro. That thou art banish'd: oh that's the newes,   1287
 *that's all one, if he be but one knaue: He liues not now 1333
 La. That's as much as to say (*Can she so?*)   1370
 La. That's as much as to say *Bastard-vertues*: that   1381
 La. Of her tongue she cannot; for that's writ downe   1410
 La. That's monstrous: oh that that were out.   1426
 Val. My friends. | 1.*Out.* That's not so, sir: we are your enemies. 1553
 This Letter: that's her chamber: Tell my Lady,   1907
 Iul. I thinke she doth: and that's her cause of sorrow. 1968
 There is our Captaine: Wee'll follow him that's fled, 2112
 And that's farre worse then none: better haue none 2172
 Val. Thou co(m)mon friend, that's without faith or loue, 2187

THAWD = 1

 (That I did loue, for now my loue is thaw'd,   855

THE *see also* th', y = 282*101

THEE *l.*19 23 31 55 59 61 64 65 96 147 190 275 *376 647 811 827 894
 *898 900 *916 918 *919 *923 977 1091 1118 1128 1130 1141 1153 1196
 1206 1220 1225 1232 1235 1309 1322 1323 1327 1356 1358 *1398 1432
 *1435 1463 1465 1612 1613 1620 1621 1726 1728 1788 1802 1805 *1855
 1859 1860 1878 1882 1889 1890 1946 1994 1997 2022 2025 2117 2139
 2182 2194 2204 2209 2230 2256 2258 2268 2270 2285 = 75*10

THEEUERY = 1

 It's an honourable kinde of theeuery.   1586

THEIR *l.*160 *184 *185 309 310 344 351 694 825 950 966 1159 1171 1212
 1215 1219 *1382 1530 2032 2033 2135 2235 *2236 2282 2286 = 22*5

THEIRS = 1

 This loue of theirs, my selfe haue often seene,   1093

THEM *see also* 'em, rest-them *l.*68 151 261 288 293 294 296 *345 485 514
 517 518 519 740 *742 *774 775 787 891 949 950 *1028 1048 1123 1125
 1211 1214 1215 1216 1276 1296 *1297 1355 1585 *1692 2055 2067 2068
 2081 2138 2281 2282 2285 2286 = 40*6

THEN *l.*10 27 37 76 *80 *83 *109 155 174 201 228 233 242 326 *399 467
 *472 523 573 583 586 *603 659 675 680 733 743 804 821 844 887 891
 906 911 952 1008 1019 1023 *1037 1039 1088 1127 1147 1160 1179 1186
 1202 1229 1231 1233 *1240 1265 1267 1277 *1340 *1344 1350 *1375
 *1378 *1414 1415 1419 *1420 *1422 *1423 1425 1427 1431 *1432 *1435
 1466 1484 1557 1590 1673 *1678 *1834 1876 1941 1970 2043 2051 2055
 2078 2096 2098 2100 2105 2124 2145 2146 2156 2168 2172 2173 2203
 2235 *2236 2269 *2293 = 79*22

THENCE = 5

 And throw it thence into the raging Sea.   282
 To any happy messenger from thence.   703
 And thence she cannot be conuay'd away.   1106
 1.*Out.* What, were you banish'd thence?   1569
 Sil. Goe to thy Ladies graue and call hers thence,   1741

THERE *l.*58 199 248 255 310 332 *353 *358 367 530 *552 *611 *621 790
 867 947 1012 1121 1150 1249 1251 *1286 1306 1363 *1416 *1548 1566
 1672 *1839 1938 1948 1997 2020 2086 2112 2159 = 27*9

THEREBY = 1

 I gaue him gentle lookes, thereby to finde   1100

THEREFORE = 14*4

 Master seekes not me: therefore I am no Sheepe.   92
 followes not thee: therefore thou art a Sheepe.   96
 He is in hast, therefore I pray you go.   391

THEREFORE *cont.*

Now therefore would I haue thee to my Tutor	1153
*onely carry, therefore is shee better then a Iade. *Item.*	1344
*indeede know not their fathers; and therefore haue no | names.	1382
*couer of the salt, hides the salt, and therefore it is more	1421
Therefore it must with circumstance be spoken	1482
Therefore the office is indifferent,	1490
Th. Therefore, as you vnwinde her loue from him;	1497
Therefore, sweet *Protheus*, my direction-giuer,	1536
Therefore, aboue the rest, we parley to you:	1606
*As big as ten of yours, & therefore the guift the greater.	1877
Therefore know thee, for this I entertaine thee.	1889
Therefore I know she is about my height,	1985
Therefore I pray you stand, not to discourse,	2088
Therefore be gone, sollicit me no more.	2161
I claime her not, and therefore she is thine.	2262

THEREIN = 2

But since thou lou'st; loue still, and thriue therein,	12
Val. My youthfull trauaile, therein made me happy,	1580

THEREOF = 1*1

Onely, in lieu thereof, dispatch me hence:	1063
La. And thereof comes the prouerbe: (*Blessing of | your heart, you brew good Ale.*)	1367

THERES = 1

There's not a haire on's head, but 'tis a *Valentine*.	1262

THERETO = 1

Pro. Why this it is: my heart accords thereto,	392

THEREWITHALL = 2

Pro. Well: giue her that Ring, and therewithall	1906
That my poore Mistris moued therewithall,	1991

THERS = 1

Ther's some great matter she'ld employ me in.	1771

THESE *l.**292 313 *413 427 *432 840 1047 1551 1559 1598 1661 1864 2087 2135 2206 2279 = 13*4

THESUS = 1

For *Thesus* periury, and vniust flight;	1989

THEY = 31*5

THEYRE = 1

When women cannot loue, where they're belou'd.	2165

THICKET = 1

The Thicket is beset, he cannot scape.	2113

THINE = 6

Duke. Protheus, I thank thee for thine honest care,	1091
Duk. A cloake as long as thine will serue the turne? | *Val.* I my good Lord.	1200
Or at the least, in hers, sepulcher thine.	1742
Doe not name *Siluia* thine: if once againe,	2255
I claime her not, and therefore she is thine.	2262
Duke. I grant it (for thine owne) what ere it be.	2278

THING = 7*4

Sweet Ornament, that deckes a thing diuine, | Ah *Siluia, Siluia*.	401
Val. Should I haue wish'd a thing, it had beene he.	732
Beares no impression of the thing it was.)	857
That longs for euery thing that he can come by.	1194
*keepe shut: Now, of another thing shee may, and that | cannot I helpe. Well, proceede.	1412
2.*Out.* Tell vs this: haue you any thing to take to?	1588

THING *cont.*

She excels each mortall thing	1675
*Ho. You would haue them alwaies play but one thing.	1692
Iu. I would alwaies haue one play but one thing.	1693
*thing, when a Cur cannot keepe himselfe in all compa-|nies:	1831
*I did the thing you wot of: he makes me no more adoe,	1847

THINGS = 4*1

I see things too, although you iudge I winke.	298
Val. Are all these things perceiu'd in me?	427
I will; for good things should be praised.	1408
Three things, that women highly hold in hate.	1479
*things. If I had not had more wit then he, to take a fault	1834

THINK = *3

*Lu. Sir *Valentines* page: & sent I think from *Protheus*;	191
*Sil. Perchance you think too much of so much pains?	502
*Duke. I think the Boy hath grace in him, he blushes.	2292

THINKE = 25*7

Thinke on thy *Protheus,* when thou (hap'ly) seest	15
Sp. Truely Sir, I thinke you'll hardly win her.	134
Lu. Then thus: of many good, I thinke him best.	174
I thinke him so, because I thinke him so.	177
Lu. Yet he, of all the rest, I thinke best loues ye.	181
Pan. I thinke your Lordship is not ignorant	327
*Pan. 'Twere good, I thinke, your Lordship sent him | (thither,	331
looke on you, I can hardly thinke you my Master.	426
*Court: I thinke *Crab* my dog, be the sowrest natured	597
And I thinke, no other treasure to giue your followers:	693
I thinke 'tis no vn-welcome newes to you.	731
*Val. Nay sure, I thinke she holds them prisoners stil.	742
*Luc. If you thinke so, then stay at home, and go not.	1037
And thinke my patience, (more then thy desert)	1229
Vnlesse it be to thinke that she is by	1246
*the wit to thinke my Master is a kinde of knaue: but	1332
Du. And also, I thinke, thou art not ignorant	1471
Du. I, but she'll thinke, that it is spoke in hate.	1480
She bids me thinke how I haue bin forsworne	1634
Trust me, I thinke 'tis almost day.	1764
Thinke not I flatter (for I sweare I doe not)	1782
But thinke vpon my griefe (a Ladies griefe)	1798
*vpon me that he did, I thinke verily hee had bin hang'd	1835
She is dead belike? | *Pro.* Not so: I thinke she liues.	1894
To thinke vpon her woes, I doe protest	1965
*Iul. I thinke she doth: and that's her cause of sorrow.	1968
When she did thinke my Master lou'd her well;	1971
I weepe my selfe to thinke vpon thy words:	1996
Here is her Picture: let me see, I thinke	2004
And thinke the worthy of an Empresse loue:	2268
What thinke you of this Page (my Lord?)	2291

THINKES = 5

Me thinkes should not be chronicled for wise.	45
And yet me thinkes I do not like this tune.	249
Me thinkes my zeale to *Valentine* is cold,	858
Du. So I beleeue: but *Thurio* thinkes not so:	1462
Iul. Because, me thinkes that she lou'd you as well	1900

THINKING = 1

And thinking on it, makes me cry alas.	1905

THINKS = *2
  Ho. Now, my yong guest; me thinks your' allycholly; 1651
  Sil. Belike she thinks that *Protheus* hath forsook her? 1967
THINKST = 5*1
  Iu. What thinkst thou of the faire sir *Eglamoure*? 162
  Iu. What think'st thou of the rich *Mercatio*? 165
  Iu. What think'st thou of the gentle *Protheus*? 167
  What thou think'st meet, and is most mannerly. 1033
  Think'st thou I am so shallow, so conceitlesse, 1720
  *think'st not of this now: nay, I remember the tricke you 1853
THIRD = *1
  *third) hang him vp (saies the Duke.) I hauing bin ac-|quainted 1842
THIS *l*.86 142 *169 187 211 249 258 320 386 392 *399 508 559 572 573 589
  *593 *594 *601 *606 *607 *609 *610 *611 *613 *623 681 725 728 737
  753 796 812 818 *875 934 962 972 1080 1093 1102 1111 1116 1118 1141
  *1149 1193 1207 1220 1231 1289 1358 1361 *1396 1452 1495 1502 1507
  1533 1534 1535 1583 1588 1609 1694 1695 1717 1724 1728 1769 1812
  *1849 *1853 1873 1889 1890 1907 1918 1939 1941 1942 1945 1953 1997
  2005 2006 2016 2017 2086 2093 2105 2106 2117 2123 2134 2139 2140
  2145 2146 2147 2216 2218 2221 2222 2230 2243 2291 = 90*20
THITHER = 4
  Pro. And thither will I bring thee *Valentine*. 59
  Pan. 'Twere good, I thinke, your Lordship sent him | (thither, 331
  How shall I best conuey the Ladder thither? 1197
  While I (their King) that thither them importune 1215
THOSE *l*.233 1295 2169 = 3
THOU *see also* y *l*.12 14 15 18 70 *94 96 *98 *135 155 162 165 167 *178
  228 319 336 337 368 371 *376 377 436 438 *440 445 *455 *627 *628 638
  639 649 809 828 832 *881 894 895 896 *907 910 *913 915 *920 *921
  *923 925 936 944 972 993 994 999 1001 1027 1032 1033 1055 1102 1129
  1190 1222 1223 1225 1233 1239 1260 1270 1287 *1307 1311 1312 1314
  1318 1325 1327 1352 1356 1361 *1435 *1438 1464 1468 1471 1534 *1610
  1614 *1615 1719 1720 1735 1781 1784 1791 *1852 *1856 *1857 1862
  1873 1880 1896 1899 1910 1912 1959 1963 *1998 2018 2019 2111 2128
  2133 *2152 2168 2171 2174 2185 *2187 2189 2191 *2222 2229 2231 2263
  2264 2273 2274 2285 2286 = 110*30
THOUDST = 1
  Thou hast no faith left now, vnlesse thou'dst two, 2171
THOUGH = 6*2
  Speed. I, but hearken sir: though the Cameleon Loue 562
  And though my selfe haue beene an idle Trewant, 714
  Lau. Why, I tell thee, I care not, though hee burne 919
  Though nere so blacke, say they haue Angells faces, 1172
  Thy letters may be here, though thou art hence, 1318
  As thou lou'st *Siluia* (though not for thy selfe) 1325
  Though his false finger haue prophan'd the Ring, 1957
  (Though you respect not aught your seruant doth) 2141
THOUGHT = 3*1
  *Made Wit with musing, weake; hart sick with thought. 73
  Lu. I: if you thought your loue not cast away. 179
  And where I thought the remnant of mine age 1143
  If I in thought felt not her very sorrow. 1993
THOUGHTS = 8
  Whose high emperious thoughts haue punish'd me 782
  Who art the Table wherein all my thoughts 978
  His loue sincere, his thoughts immaculate, 1051
  My thoughts do harbour with my Siluia nightly, 1210

THOUGHTS *cont.*

My Herald Thoughts, in thy pure bosome rest-them,	1214
And manage it, against despairing thoughts:	1317
A little time will melt her frozen thoughts,	1455
One *Iulia*, that his changing thoughts forget	1940

THOULT = *1

Pant. Tut, man: I meane thou'lt loose the flood, and	634

THOUSAND = 9*2

And yet a thousand times it answer's no. | *Exeunt. Finis.*	393
Val. Madam & Mistres, a thousand good-morrows.	489
Sil. Sir *Valentine*, and seruant, to you two thousand.	492
(Please you command) a thousand times as much: | And yet---	504
*thou shalt haue fiue thousand welcomes: But sirha, how	881
With twenty thousand soule-confirming oathes.	945
A thousand oathes, an Ocean of his teares,	1044
Sil. Sir *Eglamore*, a thousand times good morrow.	1776
For I haue heard him say a thousand times,	1955
Sil. A thousand more mischances then this one	2105
Into a thousand oathes; and all those oathes,	2169

THREATS = 1

With many bitter threats of biding there.	1306

THREE = 2*2

Three things, that women highly hold in hate.	1479
*a puppy: one that I sau'd from drowning, when three or	1824
*Hee thrusts me himselfe into the company of three or	1837
Egl. Feare not: the Forrest is not three leagues off,	2038

THREEFOLD = *1

*'Tis threefold too little for carrying a letter to your louer	113

THREE-FOLD = 1

Prouokes me to this three-fold periurie.	934

THREW = 1

And threw her Sun-expelling Masque away,	1974

THRICE = 1*1

But twice, or thrice, was *Protheus* written downe:	277
*mine, twice or thrice in that last Article: rehearse that | once more.	1417

THRIUE = 1

But since thou lou'st; loue still, and thriue therein,	12

THRIUES = *1

Val. How does your Lady? & how thriues your loue?	777

THROUGH = 2*2

*and shine through you like the water in an Vrinall: that	433
Come, Ile conuey thee through the City-gate.	1322
As he, in pennance wander'd through the Forrest:	2082
*Fils him with faults: makes him run through all th'sins;	2238

THROUGHLY = 1

Shall lodge thee till thy wound be throughly heal'd;	275

THROW = 2*1

I throw thy name against the bruzing-stones,	271
And throw it thence into the raging Sea.	282
*3.*Out*. Stand sir, and throw vs that you haue about'ye.	1549

THRUST = 1*1

*An vnmannerly slaue, that will thrust himselfe into se- |crets:	1443
Thrust from the company of awfull men.	1592

THRUSTS = *1

*Hee thrusts me himselfe into the company of three or	1837

THU = 21*3

THUR = 2*1
THURIO see also Th., Thu., Thur. = 28*2

Enter Valentine, Siluia, Thurio, Speed, Duke, Protheus.	654
Spee. Master, Sir *Thurio* frownes on you. | *Val.* I Boy, it's for loue.	657
Sil. What, angry, Sir *Thurio*, do you change colour?	677
*Sir *Thurio* borrows his wit from your Ladiships lookes,	688
Siluia, I speake to you, and you Sir *Thurio*,	734
Val. To see such Louers, *Thurio*, as your selfe,	747
Sil. I wait vpon his pleasure: Come Sir *Thurio*,	768
For *Thurio* he intends shall wed his daughter,	968
Enter Duke, Thurio, Protheus, Valentine, | *Launce, Speed.*	1068
Duke. Sir *Thurio*, giue vs leaue (I pray) a while,	1070
On *Thurio*, whom your gentle daughter hates,	1083
To match my friend Sir *Thurio*, to my daughter.	1131
Enter Duke, Thurio, Protheus.	1446
Du. Sir *Thurio*, feare not, but that she will loue you	1447
Du. So I beleeue: but *Thurio* thinkes not so:	1462
The match betweene sir *Thurio*, and my daughter? | *Pro.* I doe my Lord.	1469
The loue of *Valentine*, and loue sir *Thurio*?	1476
It followes not that she will loue sir *Thurio*.	1496
But you sir *Thurio*, are not sharpe enough:	1514
Enter Protheus, Thurio, Iulia, Host, Musitian, Siluia.	1624
And now I must be as vniust to *Thurio*,	1626
But here comes *Thurio*; now must we to her window,	1640
Pro. I gentle *Thurio*, for you know that loue	1643
Pro. Sir *Thurio*, feare not you, I will so pleade,	1703
Vaine *Thurio* (whom my very soule abhor'd.)	1787
Enter Thurio, Protheus, Iulia, Duke.	2041
Du. How now sir *Protheus*; how now *Thurio*?	2072
**Enter Valentine, Protheus, Siluia, Iulia, Duke, Thurio,* | *Out-lawes.*	2120
Val. Thurio giue backe; or else embrace thy death:	2253
Thurio: a foolish riuall to Valentine.	2306

THURIOS = 1

By some slie tricke, blunt *Thurio's* dull proceeding.	970

THUS = 12*3

Should censure thus on louely Gentlemen.	172
Lu. Then thus: of many good, I thinke him best.	174
And thus I search it with a soueraigne kisse.	276
Thus will I fold them, one vpon another;	288
Muse not that I thus sodainly proceed;	366
**Pro.* Thus haue I shund the fire, for feare of burning,	380
That makes me reasonlesse, to reason thus?	853
That thus without aduice begin to loue her?	863
**Lau.* Marry thus, when it stands well with him, it | stands well with her.	892
If I loose them, thus finde I by their losse,	950
And should she thus be stolne away from you,	1084
Thus (for my duties sake) I rather chose	1086
I am thus early come, to know what seruice	1779
*taught him (euen as one would say precisely, thus I	1826
To which I thus subscribe: Sir *Valentine*,	2272

THWARTED = 1

If crooked fortune had not thwarted me.	1568

THY *l.*6 7 8 11 15 16 17 18 20 21 62 63 87 *95 142 159 270 271 272 275
336 572 578 582 *626 *635 *636 *637 639 641 840 *874 882 *916 926
937 1061 1101 1202 1206 1214 1224 1228 1229 1230 1237 1238 1239
1288 1304 1314 1315 1318 1320 1324 1325 1326 *1360 1362 1363 *1432

THY *cont.*
  1535 1540 1622 1721 1722 1723 1725 1726 1733 1734 1736 1739 1741
  1788 1789 1790 1795 1859 1886 1913 1996 *1998 2018 2021 2022 2132
  2133 *2152 2167 2168 2174 2195 2227 2253 2267 2271 2274 = 91*15
THYSELFE *see* selfe
TIDE = 8*3

The tide is now; nay, not thy tide of teares,	582
That tide will stay me longer then I should,	583
the Tide, if you tarry any longer.	629
Laun. It is no matter if the tide were lost, for it is the	630
vnkindest Tide, that euer any man tide.	631
Panth. What's the vnkindest tide?	632
Lau. Why, he that's tide here, *Crab* my dog.	633
Laun. Loose the Tide, and the voyage, and the Ma-|ster,	643
*and the Seruice, and the tide: why man, if the Riuer	644

TILL = 6*2

Shall lodge thee till thy wound be throughly heal'd;	275
Till I haue found each letter, in the Letter,	279
*vndon till hee be hang'd, nor neuer welcome to a place,	876
*till some certaine shot be paid, and the Hostesse say wel-|come.	877
Luc. Better forbeare, till *Protheus* make returne.	989
Till the last step haue brought me to my Loue,	1011
Write till your inke be dry: and with your teares	1521
Pro. We'll wait vpon your Grace, till after Supper,	1542

TILTS = 1

There shall he practise Tilts, and Turnaments;	332

TIME = 25

But wherefore waste I time to counsaile thee	55
Made me neglect my Studies, loose my time;	71
Iul. Is't neere dinner time? | *Lu.* I would it were,	222
To let him spend his time no more at home;	316
I haue consider'd well, his losse of time,	321
And perfected by the swift course of time:	325
And in good time: now will we breake with him.	346
I am resolu'd, that thou shalt spend some time	368
Or else for want of idle time, could not againe reply,	556
Why muse you sir, 'tis dinner time. | *Val.* I haue dyn'd.	560
Val. You haue said Sir. | *Thu.* I Sir, and done too for this time.	681
Omitting the sweet benefit of time	715
And heere he meanes to spend his time a while,	730
By longing for that food so long a time.	992
Of greater time then I shall shew to be.	1023
Besides the fashion of the time is chang'd)	1155
Will giue thee time to leaue our royall Court,	1235
Time is the Nurse, and breeder of all good;	1313
The time now serues not to expostulate,	1321
A little time will melt her frozen thoughts,	1455
Pro. A little time (my Lord) will kill that griefe.	1461
Euen for this time I spend in talking to thee.	1728
And at that time I made her weepe a good,	1986
Vnlesse it be to come before their time,	2032
The priuate wound is deepest: oh time, most accurst.	2196

TIMELESSE = 1

(Being vnpreuented) to your timelesse graue.	1090

TIMES = 5

And yet a thousand times it answer's no. | *Exeunt. Finis.*	393
(Please you command) a thousand times as much: | And yet---	504

TIMES *cont.*
    Sil. Sir *Eglamore*, a thousand times good morrow.   1776
    For I haue heard him say a thousand times,   1955
    That I haue wept a hundred seuerall times.   1966
TINCTURE = 1
    And pinch'd the lilly-tincture of her face,   1976
TIRE *see* tyre
TIS *l.*28 42 *113 170 197 250 *354 *498 *535 554 560 *611 *621 685 731
    864 *909 1130 1165 1167 1221 1262 *1336 *1337 *1338 1486 1764 *1830
    1885 1904 2018 2054 2081 2164 2216 *2236 2297 = 25*14
TO *see also* t', too = 376*67, 1
    Val. And I will help thee to prefer her to: 811
TODAY *see* day
TOGETHER = 2*1
    Pro. And that set together is noddy.   119
    Sp. Now you haue taken the paines to set it toge-|ther, take it for
    your paines.   120
    We haue conuerst, and spent our howres together,   713
TOKEN = 1*1
    Giue her no token but stones, for she's as hard as steele.   140
    Iul. It seemes you lou'd not her, not leaue her token: 1893
TOLD = 2
    Val. This is the Gentleman I told your Ladiship   737
    Ho. I tell you what *Launce* his man told me,   1696
TOMORROW *see* morrow
TONGUE = 5*1
    Laun. For feare thou shouldst loose thy tongue.   639
    Panth. Where should I loose my tongue?   640
    Fie, fie, vnreuerend tongue, to call her bad,   943
    That man that hath a tongue, I say is no man,   1173
    If with his tongue he cannot win a woman.   1174
    La. Of her tongue she cannot; for that's writ downe   1410
TONGUES = 1
    2.*Out*. Haue you the Tongues?   1579
TOO *see also* to = 22*5
    Pro. Here's too small a Pasture for such store of | Muttons.   103
    *'Tis threefold too little for carrying a letter to your louer   113
    Lu. It is too heauy for so light a tune.   241
    Iu. You doe not? | *Lu*. No (Madam) tis too sharpe.   250
    Iu. You (Minion) are too saucie.   252
    Lu. Nay, now you are too flat;   253
    And marre the concord, with too harsh a descant: 254
    I see things too, although you iudge I winke.   298
    Val. Well: you'll still be too forward.   408
    Speed. And yet I was last chidden for being too slow.   409
    Sil. Perchance you think too much of so much pains?   502
    Val. You haue said Sir. | *Thu*. I Sir, and done too for this time.   681
    Sil. Too low a Mistres for so high a seruant.   756
    Pro. Not so, sweet Lady, but too meane a seruant   757
    When you haue done, we looke too heare from you.   771
    O, but I loue his Lady too-too much,   860
    Lau. I, and what I do too: looke thee, Ile but leane,   898
    Sp. Item, she is proud. | *La*. Out with that too: 1399
    Sp. Item, she is too liberall.   1409
    But *Siluia* is too faire, too true, too holy,   1629
    Let's tune: and too it lustily a while.   1650
    Vnlesse I flatter with my selfe too much.   2008

TOO *cont.*
Thu. What? that my leg is too long?	2045
Pro. No, that it is too little.	2046
Then plurall faith, which is too much by one:	2173

TOOKE = 2*1
Iu. What is't that you | Tooke vp so gingerly?	226
*seru'd me, when I tooke my leaue of Madam *Siluia*: did	1854
Be thou asham'd that I haue tooke vpon me,	2231

TOO-MUCH = 1
Which (all too-much) I haue bestowed on thee.	1232

TOO-TOO = 1
O, but I loue his Lady too-too much,	860

TORMENT = 1*1
Torment me for my Loues forgetfulnesse:	580
Val. And why not death, rather then liuing torment?	1240

TORMENTS = 1
Val. For that which now torments me to rehearse;	1572

TOUCH = 5
Didst thou but know the inly touch of Loue,	993
That touch me neere: wherein thou must be secret.	1129
Whose golden touch could soften steele and stones;	1525
Val. Ruffian: let goe that rude vnciuill touch,	2184
Take but possession of her, with a Touch:	2257

TOWARD = 1
That leads toward *Mantua*, whether they are fled:	2091

TOWNES = 1
I better brooke then flourishing peopled Townes:	2124

TOWRE = 2
I nightly lodge her in an vpper Towre,	1104
Would serue to scale another *Hero's* towre,	1188

TOYES = 1
Iul. As little by such toyes, as may be possible:	239

TRAINE = 1
To beare my Ladies traine, lest the base earth	813

TRAITOR = 1
Vnlesse I proue false traitor to my selfe.	1926

TRAMPLING = 1
Trampling contemptuously on thy disdaine.	272

TRANSGRESSION = 1
Her true perfection, or my false transgression?	852

TRAUAILE = 3
Some rare note-worthy obiect in thy trauaile.	16
In hauing knowne no trauaile in his youth.	318
Val. My youthfull trauaile, therein made me happy,	1580

TRAUAILERS = 1
That all the Trauailers doe feare so much.	1552

TRAUELL = 1
2.*Out.* Whether trauell you? | *Val.* To *Verona*.	1562

TREACHEROUS = 1
For such is a friend now: treacherous man,	2188

TREACHERY = 2
Without some treachery vs'd to *Valentine*.	961
Without false vantage, or base treachery.	1575

TREASURE = 2
And I thinke, no other treasure to giue your followers:	693
And show thee all the Treasure we haue got;	1621

TRENCHED = 1
Trenched in ice, which with an houres heate   1453
TRENCHER = *1
*Trencher, and steales her Capons-leg: O, 'tis a foule   1830
TREWANT = 1
And though my selfe haue beene an idle Trewant,   714
TRICKE = 2*1
By some slie tricke, blunt *Thurio's* dull proceeding.   970
*think'st not of this now: nay, I remember the tricke you   1853
*Gentlewomans farthingale? did'st thou euer see me doe | such a tricke? 1857
TRIFLE = 1
Alas, how loue can trifle with it selfe: 2003
TRIMD = 1
And I was trim'd in Madam *Iulias* gowne,   1982
TRIUMPHES = 1
With Triumphes, Mirth, and rare solemnity.   2288
TROUBLE = 2
Iu. This babble shall not henceforth trouble me;   258
Meaning henceforth to trouble you no more.   509
TRUE = 15*2
Val. 'Tis true; for you are ouer-bootes in loue,   28
Pro. True: and thy Master a Shepheard.   87
Speed. True sir: I was in loue with my bed, I thanke   474
Pro. Here is my hand, for my true constancie: 576
I, so true loue should doe: it cannot speake,   585
Her true perfection, or my false transgression?   852
Spee. But tell me true, wil't be a match?   902
But *Siluia* is too faire, too true, too holy,   1629
When I protest true loyalty to her,   1631
And to your shadow, will I make true loue.   1750
I am my Masters true confirmed Loue,   1924
But cannot be true seruant to my Master,   1925
Thu. 'Tis true, such Pearles as put out Ladies eyes,   2054
Iul. True: from a Gentleman, to a foole.   2065
'Tis true: for Frier *Laurence* met them both   2081
Thou Counterfeyt, to thy true friend.   2174
Pro. Then men their minds? tis true: oh heuen, were man 2236
TRUELY = 2
Sp. Truely Sir, I thinke you'll hardly win her.   134
I tender't heere: I doe as truely suffer, | As ere I did commit. 2201
TRUER = 1
But truer starres did gouerne *Protheus* birth,   1049
TRUE-DEUOTED = 1
Iul. A true-deuoted Pilgrime is not weary   984
TRUE-LOUE = 2
With twentie od-conceited true-loue knots: 1021
As when thy Lady, and thy true-loue dide,   1790
TRUST = 6
Now trust me, 'tis an office of great worth,   197
Val. Now trust me (Madam) it came hardly-off   499
Duk. No, trust me, She is peeuish, sullen, froward,   1137
Du. And *Protheus*, we dare trust you in this kinde,   1502
Trust me, I thinke 'tis almost day.   1764
I am sorry I must neuer trust thee more,   2194
TRUSTED = 1
Who should be trusted, when ones right hand   2192

TRUSTING = 1
For 'tis no trusting to yond foolish Lowt;   1885
TRUTH = 5
For truth hath better deeds, then words to grace it.   586
Val. Then speake the truth by her; if not diuine,   804
To beare a hard opinion of his truth: 1056
Pro. One (Lady) if you knew his pure hearts truth,   1711
Witnesse good bringing vp, fortune, and truth: 1888
TRY = 3
Some to the warres, to try their fortune there;   310
La. I will try thee: tell me this: who begot thee?   1358
Sp. Come foole, come: try me in thy paper.   1362
TRYED = 1
Not being tryed, and tutord in the world: 323
TUNE = 9
Lu. That I might sing it (Madam) to a tune: 237
Best sing it to the tune of *Light O, Loue*.   240
Lu. It is too heauy for so light a tune.   241
Lu. Keepe tune there still; so you will sing it out: 248
And yet me thinkes I do not like this tune.   249
Tune a deploring dumpe: the nights dead silence   1531
Let's tune: and too it lustily a while.   1650
Ho. How, out of tune on the strings.   1683
Tune my distresses, and record my woes.   2127
TUNEABLE = 1
For they are harsh, vn-tuneable, and bad.   1278
TURMOILE = 1
And there Ile rest, as after much turmoile   1012
TURN = *1
Val. Why any cloake will serue the turn (my Lord)   1204
TURNAMENTS = 1
There shall he practise Tilts, and Turnaments;   332
TURND = 1
· Is turn'd to folly, blasting in the Bud,   52
TURNE = 5
Iul. If you turne not: you will return the sooner: 571
And turne her out, to who will take her in: 1146
Duk. A cloake as long as thine will serue the turne? | *Val*. I my good
Lord.   1200
that going will scarce serue the turne.   1439
I haue a Sonnet, that will serue the turne   1539
TURNES = 1
A Slaue, that still an end, turnes me to shame: 1881
TUT = *1
Pant. Tut, man: I meane thou'lt loose the flood, and   634
TUTOR = 2
He being her Pupill, to become her Tutor.   529
Now therefore would I haue thee to my Tutor   1153
TUTORD = 1
Not being tryed, and tutord in the world: 323
TWAS = 2*1
Pan. 'Twas of his Nephew *Protheus*, your Sonne.   304
*(quoth he) you doe him the more wrong (quoth I) 'twas   1846
(Madam) 'twas *Ariadne*, passioning   1988
TWENTIE = 1
With twentie od-conceited true-loue knots: 1021

TWENTY = 5
    With twenty watchfull, weary, tedious nights;   35
    Sp. Twenty to one then, he is ship'd already,   76
    Val. Why Lady, Loue hath twenty paire of eyes.   745
    As twenty Seas, if all their sand were pearle,   825
    With twenty thousand soule-confirming oathes.   945
TWERE = 3*3
    Pro. Nay, in that you are astray: 'twere best pound | you.   107
    Pan. 'Twere good, I thinke, your Lordship sent him | (thither,   331
    Spee. 'Twere good you knockt him.   661
    Iu. 'Twere false, if I should speake it;   1731
    Iul. If 'twere a substance you would sure deceiue it,   1751
    'Twere pitty two such friends should be long foes.   2244
TWICE = 2*1
    But twice, or thrice, was *Protheus* written downe: 277
    Loe, here in one line is his name twice writ: 283
    *mine, twice or thrice in that last Article: rehearse that | once more.   1417
TWILL = *1
    Launce. Nay, 'twill bee this howre ere I haue done   593
TWINKLING = 1
    At first I did adore a twinkling Starre,   938
TWITS = 1
    She twits me with my falsehood to my friend;   1632
TWO = 7*1
    Pro. May't please your Lordship, 'tis a word or two   354
    Please you deliberate a day or two.   375
    Sil. Sir *Valentine*, and seruant, to you two thousand.   492
    Where haue you bin these two dayes loytering?   1864
    Thou hast no faith left now, vnlesse thou'dst two,   2171
    'Twere pitty two such friends should be long foes.   2244
    Valentine. | *Protheus. the two Gentlemen.*   2303
    THE | Two Gentlemen of Verona.   2317
TYGERS = 1
    Make Tygers tame, and huge *Leuiathans*   1526
TYRE = 1
    If I had such a Tyre, this face of mine   2005
VAINE = 2
    Be gone, I will not heare thy vaine excuse,   1238
    Vaine *Thurio* (whom my very soule abhor'd.)   1787
VAL = 120*27
VALEN = 1
VALENTINE *see also Val., Valen* = 3,62*1

    Pro. Wilt thou be gone? Sweet *Valentine* adew,   14
    For I will be thy beades-man, *Valentine*.   21
    Pro. And thither will I bring thee *Valentine*.   59
    How his companion, youthfull *Valentine*,   328
    Of commendations sent from *Valentine*;   355
    Enter Valentine, Speed, Siluia.   396
    Sil. Sir *Valentine*, and seruant, to you two thousand.   492
    Enter Valentine, Siluia,. Thurio, Speed, Duke, Protheus.   654
    Sir *Valentine*, your father is in good health,   699
    For *Valentine*, I need not cite him to it,   735
    Pro. Why *Valentine*, what Bragadisme is this?   818
    Me thinkes my zeale to *Valentine* is cold,   858
    Iulia I loose, and *Valentine* I loose,   948
    For *Valentine*, my selfe: for *Iulia*, *Siluia*.   951
    And *Valentine* Ile hold an Enemie,   958

VALENTINE *cont.*

Without some treachery vs'd to *Valentine*.	961
Who (all inrag'd) will banish *Valentine*:	967
But *Valentine* being gon, Ile quickely crosse	969
Enter Duke, Thurio, Protheus, Valentine, | *Launce, Speed.*	1068
Know (worthy Prince) Sir *Valentine* my friend	1079
Sir *Valentine* her companie, and my Court.	1096
Pro. Adiew, my Lord, Sir *Valentine* is comming.	1119
Duk. Sir *Valentine*, whether away so fast?	1120
There's not a haire on's head, but 'tis a *Valentine*.	1262
Pro. Valentine? | *Val.* No.	1263
Pro. Sirha, I say forbeare: friend *Valentine*, a word.	1274
Val. Is *Siluia* dead? | *Pro.* No, *Valentine*.	1279
Val. No *Valentine* indeed, for sacred *Siluia*,	1281
Hath she forsworne me? | *Pro.* No, *Valentine*.	1282
Val. No *Valentine*, if *Siluia* haue forsworne me.	1284
But *Valentine*, if he be tane, must die.	1302
Pro. Goe sirha, finde him out: Come *Valentine*.	1329
Val. Oh my deere *Siluia*; haplesse *Valentine*.	1330
Now *Valentine* is banish'd from her sight.	1448
And worthlesse *Valentine* shall be forgot.	1456
Pro. She did my Lord, when *Valentine* was here.	1473
The loue of *Valentine*, and loue sir *Thurio*?	1476
Pro. The best way is, to slander *Valentine*,	1477
But say this weede her loue from *Valentine*,	1495
As you, in worth dispraise, sir *Valentine*.	1501
To hate yong *Valentine*, and loue my friend.	1512
Enter Valentine, Speed, and certaine Out-lawes.	1546
Pro. Already haue I bin false to *Valentine*,	1625
Sil. Say that she be: yet *Valentine* thy friend	1733
Pro. I likewise heare that *Valentine* is dead.	1737
I beare vnto the banish'd *Valentine*:	1785
Sir *Eglamoure*: I would to *Valentine*	1792
Du. Why then | She's fled vnto that pezant, *Valentine*;	2078
Sil. O *Valentine*: this I endure for thee. | *Exeunt.*	2117
*Enter Valentine, Protheus, Siluia, Iulia, Duke, Thurio, | *Out-lawes.*	2120
Withdraw thee *Valentine*: who's this comes heere?	2139
Oh heauen be iudge how I loue *Valentine*,	2157
Thou friend of an ill fashion. | *Pro. Valentine.*	2185
Forgiue me *Valentine*: if hearty sorrow	2199
Your Grace is welcome to a man disgrac'd, | Banished *Valentine*.	2249
Duke. Sir *Valentine*?	2251
Thur. Sir *Valentine*, I care not for her, I:	2259
I doe applaud thy spirit, *Valentine*,	2267
To which I thus subscribe: Sir *Valentine*,	2272
Thurio: a foolish riuall to Valentine.	2306
Out-lawes with Valentine.	2309
Speed: a clownish seruant to Valentine.	2310
Siluia: beloued of Valentine.	2314

VALENTINES = 2*1

*Lu. Sir *Valentines* page: & sent I think from *Protheus*;	191
It is mine, or *Valentines* praise?	851
Because we know (on *Valentines* report)	1504

VALENTINUS = 1

With *Valentinus*, in the Emperors Court:	369

VALERIUS = 1

But *Moyses* and *Valerius* follow him:	2110

VALIANT = 1
Valiant, wise, remorse-full, well accomplish'd.   1783
VALOUR = 1
Thu. What sayes she to my valour?   2060
VANISHED = *1
Lau. Sir, there is a proclamation, y you are vanished.   1286
VANQUISHED = 1
Or else a wit, by folly vanquished.   39
VANTAGE = 2
And with the vantage of mine owne excuse   384
Without false vantage, or base treachery.   1575
VENGANCE = *1
*a veng'ance on't, there 'tis: Nor sir, this staffe is my si-|ster: 611
VENTURE = 1
That I may venture to depart alone.   1806
VERDURE = 1
Loosing his verdure, euen in the prime,   53
VERILY = *1
*vpon me that he did, I thinke verily hee had bin hang'd   1835
VERONA = 5
Duk. There is a Lady in *Verona* heere   1150
2.*Out.* Whether trauell you? | *Val.* To *Verona.*   1562
My selfe was from *Verona* banished,   1593
Verona shall not hold thee: heere she stands,   2256
THE | Two Gentlemen of Verona.   2317
VERTUE = 3*3
Is full of Vertue, Bounty, Worth, and Qualities   1134
*She can milke, looke you, a sweet vertue in a maid with | cleane
hands.   1345
La. A speciall vertue: for then shee neede not be | wash'd, and
scowr'd.   1375
To be slow in words, is a womans onely vertue: 1397
*I pray thee out with't, and place it for her chiefe vertue.   1398
To make a vertue of necessity,   1608
VERTUES = 2*1
Sp. Item, she hath many namelesse vertues.   1380
La. That's as much as to say *Bastard-vertues*: that   1381
La. Close at the heeles of her vertues.   1385
VERTUOUS = 1
A vertuous gentlewoman, milde, and beautifull.   2000
VERTUOUSLY = 1
Which, since I know they vertuously are plac'd,   1808
VERY = 14*3
Pro. Indeede a Sheepe doth very often stray,   78
Sp. Marry Sir, the letter very orderly,   125
Sil. I thanke you (gentle Seruant) 'tis very Clerkly-|(done.   498
I writ at randome, very doubtfully.   501
Sil. Yes, yes: the lines are very queintly writ,   513
*weeping: all the kinde of the *Launces*, haue this very   594
*one teare: he is a stone, a very pibble stone, and has no   602
Vpon the very naked name of Loue.   794
Lau. Marry after they cloas'd in earnest, they parted | very fairely in
iest.   883
Duk. This very night; for Loue is like a childe   1193
Especially against his very friend.   1487
Iu. Not so: but yet | So false that he grieues my very heart-strings.   1684
Sil. I am very loath to be your Idoll Sir;   1753

VERY *cont.*

Vaine *Thurio* (whom my very soule abhor'd.)	1787
That with his very heart despiseth me?	1915
If I in thought felt not her very sorrow.	1993
And now it is about the very houre	2029

VESTURE = 1

Should from her vesture chance to steale a kisse,	814

VEXATION = 1

It would be much vexation to your age.	1085

VEXE = 1

Away, I say: stayest thou to vexe me here;	1880

VICE = *1

Sp. Well, your old vice still: mistake the word: what | newes then in your paper?	1350

VICES = 1*1

Sp. Here follow her vices.	1384
La. Oh villaine, that set this downe among her vices;	1396

VICTUALS = *1

*victuals; and would faine haue meate: oh bee not like	564

VIEW = 1

And would not force the letter to my view?	208

VILE = 1

3.*Out*. No, we detest such vile base practises.	1619

VILLAINE = 2*1

Pro. Villaine, forbeare.	1272
La. Oh villaine, that set this downe among her vices;	1396
Val. Peace villaine.	1587

VILLAINES = 1

Sp. Sir we are vndone; these are the Villaines	1551

VISIBLY = 1

Are visibly Character'd, and engrau'd,	979

VISIT = 1

Visit by night your Ladies chamber-window	1529

VISITE = 1

And I likewise will visite thee with mine.	64

VNADUISD = 1

Pardon me (Madam) I haue vnaduis'd	1943

VNCERTAINE = 1

The vncertaine glory of an Aprill day,	387

VNCIUILL = 2

To keepe them from vnciuill outrages.	2138
Val. Ruffian: let goe that rude vnciuill touch,	2184

VNCOMPASSIONATE = 1

Could penetrate her vncompassionate Sire;	1301

VNDER *see also* stand-vnder = 4*1

Spee. It stands vnder thee indeed.	900
Lau. Why, stand-vnder: and vnder-stand is all one.	901
Vnder a cloake, that is of any length.	1199
Vnder the colour of commending him,	1627
*foure gentleman-like-dogs, vnder the Dukes table: hee	1838

VNDERGOE = 1

Would I not vndergoe, for one calme looke:	2163

VNDERSTAND = 1

Spee. What an asse art thou, I vnderstand thee not.	894

VNDERSTANDS = 2

My staffe vnderstands me? | *Spee*. What thou saist?	896
and my staffe vnderstands me.	899

VNDERTAKE = 2
How with my honour I may vndertake   981
Du. Then you must vndertake to slander him.   1484
VNDERTAKING = 1
For vndertaking so vnstaid a iourney?   1035
VNDER-STAND = 1
Lau. Why, stand-vnder: and vnder-stand is all one.   901
VNDESERUING = 1
Done to me (vndeseruing as I am)   1076
VNDON = *1
*vndon till hee be hang'd, nor neuer welcome to a place,   876
VNDONE = 1
Sp. Sir we are vndone; these are the Villaines   1551
VNFREQUENTED = 1
This shadowy desert, vnfrequented woods   2123
VNGARTERD = *1
*to haue, when you chidde at Sir *Protheus*, for going vn-|garter'd.   465
VNGOUERND = 1
Such as the fury of vngouern'd youth   1591
VNHAPPY = 5*1
And now am I (vnhappy Messenger)   1920
Haue some vnhappy passenger in chace;   2136
Sil. O miserable, vnhappy that I am.   2149
Pro. Vnhappy were you (Madam) ere I came: 2150
Sil. By thy approach thou mak'st me most vnhappy.   2152
Iul. Oh me vnhappy.   2210
VNHEEDFULLY = 1
Luc. I Madam, so you stumble not vnheedfully.   156
VNHOLY = 1
To keepe me from a most vnholy match,   1800
VNIUERSITIES = 1
Some, to the studious Vniuersities;   312
VNIUST = 2
And now I must be as vniust to *Thurio*,   1626
For *Thesus* periury, and vniust flight;   1989
VNKINDE = 1
Looke, here is writ, kinde *Iulia*: vnkinde *Iulia*,   269
VNKINDEST = 2
vnkindest Tide, that euer any man tide.   631
Panth. What's the vnkindest tide?   632
VNKNOWN = 1
'Tis not vnknown to thee, that I haue sought   1130
VNLES = *1
Val. No more: vnles the next word that thou speak'st   1307
VNLESSE = 8
Vnlesse it haue a false Interpreter.   235
Vnlesse you haue a cod-peece to stick pins on.   1031
Vnlesse it be to thinke that she is by   1246
Vnlesse I looke on *Siluia* in the day,   1250
Vnlesse I proue false traitor to my selfe.   1926
Vnlesse I flatter with my selfe too much.   2008
Vnlesse it be to come before their time,   2032
Thou hast no faith left now, vnlesse thou'dst two,   2171
VNMANNERLY = *1
*An vnmannerly slaue, that will thrust himselfe into se-|crets: 1443
VNPREUENTED = 1
(Being vnpreuented) to your timelesse graue.   1090

VNREUEREND = 1
Fie, fie, vnreuerend tongue, to call her bad,   943
VNRULY = 1
Iu. The meane is dround with you vnruly base.   256
VNSEEING = 1
I should haue scratch'd out your vnseeing eyes,   2024
VNSEENE = 1
Speed. Oh lest vnseene: inscrutible: inuisible,   526
VNSOUNDED = 1
Forsake vnsounded deepes, to dance on Sands.   1527
VNSTAID = 1
For vndertaking so vnstaid a iourney?   1035
VNTO = 12*1
Vnto a ragged, fearefull, hanging Rocke,   281
Vnto the secret, nameles friend of yours: 495
*Her self hath taught her Loue himself, to write vnto her | (louer.   558
I must vnto the Road, to dis-embarque   842
For, loue of you, not hate vnto my friend,   1115
Vnto a youthfull Gentleman of worth,   1176
And heire and Neece, alide vnto the Duke.   1595
Who, in my moode, I stab'd vnto the heart.   1597
Often resort vnto this Gentlewoman?   1695
I beare vnto the banish'd *Valentine*:   1785
Your message done, hye home vnto my chamber,   1909
Du. Why then | She's fled vnto that pezant, *Valentine*;   2078
Pro. But how cam'st thou by this ring? at my depart | I gaue this vnto
Iulia.   2222
VNWILLING = 1
Which I was much vnwilling to proceed in,   496
VNWILLINGLY = 1
But (since vnwillingly) take them againe. | Nay, take them.   514
VNWINDE = 1
Th. Therefore, as you vnwinde her loue from him;   1497
VNWORTHILY = 1
And so (vnworthily) disgrace the man   1098
VNWORTHY = 1
That I (vnworthy body as I am)   171
VN-HEEDFULL = 1
Vn-heedfull vowes may heedfully be broken,   940
VN-MELLOWED = 1
His head vn-mellowed, but his Iudgement ripe;   720
VN-REUERST = 1
(Which vn-reuerst stands in effectuall force)   1293
VN-RIUALD = 1
Plead a new state in thy vn-riual'd merit,   2271
VN-SEENE = 1
Here can I sit alone, vn-seene of any,   2125
VN-TUNEABLE = 1
For they are harsh, vn-tuneable, and bad.   1278
VN-WELCOME = 1
I thinke 'tis no vn-welcome newes to you.   731
VOICE = 1
You would quickly learne to know him by his voice.   1712
VOLLY = *1
Sil. A fine volly of words, gentleme(n), & quickly shot off   684
VOTARY = 2
That art a votary to fond desire?   56

VOTARY *cont.*
You are already loues firme votary,   1505
VOUCHSAFE = 2
Vouchsafe me yet your Picture for my loue,   1745
Vouchsafe me for my meed, but one faire looke: 2144
VOW = 1
That vs'd me so: or else by *Ioue*, I vow,   2023
VOWDST = 1
Vpon whose Graue thou vow'dst pure chastitie: 1791
VOWES = 4
Vn-heedfull vowes may heedfully be broken,   940
Should be full fraught with seruiceable vowes.   1517
When to her beauty I commend my vowes,   1633
That has't deceiu'd so many with thy vowes?   1722
VOYAGE = *3
*in loosing the flood, loose thy voyage, and in loosing thy   635
*voyage, loose thy Master, and in loosing thy Master,   636
Laun. Loose the Tide, and the voyage, and the Ma-|ster,   643
VP = 10*5
Iu. What is't that you | Tooke vp so gingerly?   226
Lu. To take a paper vp, that I let fall.   230
Iu. If you respect them; best to take them vp.   293
Lu. Nay, I was taken vp, for laying them downe.   294
*there 'tis; heere's my mothers breath vp and downe: 621
Iul. The more thou dam'st it vp, the more it burnes: 999
Iul. No girle, Ile knit it vp in silken strings,   1020
To cast vp, with a paire of anchoring hookes,   1187
But neither bended knees, pure hands held vp,   1299
*him (looke you) it goes hard: one that I brought vp of   1823
*third) hang him vp (saies the Duke.) I hauing bin ac-|quainted   1842
*thou see me heaue vp my leg, and make water against a   1856
Witnesse good bringing vp, fortune, and truth: 1888
Come shadow, come, and take this shadow vp,   2017
*Why wag: how now? what's the matter? look vp: speak.   2213
VPON = 32*2
Pro. Vpon some booke I loue, I'le pray for thee.   23
And not vpon your Maid.   225
Thus will I fold them, one vpon another;   288
Vpon some other pawne for fealty.   741
Vpon a homely obiect, Loue can winke.   748
Sil. I wait vpon his pleasure: Come Sir *Thurio*,   768
Pro. Wee'll both attend vpon your Ladiship.   772
Vpon the very naked name of Loue.   794
Because thou seest me doate vpon my loue: 828
To furnish me vpon my longing iourney: 1060
Duke. Vpon mine Honor, he shall neuer know   1117
(Vpon aduice) hath drawne my loue from her,   1142
I pray thee let me feele thy cloake vpon me.   1206
And feed vpon the shadow of perfection.   1247
There is no day for me to looke vpon.   1251
Val. Oh, I haue fed vpon this woe already,   1289
With them vpon her knees, her humble selfe,   1296
Haue some malignant power vpon my life: 1308
Let me not liue, to looke vpon your Grace.   1467
Vpon this warrant, shall you haue accesse,   1507
Pro. Say that vpon the altar of her beauty   1519
Pro. We'll wait vpon your Grace, till after Supper,   1542

VPON *cont.*

Vpon the dull earth dwelling.	1676
Vpon whose Graue thou vow'dst pure chastitie:	1791
Vpon whose faith and honor, I repose.	1796
But thinke vpon my griefe (a Ladies griefe)	1798
*I would haue (as one should say) one that takes vp-|on	1832
*vpon me that he did, I thinke verily hee had bin hang'd	1835
Sil. There, hold: | I will not looke vpon your Masters lines:	1948
To thinke vpon her woes, I doe protest	1965
I weepe my selfe to thinke vpon thy words:	1996
Vpon the rising of the Mountaine foote	2090
Be thou asham'd that I haue tooke vpon me,	2231
I dare thee, but to breath vpon my Loue.	2258

VPPER = 1

I nightly lodge her in an vpper Towre,	1104

VRGE = 1

Vrge not my fathers anger (*Eglamoure*)	1797

VRINALL = *1

*and shine through you like the water in an Vrinall: that	433

VRSULA = 1

Sil. Vrsula, bring my Picture there,	1938

VS *see also* let's *l.**60 168 291 1070 1537 *1549 1588 1590 1611 1620 1642 1673 1677 2109 2287 = 13*2

VSD = 2

Without some treachery vs'd to *Valentine*.	961
That vs'd me so: or else by *Ioue*, I vow,	2023

VSE = 8

Made vse, and faire aduantage of his daies:	718
Some necessaries, that I needs must vse,	843
If not, to compasse her Ile vse my skill. | *Exeunt*.	869
Iul. Base men, that vse them to so base effect;	1048
Val. When would you vse it? pray sir, tell me that.	1192
Ile vse thee kindly, for thy Mistris sake	2022
And will not vse a woman lawlesly.	2116
Val. How vse doth breed a habit in a man?	2122

VTTER = 1

My dutie pricks me on to vtter that	1077

W = *1

*to Madam *Siluia*: w (out of my neglect) was neuer done.	2215

WAG = *1

*Why wag: how now? what's the matter? look vp: speak.	2213

WAGES = *3

*for wages followest thy Master, thy Master for wages	95
*for she is her Masters maid, and serues for wages. Shee	1339

WAIES = 1

And for the waies are dangerous to passe,	1794

WAIGHTING-WOMAN = 1

Lucetta: waighting-woman to Iulia. | FINIS.	2315

WAIT = 3

Sil. I wait vpon his pleasure: Come Sir *Thurio*,	768
Pro. We'll wait vpon your Grace, till after Supper,	1542
That wait for execution in the morne.	1759

WAKE = 1

Sp. Why then my hornes are his hornes, whether I | wake or sleepe.	83

WALEFULL = 1
By walefull Sonnets, whose composed Rimes   1516
WALKD = *1
*like a cocke; when you walk'd, to walke like one of the   422
WALKE = 2*2
*to walke alone like one that had the pestilence: 416
*like a cocke; when you walk'd, to walke like one of the   422
Hope is a louers staffe, walke hence with that   1316
Val. And as we walke along, I dare be bold   2289
·WALL = 1
Out at the Posterne by the Abbey wall;   2036
WAND = *1
*small as a wand: this hat is *Nan* our maid: I am the   613
WANDERD = 1
As he, in pennance wander'd through the Forrest: 2082
WANT = 4*1
*when you look'd sadly, it was for want of money: And   424
Or else for want of idle time, could not againe reply,   556
Sil. And dutie neuer yet did want his meed.   762
Because my selfe doe want my seruants fortune.   1217
As we doe in our quality much want.   1604
WANTETH = 1
There wanteth but a Meane to fill your Song.   255
WANTON = 2
Dare you presume to harbour wanton lines?   195
Thu. Nay then the wanton lyes: my face is blacke.   2051
WANTS = 2
And he wants wit, that wants resolued will,   941
WANTST = *1
Ant. Look what thou want'st shalbe sent after thee: 376
WAR = 1
Pro. Ill, when you talke of war.   2057
WARD = 1
Fie, fie: how way-ward is this foolish loue;   211
WARRANT = 4*1
Speed. Ile warrant you, 'tis as well: 554
Sil. His worth is warrant.for his welcome hether,   752
Warrant me welcome to my *Protheus*.   1046
Vpon this warrant, shall you haue accesse,   1507
Val. I warrant you (my Lord) more grace, then Boy.   2293
WARRE = 1
Warre with good counsaile; set the world at nought;   72
WARRES = 1
Some to the warres, to try their fortune there;   310
WAS *see also* 'twas = 31*12
WASH = 1
Sp. Item, she can wash and scoure.   1374
WASHD = 1
La. A speciall vertue: for then shee neede not be | wash'd, and
scowr'd.   1375
WASPES = 1
Iniurious Waspes, to feede on such sweet hony,   266
WASTE = 1
But wherefore waste I time to counsaile thee   55
WATCH = *1
*to fast, like one that takes diet: to watch, like one that   419

WATCHD = 1
   That ere I watch'd, and the most heauiest.   1766
WATCHERS = 1
   And made them watchers of mine owne hearts sorrow.   787
WATCHFULL = 1
   With twenty watchfull, weary, tedious nights;   35
WATER = 2*2
   *and shine through you like the water in an Vrinall: that   433
   The water, Nectar, and the Rocks pure gold.   826
   Dissolues to water, and doth loose his forme.   1454
   *thou see me heaue vp my leg, and make water against a   1856
WATER-SPANIELL = *1
   *hath more qualities then a Water-Spaniell, which is   1340
WAXED = 1
   As if but now they waxed pale for woe: 1298
WAXEN = 1
   Which like a waxen Image 'gainst a fire   856
WAY = 7
   He would haue giuen it you, but I being in the way,   192
   How could he see his way to seeke out you?   744
   Luc. Alas, the way is wearisome and long.   983
   And this way comes he with it presently.   1111
   How, and which way I may bestow my selfe   1156
   Pro. The best way is, to slander *Valentine,*   1477
   Can no way change you to a milder forme;   2179
WAYLING = *1
   *wayling: my Sister crying: our Maid howling: our   599
WAY-WARD = 1
   Fie, fie: how way-ward is this foolish loue;   211
WE = 27*3
WEAKE = 1*1
   *Made Wit with musing, weake; hart sick with thought.   73
   Du. This weake impresse of Loue, is as a figure   1452
WEALTH = 4
   Lu. Well of his wealth; but of himselfe, so, so.   166
   faults then haires, and more wealth then faults.   1415
   Sp. And more wealth then faults.   1427
   Val. Then know that I haue little wealth to loose;   1557
WEARE = 3*1
   Weare out thy youth with shapelesse idlenesse.   11
   What compasse will you weare your Farthingale?   1026
   Duk. How shall I fashion me to weare a cloake?   1205
   Thu. Ile weare a Boote, to make it somewhat roun-|(der.   2047
WEARISOME = 1
   Luc. Alas, the way is wearisome and long.   983
WEARY = 4
   With twenty watchfull, weary, tedious nights;   35
   Pro. My tales of Loue were wont to weary you,   778
   Iul. A true-deuoted Pilgrime is not weary   984
   And make a pastime of each weary step,   1010
WED = 1
   For *Thurio* he intends shall wed his daughter,   968
WEDDING = 1
   Then let her beauty be her wedding dowre: 1147
WEEDE = 1
   But say this weede her loue from *Valentine,*   1495

WEEDES = 1
Gentle *Lucetta*, fit me with such weedes   1017
WEELL = 3
Pro. Why then wee'll make exchange; | Here, take you this.   573
Pro. Wee'll both attend vpon your Ladiship.   772
There is our Captaine: Wee'll follow him that's fled,   2112
WEENING = 1
Goe base Intruder, ouer-weening Slaue,   1227
WEEP = *1
*weep like a yong wench that had buried her Grandam: 418
WEEPE = 3
To that ile speake, to that ile sigh and weepe: 1747
And at that time I made her weepe a good,   1986
I weepe my selfe to thinke vpon thy words: 1996
WEEPES = *1
*now should I kisse my Father; well, hee weepes on: 618
WEEPING = *3
*weeping: all the kinde of the *Launces*, haue this very   594
*dogge that liues: My Mother weeping: my Father   598
*should not the shooe speake a word for weeping: 617
WEEPST = *1
*matter? why weep'st thou man? away asse, you'l loose   628
WEL = *2
Val. I know it wel sir, you alwaies end ere you begin.   683
Pro. Your frends are wel, & haue the(m) much com(m)ended.   774
WELCOME = 10*4
I thinke 'tis no vn-welcome newes to you.   731
Duk. Welcome him then according to his worth: 733
Val. Welcome, deer *Protheus*: Mistris, I beseech you   750
Confirme his welcome, with some speciall fauor.   751
Sil. His worth is warrant for his welcome hether,   752
Seruant, you are welcome to a worthlesse Mistresse.   763
Sil. That you are welcome?   765
Goe with me: once more, new Seruant welcome;   769
Speed. *Launce*, by mine honesty welcome to *Padua*.   873
*not welcome. I reckon this alwaies, that a man is neuer   875
*vndon till hee be hang'd, nor neuer welcome to a place,   876
*till some certaine shot be paid, and the Hostesse say wel- | come.   877
Warrant me welcome to my *Protheus*.   1046
Your Grace is welcome to a man disgrac'd, | Banished *Valentine*.   2249
WELCOMES = *1
*thou shalt haue fiue thousand welcomes: But sirha, how   881
WELL = 47*11
Pro. A silly answere, and fitting well a Sheepe.   85
Sp. Well, I perceiue I must be faine to beare with you.   123
Pro. Well Sir: here is for your paines: what said she?   133
Lu. Well of his wealth; but of himselfe, so, so.   166
Iu. Well, let vs goe.   291
I haue consider'd well, his losse of time,   321
Ant. I know it well.   330
Ant. I like thy counsaile: well hast thou aduis'd: 336
And that thou maist perceiue how well I like it,   337
Val. Well: you'll still be too forward.   408
Val. Not so faire (boy) as well fauour'd.   443
Speed. Sir, I know that well enough.   444
Val. No (Boy) but as well as I can do them: 485
Sil. A pretty period: well: I ghesse the sequell;   506

WELL *cont.*

Speed. Ile warrant you, 'tis as well:	554
*now should I kisse my Father; well, hee weepes on:	618
*now, like a would-woman: well, I kisse her: why	620
Laun. Well, I will goe. | *Exeunt.*	651
Val. Well then, Ile double your folly. | *Thu*. How?	675
*Val. I know it well sir: you haue an Exchequer of | (words,	692
And not without desert so well reputed.	707
Val. I, my good Lord, a Son, that well deserues	709
Duk. You know him well?	711
Well, Sir: this Gentleman is come to me	728
*Lau. Marry thus, when it stands well with him, it | stands well with her.	892
*Spee. 'Tis well that I get it so: but *Launce*, how saist	909
As may beseeme some well reputed Page.	1018
Iul. That fits as well, as tell me (good my Lord)	1025
Val. I know it well (my Lord) and sure the Match	1132
*Sp. Well, your old vice still: mistake the word: what | newes then in your paper?	1350
*La. Well: that fault may be mended with a break-|fast: read on.	1388
La. Well: the best is, she hath no teeth to bite.	1405
*keepe shut: Now, of another thing shee may, and that | cannot I helpe. Well, proceede.	1412
**Well, ile haue her: and if it be a match, as nothing is | impossible.	1429
Will well become such sweet complaining grieuance:	1532
To sort some Gentlemen, well skil'd in Musicke.	1538
Pro. We'll wait vpon your Grace, till after Supper,	1542
If not: we'll make you sit, and rifle you.	1550
2.*Out*. Peace: we'll heare him.	1555
1.*Out*. We'll haue him: Sirs, a word.	1584
We'll doe thee homage, and be rul'd by thee,	1612
Come, goe with vs, we'll bring thee to our Crewes,	1620
*Ho. Come, we'll haue you merry: ile bring you where	1654
Th. Where meete we? | *Pro*. At Saint *Gregories* well. | *Th*. Farewell.	1705
But, since your falsehood shall become you well	1754
Valiant, wise, remorse-full, well accomplish'd.	1783
Pro. *Sebastian* is thy name: I like thee well,	1859
She lou'd me well, deliuer'd it to me.	1892
Iul. Because, me thinkes that she lou'd you as well	1900
Pro. Well: giue her that Ring, and therewithall	1906
Iul. Almost as well as I doe know my selfe.	1964
When she did thinke my Master lou'd her well;	1971
Thu. But well, when I discourse of loue and peace.	2058
Pro. That you are well deriu'd.	2064
Him he knew well: and guesd that it was she,	2083
They loue me well: yet I haue much to doe	2137
Thou art a Gentleman, and well deriu'd,	2273

WELL-BELOUD = 1

How happily he liues, how well-belou'd,	359

WELL-FAUOURD = *1

*Speed. That shee is not so faire, as (of you) well-fa-|uourd?	446

WELL-SPOKEN = 1

Lu. As of a Knight, well-spoken, neat, and fine;	163

WENCH = 1*2

*weep like a yong wench that had buried her Grandam:	418
But tell me (wench) how will the world repute me	1034
*La. What neede a man care for a stock with a wench,	1372

197

WENT = *1
    *foure of his blinde brothers and sisters went to it: I haue   1825
WEPT = 2*2
    *more pitty in him then a dogge: a Iew would haue wept   603
    *no eyes, looke you, wept her selfe blinde at my parting: 605
    That I haue wept a hundred seuerall times.   1966
    Wept bitterly: and would I might be dead,   1992
WERE *see also* 'twere *l.**105 164 205 222 243 264 326 *421 *431 *464
    *478 553 *630 *645 646 778 825 1133 1140 1426 1569 1576 1577 1583
    *1678 *1687 *1833 1980 2006 2016 2020 2150 *2236 2237 = 23*11
WERT = 1
    Wer't not affection chaines thy tender dayes   6
WEST = 1
    Goe thou with her to the West end of the wood,   2111
WESTERNE = 1
    Egl. The Sun begins to guild the westerne skie,   2028
WETHERCOCKE = *1
    *As a nose on a mans face, or a Wethercocke on a steeple: 527
WHAT *l.*31 62 114 *129 *133 141 162 165 167 168 *169 207 220 226 289
    *292 297 302 305 *353 357 367 370 *376 445 467 511 523 533 536 540
    542 584 649 668 670 677 *689 700 818 889 894 895 896 *898 1014 *1024
    1026 1027 1033 1059 *1149 *1162 1169 1182 1207 1244 1245 1260 1267
    1285 *1336 *1347 *1350 *1372 1431 1475 1569 1570 *1610 *1615 1663
    1690 1696 1779 1784 1805 1810 *1841 1861 1867 1873 1931 1959 2014
    2042 2045 2048 2049 2060 2063 2131 2134 *2162 2240 2278 2281 2291
    2294 2296 = 84*19
WHATS = 5*3
    *ship'd, and thou art to post after with oares; what's the   627
    Panth. What's the vnkindest tide?   632
    Now tell me *Protheus*, what's your will with me?   1072
    What Letter is this same? what's here? to *Siluia*?   1207
    What's here? *Siluia, this night I will enfranchise thee.*   1220
    *then the wit; for the greater hides the lesse: What's | next?   1423
    Sil. What's your will? | *Pro.* That I may compasse yours.   1715
    *Why wag: how now? what's the matter? look vp: speak.   2213
WHEELES = *1
    La. Then may I set the world on wheeles, when she | can spin for her
    liuing.   1378
WHEN *l.*13 15 18 215 217 *421 *422 *423 *424 *425 *465 521 544 570
    577 771 802 866 *892 987 1002 1040 1041 *1054 1075 1094 1192 1304
    1373 *1378 1473 1631 1633 1689 1790 1812 *1822 *1824 *1831 *1854
    *1855 1918 1971 1980 2057 2058 2059 *2062 2094 *2153 2165 *2166
    2192 = 36*17
WHENCE = 1*1
    Val. Now tell me: how do al from whence you came?   773
    1.Out. Whence came you? | *Val.* From *Millaine*.   1564
WHERE *l.*33 234 381 569 640 *880 947 1112 1143 1191 1213 1219 *1488
    1508 1511 1644 *1654 1698 1705 1762 1793 1814 1816 1864 1910 1930
    2034 2108 2165 *2166 2216 2308 = 27*5
WHEREFORE = 3
    But wherefore waste I time to counsaile thee   55
    Pro. Wherefore should'st thou pitty her?   1899
    Thu. Wherefore? | *Iul.* That such an Asse should owe them.   2068
WHEREIN = 3
    Wherein I sigh not (*Iulia*) for thy sake,   578
    Who art the Table wherein all my thoughts   978
    That touch me neere: wherein thou must be secret.   1129

WHEREOF = 2*1
  *In requital whereof, henceforth, carry your letters your   144
  The key whereof, my selfe haue euer kept: 1105
  The least whereof would quell a louers hope: 1637
WHEREON = 1
  Whereon, this month I haue bin hamering.   320
WHEREWITH = 1
  Wherewith my brother held you in the Cloyster?   303
WHETHER = 4*1
  *Sp. Why then my hornes are his hornes, whether I | wake or sleepe.   83
  Then tell me, whether were I best to send him?   326
  Duk. Sir Valentine, whether away so fast?   1120
  2.Out. Whether trauell you? | Val. To Verona.   1562
  That leads toward Mantua, whether they are fled: 2091
WHICH see also w l.147 159 206 210 317 388 *475 496 856 933 *1073
  1078 1089 1092 1101 1110 1156 1232 1293 1294 1312 1319 *1340 1453
  1500 1560 1572 1622 *1699 1801 1808 1887 1921 1922 1923 1951 1983
  1990 2073 2173 2272 = 37*4
WHILE = 8*2
  While other men, of slender reputation   308
  *now the dogge all this while sheds not a teare: nor   623
  And heere he meanes to spend his time a while,   730
  Duke. Sir Thurio, giue vs leaue (I pray) a while,   1070
  Which to requite, command me while I liue.   1092
  Duk. Nay then no matter: stay with me a while,   1127
  While I (their King) that thither them importune   1215
  Let's tune: and too it lustily a while.   1650
  *had not bin there (blesse the marke) a pissing while, but   1839
  Loue, lend me patience to forbeare a while.   2148
WHIP = *2
  *what cur is that (saies another) whip him out (saies the   1841
  *(quoth I) you meane to whip the dog: I marry doe I   1845
WHIPS = *2
  *goes me to the fellow that whips the dogges: friend   1844
  *but whips me out of the chamber: how many Masters   1848
WHIRLE-WINDE = *1
  *Except mine own name: That, some whirle-winde beare   280
WHISPER = 1
  To whisper, and conspire against my youth?   196
WHIT = 1
  Iu. Not a whit, when it iars so.   1689
WHITE = 1*1
  *for, looke you, she is as white as a lilly, and as   612
  Euen in the milke-white bosome of thy Loue.   1320
WHITENES = *1
  *Wringing her hands, whose whitenes so became them,   1297
WHO l.190 406 686 967 978 1146 1265 1270 *1335 1358 *1435 1597 1647
  1663 1710 1772 1876 2175 2192 2205 = 18*2
WHOLE = 1
  Lau. No; they are both as whole as a fish.   890
WHOM l.188 500 538 1083 1151 1483 1635 1734 1787 1934 = 10
WHORSON = 1
  Spee. Why, thou whorson Asse, thou mistak'st me,   915
WHOR-SON = 1
  How now you whor-son pezant,   1863
WHOS = 2
  No matter who's displeas'd, when you are gone: 1041

WHOS *cont.*
   Withdraw thee *Valentine*: who's this comes heere?   2139
WHOSE = 10*1
   Whose high emperious thoughts haue punish'd me   782
   To her, whose worth, make other worthies nothing;   820
   Whose soueraignty so oft thou hast preferd,   944
   *Wringing her hands, whose whitenes so became them,   1297
   By walefull Sonnets, whose composed Rimes   1516
   Whose golden touch could soften steele and stones;   1525
   I kil'd a man, whose death I much repent,   1573
   Vpon whose Graue thou vow'dst pure chastitie: 1791
   Vpon whose faith and honor, I repose.   1796
   Whose life's as tender to me as my soule,   2158
   For whose deare sake, thou didst then rend thy faith   2168
WHY *l.*37 *83 116 124 *135 173 180 228 244 305 392 *399 406 412 439
   461 522 524 *538 542 545 550 560 573 *604 *620 *628 633 *644 745 818
   *823 891 901 915 *916 *919 923 1019 1027 1168 1179 1186 *1204 1222
   *1240 1273 *1342 1349 1353 1428 *1432 *1440 1576 1652 1681 1896
   1914 2078 2093 2211 *2213 2218 = 47*17
WIFE = 2
   Beseeming such a Wife, as your faire daughter: 1135
   I now am full resolu'd to take a wife,   1145
WILBE = 1
   Iul. Out, out, (*Lucetta*) that wilbe illfauourd.   1029
WILDE = 2
   With willing sport to the wilde Ocean.   1007
   This fellow were a King, for our wilde faction.   1583
WILDERNESSE = 1
   And liue as we doe in this wildernesse?   1609
WILL *see also* I'le, she'll, 'twill, wee'll, we'll, you'l, you'll *l.*21 31 59 64 97
   189 202 212 234 248 286 288 289 340 346 367 488 503 507 510 518 570
   571 583 651 702 736 761 799 811 845 868 *903 904 906 956 967 1014
   1026 1034 1036 1038 1042 1108 1146 1196 1198 1200 *1204 1220 1235
   1238 1277 1290 1315 *1337 1358 1406 *1407 1408 *1432 1439 *1442
   *1443 1447 1455 1461 1496 1510 1513 1532 1533 1539 *1544 *1556 1616
   1644 1659 1703 1750 1760 1812 1817 1860 1927 1948 1951 2001 2031
   2048 2097 2099 2116 2260 2287 2296 = 89*10, 10
   And to commend their seruice to his will.   344
   Pro. As one relying on your Lordships will,   363
   Ant. My will is something sorted with his wish: 365
   And he wants wit, that wants resolued will,   941
   Now tell me *Protheus*, what's your will with me?   1072
   How she opposes her against my will?   1472
   Sil. What's your will? | *Pro.* That I may compasse yours.   1715
   Sil. You haue your wish: my will is euen this,   1717
   Thou art not ignorant what deere good will   1784
   To binde him to remember my good will: 1919
WILLING = 1
   With willing sport to the wilde Ocean.   1007
WILLINGLY = 2
   When willingly, I would haue had her here?   215
   Du. Thou know'st how willingly, I would effect   1468
WILLS = 1
   These are my mates, that make their wills their Law,   2135
WILT *see also* thou'lt *l.*14 649 809 *920 925 1223 1225 *1610 1862 = 7*2,
   2
   Iu. Come, come, wilt please you goe. *Exeunt.*   299

WILT *cont.*
    Spee. But tell me true, wil't be a match?   902
WIN = 4
    Sp. Truely Sir, I thinke you'll hardly win her.   134
    Cannot your Grace win her to fancie him?   1136
    Val. Win her with gifts, if she respect not words,   1158
    If with his tongue he cannot win a woman.   1174
WINDE = 1 *2
    Be calme (good winde) blow not a word away,   278
    *Except mine own name: That, some whirle-winde beare   280
    *were drie, I am able to fill it with my teares: if the winde   645
WINDING = 1
    And so by many winding nookes he straies   1006
WINDOW = 6
    Determin'd of: how I must climbe her window,   836
    To climbe celestiall *Siluia's* chamber window,   963
    How he her chamber-window will ascend,   1108
    Val. What letts but one may enter at her window?   1182
    Visit by night your Ladies chamber-window   1529
    But here comes *Thurio*; now must we to her window,   1640
WINGS = 2
    Loue lend me wings, to make my purpose swift   971
    Much lesse shall she that hath Loues wings to flie,   986
WINKE = 3
    I see things too, although you iudge I winke.   298
    Vpon a homely obiect, Loue can winke.   748
    For I had rather winke, then looke on them.   2055
WINTER = 1
    And make rough winter euerlastingly.   817
WIPE = 1
    You could not see to wipe my shooes.   473
WISE = 4
    Me thinkes should not be chronicled for wise.   45
    Thu. What seeme I that I am not? | *Val.* Wise.   668
    Holy, faire, and wise is she,   1665
    Valiant, wise, remorse-full, well accomplish'd.   . 1783
WISH = 6 *1
    Wish me partaker in thy happinesse,   17
    Ant. And how stand you affected to his wish?   362
    And not depending on his friendly wish.   364
    Ant. My will is something sorted with his wish: 365
    Sil. You haue your wish: my will is euen this,   1717
    As much, I wish all good befortune you.   1811
    Pro. Beare witnes (heauen) I haue my wish for euer.   2245
WISHD = 2
    Val. Should I haue wish'd a thing, it had beene he.   732
    If this be he you oft haue wish'd to heare from.   753
WISHING = 1
    Wishing me with him, partner of his fortune.   361
WIT = 9 *8
    How euer: but a folly bought with wit,   38
    Or else a wit, by folly vanquished.   39
    Euen so by Loue, the yong, and tender wit   51
    *Made Wit with musing, weake; hart sick with thought.   73
    Pro. Beshrew me, but you haue a quicke wit.   127
    *Sir *Thurio* borrows his wit from your Ladiships lookes,   688

WIT *cont.*
  Thu. Sir, if you spend word for word with me, I shall | make your wit
  bankrupt.   690
  And he wants wit, that wants resolued will,   941
  To learne his wit, t'exchange the bad for better;   942
  As thou hast lent me wit, to plot this drift. | *Exit.*   972
  *the wit to thinke my Master is a kinde of knaue: but   1332
  Sp. Item, shee hath more haire then wit, and more   1414
  Sp. Item, she hath more haire then wit.   1419
  La. More haire then wit: it may be ile proue it: The   1420
  *then the salt; the haire that couers the wit, is more   1422
  *then the wit; for the greater hides the lesse: What's | next?   1423
  *things. If I had not had more wit then he, to take a fault   1834
WITH = 121 *28
WITHALL = 1
  Val. These banish'd men, that I haue kept withall,   2279
WITHDRAW = 1
  Withdraw thee *Valentine*: who's this comes heere?   2139
WITHIN = 2 *1
  Speed. Shee is not within hearing Sir.   405
  *so without these follies, that these follies are within you,   432
  Come not within the measure of my wrath: 2254
WITHOUT = 8 *4
  Speed. They are all perceiu'd without ye.   428
  Val. Without me? they cannot.   429
  Speed. Without you? nay, that's certaine: for with-|out   430
  *so without these follies, that these follies are within you,   432
  Iulia, farewell: what, gon without a word?   584
  And not without desert so well reputed.   707
  That thus without aduice begin to loue her?   863
  Without some treachery vs'd to *Valentine*.   961
  Without apparant hazard of his life.   1185
  Without false vantage, or base treachery.   1575
  Val. Thou co(m)mon friend, that's without faith or loue,   2187
WITHT = *1
  *I pray thee out with't, and place it for her chiefe vertue.   1398
WITNES = *1
  Pro. Beare witnes (heauen) I haue my wish for euer.   2245
WITNESSE = 3
  And *Siluia* (witnesse heauen that made her faire)   954
  Suruiues; to whom (thy selfe art witnesse)   1734
  Witnesse good bringing vp, fortune, and truth: 1888
WITS = 1 *1
  *Home-keeping youth, haue euer homely wits,   5
  Inhabits in the finest wits of all.   48
WOE = 4
  There is no woe to his correction,   790
  Val. Oh, I haue fed vpon this woe already,   1289
  As if but now they waxed pale for woe: 1298
  Yet will I woe for him, but yet so coldly,   1927
WOES = 2 *1
  Val. To whom? | *Speed.* To your selfe: why, she woes you by a figure.   538
  To thinke vpon her woes, I doe protest   1965
  Tune my distresses, and record my woes.   2127
WOLD *l.*767 *1073 = *2
WOMAN = 4 *4
  *now, like a would-woman: well, I kisse her: why   620

WOMAN *cont.*

Iul. Not like a woman, for I would preuent	1015
*Val. A woman somtime scorns what best co(n)tents her.	1162
If with his tongue he cannot win a woman.	1174
**'tis I loue: and yet 'tis a woman; but what woman, I	1336
And will not vse a woman lawlesly.	2116
Lucetta: waighting-woman to Iulia. | FINIS.	2315

WOMANS = 4

Iul. Your reason? | *Lu*. I haue no other but a womans reason:	175
More then quicke words, doe moue a womans minde.	1160
To be slow in words, is a womans onely vertue:	1397
Our youth got me to play the womans part,	1981

WOMEN = 5

Three things, that women highly hold in hate.	1479
Prouided that you do no outrages | On silly women, or poore passengers.	1617
Iul. How many women would doe such a message?	1911
When women cannot loue, where they're belou'd.	2165
Women to change their shapes, then men their minds.	2235

WON = 2

If hap'ly won, perhaps a haplesse gaine;	36
If lost, why then a grieuous labour won;	37

WONDER = 1

That you will wonder what hath fortuned:	2296

WONDERS = 1

To see the wonders of the world abroad,	9

WONDRED = 1

Pan. He wondred that your Lordship	306

WONT = 2*2

**You were wont, when you laughed, to crow	421
**eyes, or your owne eyes had the lights they were wont	464
Pro. My tales of Loue were wont to weary you,	778
And that I loue him not as I was wont:	859

WOOD = 1

Goe thou with her to the West end of the wood,	2111

WOODS = 1

This shadowy desart, vnfrequented woods	2123

WOOE *see also* woe = 1

Ile wooe you like a Souldier, at armes end,	2180

WORD = 8*8

Hauing nothing but the word noddy for my paines.	126
Be calme (good winde) blow not a word away,	278
*Pro. May't please your Lordship, 'tis a word or two	354
Val. She gaue me none, except an angry word.	549
Iulia, farewell: what, gon without a word?	584
**should not the shooe speake a word for weeping:	617
**speakes a word: but see how I lay the dust with my | teares.	624
*Thu. Sir, if you spend word for word with me, I shall | make your wit bankrupt.	690
And in a word (for far behinde his worth	721
Pro. Sirha, I say forbeare: friend *Valentine*, a word.	1274
*Val. No more: vnles the next word that thou speak'st	1307
*Sp. Well, your old vice still: mistake the word: what | newes then in your paper?	1350
La. Why that word makes the faults gracious:	1428
*Du. Where your good word cannot aduantage him,	1488
1.*Out*. We'll haue him: Sirs, a word.	1584

WORDS = 12*1

Oh hatefull hands, to teare such louing words;	265
For truth hath better deeds, then words to grace it.	586
*Sil. A fine volly of words, gentleme(n), & quickly shot off	684
*Val. I know it well sir: you haue an Exchequer of | (words,	692
That they liue by your bare words.	695
As seeke to quench the fire of Loue with words.	995
His words are bonds, his oathes are oracles,	1050
Val. Win her with gifts, if she respect not words,	1158
More then quicke words, doe moue a womans minde.	1160
Sp. Item, she is slow in words.	1395
To be slow in words, is a womans onely vertue:	1397
I weepe my selfe to thinke vpon thy words:	1996
Pro. Nay, if the gentle spirit of mouing words	2178

WORLD = 6*2

To see the wonders of the world abroad,	9
Warre with good counsaile; set the world at nought;	72
Not being tryed, and tutord in the world:	323
*Val. Not for the world: why man, she is mine owne,	823
But tell me (wench) how will the world repute me	1034
And with thy daring folly burne the world?	1224
*La. Then may I set the world on wheeles, when she | can spin for her liuing.	1378
But count the world a stranger for thy sake:	2195

WORLDLY = 1

Which else, no worldly good should draw from me:	1078

WORSE = 2

Val. I would it were no worse.	553
And that's farre worse then none: better haue none	2172

WORSER = *1

*yes; it is so, it is so: it hath the worser sole: this shooe	609

WORSHIP = 5

Speed. Your worship sir, or else I mistooke.	407
Speed. Shee that your worship loues?	411
Was this the Idoll, that you worship so?	796
But now I worship a celestiall Sunne:	939
To worship shadowes, and adore false shapes,	1755

WORSHIPD = 1

Thou shalt be worship'd, kiss'd, lou'd, and ador'd;	2019

WORST = 1

'Mongst all foes that a friend should be the worst?	2197

WORTH = 10*1

Now trust me, 'tis an office of great worth,	197
To be of worth, and worthy estimation,	706
And in a word (for far behinde his worth	721
Duk. Welcome him then according to his worth:	733
Sil. His worth is warrant for his welcome hether,	752
To her, whose worth, make other worthies nothing;	820
*if not, thou art an Hebrew, a Iew, and not worth | the name of a Christian.	921
Luc. A round hose (Madam) now's not worth a pin	1030
Is full of Vertue, Bounty, Worth, and Qualities	1134
Vnto a youthfull Gentleman of worth,	1176
As you, in worth dispraise, sir Valentine.	1501

WORTHIES = 1

To her, whose worth, make other worthies nothing;	820

WORTHIEST = 1
In thy opinion which is worthiest loue? 159
WORTHLESSE = 5
Receiuing them from such a worthlesse post. *Exit.* 151
Seruant, you are welcome to a worthlesse Mistresse. 763
Pro. That you are worthlesse. 766
And worthlesse *Valentine* shall be forgot. 1456
To be corrupted with my worthlesse guifts; 1630
WORTHY = 11
Some rare note-worthy obiect in thy trauaile. 16
Worthy his youth, and noblenesse of birth. 335
To be of worth, and worthy estimation, 706
He is as worthy for an Empresse loue, 726
To haue a looke of such a worthy a Mistresse. 758
Know (worthy Prince) Sir *Valentine* my friend 1079
Eg. As many (worthy Lady) to your selfe: 1777
I doe desire thy worthy company, 1795
And thinke thee worthy of an Empresse loue: 2268
Are men endu'd with worthy qualities: 2280
And fit for great employment (worthy Lord.) 2284
WOT = *1
*I did the thing you wot of: he makes me no more adoe, 1847
WOULD *see also* she'ld *l.*8 13 150 186 192 204 208 210 215 220 222 243
261 *262 264 307 317 350 *431 *478 519 553 *564 *603 1015 1085 1089
*1149 1153 1179 1188 1189 1192 1213 1468 1637 1646 *1687 *1692 1693
1712 *1751 1786 1792 *1826 *1827 *1832 *1849 1911 1921 1922 1923
1928 1931 1941 1992 2143 2155 2163 = 46*14
WOULDST *l.*155 *178 994 1270 2191 = 4*1
WOULD-WOMAN = *1
*now, like a would-woman: well, I kisse her: why 620
WOUND = 2
Shall lodge thee till thy wound be throughly heal'd; 275
The priuate wound is deepest: oh time, most accurst. 2196
WOUNDED = 2
And here is writ, *Loue wounded Protheus.* 273
Poore wounded name: my bosome, as a bed, 274
WRACK = *1
Pro. Go, go, be gone, to saue your Ship from wrack, 146
WRATH = 2
By heauen, my wrath shall farre exceed the loue 1236
Come not within the measure of my wrath: 2254
WRATHS = 1
By Penitence th'Eternalls wrath's appeas'd: 2207
WREAKING = 1
Wreaking as little what betideth me, 1810
WREATH = *1
*learn'd (like Sir *Protheus*) to wreath your Armes like a 414
WRETCHES = 1
Pro. As wretches haue ore-night 1758
WRINGING = *2
*Catte wringing her hands, and all our house in a great 600
*Wringing her hands, whose whitenes so became them, 1297
WRIT = 14*1
Iul. Some loue of yours, hath writ to you in Rime. 236
Looke, here is writ, kinde *Iulia*: vnkinde *Iulia*, 269
And here is writ, *Loue wounded Protheus.* 273
Loe, here in one line is his name twice writ: 283

WRIT *cont.*

Val. As you inioynd me; I haue writ your Letter	494
I writ at randome, very doubtfully.	501
Sil. Yes, yes: the lines are very queintly writ,	513
Silu. I, I: you writ them Sir, at my request,	517
I would haue had them writ more mouingly:	519
Sil. And when it's writ: for my sake read it ouer,	521
Val. Why she hath not writ to me?	*Speed.* What need she,	542
Val. That's the Letter I writ to her friend.	551
For often haue you writ to her: and she in modesty,	555
Which, being writ to me, shall be deliuer'd	1319
La. Of her tongue she cannot; for that's writ downe	1410

WRITE = 6*1

To write some lines to one she loues.	481
Val. No (Madam) so it steed you, I will write	503
Val. Please you, Ile write your Ladiship another.	520
To himselfe should write the Letter?	532
When shee hath made you write to your selfe?	544
*Her self hath taught her Loue himself, to write vnto her	(louer.	558
Write till your inke be dry: and with your teares	1521

WRITERS = 2

Pro. Yet Writers say; as in the sweetest Bud,	46
Val. And Writers say; as the most forward Bud	49

WRITES = *1

Pro. There is no newes (my Lord) but that he writes	358

WRITT = 1

Speed. Are they not lamely writt?	484

WRITTEN = 1

But twice, or thrice, was *Protheus* written downe:	277

WRONG = 4*1

To wrong my friend, I shall be much forsworne.	932
Iul. Now, as thou lou'st me, do him not that wrong,	1055
To wrong him, with thy importunacy?	1736
*(quoth he) you doe him the more wrong (quoth I) 'twas	1846
Mine shall not doe his *Iulia* so much wrong.	1958

WRONGFULL = 1

That I despise thee, for thy wrongfull suite;	1726

WRONGS = 1

Poore Gentlewoman, my Master wrongs her much.	1962

Y = *7

Speed. Nay: I was riming: 'tis you y haue the reason.	535
Speed. And y letter hath she deliuer'd, & there an end.	552
*Or fearing els some messe(n)ger, y might her mind discouer	557
Sil. Haue done, haue done: here comes y gentleman.	749
Iul. Oh, know'st y not, his lookes are my soules food?	990
Lau. Sir, there is a proclamation, y you are vanished.	1286
Val. I thank your Grace, y gift hath made me happy:	2275

YE *l*.181 202 428 704 *1549 2181 = 5*1

YEARES = 1

His yeares but yong, but his experience old:	719

YEELD = 1

Sil. Oh heauen.	*Pro.* Ile force thee yeeld to my desire.	2182

YEELDE = 1

And kill the Bees that yeelde it, with your stings;	267

YELLOW = 1

Her haire is *Aburne*, mine is perfect *Yellow*;	2009

YES = 2*1

Sil. Yes, yes: the lines are very queintly writ,   513
*yes; it is so, it is so: it hath the worser sole: this shooe   609
YET = 34*8

And yet you neuer swom the *Hellespont.*   29
Pro. Yet Writers say; as in the sweetest Bud,   46
Sp. And yet it cannot ouer-take your slow purse.   128
Lu. Yet he, of all the rest, I thinke best loues ye.   181
Iul. And yet I would I had ore-look'd the Letter;   204
And yet me thinkes I do not like this tune.   249
And yet I will not, sith so prettily   286
Yet here they shall not lye, for catching cold.   295
And yet a thousand times it answer's no. | *Exeunt. Finis.*   393
Speed. And yet I was last chidden for being too slow.   409
Val. Do'st thou know her by my gazing on her, and | yet know'st her
not?   440
(Please you command) a thousand times as much: | And yet---   504
And yet I will not name it: and yet I care not.   507
And yet, take this againe: and yet I thanke you: 508
Speed. And yet you will: and yet, another yet.   510
*perplexitie, yet did not this cruell-hearted Curre shedde   601
Yet hath Sir *Protheus* (for that's his name)   717
Sil. And dutie neuer yet did want his meed.   762
Yet let her be a principalitie,   ·   805
'Tis but her picture I haue yet beheld,   864
I cannot leaue to loue; and yet I doe: 946
(A rashnesse that I euer yet haue shun'd)   1099
Launce. I am but a foole, looke you, and yet I haue   1331
*that knowes me to be in loue, yet I am in loue, but a   1334
*'tis I loue: and yet 'tis a woman; but what woman, I   1336
*will not tell my selfe: and yet 'tis a Milke-maid: yet 'tis   1337
*not a maid: for shee hath had Gossips: yet 'tis a maid,   1338
But yet I slew him manfully, in fight,   1574
Yet (Spaniel-like) the more she spurnes my loue,   1638
Iu. Not so: but yet | So false that he grieues my very heart-strings.   1684
Sil. Say that she be: yet *Valentine* thy friend   1733
Vouchsafe me yet your Picture for my loue,   1745
Yet will I woe for him, but yet so coldly,   1927
And yet the Painter flatter'd her a little,   2007
And yet she takes exceptions at your person.   2044
They loue me well: yet I haue much to doe   2137
YE-GOOD-EVN = *1

Speed. Oh, 'giue ye-good-ev'n: heer's a million of | manners.   490
YOKED = 1

And he that is so yoked by a foole,   44
YOND = 1

For 'tis no trusting to yond foolish Lowt;   1885
YONDER = 1

Thu. Yonder is *Siluia*: and *Siluia*'s mine.   2252
YONG = 4*2

How yong *Leander* crost the *Hellespont.*   25
Euen so by Loue, the yong, and tender wit   51
*weep like a yong wench that had buried her Grandam: 418
His yeares but yong, but his experience old: 719
To hate yong *Valentine*, and loue my friend.   1512
Ho. Now, my yong guest; me thinks your' allycholly;   1651

YOU = 247*77
YOUL = *1
   *matter? why weep'st thou man? away asse, you'l loose   628
YOULL = 3
   Val. So, by your circumstance, I feare you'll proue.   41
   Sp. Truely Sir, I thinke you'll hardly win her.   134
   Val. Well: you'll still be too forward.   408
YOUR *l.*40 41 43 *100 *109 *113 *120 128 *131 *133 137 138 *139 *143
   *144 *146 175 179 193 220 224 225 238 246 255 267 *290 304 306 314
   327 *331 *354 363 390 397 407 411 *414 434 *464 *468 470 *478 494
   497 511 520 524 533 *538 544 565 *616 670 673 675 *679 680 687 *688
   *689 690 693 695 699 700 704 737 747 755 760 764 *767 772 *774 *777
   795 996 1019 *1024 1026 1040 1072 1075 1080 1083 1085 1088 1090
   1121 1126 1135 1136 *1149 1285 1347 1350 1367 *1440 1457 1466 1467
   *1488 1489 1491 1506 1510 1511 1520 1521 1528 1529 1542 1553 1602
   1616 1647 *1649 1708 1709 1714 1715 1717 1744 1745 1746 1748 1750
   1753 1754 1774 1775 1777 1778 1780 1807 1817 *1868 1901 1903 1909
   1932 1939 1945 1948 1953 2024 2044 2141 2143 *2153 2249 *2275 2276
   2290 2297 2298 = 133*36, *1
   Ho. Now, my yong guest; me thinks your' allycholly;   1651
YOURS = 6*2
   Iul. Some loue of yours, hath writ to you in Rime.   236
   Sp. Why then this may be yours: for this is but one.   399
   bolder to chide you, for yours.   476
   Vnto the secret, nameles friend of yours: 495
   Val. And how doe yours? | *Pro.* I left them all in health.   775
   Sil. What's your will? | *Pro.* That I may compasse yours.   1715
   *As big as ten of yours, & therefore the guift the greater.   1877
   That done, our day of marriage shall be yours,   2299
YOURSELFE *see* selfe
YOUTH = 13*2
   *Home-keeping youth, haue euer homely wits,   5
   Weare out thy youth with shapelesse idlenesse.   11
   To whisper, and conspire against my youth?   196
   Would suffer him, to spend his youth at home,   307
   In hauing knowne no trauaile in his youth.   318
   Worthy his youth, and noblenesse of birth.   335
   Laun. Forsweare not thy selfe, sweet youth, for I am   874
   To be fantastique, may become a youth   1022
   Knowing that tender youth is soone suggested,   1103
   Such as the fury of vngouern'd youth   1591
   Ho. Why, my pretty youth? | *Iu.* He plaies false (father.)   1681
   Partly that I haue neede of such a youth,   1883
   Our youth got me to play the womans part,   1981
   Sil. She is beholding to thee (gentle youth)   1994
   Here youth: there is my purse; I giue thee this   1997
YOUTHFULL = 4
   How his companion, youthfull *Valentine*,   328
   For which, the youthfull Louer now is gone,   1110
   Vnto a youthfull Gentleman of worth,   1176
   Val. My youthfull trauaile, therein made me happy,   1580
ZEALE = 1
   Me thinkes my zeale to *Valentine* is cold,   858
& *l.**191 *489 *493 *552 *684 *774 *777 *1275 *1877 = *9
1 = 1*1
1OUT = 8

```
1OUT-L = 1
2 = 1
2OUT = 7*2
3 = 1
3OUT = 4*3
```